Course	Political Philosophies in Moral Conflict
Course Number	**2007**
	Peter Wenz

http://create.mheducation.com

ISBN-10: 1121473202   ISBN-13: 9781121473201

Contents

Credits

Note to Instructors

This book treats political philosophies as tools for understanding and expressing competing views of the state's role in people's lives. Accordingly, it introduces readers to contemporary political philosophies and their associated concepts through discussion of controversial state laws and policies, such as those concerning racial profiling, the legalization of drugs and prostitution, pollution control, physician-assisted suicide, markets in nonvital human organs, and the battered-woman defense.

The book covers two forms of democracy—aggregative and deliberative—and eleven political philosophies: theocracy, utilitarianism, libertarianism, free-market conservatism, contractarianism, communitarianism, moral conservatism, multiculturalism, feminism, environmentalism, and cosmopolitanism. Related concepts explained and used include natural law, human rights, civil liberties, private property, free markets, public goods, reflective equilibrium, social capital, and ethical relativism.

I use extensive quotations from mainstream news sources, works of history, and judicial opinions to show that discussions concern real political conflicts, to introduce authentic participant voices, and to retain reader interest through variety in writing style. I often use legal cases as illustrations because they dramatize the practical impact of competing political philosophies. Cases concern such matters as interracial marriage, abortion, school vouchers, Microsoft's restraint of trade, affirmative action, the Boy Scouts' exclusion of homosexuals, the cultural defense, and polygamy.

A book that relates political philosophies to such issues is needed because people who discuss politics (I mean non-academics on television, families around the table, and politicians in legislatures) are seldom pressed for underlying justifications, so they are often unaware of their own fundamental convictions. But should they be pressed, different people would express different foundational views. "Because it will maximize happiness" is one utilitarian bottom line. "Because it will maximize economic opportunity" is the bottom line for most free-market conservatives.

"Because we are just one species among many" is the bottom line for many environmentalists. "Because that's what God says is right" is the bottom line for theocrats. "Because one culture's values cannot be imposed on others'" is the bottom line for multiculturalists. "Because no one would agree to that if she put herself in the other person's shoes" is the bottom line for contractarians. "Because some human needs and aspirations are universal" is the bottom line for cosmopolitans—and so on. Since people's justifications for their views on controversial political topics rely on such bottom-line beliefs, investigation of underlying political philosophies and the concepts needed for their full comprehension can aid society's mainstream political conversation. The present book offers such aid.

The Introduction illustrates the book's method. Philosophical material appears only after its utility in political discussion is manifest. The Introduction begins with *Newsweek's* account of the 1992 Los Angeles Riots to make Hobbes's point about the need for state-enforced laws. Max Weber's definition of the state follows. But police must be limited, as Amadou Diallo's death in New York City and scandals at the Rampart police station in Los Angeles make clear. In addition, Soviet oppression suggests that we want liberty as well as security. I then give brief sketches of several political philosophies, including libertarian, theocratic, utilitarian, free-market conservative, and liberal contractarian views, to give readers a foretaste of some philosophies explored in the book and to provide examples of the book's method. Readers see the need for logical consistency through a consideration of arguments concerning rodeos and bullfights. The concept of reflective equilibrium is introduced and applied. The Introduction ends, as do all the chapters, with Judgment Calls, puzzling scenarios, cases, and arguments to ponder and discuss.

Subsequent chapters have the following general structure: Each begins with an illustration of a social problem or an issue likely of interest to readers. A political philosophy, with some attendant terminology and distinctions, is then introduced to provide reasonable guidance in the matter at hand. Additional interesting cases and other considerations show the philosophy's limitations: how the philosophy is helpful in treating some range of cases, but many important problems remain outside its range. It cannot be the *sole* bottom line in *all* political discussions. Later chapters introduce additional philosophies to address certain problems without denying the worth of ideas considered earlier; thus the book is cumulative. Readers accumulate knowledge of philosophies and concepts they can use as a tool to understand new situations, and they are challenged to apply the right tool to different situations and justify their choice to people with different views. Readers can construct their own political philosophies by building on the strengths of the philosophies presented while also recognizing their limits. They improve their political thinking and their potential for political communication and effectiveness by DOING, not just reading about, political philosophy.

This practical, pragmatist orientation explains why I do not discuss anarchism in any depth. No position in serious, practical, contemporary political debate rests on the bottom-line belief that we should abolish all states, which is classic anarchism, or maintains that all states are morally illegitimate, the claim of some current anarchists. The minimal state is advocated seriously, and I cover this topic in two chapters on libertarianism, which is a live political option, especially after 9/11, anarchism is not. For similar reasons, I do not discuss Marxism, but I connect egalitarian views to deliberative democracy and Rawls.

The text as a whole centers on the liberal contractarian view of John Rawls. Each chapter before the central chapter on Rawls considers a major element in Rawls's theory, such as rights and liberties in Rawls's first principle of justice, property rights in the second principle, and reasonable pluralism. Each later chapter extends Rawls's views via discussions of the views of many feminists and multiculturalists, or challenges them via discussions of the views of communitarians, moral conservatives, environmentalists, and cosmopolitans.

This book argues for several theses. First, conflicts among political philosophies underlie many political controversies. Second, reflective equilibrium is the proper method for evaluating political philosophies. Third, no one political philosophy answers all issues adequately, so a pluralistic political philosophy, which I call *political principlism,* is needed. Fourth, most of the popular political philosophies contain important elements for inclusion in a pluralistic philosophy. For example, hedonistic utilitarianism is inadequate as a complete political philosophy, but human happiness remains an important political consideration. Finally, political pluralism can be principled and consistent, rather than just an eclectic blend of inconsistent elements.

I have tried to keep my writing style simple without compromising complexity of thought, making the book both accessible and intellectually challenging for most readers. The book consists of an Introduction, 11 chapters, and a Conclusion—13 segments of roughly equal length that can be used alone or with other material for 13 weeks of class reading.

In sum, this book will inform, stimulate, and sometimes amuse students as it lays foundations for interesting and productive class discussions.

 # Introduction

The **political philosophies*** discussed in this book *concern the foundations and the functions of the* **government.** *Such philosophies organize people's views about the need for, and the proper role of, the* **state.** *They attempt to explain in persuasive and consistent ways which laws and public policies are appropriate and which are not.* Such philosophical explanation is important. Governments tell people what they can and cannot do; they compel people to pay taxes and sometimes to serve in the military; they often punish people who disobey the law. Such intrusions on individual freedom seem to require justification, which political philosophies supply.

This book examines several philosophies, assessing their strengths and weaknesses. One goal is to help readers recognize, adopt, or construct their own philosophies, which they can then use for political understanding and effectiveness.

Employing a series of examples, this introduction explains why diverse political philosophies exist and compete with one another, what is at stake in the competition, and how reason, when used to evaluate philosophies, can make the competition generally beneficial to individuals and to society (through improved democratic decision making).

A Dangerous World

Almost everyone agrees that people need governments in part for self-protection in a dangerous world. The violence that engulfed Los Angeles in 1992 illustrates one type of danger. A riot followed the acquittal of four white police officers who had been caught on videotape beating African-American Rodney King. *Newsweek* reported:

> "We've got shooting all over the city." Like bulletins from a war zone, the words and images came flying out of a city going up in smoke and

---

* Terms printed in bold are defined in the Glossary at the end of the text.

flames.... Downtown, a mob of blacks, whites, and Hispanics torched the guardhouse outside police headquarters, lit a fire in city hall, then trashed the criminal courts building. Across town, hammers banged down storefront security gates.[1]

Looters of all races owned the streets, storefronts, and malls. Blond kids loaded their Volkswagen with stereo gear; a Yuppie jumped out of his BMW and scrounged through a gutted Radio Shack.... Filipinos in a banged-up old clunker stocked up on baseball mitts and sneakers. Hispanic mothers with children browsed the gaping chain drug marts and clothing stores.[2]

Richard Cunningham ..., a clerk ..., shook his head. "They want to live the lifestyle they see people on TV living," he said. "They see people with big old houses, nice cars, all the stereo equipment they want, and now that it's free, they're gonna get it."[3]

After 72 hours, 44 dead, 2,000 wounded, and $1 billion in damages, police restored order, reinforcing belief in the importance of law enforcement. If, as the Preamble to the United States Constitution puts it, a major goal of government is to "insure domestic Tranquility," armed police are often necessary. They were in short supply when disturbances began.

At 2:30 [P.M.], about an hour before the jury rendered the verdict, bean counters worried about overtime let 1,000 officers go off duty. At South Central's 77th Division, there were fewer than three dozen cops. At 6:30 [Chief of Police] Gates was nowhere to be found.... No one ordered a "mobilization" until about 7:30. Gates did not get back until about 9 P.M. Only then did the LAPD lurch into action.... But ... it took a lot of time to get off-duty cops back, and the blue line was spread so thin it frightened no one.... By 10 P.M., 25 square blocks of central Los Angeles were ablaze.... Buses and trains stopped running. Schools closed. In a panicky rush to get out of town, drivers clogged the freeways.... Stores and offices shut their doors. The smoke from 1,000 fires grew so dense that air-traffic controllers could keep open only one runway at Los Angeles International Airport.[4]

Mayhem in the absence of adequate police protection is what Thomas Hobbes, a 17th-century English philosopher and political theorist, would have expected. He experienced anarchy during the English Civil War

1. "The Siege of L.A.," *Newsweek,* Vol. CXIX, No. 19 (May 11, 1992), p. 30.
2. "The Siege of L.A.," p. 36.
3. "The Siege of L.A.," p. 37.
4. "The Siege of L.A.," pp. 35–36.

(1642–1649) and wrote in his major work, *Leviathan* (1651), that without law enforcement robbery and murder are normal.

> If any two men desire the same thing, which nevertheless they cannot both enjoy, they become enemies . . . ; and from hence it comes to pass that . . . if one plant, sow, build, or possess a convenient seat, others may probably be expected to come prepared with forces united to dispossess and deprive him, not only of the fruit of his labor, but also of his life or liberty.[5]

According to Hobbes, without law enforcement to make people fear the consequences of harming others, people live in a condition "called war . . . , a war . . . of every man against every man. . . . In such condition there is no place for industry, because the fruit thereof is uncertain: and consequently" there is no agriculture, science, navigation, imported products, or comfortable living.[6]

Increasing poverty was among the worries in Los Angeles that *Newsweek* reported:

> Thomas Hill, owner of a [riot-trashed] shop on Western Avenue [remarked,] "I'm a businessman and I've got a family to support. I'll never come back here again." Watts never recovered from the 1965 riots. Now [from 1992 onward], predicts sociologist [Joel] Kotkin [of the city's Center for the New West], "South-Central L.A. [where the riot started] will become an economic Mojave Desert."[7]
>
> Looking on in disgust, Hector Ybarra said, "Where we gonna shop tomorrow? Where those people gonna live?"[8]
>
> The arsonists concentrated on stores owned by Koreans, who sell most of the food in the neighborhood. "What are people who don't have cars going to do to get food?" [South-Central L.A. resident] Wanda Mitchell wondered. Many of the businesses will not be rebuilt, and life at ground zero will never be the same.[9]

Failure of law enforcement impoverishes life. Lawlessness endangers life as well. *Newsweek* writer Tom Morganthau noted shortly after the riot:

> South-Central L.A., where [the] troubles began, is ground zero for . . . crack cocaine and . . . the nationwide underground market for guns. South-Central is a vast residential cage in which most of

---

5. Thomas Hobbes, *Leviathan* (Indianapolis: The Bobbs-Merrill Company, 1958), p. 105.
6. Hobbes, pp. 106–07.
7. "The Siege of L.A.," p. 38.
8. "The Siege of L.A.," p. 37.
9. "The Siege of L.A.," p. 35.

the population is held prisoner by an armed and dangerous minority—an estimated 100,000 "gangbangers," many of whom are still in their teens. . . . Law-abiding citizens cower behind locked doors and barred windows, fearful of going outside. . . . Homicide is now the leading cause of death for black men between the ages of 15 and 34.[10]

As Hobbes pointed out, *without the rule of law, "the life of man is solitary, poor, nasty, brutish, and short."*[11] Hobbes believed that life is so bad in what he called "the state of nature," a situation without effective law enforcement, that he endorsed creating a sovereign, whom he called the Leviathan, to make rules that everyone should obey. However, as the Los Angeles riots illustrate, people are sometimes unwilling to listen to reason or to abide by sensible rules. To meet this problem, the Leviathan must have enough force to overpower those who would defy the law. Hobbes recommends that people relinquish their power to the Leviathan so he will have the wherewithal to maintain law and order by force if necessary. The Sovereign State of California performed this role when it eventually deployed enough police officers and National Guard personnel to quell the Los Angeles riot and protect both people and property from further harm.

According to Hobbes, then, governments are founded primarily on the need for security, and their main function is to provide protection. Only an organization that can wield more power than anyone else in society can provide needed protection, so Hobbes endorsed creation of a state. German sociologist Max Weber (1856–1920) regarded the **state** as *the organization in society that can wield more power than can any other organization and that claims the right to determine how force may be used in that society.* This definition does not mean that the state *alone* may use force. In football, for example, defensive players are allowed to tackle offensive players who have the ball, and offensive players are allowed to block tacklers. These are uses of force. But the state determines what *kind* of force is legal. Even if the National Football League had no objections, state law forbids football players to stab or shoot one another. Almost everyone today accepts the need for states, state laws, and state law enforcement. But few people today accept Hobbes's political philosophy.

---

10. Tom Morganthau, "The Price of Neglect," *Newsweek*, Vol. CXIX, No. 19 (May 11, 1992), pp. 54–55.
11. Hobbes, p. 107. Emphasis added.

Limited Government

Hobbes considered anarchy so dangerous that self-preservation justified granting the government unlimited power. *Some political philosophers reject Hobbes's view and formulate competing philosophies out of fear that unlimited state power will be abused.*

Abuse of power occurred in Los Angeles during the 1990s. Police concerned about gang violence established a special antigang unit, Community Resources Against Street Hoodlums (CRASH), at the Rampart Police Station. It was allowed to arrest suspected gang members for such offenses as blocking sidewalks and carrying pagers. Officers carried shotguns and assault rifles. According to *Time* magazine's Adam Cohen, "In the '90s the CRASH unit certainly lived up to its name, with a confrontational style of policing that aggressively took back the streets. It seemed to be getting results. In the 1960s the area had 170 murders a year. [In 1999] there were just 33."[12]

Former Rampart police officer Rafael Perez testified to the down side of aggressive policing. Police increasingly broke the law. In one 1996 incident Perez and his partner shot an admitted gang member, Javier Francisco Ovando, who was unarmed. The officers "planted a rifle . . . to make it look as if Ovando had attacked the police. Ovando was paralyzed, and may never walk again. The judge at the trial lambasted Ovando . . . for endangering the lives of two hero policemen, before sentencing him to 23 years in prison." After Perez admitted to planting the rifle, Ovando was released, but he had already served 2 years and 11 months. Reporter Cohen continues:

> Perez also claims to have helped cover up two other unjustified shootings. In one, he says, he watched police plant a gun next to Juan Saldana, 21, whom they had just shot. Perez says the cops delayed calling an ambulance for Saldana while they worked with a supervisor on getting their stories straight. Saldana ended up bleeding to death.[13]

In another case, Alex Sanchez, a former gang member who changed sides and began opposing gang violence, was threatened with deportation to his native El Salvador because he was an alibi witness for Jose Rodriguez, a 15-year-old accused of murder. "Sanchez says the police want to deport him because he was with Rodriguez at the time of the killing . . . and because he knows how the cops operate."[14] L.A. police may often have silenced immigrant witnesses of police misconduct by threatening deportation.

---

12. Adam Cohen, "Gangsta Cops," *Time*, Vol. 155, No. 9 (March 6, 2000), pp. 30–34, at 31.
13. Cohen, p. 32.
14. Cohen, p. 33.

Los Angeles attorney Gregory Yates claimed that "the cases he has seen so far point to 'systematic corruption' in the ranks of the L.A.P.D. One disturbing pattern: many of his clients have told him arresting officers tried to recruit them to sell drugs."[15]

According to L.A. Police Chief Bernard Parks, Chief Gates's successor, corruption often begins with officers "trying to impress supervisors." This problem is not limited to L.A.P.D.

> Law enforcement experts say police nationwide are too often told by their supervisors, or by prosecutors and politicians, that the only thing that matters is getting a conviction. "The seed of corruption begins when cops are asked to fill in the blanks for district attorneys to make cases," says Gene O'Donnell, a professor at New York City's John Jay College of Criminal Justice and a former cop. "If they don't remember, there's a tremendous pressure for them to make it up." O'Donnell says one of the most common refrains he hears from police is that "this job is not on the level." Police then often find themselves adapting to a corrupt system.[16]

Besides becoming criminals themselves, police sometimes become so zealous that they mistakenly kill innocent people who have no relationship to crime at all. New York City, for example, established an elite Street Crimes Unit (SCU) with the motto, "We Own the Night." Like L.A.'s CRASH unit, writes *Time* reporter Howard Chua-Eoan, "It had been tremendously successful. Though making up less than 2% of the police force, the SCU accounted for more than 20% of the city's gun arrests. . . ."[17] But this success was achieved through very aggressive police tactics that sometimes included literally shooting first and investigating later. In this context Amadou Diallo was killed in a hail of 41 bullets shot by four police officers in plain clothes. Nineteen of these hit the unarmed Diallo as he stood at his front door reaching for his wallet, which police claimed they mistook for a gun. The four officers were acquitted on all charges of misconduct.

In sum, *if the goal of the state is to protect people, state law-enforcement efforts must be limited by the rule of law.* An unlimited government crackdown on crime may threaten innocent people more than it protects them. In addition, police are not immune to the temptations that produce destructive anarchy in the absence of law enforcement.

---

15. Cohen, p. 33.

16. Cohen, p. 33.

17. Howard Chua-Eoan, "Black and Blue," *Time*, Vol. 155, No. 9 (March 6, 2000), pp. 24–29, at 26.

Even when the only value is security, different, competing political philosophies reflect different levels of concern about general anarchy, on the one hand, and possible police error and corruption, on the other. People who are most afraid of street crime or terrorism, for example, lean toward Hobbes's view and want few limits on law-enforcement officials. People who are more afraid of police misconduct or mistakes favor increased safeguards for defendants. The difference is practical and important. Few Americans want more crime, but *people subject to recurrent police misconduct or government mistreatment are liable to kick up a dangerous storm.*

The 1992 Los Angeles riot illustrates this fact. The riot began when it seemed that the state would not address police misconduct. Videotape showed four police officers hitting Rodney King 56 times during an arrest on March 3, 1991. The evidence of police brutality seemed clear. However, according to *Newsweek,*

> defense lawyers turned what had looked like a clear case of police brutality into a shrewd exercise in reverse English. Pretrial publicity was relentless. The defense got a change of venue from Los Angeles to Simi Valley, a comfortable, white middle-class suburb favored by officers retiring from the LAPD. Even so, the evidence looked overwhelming. In addition to the video, prosecutors had transcripts of conversations in which Officers Laurence Powell, Timothy Wind, and Sgt. Stacy Koon talked about "a Big Time use of force." ("I haven't beaten anyone this bad in a long time.") Then the fourth defendant, Officer Theodore Briseno, testified *against* the others.[18]
>
> The latter part of the videotape potentially was the most damaging to the four police officers. King is virtually motionless on the ground and is offering no visible resistance. But the officers, according to their lawyers, continued to beat King because he refused to comply with their demands.[19]

The officers' acquittal convinced many that the criminal justice system is unjust because it allowed state-authorized police brutality against African Americans to go unpunished.

> Not since the 1960s had so many people talked so furiously about "the system" and the way it ran down the powerless. . . . After the verdict, a Washington Post/ABC News Poll showed that three quarters of the whites questioned agreed with the all-but-unanimous feeling of African Americans that the system of justice was loaded against them.[20]

---

18. "The Siege of L.A.," p. 31. Emphasis in original.
19. Bob Cohn and David A. Kaplan, "How the Defense Dissected the Tape," *Newsweek,* Vol. CXIX, No. 19 (May 11, 1992), pp. 36–37, at 37.
20. "The Siege of L.A.," p. 38.

This feeling sparked the riot. The feeling is based not on paranoid fantasy, but on real-life experiences. In one of her *Newsweek* columns, Anna Quindlen poses this riddle:

> Why was the internationally known Princeton professor stopped for driving too slowly on a street where the speed limit was 25 miles per hour? How come a Maryland state trooper demanded to search the car of a lawyer who graduated from Harvard? And why were an accomplished actor, a Columbia administrator, a graduate student, and a merchandiser for Donna Karan arrested together in New York although none of them had done anything wrong?
>
> The answer is elementary: all of the men were black. In some twisted sense, they were the lucky ones. They were only humiliated. Not, like Rodney King, beaten bloody. . . . Not, like Amadou Diallo, killed in a gray blizzard of bullets.[21]

One result of blacks experiencing police racism is, according to *Newsweek*'s Ellis Cose, that "black jurors are less likely than whites to believe police testimony—at least when that testimony conflicts with that of a defendant." Law professor Sheri Lynn Johnson adds, "The people who have the most experience with police find them the most biased."[22] As a result, jurors from minority communities may disbelieve police testimony and acquit guilty defendants, as possibly happened when former football star O. J. Simpson was acquitted of double homicide.

Crime control, a major function of government, is impaired when the public distrusts the police and the courts. Different beliefs about how best to control crime, whether through more aggressive policing or more stringent oversight of police, rest on different views about how government institutions work. *People more confident of police integrity favor more aggressive policing, whereas those more impressed by police misconduct and more fearful of violent community backlash want more oversight of police.*

The Value of Liberty

Different political philosophies reflect not only different beliefs about how political institutions are likely to operate but also different views about the relative importance of competing values. Every political philosophy includes security as a value, but some philosophies are more concerned

---

21. Anna Quindlen, "The Problem of the Color Line," *Newsweek*, Vol. CXXXV, No. 11 (March 13, 2000), p. 76.
22. Ellis Cose, "The Long Shadow of Amadou Diallo," *Newsweek*, Vol. CXXXV, No. 11 (March 13, 2000), p. 54.

than others are to promote individual liberty as well. Liberty requires security because people have little freedom when they are constantly threatened by lawless aggression. But according to **libertarianism,** security is a means whereas liberty is the end or the goal. *The main foundation of government, libertarians contend, is the human desire for liberty, and the main function of government is to guarantee liberty.* Libertarians reject exclusive preoccupation with security because it can endanger liberty. The former Soviet Union illustrates this problem.

A communist state that existed from 1917 to 1991, the Soviet Union provided a high degree of security against general anarchy but was itself oppressive, denying to its people liberties we take for granted. For example, the Soviet Union forbade writers from publishing material that it found embarrassing. Boris Pasternak was not allowed to publish his novel *Doctor Zhivago* in the Soviet Union because its account of the Russian Revolution of 1917 portrayed some communists as ruthless. The novel was spirited out of the country and published first in Italy in 1957 and then in other Western countries. Pasternak won the Nobel Prize for Literature in 1958 but in retaliation was threatened with forced emigration, which would mean separation for the rest of his life from his country, friends, colleagues, and most of his family. Pasternak wrote to the head of the Soviet government, Nikita Khrushchev: "Leaving my motherland would be equal to death for me, and that is why I ask that you do not take such extreme measures in this case."[23] The author was allowed to live in the Soviet Union until he died two years later.

Others who disagreed with the Soviet government were not so lucky. Jaures Medvedev, a biologist, supported the Darwinian theory of evolution by natural selection against the government's favored view, evolution by personal effort and social conditioning. In 1970 the novelist Alexander Solzhenitsyn described the state's treatment of Medvedev:

> A healthy man is accosted by two policemen and two doctors without either a warrant for his arrest or a medical justification. The doctors declare that the man is crazy, the policemen shout: "Stand up! We are an organ of force!" His arms are bound, and they take him to a madhouse. This can happen tomorrow to any one of us. As a matter of fact, it has just happened to Jaures Medvedev, a geneticist and publicist, a man with a sharp, subtle, brilliant intelligence and a good soul. . . . If only this were the first case! But this type of thing has become the rule with us. . . . Servile and unscrupulous psychiatrists

---

23. Cornelia Gerstenmaier, *The Voices of the Silent,* translated from the German by Susan Kecker, (New York: Hart Publishing Co., 1972), p. 50.

define the concern about social problems . . . as "mental illness. . . ." It is high time we realized that the forced confinement of free-thinking, healthy people in an insane asylum is spiritual murder. It is a variation of the gas chamber, only more cruel; the tortures of its victims are more malicious and more prolonged.[24]

Soviet physicist and winner of the 1975 Nobel Peace Prize, Andrei Sakharov, was punished without trial for his opposition to the 1979 Soviet invasion of Afghanistan. He supported a boycott of the Olympic games being held that year in Moscow, writing: "The ancient rules of the Olympics called for suspension of hostilities during the games. The USSR should withdraw its troops from Afghanistan. If it doesn't, the Olympic Committee should refuse to hold the games in a country that is waging war."[25]

Sakharov was stripped of all his state honors and awards and forced to move to Gorky, a city closed to foreigners. Upon arrival he received these orders:

You are forbidden to go beyond the city limits of Gorky. You'll be kept under surveillance, and you are forbidden to meet with or contact foreigners or criminal elements. The MVD [Ministry of Internal Affairs, or Secret Police] will let you know when you're required to check in with Comrade Glossen at their headquarters on Gornaya Street. They're empowered to have the police bring you in if you fail to answer their summons. If you have any questions, call the KGB [Committee for State Security]. . . .[26]

Sakharov was a famous man, so his punishment (without trial) was relatively light. Others disfavored by the state were sent to harsh labor camps, called *gulags*. Sakharov recalls descriptions given by Solzhenitsyn in his novel *The Gulag Archipelago*.

A somber world of gray camps surrounded by barbed wire, investigators' offices, and torture chambers flooded with merciless electric lights, icy mines in Kolyma and Norilsk. This was the fate of millions of our fellow countrymen, the obverse of the enthusiasm and glorious achievements celebrated in official song and story.[27]

Some Soviet citizens maintained a sense of humor in the face of state repression. They joked: In the Soviet Union we have freedom of speech and

---

24. Gerstenmaier, pp. 395–97.
25. Andrei Sakharov, *Memoirs,* translated from the Russian by Richard Lourie, (New York: Alfred A. Knopf, 1990), p. 509.
26. Sakharov, p. 515.
27. Sakharov, p. 406.

freedom of assembly just like in America. Only in America you have freedom *after* speech and *after* assembly.

Stressing the value of liberty, libertarians oppose restrictions on the freedoms of speech and assembly, believing that in general, as in the former Soviet Union, state oppression is more likely than are free speech and assembly to jeopardize individual security.

God's Will and Natural Law

These beliefs about free speech accord with the views of most Americans. The libertarian political philosophy is controversial, however, because it treats all other human activities the same way it treats speech. **People should be free to do whatever they want so long as they do no direct harm to others without their consent.** Some people object to this political philosophy when the issue is physician-assisted suicide (PAS), because they believe that God forbids all suicide. This introduces a third political philosophy in competition with libertarian and Hobbesian views, the **theocratic view.**

Dr. Timothy Quill's account of a patient with acute myelomonocytic leukemia illustrates what is at stake in this conflict of political philosophies:

> Diane . . . was raised in an alcoholic family . . . , had vaginal cancer as a young woman, [and] had struggled with depression and her own alcoholism. I had come to know, respect, and admire her over the previous eight years as she confronted these problems and gradually overcame them. . . . As she took control of her life, she developed a strong sense of independence and confidence. . . . In the previous three-and-one-half years. . . , she was completely abstinent from alcohol, she had established much deeper connections with her husband [and] college-age son, and . . . felt she was really living fully for the first time.[28]

Then she contracted acute leukemia. A long and painful course of treatments was available, but it offered only a 25% chance of cure. "In fact," Dr. Quill notes, "the last four patients with acute leukemia at our hospital had died very painful deaths in the hospital during various stages of treatment."[29] Diane quite reasonably decided to forgo therapy and

---

28. Timothy E. Quill, "Death and Dignity: A Case of Individualized Decision Making," in *Ethical Issues in Modern Medicine*, 6th ed., Bonnie Steinbock, John D. Arras, and Alex John London, Eds. (New York: McGraw-Hill, 2003), pp. 377–80, at 377. Originally in *The New England Journal of Medicine* 324, No. 10, March 7, 1991, pp. 691–94.
29. Quill, p. 378.

wanted "to maintain control of herself and her own dignity during the time remaining to her. When this was no longer possible, she clearly wanted to die." She did not want to live in a stupor under so-called comfort care, as she found this undignified. "When the time came, she wanted to take her life in the least painful way possible."[30]

Both Dr. Quill and Diane's family thought this was reasonable, but laws against physician-assisted suicide precluded Dr. Quill from directly helping Diane kill herself. Are these laws just, or should competent adults be allowed to seek help, and doctors be allowed to give help, in cases like Diane's? Libertarians, whose views are examined more fully in Chapters 3 and 4, think they should. It is Diane's life, so she should be free to do what she wants, even kill herself, so long as she harms no one else.

Some theocratic political philosophers would reject this libertarian principle. Theocrats maintain that *governments are properly founded on God's will, and their primary function is to further the realization of God's plan for the world.* Theocrats who believe that God forbids all suicide oppose legalizing PAS. As evidence that God forbids suicide, they might claim that fighting for life is universal in nature, so people who commit suicide are breaking the **natural law.** Assuming that God created nature and that natural laws reflect God's will, the unnaturalness of suicide shows that it contravenes the will of God. For people with this view, discussed at greater length in Chapter 1, the state acts justly when it restricts liberty to promote God's plan for humanity.

Hobbes rejected theocracy because he thought it led to sectarian violence and insecurity. During his lifetime, people in England fought a bloody civil war largely over which religious view the state should endorse. Hobbes worried, in other words, about the practicality of settling political controversies with religious beliefs. He was concerned about how political institutions operate, and citizens respond, in practice. Libertarians, by contrast, reject theocracy because it limits individual liberty. They do not want the government restricting their freedom on the basis of religious beliefs that they may not share. They value individual liberty over religious claims.

Utilitarianism and "Spheres of Justice"

Utilitarianism, discussed at greater length in Chapter 2, is a fourth major approach to political philosophy. It stresses a value different from security, obedience to God, and maximum individual liberty. Utilitarians believe that governments exist to promote the greatest good in society. *Promoting*

---

30. Quill, p. 379.

maximum happiness or the greatest satisfaction of human preferences is both the foundation and the function of the state. Utilitarians would favor legalizing PAS if they thought this would maximize happiness or preference satisfaction. They would favor a state-imposed religion, too, if they thought it would maximize happiness or preference satisfaction, but few utilitarians believe that theocracy promotes utilitarian goals.

Happiness and preference satisfaction seem good, so why are not all people utilitarians? First, some religious people believe that all humans are born with original sin. They worry that satisfying people's preferences will lead to immoral behavior because original sin influences people to prefer to disobey God. Some proponents of theocracy oppose utilitarianism for this reason.

Secular reasons for rejecting utilitarianism come from its implications in certain kinds of cases. Consider, for example, organ transplantation, a medical technique that helps people extend their lives under conditions that previously led to certain death. A person with a failing organ can receive a replacement from someone else. Most often, the donor or the donor's family consents to this transfer of organ from donor to recipient.

Unfortunately, there is a shortage of donated organs for transplant, resulting in many unnecessary deaths each year. Belgium responds to this problem with a law that presumes consent to be an organ donor. "Under its provisions," David Rothman writes in the *New York Review of Books*, "you must formally register your unwillingness to serve as a donor; otherwise, upon your death, physicians are free to transplant your organs." Rothman continues:

> When a death occurs, the hospital checks the computer base, and unless your name appears on it, surgeons may use your organs, notwithstanding your family's objections. I was told by health professionals in Belgium that many citizens privately fear that if they should ever need an organ, and another patient simultaneously needs one as well, the surgeons will check the computer and give the organ to the one who did not refuse to be a donor. There is no evidence that surgeons actually do this; still many people feel it is better to be safe than sorry, and so they do not register any objections.[31]

As a result of this system, Belgium does not have the shortage of donated organs that persists in the United States and elsewhere in Europe. From the utilitarian perspective, this is good because it maximizes happiness or the satisfaction of human preferences. But is it right that upon

---

31. David J. Rothman, "The International Organ Traffic," *The New York Review of Books,* March 26, 1998, pp. 14–17, at 15.

your death your body parts are presumed to be the property of others, even over family objections? Libertarians who believe that people own their bodies the way they own objects may object to the presumption that upon death their bodies belong to others. Utilitarians, by contrast, object to people dying needlessly for lack of donated organs. Both sides make sense, and we must choose between them.

China addresses the problem differently. "It has adopted the tactic of harvesting the organs of executed prisoners." Rothman writes:

> Immediately before the execution, the physician sedates the prisoner and then inserts both a breathing tube in his lungs and a catheter in one of his veins. The prisoner is then executed with a bullet to his head; the physician immediately moves to stem the blood flow, attach a respirator to the breathing tube, and inject drugs into the catheter so as to increase blood pressure and cardiac output. With the organs thus maintained, the body is transported to a hospital where the donor is waiting and the surgery is performed.[32]

As Rothman notes, "China's system has its defenders. Why waste the organs? Why deprive prisoners of the opportunity to do a final act of goodness?"[33]

But is this right? Should a death-row inmate's execution date be determined by someone else's need for a heart transplant? If two prisoners are on death row, should one be executed first because he is a better tissue match for a person with a failing heart? Utilitarians may not be troubled by this, but some others are. Rothman reports:

> Several years ago a heart transplant surgeon told me that he had just been invited to China to perform a transplant; accustomed to long waiting periods in America, he asked how he could be certain that a heart would be available when he arrived. His would-be hosts told him they would schedule an execution to fit with his travel schedule. He turned down the invitation.[34]

Those of us who believe that we, too, would have turned down the invitation may be following a political philosophy like Michael Walzer's, according to which different "spheres of justice" should not be confused with one another. Medical needs, which are in one sphere, should not affect application of the death penalty, which is in a different sphere. Executions

---

32. Rothman, pp. 15–16. In the last sentence, Rothman probably means that the patient or recipient, rather than the donor, is waiting at the hospital.
33. Rothman, p. 16.
34. Rothman, p. 16.

should follow upon completion of the criminal appeals process. It is simply wrong, on this view, to gear the operation of one sphere of justice to meet needs in a different sphere. Walzer's ideas are discussed in Chapter 7.

An additional consideration is distrust of government. Like libertarians, many people fear government corruption. They may worry that in the rush to obtain organs for transplantation, an innocent person might be executed before an exonerating appeal is completed. Utilitarians may worry little about this if they are optimistic about accuracy and integrity in government decision making, or a great deal if they are pessimistic.

The Free Market and Liberal Equality

Some political philosophies stress the importance of economics. One of these, the fifth political philosophy introduced so far, claims that *free markets promote efficiency, efficiency leads to affluence, and the state's primary jobs are protecting rights and fostering affluence.* This is **free-market conservatism,** discussed in Chapter 5, which suggests a commercial approach to obtaining organs for transplantation. In our global economy some people are so poor that they will sell a nonvital organ, such as a kidney, if the price is right. Scarcity lessens, efficiency increases, and the economy grows when willing sellers profit from commercial transactions with willing buyers. In this case, buyers get kidneys so they can live longer, and sellers get the money they need. Sellers use this money to buy what they want and need, creating jobs for other people, many of whom are also poor. It is a win-win situation that promotes general affluence, giving everyone as much as possible of what they want. Free market conservatism suggests legalizing the sale of nonvital organs.

Some people might argue that selling kidneys should remain illegal because it jeopardizes the sellers' health, but Rothman cites evidence that it does not.

> A University of Minnesota transplant team compared 78 kidney donors with their siblings 20 years or more after the surgery took place, and found no significant differences between them in health. . . . Why ban the sale of kidneys when the sale of other body parts, including semen, female eggs, hair, and blood, is allowed in many countries? The argument that these are renewable body parts is not persuasive if life without a kidney does not compromise health. Finally, transplant surgeons, nurses, and social workers, as well as transplant retrieval teams and the hospitals, are all paid for their work. Why should only the donor and the donor's family go without compensation?

In spite of its illegality, the sale of kidneys continues in India,

> which has an abundant supply of kidneys because physicians and brokers bring together the desperately poor with the desperately ill. The sellers include impoverished villagers, slum dwellers, power-loom operators, manual laborers, and daughters-in-law with small dowries. The buyers come from Egypt, Kuwait, Oman, and other Gulf States, and from India's enormous middle class.

Is it wrong to allow a free market in kidneys? "Every world medical organization opposes the sale of organs."[35] Or is it wrong to interfere with market forces that tend in general and in this case to promote economic growth and affluence? Free-market conservatives favor economic growth and affluence.

Libertarians may also favor a free market in nonvital organs, but for a reason different from that used by free-market conservatives. Libertarians are not focused on economic growth and affluence but on individual rights. People have a right to their bodies and should be able to do what they want with them. They should be allowed to sell a nonvital organ if they want to; it is *their* organ. Because libertarians favor individual liberty, they generally favor free markets, which allow people to exercise liberty, the liberty freely to exchange goods and services. So libertarians may join free-market conservatives in favoring a free market in nonvital organs, but they join to vindicate the individual rights of buyer and seller to do what they want with their own property, not to promote economic growth and affluence.

Proponents of **liberal contractarianism,** discussed in Chapter 6, might oppose such a market because they think it exploits desperately poor people. *Liberals are not libertarians.* Liberals share with libertarians an interest in promoting individual rights and with free-market conservatives an interest in promoting affluence. Liberals agree with both that free markets are generally useful as expressions of individual rights and as means of promoting affluence. But *liberals part company with libertarians and free-market conservatives over the issue of inequality. Liberals oppose great economic inequality. It is wrong, they think, for some people to be much wealthier than others if this results in some poor people lacking necessities while rich people have luxuries. Free markets tend to produce extremes of poverty and wealth, so liberals qualify their support for free markets by endorsing government regulations aimed at reducing gaps between rich and poor.* Liberals may believe that the desire of some people

---

35. Rothman, p. 16.

to sell their kidneys shows that disparities between haves and have-nots are too great. Kidney sales should remain illegal while the state intervenes in the economy to help desperately poor people.

Theocrats may join liberals on this matter if they believe, as many do, that God disfavors extremes of poverty and wealth. Pope John Paul II, for example, often expressed the view that gaps between rich and poor should be reduced. Other theocrats, however, may interpret God's will differently.

In sum, libertarians and free-market conservatives would not interfere with a free market in kidneys because, even if the free market rests on great disparities of wealth, they do not think such disparities are necessarily unjust. Instead, libertarians worry that attempts to eliminate disparities will impair individual freedom, and free-market conservatives worry that such attempts will cripple economic progress. Liberals, by contrast, would curtail individual freedom and economic growth to promote more equality. They are joined by some, but not all, theocrats.

How to Choose a Political Philosophy

We see that several political philosophies (and there are more where those came from) compete for our allegiance. Each is a general perspective on state methods and goals. Each attempts to apply a unified, coherent vision to political issues, although *individual thinkers who share a general perspective often differ about details.*

All these philosophies favor security, but they differ on how to ensure it and on its importance compared to other values, including liberty, righteousness (in the sight of God), preference satisfaction, affluence (from free market competition), and equality. The stakes in choosing among political philosophies are high because the philosophy that guides the government affects: whether doctors can help people commit suicide; whether people can criticize the government; whether police corruption can be combated effectively; whether gaps between rich and poor should be allowed to become or remain enormous; whether wealth is society's highest value; and a host of other matters. How should we choose among competing political philosophies?

We should start with our current beliefs about morality and politics. We all have many such beliefs acquired from family, religion, civic groups, school, friends, and so on. Different people often have different beliefs. Each person should start with her own views and retain them until given good reasons to change her mind.

The requirement of logical consistency often justifies altering one's views. Here is an example. In Illinois, where I live, and in most of the

United States, bullfighting is illegal, even so-called American-style bull-fighting, which does not include killing the bull. Picadors poke the bull, clowns run in and out taunting the bull, and a matador gets the bull to charge his red cape, but in the end the bull leaves the arena slightly injured and frustrated, but otherwise healthy. Why is this illegal? Suppose that you favor the ban on bullfighting because you care about animals and consider even American-style bullfighting cruelty to animals. But now someone points out that rodeos are legal and cause animals as much suffering as (American-style) bullfighting. Broncos do not buck because they are happy. A strap is tightened around what we politely call "sensitive areas" causing great pain, which results in bucking. How can a person consistently object to bullfighting as animal cruelty but not to rodeos?

One response is to look for differences between the two that justify their different treatment. For example, if bullfighting involved significantly more cruelty than rodeos, there would be reason to ban the former but not the latter. However, we have no reason to believe that American-style bullfighting harms or hurts animals more than rodeos do.

Another possible difference that may justify allowing one and prohibiting the other concerns the economy. Rodeos, although cruel to animals, are a big business and help sustain economic prosperity, whereas bull-fighting does not. However, this reasoning is lame; bullfighting sustains the economy where it is legal. If cruelty to animals is justified by economic growth, both rodeos and bullfighting should be legal.

The majority culture is another way of differentiating rodeos from bull-fights. In North America rodeos are part of the majority population's culture, whereas bullfights are not, so perhaps only rodeos should be allowed. But even if this reasoning explains why, as a matter of fact, rodeos are legal and bullfights illegal, it justifies their different treatment on the basis of either **ethnocentrism,** the denigration of other cultures, or belief in the need for cultural uniformity, with attendant limitations on individual liberty.

Some people favor cultural uniformity or endorse ethnocentrism. They can attain consistency by claiming that rodeos are all right, whereas bull-fights are not, simply because one reflects the majority, and the other a minority, culture. Others reject this way of reaching consistency because they believe that laws should not favor the cultural practices of the majority and outlaw those of the minority without good reasons to believe that the majority's cultural practices are superior. Otherwise, they think, minority ethnic groups will suffer unjustified prejudice. (We discuss multi-culturalism in Chapter 8.)

This case illustrates five things. First, although we come to the study of political philosophy with certain assumptions and beliefs, they may not be compatible with one another. Acceptance of rodeos may not be compatible with rejection of bullfights. A state of consistency among all our beliefs, which philosophers call **reflective equilibrium,** is an aspiration, not a starting point. Second, attempts to demonstrate or to attain reflective equilibrium often require increased awareness of facts and assumptions. We may have long objected to animal cruelty and would complain about a neighbor who beats his dog but were unaware that people inflict pain on broncos to get them to buck.

Third, consistency can be achieved by altering one or more of our beliefs. In the case of rodeos and bullfighting, for example, consistency can be achieved by considering both practices to involve so much animal cruelty that both should be illegal. For most people, this involves changing one's view of rodeos from positive to negative. Fourth, there is more than one way to achieve reflective equilibrium. Instead of changing one's views about rodeos, consistency could be achieved by deciding that cruelty to animals is not bad (a moral judgment), or that even if it is bad the state should not try to prevent it (a judgment in political philosophy). In this case, both rodeos and bullfights should be legal. For most people, this involves changing beliefs about animal cruelty or the state's role in its prevention, and the acceptability of bullfighting.

Finally, not all beliefs that I hold and might change are on the same level of generality. If I change my view and decide that there is nothing wrong with cruelty to animals (a belief about a general moral principle), consistency requires that I not object, except to the noise, the next time my neighbor beats his dog. I should keep my judgments about particular events compatible with my general moral principles.

The same consistency between general views and particular applications is needed in political philosophy. If I think it appropriate for the state generally to suppress the cruel treatment of animals, I endorse state intervention to prevent individual acts of cruelty (my neighbor beating his dog) and practices that are equally cruel (rodeos and bullfights), unless there are good reasons to allow them. If I think the state's primary responsibility is to protect people and foster economic growth, I may find good reasons to allow rodeos and bullfights but not my neighbor's cruel treatment of his dog. However, I might so abhor cruelty to animals that this implication of free market conservatism convinces me to modify my views about the state's proper role.

In sum, *we choose political philosophies by using reason to test the compatibility of a political philosophy's implications with what we consider morally right and politically appropriate.* We alter our moral judgments and political philosophies as needed to attain reflective equilibrium.

The method of reflective equilibrium is so attractive and commonsensical that I have used it extensively already in this Introduction to evaluate different political philosophies without having to call attention to it. Consider this example of its use so far. Hobbes's philosophy seemed initially attractive because it emphasizes the need for security in a dangerous world. However, if it implies that states can legitimately pursue security by limiting free speech, as the former Soviet Union did, most people will reject Hobbes's philosophy as an overall perspective on the foundations and functions of government. If Hobbes's view allows states to curtail free speech, one must, to attain reflective equilibrium, either accept such limitations on free speech or reject (or modify) Hobbes's philosophy.

The dictatorial implications of Hobbes's views, combined with problems of police corruption and other forms of state-sponsored misconduct, convince some people to agree with libertarianism that the only legitimate goal of government is promotion of individual liberty. But others balk at the libertarian philosophy's implication that doctors should be able to prescribe lethal drugs to cancer patients who want to commit suicide. Even more people would probably oppose legalizing lethal drugs completely, enabling willing adults to commit suicide without a doctor's prescription whether they are sick or not. If libertarianism implies this policy (see Chapter 3) it will lose the support of many. But some people may be so impressed with libertarianism that they will change their views about drug legalization. Logical consistency can be reached either way. My point here is that whatever people decide about these issues, their quest for consistency constitutes an attempt to attain reflective equilibrium.

Logical Consistency and Justice

Justice requires *giving each person her due* and *treating like cases alike.* People are commonly aggrieved when, for no good reason, they are singled out for especially harsh treatment or are denied benefits available to others. If everyone else in the office but me gets two weeks paid vacation, I will think this unjust (I am not getting my due; management should treat like cases alike) unless there are relevant differences that justify different treatment. If only full-time employees get two weeks paid vacation and I am the only part-time worker in the office, this may justify denying me a benefit available to others. Management is treating like cases alike (all full-time employees) and me differently because there is a relevant difference between the others and me.

As this case illustrates, justice requires consistency of the sort that reflective equilibrium provides. As we examine competing political philosophies to determine their implications and whether we can accept those implications with logical consistency, we are seeking not only reflective equilibrium but justice.

This statement does not mean that all political philosophies are **theories of justice,** *explicit, general accounts of what people are due and which differences justify different treatment.* John Rawls's liberal contractarianism is a theory of justice, as are some libertarian, feminist, multicultural, and cosmopolitan views. Other philosophies are not theories of justice but nevertheless have implications regarding justice and claim compatibility with justice. Each philosophy has views about what people are due and which differences among people and situations are relevant to different treatment. They differ from one another about what people are due, why it is due, and which differences among people are relevant, but all oppose injustice. They all oppose treating people differently for no good reason; they all support treating like cases alike. We judge them largely by deciding if we can accept all their implications on these and other matters.

Political philosophies have a practical reason for claiming that their views are just, that they give all people what they are due. When people believe that they are being treated unjustly, we have already seen, they are tempted to break the law. If enough people believe the state is seriously unjust, the society may become ungovernable. Inconsistent treatment can provoke lawlessness.

Religion is a sensitive matter for many people, so consistent treatment of people regardless of religious belief is generally necessary for long-term social and political stability. But accusations of injustice related to religion can surface when all people are denied what only people in a particular religious group desire. This was the situation when the Church of Jesus Christ of Latter-Day Saints was forced in the 19th century to give up the practice of one man marrying more than one woman. This issue illustrates the importance of seeking reflective equilibrium when searching for justice.

Was the prohibition of polygamy just? Does it remain just? Most Americans believe that people should be free to practice religion without state interference, except as needed to protect others from harm, and that adults should be able to influence their own destiny by making religious and marital commitments. These views suggest that competent, willing adults whose religion commands polygamy should be permitted to practice it.[36]

---

36. Of course, since Mormons renounced polygamy in 1890, anyone seeking such marriage today could not be a practicing Mormon. But we can imagine people from a splinter sect wanting to return to polygamous practices common among Mormons between 1840 and 1890.

However, since the Old Testament era, when polygamy was common, our culture has adopted monogamy as the norm. We hold monogamous marriage in high moral esteem and celebrate romantic monogamy in novels, plays, cinema, and song. But its enforcement on those who prefer polygamy for religious reasons seems inconsistent with our beliefs about religious freedom and individual self-determination. This kind of inconsistency seems to place unjustified burdens on some people. *Inconsistency can embody unjustified prejudice. Consistency is needed to treat everyone justly.*

Recognizing that justice requires consistency, people favoring the ban on polygamy could try to attain reflective equilibrium by examining the issue more carefully. They might note that religious freedom and individual self-determination typically extend only to competent adults. Polygamy opponents may then alter their beliefs about tests for competence. Ordinarily, we assume that adults are competent unless a psychiatrist declares otherwise after scientific observations or tests. This is the view that people opposed to polygamy may alter. They may deny that any competent woman in our society would ever agree to share a husband. Regardless of her age, and without any scientific, psychiatric evidence, a woman's agreement to be a co-wife in a polygamous marriage is sufficient evidence of her incompetence. So, they would argue, religious freedom and individual self-determination for competent people is consistent with the ban on polygamy.

This does not settle the matter, however, because proponents of polygamy could challenge the claim that willingness to enter a polygamous marriage establishes incompetence. Why make this claim? It seems like an **ad hoc assumption,** *a belief that people adopt without any good reason except to win an argument.* Ad hoc assumptions can embody the kind of unjust prejudice that requiring consistency is designed to overcome. To make their competency assumption reasonable instead of ad hoc, opponents of polygamy must relate it to a larger group of situations. The larger group could be all those situations in which people make choices that others find irrational; opponents of polygamy assume that women willing to be co-wives are incompetent because their marital choice seems irrational.

This opens a can of worms. What is the test for irrationality? In this case it seems to be merely that some people think what other people want to do, be a co-wife, is senseless or self-destructive. Do opponents of polygamy want consistently to claim that people are irrational and therefore incompetent to make their own decisions whenever other people find their choices senseless or self-destructive? Such a standard would remove decision-making power from many young adults with pierced tongues or romantic attachments to losers because others find their choices senseless or self-destructive. Do opponents of polygamy want to declare such people incompetent and limit choices of adornments and mates? Few Americans would consistently endorse such limitations of freedom.

Opponents of polygamy might claim at this point that many people are narrow-minded, so their views about adornments and mates do not set the standard for irrationality and incompetence. But there are broad-minded people as well who properly appreciate the difference between rationality and irrationality. These people should set and apply standards of competence for everyone. Opponents of polygamy claim that they are among these broad-minded people. Is this ad hoc, or what?

As the foregoing discussion suggests, achieving reflective equilibrium is not easy. We start with views about particular kinds of cases, such as a negative view about polygamous marriage, and beliefs about political principles, for example, that competent people should be accorded freedom regarding religion and marriage. Because there is an apparent inconsistency, achieving reflective equilibrium requires altering one or more of our opinions. But the alteration must not be ad hoc. We must be able to apply it to other relevant areas, such as the choice of adornments and mates, without creating new inconsistencies in our thinking regarding those areas. In the present case, opponents of polygamy have more work to do.

Theses and Benefits

This book as a whole argues for several theses, seven in all. First, as my examples already indicate, conflicts among political philosophies underlie many political controversies. Second, reflective equilibrium is the proper method for evaluating individual judgments and political philosophies. Third, several political philosophies provide valuable insights into the resolution of political controversies; they are helpful in treating some range of cases. But additional controversies lie outside that range, so no one political philosophy provides an adequate foundation for the reasonable resolution of all controversies. The fourth thesis follows from the third; a **pluralistic political philosophy** is necessary. This is a philosophy that draws important insights from several philosophies.

Fifth, political pluralism can be principled and consistent, rather than just an eclectic blend of inconsistent views. This thesis resembles **principlism** in ethics, according to which *we should guide our conduct by several* *independent moral principles. None of these principles is basic in the sense that all the others can be derived from it. In addition, no single order of priority or importance among the principles covers all situations; one principle might be more important in one situation and another in a different situation.* When the principles involved derive from different political philosophies, the result is a pluralistic political philosophy that I call **political principlism.**[37]

Sixth, more than one reasonable pluralistic political philosophy is possible. I will continue throughout the book to indicate situations in which I can imagine reasonable people having different views. Even where I present a strong opinion, readers should consider whether reasonable alternatives exist.

Finally, political philosophy provides benefits for individuals and society. *Individuals using reason to choose among competing political philosophies help themselves personally and improve democratic decision making.* Here is how this may apply to you. Assuming that I am correct that no ready-made political philosophy is adequate for all purposes, reason suggests that you create your own pluralistic view, using input from different philosophies and avoiding inconsistency by including justifications for using different philosophies in different contexts. If you apply those justifications consistently, you will have approached or achieved reflective equilibrium.

You may wonder how a political philosophy held in reflective equilibrium will help you if lacking one has not crippled your life so far. First, *developing a political philosophy improves self-awareness.* We all think about politics at least some of the time, and when we do we implicitly use political philosophies, mostly the ones included in this book. Of course, we seldom think, "I'll use a Hobbesian approach to this issue," but such an approach may be in the back of our minds in the form of implicit assumptions and habitual patterns of thought. Such assumptions and thought patterns influence our perceptions of justice and our reactions to public policies, but mostly unconsciously. *Reasoning about political philosophies will help you become more aware of your own political reasoning.*

You might think that if you are guided by a certain philosophy you would surely be aware of it. Reflection on language, however, shows that this may not be so. We all follow complex rules of grammar in our native language without being consciously aware of those rules and without

---

37. See Peter S. Wenz, *Environmental Justice* (Albany: State University of New York Press, 1988), pp. 313–16 for an account of moral pluralism or principlism.

being able to explain them to foreigners. Studying language improves self-awareness by making us conscious of rules we generally use unconsciously. Similarly, studying political philosophy makes us more aware of views about the foundations and the functions of government that we have been using all along.

Reasoning about political philosophy also helps reduce confusion in political thinking. As noted already, we often draw from more than one political philosophy, depending on context. For example, to promote economic growth, someone may favor free markets and oppose government "meddling" in the economy. At the same time, however, he may want some special protections for women, such as a law requiring that all health insurance policies, including private health insurance, pay for women to stay in the hospital at least 24 hours after delivering a baby. Because such a requirement interferes with the free market in medical insurance, this person is not in reflective equilibrium. His thinking requires some addition or modification to be consistent. The modification could be a justification for making health insurance an area where some other value is more important than free market efficiency, or it could be an argument that the free market is not efficient in the context of health care, or something else. Without political philosophy, which helps expose the problem, confusion may persist. In sum, *by revealing confusions, political philosophy helps you make more coherent political decisions.*

Studying political philosophy can broaden your perspective. People typically start with a bundle of moral and political views that are not entirely coherent. In the process of working toward reflective equilibrium they encounter suggestions that they had never heard of before. Some of these may come from minority communities or foreign cultures. (See Chapter 8 on multiculturalism.) More familiar ideas, too, take on new meaning when needed to make our political views coherent in the face of apparent inconsistencies.

Political communication and democratic decision making benefit when people articulate clear, coherent political philosophies. When people are more aware of their thoughts and have eliminated confusions, they are better able to communicate their thinking to others. Improved communication enables others to respond with reasoned criticism, which can lead to further refinement of thought. Without the kind of reflection that political philosophy encourages, people are more likely to make ad hoc assumptions and try merely to win an argument instead of seek the kind of genuine understanding typical of democracy at its best. In sum, *political philosophy promotes the intelligent public discussion of controversial political issues, which is essential to thriving democracies.*

What is more, *those who can thoroughly articulate their reasoning are more effective in political debates.* We cannot expect others to be convinced by our arguments unless we make our reasoning clear to them, and clarity requires demonstrating the consistency of our thinking. Also, because people who study political philosophy can articulate their views completely, they can answer objections clearly and coherently. *Studying political philosophy will make you more effective in political discussions.*

Political effectiveness is important because politics influence your life. The availability of an organ that you or a loved one may need for a transplant may be affected by our adopting Belgium's system of organ procurement. The legal availability of abortion, marijuana, and physician-assisted suicide are also determined politically. Most of us pay taxes, and politics determines, for example, whether or not the rich are taxed at a higher percentage rate than the poor are taxed. Schooling is important, and politics determines whether there will be enough tax money for quality schools, whether government vouchers will be available for people to use in religious schools if they so choose, and whether race may be used as a factor in admission decisions at elite schools. Politics determines also what kind of gun you can legally purchase and whether you can marry someone of the same sex. In sum, *politics affects everyone's life in important ways, so political effectiveness is generally helpful.*

Many philosophies are considered in this work. In addition to covering Hobbes's view, theocratic theories, utilitarianism, libertarianism, free market conservatism, and liberal contractarianism, which have already been introduced, the book discusses communitarianism, multiculturalism, feminism, environmentalism, and cosmopolitanism. Some of these terms may be new to you, but many of the ideas are familiar, because each philosophy emphasizes values held by many people in our society that influence what they want and expect from the state. Everyone wants and expects security, Hobbes's predominant concern. Other political philosophies add one or more additional concerns. Free-market conservatives emphasize affluence through free market activity, which they want and expect the state to promote. Utilitarians make similar demands on the state to promote maximum happiness or preference satisfaction. Libertarians favor maximum individual liberty, and multiculturalists want the state to promote harmonious interaction among a culturally diverse population. Each philosophy, in my view, contains valuable insights. My goal is to help you draw on these philosophies to form your own consistent political philosophy to use in reasoned political discussion.

JUDGMENT CALLS

1. Consider the following argument against polygamy: justice between genders is important in our society, so we should enforce gender fairness on all religions. The Church of Jesus Christ of Latter-Day Saints used to allow a man to have more than one wife but did not allow a woman to have more than one husband, so its practice of polygamy was unjust to women. We should reject any practice, whether religiously motivated or not, that is unjust to women, polygamy included. What problems may this argument pose regarding reflective equilibrium?

2. Consider another argument against polygamy. Polygamy in any segment of the population would undermine the institution of marriage in society generally and would harm many people who do not desire polygamy for religious reasons. Religious freedom and individual self-determination may be curtailed when necessary to protect others.

3. Consider this argument. Almost all women who now desire polygamous marriages were raised in splinter groups related to, but not part of, the Church of Jesus Christ of Latter-Day Saints. They were brainwashed to want what no mentally competent women would otherwise accept. This history of brainwashing justifies denying the competence of women who would agree to be co-wives.

4. Most Americans, because we favor free speech, believe that the Soviets treated Boris Pasternak unjustly when they threatened to deport him for having published a novel that Communist Party officials found offensive and embarrassing. But we, too, condemn some forms of expression because others find them offensive and embarrassing. Consider workers in an auto assembly plant. Suppose male workers often tell jokes that female colleagues cannot help overhearing. These jokes make frequent, derogatory reference to specifically female anatomy and bodily functions. Some women find this work environment so hostile that they give up high-paying jobs to protect their sense of dignity. Are the men behaving unjustly, or is it unjust to censor their "joking" at work?

5. Some poor people sell nonvital organs, such as kidneys, to feed their families. What if they wanted to sell vital organs, such as their heart and liver, to leave a financial legacy to their otherwise poverty-stricken family? Should this be allowed? What would libertarians, utilitarians, and free-market conservatives think?

1   God's Will and Natural Law

using religion as source of justification

In 1776 the authors of the United States' Declaration of Independence appealed to God and to God's natural law to justify political divorce from Great Britain. The colonies claimed "the separate and equal station to which the Laws of Nature and of Nature's God entitled them. . . ." The Declaration continued, "We hold these truths to be self-evident, that all men are created equal, that they are endowed by their Creator with certain unalienable Rights, that among these are Life, Liberty and the pursuit of Happiness. That to secure these rights, Governments are instituted among Men. . . ."[1]

Fast-forward to a presidential address shortly after the terrorist attacks of September 11, 2001. Religious thought is still central to American political justifications. President Bush said, "Freedom and fear, justice and cruelty, have always been at war, and we know that God is not neutral between them. Fellow citizens, we'll meet violence with patient justice, assured of the rightness of our cause and confident of the victories to come."[2] Bush seems "assured of the rightness of our cause" (the fight against terrorism) because it promotes what God values—freedom and justice.

The President's State of the Union Address in 2003 contemplated war with Iraq. Mr. Bush promised to bring freedom to the Iraqi people. "Freedom," the President declared, "is the right of every person and the future of every nation. The liberty we prize is not America's gift to the world, it is God's gift to humanity." So America delivers God's gift to the Iraqi people when it sets them free.[3]

---

1. *The Declaration of Independence*, Sam Fink, Ed. (New York: Scholastic Inc., 2002), p. 146.
2. President George W. Bush, "President Bush Addresses the Nation," washington post.com.text, p. 10 of 10. Speech delivered September 20, 2001. File accessed June 27, 2002.
3. www.whitehouse.gov/news/releases/2003/01/20030128-19.html, p. 10 of 10.

The present chapter discusses the glories and perils of justifying political action by appealing to God's will and natural law. *Because religion often inspires people to moral heights, it is a valuable component of American political life. Yet religious justifications and related natural law reasoning can divide and endanger a religiously pluralistic society. Fruitful debate and domestic tranquility are more likely when people give secular reasons for their views and limit their appeals to God's will and natural law.*

The Fight against Jim Crow

Religious beliefs can be politically relevant and important. As defined in the Introduction, reflective equilibrium is a state of consistency among all a person's beliefs. So, *when religious people, such as President Bush, think about politics, they should seek consistency among all their political beliefs, including those that are religious.* When asked during his third debate with Senator Kerry about the role of religion in his presidency, Mr. Bush said this:

> When I make decisions I stand on principle. And the principles are derived from who I am. I believe we ought to love our neighbor like we love ourself. That's manifest in public policy through the faith-based initiative where we've unleashed the armies of compassion to help people who hurt. I believe that God wants everybody to be free. That's what I believe. And that's one part of my foreign policy. In Afghanistan I believe that the freedom there is a gift from the Almighty. . . . And so my principles that I make decisions on are a part of me. And religion is a part of me.[4]

This statement seems to endorse consistency in reflective equilibrium between religious beliefs and secular policies, thereby finding a legitimate role for religion in politics. Consequently, when discussing political matters with religious people, we should appeal to their religious convictions along with their other beliefs in attempts to persuade them that our view is one they should adopt in order to make their own political thinking more consistent. This is what Dr. Martin Luther King, Jr. did so successfully. *The American civil rights movement exemplifies the glory of religion in politics.*

The civil rights movement opposed **Jim Crow.** Originally, writes historian Nancy Shuker, the name Jim Crow referred to "a fictitious person . . . , a creation of white entertainers who performed songs and dances in blackface and an exaggerated Southern dialect." Eventually, Jim Crow

---

4. www.nytimes.com/2004/10/14/politics/campaign/14text.html, p. 17.

30 Chapter 1: God's Will and Natural Law

started off as a way to demean African Americans

came to represent *all laws and customs in the American South designed to segregate and humiliate black people.* Shuker continues:

> Throughout the South, railroad stations had black waiting rooms and white waiting rooms, black restrooms and white restrooms, even black water fountains and white water fountains. Movie houses—if they had a section for black people, usually in the last rows of the top balcony—made the negroes enter through a side door. Public swimming pools and parks were for whites only. Restaurants—unless they were in the black sections of town—did not serve blacks at all. Blacks were forced to take the freight elevator in department stores. Downtown drug stores with soda fountains did not serve blacks at the counter. A negro, or "colored person"—as black people were referred to then—might be served a soda or an ice cream from a window at the side of the store.
>
> If a black family took a car trip to another town, they had to plan carefully to make stops in places where they had family or friends. No hotel or motel would accommodate black people anywhere in the South. And there were few black restaurants on the road.[5]

When traveling by bus, blacks were required to sit in the back, recalls Harold Middlebrook, youth pastor at Ebenezer Baptist Church in Atlanta, Georgia.

> When I got on the bus, the signs said, "Coloreds seat from the rear forward." Then it said, "Whites seat from the front back." I can remember getting on the bus, and white man sitting, and there was an empty seat in front of him, he refused to move up. And all of the seats behind him were filled. So I had to stand. But I couldn't sit.[6]

Coretta Scott King, the widow of civil rights leader Dr. Martin Luther King, Jr., recalls the sad day when their daughter Yoki learned about Jim Crow.

> A new amusement park had been built in Atlanta, called Funtown, and it was advertised extensively. My children would watch television and see so many commercials for Funtown that they even learned to sing the lyrics of the song.
>
> They would plead with us to take them, and we would keep making excuses, not wanting to tell them that the television invitations

---

5. Nancy Shuker, *Martin Luther King* (New York: Chelsea House Publishers, 1985), pp. 23–24. Found in Russell Moldovan, *Martin Luther King, Jr.: An Oral History of His Religious Witness and His Life* (San Francisco: International Scholars Publications, 1999), p. 55.

6. Moldovan, p. 60.

were not meant for black children . . . until finally Yoki, who was about six at the time, said, "You just don't want to take me to Funtown."

I hated the hurt look in her eyes, and I told her, "Yolanda, Funtown was built by people who decided that they did not want colored people to come there. . . . You see, we are colored."

This was her first emotional realization and understanding of being black in a white world.[7]

The modern **civil rights movement** began *organized protests against Jim Crow* in 1955. In 1960 black students at the Agricultural and Technical College of North Carolina in Greensboro began sitting at the Woolworth's five-and-ten lunch counter, demanding service reserved for whites. "Day after day," Coretta King writes,

they went back and sat, joined by both black and white students coming from the Women's College of the University of North Carolina and Bennett College.

The wire services picked up the story, and the Movement spread like a forest fire. Within two weeks black and white students in college towns south from Virginia to Florida and west to Louisiana, organized sit-ins. Some were arrested, but this merely spread the flames.

The sit-in movement caught on in Atlanta in the fall of 1960. . . . Their main target in Atlanta was Rich's Department Store, one of the largest in the South. They invited Martin to sit-in at the lunch counter with them, and of course he accepted with alacrity.[8]

Reverend King was arrested for his crime and nearly spent six months at hard labor.

Some reactions to civil rights protests were violent. In May 1961 the Congress on Racial Equality (CORE) conducted the first Freedom Rides to desegregate interstate buses and bus terminals in the South. Here is Coretta King's account:

On May 4 pairs of white and black volunteers, with a white observer from CORE, took Greyhound and Trailways buses for a trip through Virginia, the Carolinas, Georgia, Alabama, and Mississippi to New Orleans.

This well-advertised project seemed to infuriate southern reactionaries beyond all reason. Bands of raging whites attacked the buses in cities in the deep southern states. The riders were hauled

---

7. Coretta Scott King, *My Life with Martin Luther King, Jr.* (New York: Avon Books, 1969), pp. 218–19.
8. King, pp. 195–97.

off, beaten up, and thrown into jails. In Anniston, Alabama, a roaring crowd attacked a Greyhound bus, smashed its windows with iron bars, punctured the tires, and threw an incendiary bomb into it. The bus was destroyed.[9]

This was the reaction to blacks and whites simply riding a bus together.

In 1963 the Southern Christian Leadership Conference (SCLC) began working in Birmingham, Alabama, to desegregate lunch counters, dressing rooms, and rest rooms and to reform hiring practices at Birmingham's big downtown stores. Mrs. King recalls:

> The protest started on April 3, 1963, with lunch counter sit-ins. In the first three days alone, thirty-five people were arrested. On Saturday, April 6, an orderly march of carefully selected demonstrators moved toward City Hall. They were stopped three blocks from their goal. Forty-two people were arrested for parading without a permit.
>
> After that, demonstrations were staged every day with increasing strength. . . . Between four and five hundred black people were arrested, and though some got out on bail, about three hundred remained in jail.
>
> On Wednesday . . . city officials obtained an injunction against the demonstrators, but it was issued by an Alabama state court, not a federal court. Martin promptly announced that the injunction would be disobeyed.[10]

Reverend King spent eight days in the Birmingham City Jail. Upon his release he decided to enlist "the black children of Birmingham in the crusade for freedom." On May 3, the second day of the children's protest, the Commissioner of Public Safety, Eugene (Bull) Connor, placed police in the path of the children's march.

> As a thousand children and teen-agers marched . . . , [Connor] ordered the fire hoses opened. Jets of water under a hundred pounds of pressure knocked the children flat, ripping the clothes off some of them. Then Connor unleashed the police dogs—they ran wild, biting the children.
>
> Tremendous moral pressure [built] up in the nation. The newspaper and television pictures of the young people prostrated by fire hoses, beaten up, and bitten by dogs brought a storm of telegrams to the White House.[11]

---

9. King, p. 205.
10. King, pp. 226–27.
11. King, pp. 234–35.

President Kennedy's intervention enabled Dr. King to negotiate successfully with downtown merchants. The Birmingham protesters achieved all their original goals.

God's Will Be Done on Earth

During his eight-day incarceration in Birmingham in April, 1963, Reverend King wrote a "Letter from Birmingham City Jail" to reply to some white clergymen who criticized the on-going civil rights protests in their city. He responded to the criticism that the protests are poorly timed by writing: "We have waited for more than 340 years for our constitutional and God-given rights."[12] He answered the criticism that the protests were illegal by invoking the Christian tradition of natural law:

> There are two types of laws: there are *just* and there are *unjust* laws. I would agree with Saint Augustine that "an unjust law is no law at all."
>
> Now what is the difference between the two? How does one determine when a law is just or unjust? A just law is a man-made code that squares with the moral law or the law of God. An unjust law is a code that is out of harmony with the moral law. To put it in the terms of Saint Thomas Aquinas, an unjust law is a human law that is not rooted in eternal and natural law. Any law that uplifts human personality is just. Any law that degrades human personality is unjust. . . . So segregation is not only politically, economically, and sociologically unsound, but it is morally wrong and sinful.
>
> Let us turn to a more concrete example of just and unjust laws. . . . I was arrested Friday on a charge of parading without a permit. Now there is nothing wrong with an ordinance which requires a permit for a parade, but when the ordinance is used to preserve segregation and to deny citizens the First Amendment privilege of peaceful assembly and peaceful protest, then it becomes unjust [and peaceful disobedience is justified].
>
> Of course, there is nothing new about this kind of civil disobedience. It was seen sublimely in the refusal of Shadrach, Meshach, and Abendego to obey the laws of Nebuchadnezzar, because a higher moral law was involved. It was practiced superbly by the early Christians. . . .[13]
>
> Wherever the early Christians entered a town the power structure got disturbed and immediately sought to convict them for being

---

12. James Melvin Washington, Ed., *A Testament of Hope: The Essential Writings of Martin Luther King, Jr.* (New York: Harper and Row, 1986), p. 292.

13. Washington, pp. 293–94. Emphasis in original.

"disturbers of the peace" and "outside agitators." But they went on with the conviction that they were "a colony of heaven," and had to obey God rather than man.[14]

In our own day, too, King maintains, we must do God's will. "We must come to see that human progress never rolls in on wheels of inevitability. It comes through the tireless efforts and persistent work of men willing to be co-workers with God. . . ."[15]

Dr. King was a Christian minister, so he properly combined his religious convictions with his other beliefs when formulating and defending his views about racial segregation and appropriate methods of opposing it. He could not otherwise attain reflective equilibrium. Neither could the clergymen to whom Reverend King wrote his "Letter from Birmingham City Jail." King appropriately presented his views to religious readers as ones they should share, because, he claimed, these views cohere best with traditional Christian beliefs about God's will and natural law.

Almost everyone today agrees that Jim Crow laws and practices were abhorrent and the civil rights movement was justified. Appeals to God's will and natural law helped to improve the United States. Yet, such appeals raise difficulties as well owing to the different roles that secular and religious beliefs play in society.

Secular and Religious Beliefs

The First Amendment to the Constitution of the United States begins, "Congress shall make no law respecting an establishment of religion. . . ." Interpreting this **Establishment Clause** has required the Supreme Court to distinguish secular from religious matters to determine if a certain practice is or is not an establishment of religion. The court maintains that unlike specifically religious practices, secular practices are, in Justice William Brennan's words, "interwoven . . . deeply into the fabric of our civil polity."[16] Chief Justice Warren Burger used similar language when confronted with the question whether tax exempt status for religious charities violates the Establishment Clause. It does not because the practice of treating religious charities the same as other charities is "embedded in the fabric of our national life."[17]

---

14. Washington, p. 300.
15. Washington, p. 296.
16. *Abington School District v. Schempp*, 374 U.S. 203 (1963), at 303.
17. *Walz v. Tax Commission*, 397 U.S. 664 (1970), at 676.

Religion: optional, can be a part of life but not integral

Secular: part of social fabric → integral to function

I believe this is the key to understanding the difference *for politics* between secular and religious beliefs and values. *Beliefs and values are secular when they are part of the social fabric that holds society together, enabling it to maintain the way of life common to its people.*[18] Religious beliefs and values, by contrast, are not integral to our common way of life. (1) Some are unnecessary for our common way of life but do not interfere with it. (2) Other religious beliefs or values conflict with our way of life. Finally, (3) some beliefs and values are religious as well as secular. They are secular because they are integral to our way of life, but religious insofar as they are or were held by some people on religious grounds. Let us consider values first, then beliefs of fact.

Secular values include many rules and principles of conduct needed for people in society to get along peacefully with one another. These include prohibitions of murder, assault, and theft. Without widespread respect for these prohibitions, society would resemble Hobbes's state of nature.

As long as it doesn't pose a social disruption, it can be optional

Contrast such rules and principles with prohibitions against eating pork, eating meat on Friday, or cutting one's beard. Industrial societies can thrive without agreement on these matters. Some people can adhere to these restrictions while others do not without social disruption. This indicates that these prohibitions are not secular rules or principles. If they are associated with a religious tradition or text, they are religious beliefs of the first type; otherwise they are benign eccentricities.

Toleration of religious practices and individual eccentricities that deviate from the norm but do not otherwise endanger people is a secular value. Forcing people to eat what their religion forbids, for example, can provoke sectarian violence that interferes with our common way of life. In addition, individual liberty is a fundamental feature of our common way of life. Such liberty requires tolerating benign eccentricities.

Some religions do not advocate the toleration that our way of life requires. Suppose someone has a religious belief that no man should cut his beard and that it is the state's responsibility to enforce this regulation. Such religious beliefs fall into the second category, they conflict with our common way of life because, in this case, they deny liberties integral to that way of life.

Finally, there are secular values (integral to our way of life) that are also religious insofar as they are or were held on religious grounds. Justice Brennan writes, "Nearly every criminal law on the books can be traced to

---

18. I first developed many of the views in this section in an earlier book. See Peter S. Wenz, *Abortion Rights as Religious Freedom* (Philadelphia: Temple University Press, 1992), especially pp. 119–30.

36 Chapter 1: God's Will and Natural Law

some religious principle or inspiration. But that does not make the present enforcement of the criminal law in any sense an establishment of religion, simply because it accords with widely held religious principles."[19] Laws against murder and theft enforce two of the Ten Commandments, but as we saw in the Introduction, they are also needed to make social life tolerable. So they now have a secular basis. Similarly, literacy may have been valued originally for a religious reason, to help people know the word of God in the Bible. But it now has a secular purpose. An industrial society cannot maintain itself without a generally literate population. Similarly, the value of racial equality, for which Dr. King argued on religious as well as secular grounds, is now a secular value. It is hard to imagine a peaceful, prosperous America where Jim Crow prevails. But racial equality remains a religious value for people who believe it implicit in God's love for His children.

Beliefs of fact can also be religious. Consider the belief that there exists a benevolent, all-powerful God who offers eternal life as a reward for religious faith. People who believe that such a God exists can interact productively with those who deny God's existence, as can people who believe in life after death with those who disbelieve. These are religious beliefs of the first variety; they are not required by, but they are compatible with, our common way of life.

Some other religiously inspired beliefs of fact conflict with our common way of life. Consider the belief, based on a certain biblical interpretation, that Earth is less than 10,000 years old. This belief conflicts with beliefs in mainstream geology that Earth is billions of years old. Mainstream geological theories are used to explore for oil and natural gas, find important minerals, and identify areas prone to earthquakes. Oil, natural gas, and minerals are integral to our common way of life, so beliefs used to find them are also integral to our common way of life, and are therefore secular. In addition, mitigating earthquake damage serves secular values by protecting lives and property. Of course, not everyone has to believe that Earth is old for geology to serve society, only professionals in the field do. But the beliefs of these professionals and those who find their views credible are secular. Belief that Earth is only 10,000 years old is a religious belief of the second variety because its general acceptance would tend to undermine the continuation of our common way of life. For this reason, public schools reasonably teach the secular view.

Not only geology, but the scientific method that it employs, is secular because many discoveries in science underpin technological developments

---

19. *Abington*, at 303.

integral to our common way of life, such as telephones, computers, cars, bridges, airplanes, and satellite communications. This implies that beliefs do not have to be certain to be secular. Scientific investigations leave many uncertainties, hence the continuing need for research. But the scientific method, unlike the methods of obtaining factual information by reading the stars or the Bible, is integral to our common way of life. We could perpetuate our society quite well if no one ever consulted the stars or the Bible for factual information, but we could not do so if we forsook the scientific method.

Reason and Faith

One sign that a belief is a religious belief of the first variety (society can thrive without agreement on the matter) is the inability of common sense or scientific reason to favor one side more than the other. Consider the existence of God, defined as an all-powerful, benevolent creator who favors human flourishing. Some people say that evidence of such a being lies in the beauty of the world, the extraordinary suitability of Earth's climate and chemical composition to life, and the abilities of human beings to read, do mathematics, and write poetry, none of which were obviously necessary for survival during evolution. However, Earth may seem beautiful to us because we evolved here and our aesthetic appreciation, like the attraction of one rhinoceros for another, contributes to our species' survival. Second, Earth's climate and chemical composition might exist by chance rather than design. Because the number of planets in the universe is so large, extraordinary circumstances are likely to exist somewhere, and Earth just happens to be the site for circumstances conducive to life. Third, the human abilities to read, do math, and write poetry might have evolutionary advantage, or be tied genetically to traits that have evolutionary advantage. Finally, if God is good, why do innocent children die of incurable cancer and other bad things happen to good people? In sum, evidence can be given for and against belief in God.

The point here is that the methods of science and reason that help people understand nature in ways that contribute to our common way of life, the methods used in geology, biology, medicine, and the like cannot be used to favor one side more than the other regarding God's existence. It is not just that scientific reason is unable to settle the issue right now with certainty; science is inconclusive at any given time about many matters, and certainty is an elusive ideal. But on questions of secular science, people can imagine evidence that would and should incline unbiased minds toward one side rather than the other, even if some uncertainty remains. This is where religious matters, such as the issue of God's existence, differ. Every bit of evidence or reasoning on one side can be countered by the other side with evidence and reasoning of equal significance to unbiased minds. *Nothing that anyone is even trying to find or show would, by the standards of scientific methodology integral to our common way of life, convince an unbiased mind one way or the other regarding God's existence.*

This should come as no surprise. We depend as a society on the fruits of science, so unbiased minds must be swayed by what society considers valid science. Agreement about scientific reasoning underlies the general acceptance of many programs, such as inoculation programs in schools and safety standards at work, that provide secular benefits. We cannot agree to disagree about mainstream scientific method because disagreement threatens social disruption and endangers other values integral to our common way of life, such as health and safety. If people are allowed to reject science as they are allowed to reject God, they may refuse inoculations for their children and, in the view of authorities and other parents, endanger the health of other children. Social cooperation can easily break down when parents think their children are endangered.

Belief in God, by contrast, is a religious matter of the first variety, one on which people can agree to disagree. We do not need to accept common standards of evidence that enable one side to convince the other because we do not need the agreement that such standards would foster. So the common view in our society that religion is a matter of faith, not science, and that people have a right to their different faiths, is related to the fact that religious beliefs of the first variety are matters on which people can disagree without endangering our common way of life. Of course, in societies very different from our own, different methodologies and beliefs may be secular and different ones religious. It all depends on what methodologies and beliefs are needed to maintain their common way of life. In the extreme case of a society whose common way of life is based on beliefs about God or other supernatural entities, the distinction between "secular" and "religious," as we understand them, disappears. But here we confine ourselves to the United States and other industrial societies where belief in an all-powerful, benevolent deity is optional, because it is not integral to our common way of life.

In keeping with this view, *the Supreme Court of the United States has used the inadequacy of what counts as reason in our society to determine the truth of a belief as evidence that the belief is religious.* One case concerns conscientious objection to military service. At one time, young men in the United States were required to serve in the military unless they had some acceptable justification for exemption. One justification made acceptable by the Selective Service Act was objection "to participation in war in any form" by reason of "religious training and belief." Congress specified that "the term 'religious training and belief' does not include essentially political, sociological, or philosophical views. . . ."[20]

One young man, Mr. Gillette, claimed to be a conscientious objector but did not object to "war in any form." Instead, he objected to serving in the military because he believed the war in Vietnam, which was taking place at the time, was unjust. After being "convicted of willful failure to report for induction into the armed forces," he appealed to have his conviction overturned.[21]

Justice Thurgood Marshall, writing for the Supreme Court, accepted the distinction made by Congress between religious beliefs and "essentially political, sociological, or philosophical views. . . ." He wrote, "opposition to a particular war may more likely be political and nonconscientious, than otherwise. . . ."[22] It is political because it depends on such consideration as

> whether the purposes of the war are . . . ultimately defensive and pacific, or otherwise; whether the conflict is legal, or its prosecution decided upon by legal means. . . . A war may be thought "just" or not depending on one's assessment of these factors and many more: the character of the foe, or of allies; the place the war is fought; the likelihood that a military clash will issue in benefits, of various kinds, enough to override the inevitable costs of conflict.[23]

Marshall's distinction between what is political and what is religiously conscientious corresponds to the distinction between what is secular and religious as explained above. Political judgments depend on beliefs that people can investigate and challenge using our society's ordinary methods of inquiry to determine whether, for example, a given war is necessary, legal, and likely to succeed. Where religion is concerned, by contrast, no such reasons exist. Marshall referred to an earlier appellate decision on this issue in which Judge Augustus Hand wrote, "religious belief arises from a sense of the inadequacy of reason."[24] Exactly.

Well, almost exactly. Hand adequately describes only religious beliefs of the first variety, beliefs that are not essential for social cooperation and

---

20. *Gillette v. United States*, 401 U.S. 437 (1970), at 441-42, notes 4 and 5.
21. *Gillette*, at 439.
22. *Gillette*, at 455.
23. *Gillette*, at 455, note 21.
24. *United States v. Kauten*, 133 F.2nd 703 (1943), at 707.

our society's common way of life. Some other beliefs, such as belief that inoculations are unnecessary because faith in God cures all illness, are religious beliefs of the second variety. They endanger social cooperation and conflict with scientific methods of investigation integral to our common way of life. Such beliefs gain support from faith alone and are designated religious for precisely this reason.

In conclusion, some beliefs are religious because scientific reason cannot incline unbiased minds for or against (the first variety), whereas others (the second variety) are religious because they are held in the face of the kind of scientific reasoning that underpins social cooperation and our common way of life. In addition, some beliefs (the third variety) are secular, such as the belief that racial prejudice is wrong, but are held by some people on religious grounds instead of, or in addition to, secular grounds. Secular beliefs of fact can also be held on religious instead of secular grounds. For example, someone may believe in biblical rather than geological evidence that birds existed on Earth before the existence of human beings. Because secular sources of knowledge confirm the belief, it poses no danger to social cooperation or our common way of life.

Two more points are in order. First, to say that scientific reason cannot incline unbiased minds for or against religious beliefs of the first variety is not to say that reason is entirely inapplicable to such beliefs. People with such religious beliefs can, and if they want to be logical should, use reason to reach reflective equilibrium among their religious beliefs and between their religious and secular beliefs.

Second, *the inadequacy of reason to verify religious beliefs of the first variety does not mean that such beliefs are false. Secular investigation and reasoning can no more refute than uphold such religious beliefs.* God really may (or may not) exist. There really may (or may not) be life after death. Good people really may (or may not) be rewarded for good works or faith or both. None of these matters can be settled by secular arguments, but some views may yet be true and others false.

Disparate Traditions of Biblical Interpretation

Many people believe strongly that they have the true religion and that our country risks disaster when its laws and public policies ignore God's will. Some of these people, theocrats, would impose their religious views on society at large, believing that society exhibits dangerous tendencies toward immorality. They point to drug abuse, homosexuality, and abortion as examples of moral degeneration produced by uncertainties inherent in **humanistic ethics,** *ethics based entirely on human reason and emotion.*

Theocrats believe that society should follow God's commands, as theocrats understand them, to know with certainty the difference between right and wrong.

I find this view untenable in part because religious people differ among themselves about God's will and the conduct He requires. *The five avenues of access to God's will in the Judeo-Christian religious tradition—the Bible, history, personal revelation, prayerful meditation, and natural law—often lead religious people of good will to opposite positions on politically controversial matters.* I claim that when religious thinkers consult these means of access to God's will, they are actually seeking reflective equilibrium, as they should. *They reach different conclusions about God's will because their other beliefs differ. This undercuts claims that religion provides a more secure, certain, universal, and stable guide to ethics than humanistic reason. Like humanistic ethics, religious ethics incorporates traditions and social norms that vary according to group, time, and place.*

Consider first the influence of disparate group traditions on interpretations of the Bible, the Old and New Testaments. In Deuteronomy 12:23, God tells people when they eat meat they should not eat blood; "for the blood is the life; and you shall not eat the life with the flesh."[25] Traditional Jews interpret the verse to require that meat be cooked well done. But the traditional interpretation among Jehovah's Witnesses holds that the verse forbids life-saving transfusions of whole blood. Jehovah's Witnesses often refuse blood transfusions because they think violating God's command jeopardizes their immortal souls. The tradition among most Christians, by contrast, is to ignore this passage. This is interpretation through a group's tradition of selective attention.

Another example of different traditional interpretations comes from the command by God in Genesis 1:28 to "be fruitful and multiply and fill the earth." Some religious groups, such as Roman Catholics, think that this means human beings should never use any kind of birth control except periodic abstinence. Many other Christians find no moral guidance in this passage. Again, this is interpretation through a group's tradition of selective attention. In the 1950s, Connecticut law seemed to reflect the belief that God forbids contraception. "Any person who uses any drug, medicinal article or instrument for the purposes of preventing conception shall be fined not less than 50 dollars or imprisoned not less than 60 days nor more than one year or be both fined and imprisoned."[26]

---

25. *The Holy Bible,* The Standard Revised Version (New York: Thomas Nelson and Sons, 1953). Verses are cited in the text.
26. *Griswold v. Connecticut,* 381 U.S. 479, at 480.

42   Chapter 1: God's Will and Natural Law

The United States Supreme Court declared the law an unconstitutional invasion of privacy. They did not remark that the law probably reflected a particular tradition of biblical interpretation that many people do not share.

Disparate interpretations of Exodus 23:19 also exemplify the influence of group traditions. God says: "You shall not boil a kid [a young goat] in its mother's milk." Traditional Jews base many rules of kosher eating upon this verse. They do not eat milk and meat products at the same meal. At milk meals they use dishes, pots, pans, and flatware different from those used at meat meals. They wash milk and meat dishes, pots, pans, and flatware in different sinks. Christians generally ignore the verse about not cooking a kid in its mother's milk, acting as if it did not exist.

Traditional Jews recognize that their interpretation is not compelled by the words of the Bible. Rabbis even joke about an imagined conversation between God and Moses:

> GOD: You shall not boil a kid in its mother's milk.
>
> MOSES: You mean we should not eat milk and meat at the same meal?
>
> GOD: You shall not boil a kid in its mother's milk.
>
> MOSES: You mean we should have separate dishes for milk and meat meals?
>
> GOD: You shall not boil a kid in its mother's milk.
>
> MOSES: You mean we should have separate flatware and serving dishes for milk and meat meals?
>
> GOD: You shall not boil a kid in its mother's milk.
>
> MOSES: You mean we should have separate sinks for washing the dishes, pots, pans, and flatware of milk and meat meals?
>
> GOD: O.K. Have it your way.[27]

Such traditions are poor bases for public policy. In a society with a Jewish majority, such as Israel, non-Jews would certainly resent imposition of this traditional interpretation on society at large, for example, through laws that require all restaurants to keep kosher. Public health requirements on restaurants, by contrast, justified by science-based reasons concerning communicable diseases, would be entirely acceptable.

---

27. I owe this example to Rabbi Barry Marks of Temple Israel, Springfield, Illinois.

Social Morality and Biblical Interpretation

A second source of different biblical interpretations is a community's current or emerging social morality. In these cases, the Bible is used to reinforce people's preexisting moral beliefs, whether those beliefs favor the status quo or reform. As we have seen, religious thinkers properly integrate their religious with their secular views in quest of reflective equilibrium. An inevitable result is that religious people with different secular moral views interpret the Bible differently, so biblical bases for public policy are no more secure, certain, universal, or stable than secular bases are.

A striking example of the Bible's perceived meaning reflecting social morality concerns race relations. Before the Civil War, many proslavery Americans in the South interpreted the Bible to endorse slavery. Yet it is hard to imagine a more odious practice.

> A slave entered the world in a one-room dirt floored shack. Drafty in winter, reeking in summer, slave cabins bred pneumonia, typhus, cholera, tuberculosis. The child who survived to be sent to the fields at 12 was likely to have rotten teeth, worms, dysentery, malaria. Fewer than four out of 100 slaves lived to be 60.
>
> On the auction block, blacks were made to jump and dance to demonstrate their sprightliness and good cheer, were often stripped to show how strong they were, how little whipping they needed. "The customers would feel our bodies," an exslave recalled, "and make us show our teeth, precisely as a jockey examines a horse." Since slave marriages had no legal status, preachers changed the wedding vows to read, "until death or *distance* do you part."
>
> "Them days was hell," [one] woman remembered. "Babies was snatched from their mother's breast and sold. . . . Childrens was separated from sisters and brothers and never saw each other agin. Course they cried. You think they not cry when they was sold like cattle?"[28]

Slavery was worse than Jim Crow, which Martin Luther King, Jr. found abhorrent to God's will. Yet slavery had Christian religious defenders as well as opponents.

When Africans and African Americans were held as slaves, leading interpretations of the Bible found slavery to be commanded by God. The Bible clearly endorses the slavery practiced by Hebrews in biblical times.

> You may buy male and female slaves from among the nations that are about you. You may also buy from among the strangers who

---

28. Geoffrey C. Ward, Rick Burns, and Ken Burns, *The Civil War* (New York: Alfred A. Knopf), front flap, in Moldovan, p. 56.

sojourn with you and their families that are with you, who have been born in your land; and they may be your property. You may bequeath them to your sons after you, to inherit as a possession for ever. (Leviticus 25:44–46)

Many Christians in the United States believed that the Bible not only allows slavery but also promotes the enslavement of Africans and African Americans in the United States. One biblical source often cited was the story of Noah; historian Winthrop Jordan explains:

> The original story . . . was that after the Flood, Ham had looked upon his father's nakedness as Noah lay drunk in his tent, but the other two sons, Shem and Japheth, had covered their father without looking upon him; when Noah awoke he cursed Canaan, son of Ham, saying that he would be a "servant of servants" unto his brothers.[29]

The fact that *black* people are slaves, that the descendents of Canaan are black, is explained by Jordan as stemming from the fact that the name 'Ham' "originally connoted both 'dark' and 'hot.'"[30]

The great English jurist Sir Edward Coke (1552–1634) justified slavery on these grounds: "This is assured, that Bondage or Servitude was first inflicted for dishonouring of Parents: For Cham [Ham] the Father of Canaan . . . seeing the nakedness of his Father Noah, and shewing it in Derision to his Brethren, was therefore punished in his Son Canaan with Bondage." So whites enslaving blacks accords with God's will.

Few people in the United States interpret the Bible this way today because we live in a society that rejects slavery as morally repugnant. We tend to ignore those passages in the Bible where slavery is endorsed (interpretation by selective attention) and see no implications regarding slavery in the story of Noah. This is because we have a different social context, one with antislavery values. The words of the Bible have not changed, but their meaning for readers of good will has changed owing to changes in social values. Biblical interpretation in reflective equilibrium requires incorporation of these values.

Interpretations may promote emerging values instead of reinforce established views. Although slave owners appealed to the Bible, so did abolitionists. *David Walker's Appeal,* for example, asked in 1829:

> How can the preachers and people of America believe the Bible? Does it teach them any distinction on account of a man's colour?

---

29. Winthrop D. Jordan, *White over Black: American Attitudes Toward the Negro, 1550–1812* (Chapel Hill: University of North Carolina Press, 1968), p. 17.

30. Jordan, p. 19.

> Hearken, Americans! To the injunctions of our Lord and Master, to his humble followers.
>
> "Go ye, therefore, and teach all nations, baptizing them in the name of the Father, and of the Son, and of the Holy Ghost."
>
> I declare, that the very face of these injunctions appear to . . . not show the slightest degree of distinction [according to color].[31]

James G. Birney's *Letter to the Ministers and Elders* (1834) and Theodore Weld's *The Bible against Slavery* (1837) also used Christian arguments against slavery.[32]

Another example of using the Bible to promote moral and political reform is Martin Luther King, Jr.'s use of the Bible to argue against Jim Crow. However, whether people use the Bible to reinforce the moral status quo or promote reform, they are using the Bible to add weight to beliefs they consider defensible on secular grounds. They are properly seeking reflective equilibrium among all their views.

Controversies about homosexuality illustrate this point as well. Homosexuals increasingly seek laws to end discrimination on the basis of sexual orientation. Some other people favor such discrimination because they find homosexuality morally offensive and socially dangerous. The two sides interpret the Bible differently.

Opponents of homosexuality point to Bible verses in which God lays down rules of sexual conduct and punishments for their breach:

> If a man commits adultery with the wife of his neighbor, both the adulterer and the adulteress shall be put to death. The man who lies with his father's wife has uncovered his father's nakedness; both of them shall be put to death, their blood is upon them. If a man lies with his daughter-in-law, both of them shall be put to death; they have committed incest, their blood is upon them. If a man lies with a male as with a woman, both of them have committed an abomination; they shall be put to death, their blood is upon them. (Leviticus, 20:10–13)

Besides showing that the Bible anticipates many soap opera plots, these verses suggest that homosexuality is particularly bad. It alone is called "an abomination."

The New Testament echoes this view. Saint Paul writes that because people spurned God, "God gave them up to dishonorable passions. Their women exchanged natural relations for unnatural, and the men likewise

---

31. David Walker, *David Walker's Appeal* (New York: Hill and Wang, 1995), pp. 41–42.
32. See John Hope Franklin and Alfred A. Moss, Jr., *From Slavery to Freedom: A History of African Americans*, 7th ed. (New York: McGraw-Hill, 1994), p. 173.

gave up natural relations with women and were consumed with passion for one another, men committing shameless acts with men . . ." (Romans 1:26–27). Homosexuality seems to violate God's law.

The Hebrew Scriptures indicate also that failure to obey God can result in physical calamity.

> If you will not obey the voice of the Lord your God . . . the Lord will smite you with consumption, and with fever, inflammation, and fiery heat, and with drought, and with blasting, and with mildew. . . . The Lord will make the rain of your land powder and dust; from heaven it shall come down upon you until you are destroyed. (Deut. 28:15, 22, and 24)

With this in mind, some religious people oppose not only laws designed to protect homosexuals from discrimination but also any demonstrations of "gay pride." When Orlando, Florida, permitted the display of "gay days" flags on street-lamp poles, Reverend Pat Robertson said on "The 700 Club" program:

> The Apostle Paul made it abundantly clear in the Book of Romans that the acceptance of homosexuality is the last step in the decline of Gentile civilization. . . . I would warn Orlando that you're right in the way of some serious hurricanes, and I don't think I'd be waving those flags in God's face if I were you. . . . It'll bring about terrorist bombs; it'll bring earthquakes, tornadoes, and possibly a meteor.[33]

Some Christians, however, challenge Robertson's interpretation of St. Paul's Letter to the Romans. Patricia Beattie Jung and Ralph F. Smith claim that St. Paul was merely discussing the disruptive effects of idolatry on people who, in Paul's words, "exchanged the glory of the immortal God for images resembling mortal man or birds or animals or reptiles" (Romans 1:23). According to Jung and Smith, "Paul presupposed that all same-sex desires and behaviors among the Gentiles resulted from their insatiable lust for sexual variety, rooted ultimately in their idolatry." Paul's words do not tell us what he would think about "the just, faithful, and loving unions of homosexual persons" unrelated to idolatry and without "insatiable lust for sexual variety."[34]

---

33. Thomas B. Edsall, *The Washington Post*, June 10, 1998. Found at www.loper.org/~george/trends/1998/Jun/77.html.
34. Patricia Beattie Jung and Ralph F. Smith, *Heterosexism: An Ethical Challenge* (Albany: State University of New York Press, 1993), pp. 80–81.

In sum, *biblical interpretation is subject to all the vagaries of tradition, social morality, and prejudice that beset humanistic ethics. So biblically based religious ethics does not give people a more certain, secure, universal, or stable basis for distinguishing right from wrong than do humanistic ethics.*

Literal Interpretations of the Bible

Some people try to avoid disparate interpretations of the Bible by insisting on a literal reading. Leviticus 18:6–7, for example, says: "None of you shall approach to any that is near of kin to him, to uncover nakedness: I am the Lord. You shall not uncover the nakedness of your father, which is the nakedness of your mother; she is your mother, you shall not uncover her nakedness." Interpreting this command literally seems reasonable. Who wants to see their parents naked, anyway?

In some cases, however, a literal interpretation yields a rule that seems too harsh. Deuteronomy 17:3–6 specifies death by stoning for any-one among the Hebrew people who "has gone and served other gods and worshiped them, or the sun or the moon and any of the host of heaven." It seems here that Jews are supposed to be stoned to death if they prac-tice a different religion or worship nature. No one wants to apply this literally today, even though it would give new meaning to being stoned on Earth Day!

A Christian might think that the Old Testament is too harsh to be applied literally, but not the New Testament. However, some verses of the Gospel raise similar problems. Consider the Sermon on the Mount. Jesus says, "Do not resist one who is evil. But if any one strikes you on the right cheek, turn to him the other also; and if any one would sue you and take your coat, let him have your cloak as well . . ." (Matt. 5:39–40). Taken lit-erally, this means that Christians must submit to certain forms of physical assault and material fraud without protest and then invite further abuse of the same kind or worse. On this literal reading, it is hard to imagine criminal justice in a Christian country.

Here is another New Testament command that few American Chris-tians today would apply literally. Saint Paul wrote to the church in Corinth: "Women should keep silence in the churches. For they are not permitted to speak, but should be subordinate, as even the law says. If there is anything they desire to know, let them ask their husbands at home. For it is shameful for a woman to speak in church" (I Corinthians

14:34–35). In a country where women increasingly demand equal treatment and respect from men, a church where women could not speak would quickly be empty.

So what should one do when literal readings seem overly strict (stoning for Jews who start practicing other religions and requiring that victims of assault make themselves available for further assault) or morally obnoxious (disallowing women to speak in church)? In such cases people either resort to the kind of nonliteral interpretation already discussed or they simply ignore the biblical passage in question.

In sum, *selective attention and disparate interpretations owing to differences in traditions or social morality perpetuate disagreements about the Bible's meaning. Even among people with biblical faith it is hard to justify public policies by appealing to God's will as expressed in the Bible.*

History, Personal Revelation, and Prayerful Meditation

Other methods of access to God's will also yield disparate interpretations that reflect differences among social groups. Consider attempts to discover God's will through a consideration of history, such as the history of the Crusades. Frederick Barbarossa, a Christian king preparing for the Third Crusade in 1188, wrote to the Muslim ruler Saladin, "We require you to give back the [holy] land . . . as laid down by divine law."[35] Barbarossa thought that God wanted Muslims to transfer rule of the Holy Land to Christians, which accorded with the social consensus in his group.

Saladin replied to Frederick: "It is in God's might that we shall come out against you. . . . God willing, we will . . . take possession of all your territories. . . ."[36] In other words, God wants us to have the land, so He'll make sure we kick your butt. Saladin's opinion also reflected the social consensus in his group.

It seems that at least one of them must have been wrong, Barbarossa or Saladin. Does history give us the answer? Does the fact that Christians lost control of the Holy Land for about 700 years suggest that God was on Saladin's side? Or does the fact that Christians created the industrial

---

35. Frederick Barbarossa, "Frederick Barbarossa Threatens Saladin," in *The Crusades,* Brenda Stalcup, Ed. (San Diego: Greenhaven Press, 2000), pp. 218–219, at 219.
36. Saladin, "Saladin's Defiant Reply," in Stalcup, Ed., pp. 219–220, at 220.

revolution, which gave them the power of conquest in the 20th century, suggest that God was on the Christian side? But Muslims now rule everywhere in the Middle East outside of Israel. Moreover, the internal combustion engine is an important part of the industrial revolution, and Muslim countries control the world's greatest concentration of oil. Now, on whose side does God seem to be?

Few thinkers today believe, as did many Crusaders and their Muslim adversaries, that we know God's will by who wins a war or controls valuable resources. Evil people often succeed. In 1953 Joseph Stalin died unpunished after killing millions of his countrymen, and in the 1990s most Christian Serbs who killed and raped Bosnian Muslims escaped retribution. But no one in our society attributes their successes to God's will. In short, *we do not believe that might makes right; we do not think that the ability to impose one's will by force indicates God's favor.* The United States can defeat other countries in war, but this neither demonstrates God's will nor justifies military conquest.

Another approach to discovering God's will is **personal revelation,** *a special communication from God, such as in a dream or an apparition.* However, *we tend to accept only those personal revelations from God that reinforce values that we already hold and attribute to God.* Suppose, for example, that you heard a voice that you thought was a personal revelation. How could you tell it was not a delusion? What if the message ran counter to common morality and to what your religious training leads you to expect of God? Suppose the message was that you should kill your grandfather. This resembles God's command to Abraham that Abraham kill his son Isaac. At the last minute, according to the Bible, God substituted a lamb for Isaac, indicating that God really does not want people to kill their relatives for no good reason. Yet the message you are getting is to kill your grandfather by poisoning his food. Should you do as the voice commands and hope that God will save your grandfather as he saved Isaac by putting in a substitute at the last minute? There are no lambs around, but the neighbor's cat is handy.

I think most people would assume that the voice did not represent God at all. Rather than endanger their grandfather's life, they would go to counseling to find out why they are having delusions. (I would recommend this to my grandchildren.) On the other hand, you might be quite willing to accept as revelatory a voice telling you to attend medical school and find a cure for cancer or help build a Habitat for Humanity house. Such commands fit better with your other views held in reflective equilibrium.

Just as biblical interpretations change with changes in social morality, so do accepted revelations. An example comes from a 20th-century change in doctrine of the Church of Jesus Christ of Latter-Day Saints, that is, the Mormons.[37] Mormons always accepted blacks as full members of the church, even before the Civil War, which was one cause of violent opposition to the church in proslavery Missouri. The only limitation on blacks was their exclusion from the priesthood.

Mormons believe that prophets exist in our day and receive revelations from God. In 1978, Spencer W. Kimball, who was the 12th prophet of the church, received a revelation that the priesthood should be granted to all men regardless of race, color, ethnicity, or heritage. Owing to widespread racism in the United States before the Civil War, the exclusion of blacks from the priesthood accorded better with prevailing social attitudes about right and wrong than did their inclusion. By the 1970s, however, racism had declined and was in disrepute, so the inclusion of blacks in the Mormon priesthood accorded better with prevailing moral views than did their exclusion. Again, it seems that what people consider the word of God, whether through revelation or biblical interpretation, mostly reinforces preexisting values and perspectives, as it should among people seeking reflective equilibrium.

It is the same story with prayerful meditation. People sometimes consult the Bible and pray when they face important choices in personal and political life. President Bush is said to do so regularly.[38] Even if God does not offer revelation in such cases, it is possible that He offers inspiration. The Spirit of God, whom Christians consider the Trinity's Third Person, may guide people's thought processes on paths that accord with God's will. This is the point of such prayerful reading and reflection. The problem, however, is that the results of prayerful meditation may simply reflect the individual's religious tradition or preexisting social or moral views. In 2003, Pope John Paul II reflected prayerfully about a possible American-led war against Iraq and found that such a war was wrong. George Bush's prayerful reflection yielded opposite results. In both cases, the results accorded with the person's preexisting moral views. It is impossible to know if the Holy Spirit was actively involved.

In sum, history, personal revelation, and prayerful meditation do not yield more certain, secure, universal, or stable ethical guidance than do humanistic ethics.

---

37. My source of information on this matter is an e-mail from Dr. Kyle Weir.
38. Howard Fineman, "Bush and God," *Newsweek*, Vol. CXLI, No. 10 (March 10, 2003), pp. 22–30.

Natural Law

Christians often look to nature for indications of God's will because, they believe, God created the earth and all its inhabitants and declared the creation to be good. So, *what is natural often indicates divine commands and restrictions. Some nonreligious thinkers also look to nature for guidance, believing that what is natural tends to be good.* Whether or not it is religiously inspired, the appeal to nature for moral guidance is the **natural-law** perspective. Natural law can be an alternative or supplement to finding God's will in history, personal revelation, reflection, and Scripture, but *nature seldom provides clear guidance, whether or not it is thought to indicate God's will.*

Consider the debate over whether homosexuals should be allowed same-sex marriage. One critic offers a natural-law argument against allowing such marriages:

> Humans still reproduce from the mating of a male and a female. This is where we all come from. Our biological parents are not two men or two women. . . . Thus there is a basis in reality to distinguish heterosexual families with children as being directly part of the process of reproduction and the continuing of the human species. The reproductive process and biological parents and families do create a logical distinction that is not an arbitrary line.[39]

This seems correct, but does not help to settle the issue of allowing same-sex marriage. On the author's reasoning the government might give special help to "heterosexual families with children," because they are "directly part of the process of . . . continuing the human species." But nothing in that reasoning rules out same-sex unions. The importance of heterosexuality in nature does not imply that alternatives should be illegal.

Another natural-law argument, this one against homosexuality in general, comes from a lay Catholic group in Minnesota. They compare homosexuality to bulimia:

> Suppose someone were to decide that they were going to eat for pleasure alone and, not wanting to experience the natural result of such activity, deliberately induce vomiting to keep from gaining weight. Such an activity is not ordered towards the natural process of eating. . . . Food is meant to go on a one-way trip. The organs of digestion are designed for this process.
>
> In the same way the sexual organs are designed for certain functions. . . . The male and female bodies . . . are different. By light of

---

39. www.perkel.com/politics/issues/samesex.htm, March 19, 2003.

reason alone we can tell that the male and female organs are made for different purposes. We can also determine by reason alone what those purposes are. When someone uses his or her sexual organs for purposes other than those for which they are specifically designed, such actions are disordered. . . . It is not the way God wants us to be. We can tell by the bodies He gave us.[40]

Such natural-law arguments, like arguments based on biblical interpretation, seldom convince the uncommitted, because opposing arguments, also based on natural law, can be strong. Jung and Smith, for example, would reject the analogy between homosexuality and bulimia. They claim that nature displays many traits that are statistically abnormal, but still natural. They consider homosexuality to be in this regard like left-handedness. Left-handedness is not the statistical norm, and left-handed people were once viewed with suspicion. "Sometimes people linked left-handedness with witchcraft and amputated the offending limb," Jung and Smith write. Before the 20th century it was common to train left-handed people to switch hands. Now, however, left-handedness is considered completely natural. Similarly, Jung and Smith claim, "gay men and lesbians act naturally when they engage in homosexual conduct."[41] Maybe.

The fundamental objection to natural-law arguments is that we do not always value what is natural. Consider something that is both natural and, according to the Bible's book of Genesis, ordained by God. In response to their sin of disobedience, God expelled Adam and Eve from the Garden of Eden and said to Eve, "I will greatly multiply your pain in childbearing; in pain you shall bring forth children . . ." (Gen. 3:16). Great pain in childbirth is not only obviously natural but, for many religious people, established by God for just cause. Nevertheless, few people in our society conclude that it is good. Most pregnant women attempt to reduce pain in childbirth. No one proposes public policies, such as a ban on epidurals during delivery, designed to ensure that women experience the full measure of natural pain in childbirth.

Our culture avoids or modifies what is natural in myriad ways. Plastics do not grow on trees. They were invented in chemical laboratories and are generally useful. Animal breeders have modified domestic and agricultural animals since prehistoric times. Standard milk cows could never live in the wild without human care because they were bred by people for their milk-producing capacity in disregard of abilities to fend for themselves

---

40. "Homosexuality and the Natural Law," published by The Minnesota St. Thomas More Chapter of Catholics United for the Faith, January 2002, www.mncuf.org.
41. Jung and Smith, p. 31.

without human support. Like plastics, they would never exist on Earth without human intervention. People do not naturally fly, yet we do fly because people have invented planes. Few people object to epidurals, plastics, milk cows, or human flight simply because they are unnatural. Taken by itself, the difference between what is natural and what is unnatural is seldom morally important.

Of course, in another sense, all these products of human ingenuity are natural because human beings are part of nature, and ingenuity is part of human nature. But if something is natural when people invent it, then all distinctions between the natural and the unnatural disappear. Pain in childbirth is natural, but so is the absence of pain, because people invented epidurals. Similarly, if homosexuality is natural, then of course it is natural. If, however, it was invented by people, then because people are naturally inventive, it is still natural. The same is true of bulimia. It is a naturally ingenious way of having your cake and seeing it later.

This approach is no good because we do make a distinction between what is natural and what is unnatural. Yet—and here is the point—this distinction taken by itself does not settle policy disputes. For example, people consider bulimia a disorder not because it is unnatural but because it harms those who practice it. Similarly, controversies about epidurals center not on what is natural but on fears that they harm the baby during birth. Controversies about plastics concern not their naturalness but, for example, their manufacture, which may add health-impairing chemicals to the environment. Controversies about milk production concern the use, for example, of antibiotics that may keep cows healthy but may also endanger human health when trace amounts appear in the milk. *In general, we care less about what is natural than about what is good, valuable, or just.*

Replace Religious Arguments with Secular Arguments

As we have seen, religious views are usually combined with secular views in people's minds, and thoughtful religious people do this purposely to achieve reflective equilibrium among all their beliefs. However, to appeal to society in general, *religious people should exclude their specifically religious beliefs from their arguments regarding laws and public policies.* Instead, *they should base such arguments exclusively on beliefs that they can support with secular reasons.*

In his third debate with John Kerry, President Bush suggested that religious arguments are not sufficient in the public realm. He said, "I'm mindful in a free society that people can worship if they want to or not. You're equally an American if you choose to worship an Almighty and if you choose not to. If you're a Christian, Jew, or Muslim you're equally an American."[42] This suggests that his policies, to be appreciated by all Americans, should be justified by secular, not purely religious considerations.

Many faith-based thinkers do this. Consider, for example, the controversial claim that God does not want people to be active homosexuals. In addition to reasons based on controversial religious views, faith-based thinkers give secular reasons. Jewish historian Dennis Prager, for example, argues that allowing active homosexuals to become rabbis would make homosexuality seem legitimate, and widespread acceptance of homosexuality is bad for women. He writes: "There seems to be a direct correlation between the prevalence of male homosexuality and the relegation of women to a low societal role. At the same time, the emancipation of women has been a function of Western civilization, the civilization least tolerant of homosexuality."[43] Examples of societies in which women were suppressed while homosexuality flourished include ancient Greece, medieval France, and traditional China, according to Prager.

Philosopher William J. Bennett, opposed to homosexuality on religious grounds, also gives secular reasons that he thinks sufficient to justify his position. He focuses on denying marriage to same-sex couples. Proponents of same-sex marriage claim that it will discourage promiscuity among homosexuals, leading to more stable unions that benefit both homosexuals and society. Bennett counters, "it is not marriage that domesticates men; it is women." Men have a natural inclination toward promiscuity, according to Bennett, so the likely result of allowing homosexual marriage would be that "instead of marriage radically tempering homosexual promiscuity, same-sex marriage . . . would lead to the further legitimation of 'extramarital outlets' for all,"[44] contributing to the breakdown of the nuclear family.

Another secular reason for disallowing same-sex marriage concerns adoption, according to James Q. Wilson, Professor of Management and Public Policy. Children adopted at birth by same-sex couples may be harmed by learning "from the first years of life that [they] are, because of [their] family's position, radically different from almost all other children. . . . No one can now say how grievous this would be. We know

---

42. www.nytimes.com/2004/10/14/politics/campaign/14text.html, p. 17.

43. Denis Prager, "Judaism, Homosexuality and Civilization," *Ultimate Issues*, Vol. 6, No. 2 (April-June 1990), p. 11.

44. William J. Bennett, *The Broken Hearth: Reversing the Moral Collapse of the American Family* (New York: Doubleday, 2001), pp. 117 and 118.

that young children tease one another unmercifully; adding this dimension does not seem to be a step in the right direction."[45]

Secular reasons can also support allowing homosexuals to become rabbis, marry one another, and adopt children. For example, psychological tests show that unlike bulimia, homosexuality is not a psychological disorder. Jung and Smith write:

> The American Psychiatric Association removed homosexuality from its list of mental illnesses in 1973. Studies demonstrated that gay men and lesbians were no more or less likely to be socially dysfunctional or emotionally disturbed . . . than were heterosexual people. This judgment has received global confirmation [from] the World Health Organization. . . .[46]

If homosexuals are psychologically normal, perhaps they should be allowed to become rabbis, marry one another, and adopt children.

These claims, regardless of their merits, illustrate the possibility of replacing religious arguments about homosexuality with secular arguments. Personality tests are the commonly accepted way of testing for mental abnormality in our society. On the other side, people opposed to gay rights appeal to such commonly accepted values as opportunity for women, the socialization of children to become loyal, contributing citizens (for which the nuclear family may be essential), and the protection of adopted children from unnecessary trauma. These arguments focus debate about gay rights on considerations that can be fruitfully investigated regardless of religious differences.

The Importance of Nature and Religion

It might seem at this point that public policy discussions can dispense with natural law and religion altogether, but this is not true. First, *natural law may legitimately affect public policy discussions by distinguishing the possible from the impossible.* This is relevant because if we discover that something is beyond human capability, it makes no sense to require it of people. **Ought implies can.** *If you say that people ought to do something, you assume that they can do it; otherwise the "ought" makes no sense.*

---

45. James Q. Wilson, "Against Homosexual Marriage," *Commentary,* Vol. 101, No. 3 (March 1996), in *Taking Sides: Clashing Views on Controversial Legal Issues,* 10th ed., M. Ethan Katsh and William Rose, Eds. (Guilford, CT: McGraw-Hill/Dushkin, 2002), pp. 305–311, at 310.

46. Jung and Smith, p. 19.

Consider, for example, government programs designed to provide equal opportunity for women. Some people justify such programs on the ground that women are just as capable as men, so the fact that they occupy fewer positions of power than men do indicates unjust prejudice that the government should combat. Sociologist Steven Goldberg argues against such reasoning. Goldberg claims in *Why Men Rule* that "neuroendocrinological differences between men and women"—natural, biological differences—make men on average more emotionally predisposed than women to focus on attaining positions of prominence in hierarchical organizations. The result is that men inevitably rule because they generally put more energy into competition than women do.[47] Programs to give women equal opportunity may be justified, but not by the fact that men rule. More important, such programs should not continue until women rule equally with men, because human psychology makes this impossible.

Whether Goldberg is right or wrong, his reasoning from premise to conclusion is correct. If for biological reasons women cannot attain equal power with men in hierarchical societies such as ours, then policymakers should not try to impose such equality. Ought implies can. Programs to combat prejudice against women should not aim at the impossible goal of equal power for women (if that really is impossible).

What is natural is important also to environmentalists interested in preserving nature. Environmentalists usually want to preserve ecosystems, such as old-growth forests in the Pacific Northwest, which are not the result of human engineering. They want to preserve species in their natural habitat rather than in zoos. But the goal is to preserve certain natural things, not to rule out everything unnatural.

Caution is another reason to think about what is natural. Whether or not God created nature, human understanding of nature is limited. Many ancient civilizations were ruined by ecologically unsustainable agriculture. North Africa, for example, was the breadbasket of the Roman Empire until ancient agriculture diminished its food-producing potential. We need to know which crops are naturally suited to an area.

Attempts to manipulate nature often backfire owing to ignorance about what is natural. Rachel Carson gives many examples in *Silent Spring*:

> Many thousands of gallons of chemicals have been discharged along roadsides in the name of ragweed control. But the unfortunate truth is that blanket spraying is resulting in more ragweed, not less. Ragweed is an annual: its seedlings require open soil to become established

---

47. Steven Goldberg, *Why Men Rule: A Theory of Male Dominance* (Chicago: Open Court, 1993), pp. 64–65.

each year. Our best protection against this plant is therefore the maintenance of dense shrubs, ferns, and other perennial vegetation. Spraying frequently destroys this protective vegetation and creates open, barren areas which the ragweed hastens to fill.[48]

Fire suppression in national forests is another example. The goal was to preserve forests by suppressing all forest fires. But in the absence of human control, fires started by lightning clear away underbrush in forests. When such fires are suppressed, underbrush builds up so that when fires do eventually start, they burn much hotter and are far more destructive than any that would otherwise have occurred. Fire suppression thus increases the loss of trees to fire.

Caution is increasingly important as science and technology enable us to alter nature more radically. Consider genetic engineering. For most people, including most environmentalists, the fact that engineered plants are unnatural is no problem by itself. Traditional plant breeding also yields results different from anything nature would produce without people. But because people have been breeding plants since prehistory, few worry about its products. Genetic engineering, by contrast, is new and much more powerful. We can change plants in ways previously unimaginable. This greater deviation from nature corresponds to greater risk of unanticipated by-products. The risk of catastrophe is the main point of objecting to genetic engineering on grounds that it is unnatural. *We should be cautious when manipulating nature to avoid negative effects.*

Just as naturalness is sometimes important in political controversies even though naturalness is not always good, religion is sometimes important even though claims about what God wants cannot be decisive. First, many people feel so strongly about their religious beliefs that they would resist interference with their religious practices. As noted earlier, *toleration of all religions and religious practices that do not clearly harm others is therefore a secular norm because intolerance jeopardizes peaceful and productive social interaction.* Second, as we have seen, *the moral content of religions often inspires people to make secular improvements,* as with Martin Luther King, Jr. and the civil rights movement. However, the secular arguments King uses are appropriate in all political contexts, whereas arguments based on God's will are appropriate only in discussions among people who participate in the relevant religious tradition.

Third, people are most effective in political argument when they appeal to beliefs that others hold. *In a society such as ours, in which many people*

---

48. Rachel Carson, *Silent Spring* (New York: Fawcett, 1962), pp. 78–79.

hold religious beliefs, political arguments reasonably appeal to those beliefs. If I know, for example, that someone is a Christian who believes that God is the father of all humanity and cares equally about all human beings, then I reasonably appeal to this belief when arguing for the rich to pay higher taxes so the poor can have adequate food, shelter, or education. So Dr. King was correct to use religious considerations when addressing fellow believers.

This does not mean, however, that people should accept or reject a war based on claims about divine guidance. We must distinguish inspiration from justification. **Inspiration** concerns the origins of ideas; **justification,** by contrast, concerns their acceptability. Secular investigation can neither confirm nor deny that the idea for a public policy came from divine inspiration. But before that policy is justifiably imposed on society at large, believers and nonbelievers alike, it must have a rationale grounded in secular reasons. When war is a good idea, its merits should be clear without claims of divine inspiration. Opposition should also be justified without invoking God.

The danger of claiming divine warrant for political views is dogmatism. People who think they are serving God are often unwilling to listen to others or compromise. Whatever God wants must be absolutely correct, they often reason, so negotiation and compromise are inappropriate. Without negotiation and compromise, however, many conflicts worsen, leading to violence and prolonged human suffering. So, even though secular thought cannot rule out the possibility of good public policies originating in divine inspiration, people who favor domestic tranquility in a pluralistic society try to avoid mixing religion and politics.

CONCLUSION

This was Thomas Jefferson's view. Regardless of his invocation of God in the Declaration of Independence, Jefferson believed that public policies must be judged on secular grounds. Twenty-five years after he wrote the Declaration and shortly after he became president of the United States, Jefferson received a letter from Baptists in Danbury, Connecticut, complaining of religious persecution by the state's majority Congregationalist establishment. Jefferson's sympathetic reply quoted the First Amendment to the Constitution, passed in 1791: "Congress shall make no law respecting an establishment of religion, or prohibiting the free exercise thereof." Jefferson claimed that this amendment built "a wall of separation between church and State."[49]

---

49. Andrew Lipscomb and Albert Bergh, *The Writings of Thomas Jefferson,* Vol. 16 (Washington, D.C.: Thomas Jefferson Memorial Association of the United States, 1905), p. 282. The letter is dated January 1, 1802.

The wall metaphor may be too strong, since we have found legitimate ties between religion and politics. Still, the metaphor underlines the American expectation that public policies be justified on secular grounds. We next consider secular political philosophies enmeshed in the secular reasons that people give for their political views.

JUDGMENT CALLS

1. Genetic engineering has produced a featherless chicken. How might the repugnance that some people experience at the thought of such a chicken be related to the claim that naturalness by itself is seldom important?[50]

2. What laws or public policies would follow from taking *literally* the biblical command to "be fruitful and multiply and fill the earth?" How full does the command suggest Earth become? Docs the command mean that married couples must have as many children as physically possible? Does it mean that they should have sex only in order to have children, or may they have sex at times of least fertility precisely to avoid pregnancy? If they are allowed to avoid pregnancy by timing their sex, can they do so with contraceptives? Does the command mean that every fertile man and woman should have children, or is celibacy allowed? Most important, what is there in the literal meaning of the command to answer these questions?

3. Given the practice and divine endorsement of polygamy in biblical times, how do Christians and Jews, consistent with reflective equilibrium, justify rejecting polygamy today?

4. How might Jehovah's Witnesses differentiate their refusal of blood transfusions needed to save their lives from physician-assisted suicide? What differences, if any, make a difference? Why do some people think these differences are important and others disagree?

5. Jung and Smith claim that homosexuality is like left-handedness. But right and left hands are anatomically the same, whereas the sex organs of men and women are anatomically different and only heterosexual interaction produces children.[51] How might Jung and Smith address this challenge to their claim that homosexuality is as natural as left-handedness?

---

50. See Mary Midgley, "Biotechnology and Monstrosity: Why We Should Pay Attention to the 'Yuk Factor,'" *Hastings Center Report* 30, No. 3 (September-October 2000), pp. 7–15.

51. I thank Avery Kolers for pointing this out to me. Maybe I didn't play doctor enough as a child.

2 Utilitarianism

Early one Sunday morning in November, 1959, six people were killed in the small town of Holcomb, Kansas. One of them was Herbert William Clutter. According to Truman Capote's *In Cold Blood*, the sheriff who found Mr. Clutter's body recalled:

> I took one look at Mr. Clutter, and it was hard to look again. I knew plain shooting couldn't account for that much blood. And I wasn't wrong. He'd been shot, all right . . . , with the gun held right in front of his face. But probably he was dead before he was shot. Or, anyway, dying. Because his throat had been cut, too. He was wearing striped pajamas—nothing else. His mouth was taped. . . . His ankles were tied together, but not his hands—or, rather, he'd managed, God knows how, maybe in rage or pain, to break the cord binding his hands. . . . There was a steampipe overhead, and knotted to it, dangling from it, was a piece of cord—the kind of cord the killer had used. Obviously, at some point Mr. Clutter had been tied there, strung up by his hands, and then cut down. But why? To torture him? I don't guess we'll ever know. Ever know who did it, or why, or what went on in that house that night.[1]

Revulsion at such killing transcends religious differences. Secular thought condemns it as immoral, calls for criminal laws against it, and insists that perpetrators be punished. Many other criminal laws enjoy similar support on secular grounds, including laws against armed robbery, bribery, fraud, rape, and insider trading. But what secular political philosophy accounts for such widespread consensus?

This chapter explores **utilitarianism.** This is the view, as noted in the Introduction, that governments exist to promote the greatest total good. Promoting maximum happiness or the greatest satisfaction of preferences is both the foundation and the function of government. Proponents claim that utilitarianism gives the best answers to all questions of morality and

---

1. Truman Capote, *In Cold Blood* (New York: Signet Books, 1965), pp. 80–81.

politics. We will find that utilitarianism, like religious and natural-law views, has merits but also limitations. Its concept of what is good does not always match common-sense notions; it may endorse policies that most people consider unjust; and the reasoning it requires seems to exceed human capabilities. Nevertheless, the utilitarian concern for happiness and preference satisfaction are part of any reasonable political philosophy. However, other considerations are also important.

Crime Diminishes Happiness

Jeremy Bentham (1748–1832), the founder of modern utilitarianism, claimed that increasing pleasure and avoiding pain are the only proper secular goals of moral rules, government laws, and public policies. Bentham wrote in *The Principles of Morals and Legislation* (1789): "Nature has placed mankind under the governance of two sovereign masters, *pain* and *pleasure*. It is for them alone to point out what we ought to do, as well as to determine what we shall do."[2] According to Bentham, "A thing is said to promote the interest . . . of an individual when it tends to add to the sum total of his pleasures: or, what comes to the same thing, to diminish the sum total of his pains."[3] The right thing to do is always to follow the principle of utility "which approves or disapproves of every action whatso-ever, according to the tendency which it appears to have to augment or diminish the happiness of the party whose interest is in question."[4]

For utilitarians, "the party whose interest is in question" is anyone affected by the action, law, or policy. Utilitarians endorse **altruism,** the belief that *everyone's welfare is equally important.* When we decide what to do, we should choose whatever produces the greatest good for all those affected. Our own good counts; altruism is not the same as **selflessness,** which *counts the good of everyone except the person doing the action (the agent).* Altruism requires, instead, that we count our own good, but we must count it neither more nor less than the good of anyone else. A strict utilitarian going out to the movies with friends, for example, would choose the movie that will provide maximum satisfaction for all concerned. She might want to see a movie that her friends have already seen and do not want to see again. In this case, it is her utilitarian duty to

---

2. Jeremy Bentham, *The Principles of Morals and Legislation* (New York: Hafner Press, 1948), p. 1.
3. Bentham, p. 3.
4. Bentham, p. 2.

attend a different movie if that will maximize the sum total of good in the group, her own good figuring into that sum total neither more nor less than the good of each other person in the group. The good of those not in the group can be ignored if they are not affected by the movie decision. This includes more than a billion people in China.

↗ good = pleasure

Bentham identified the good with pleasure, a view known as **hedonism.** To say that something is good means that it contributes either directly or indirectly to some kind of pleasure. Bentham's conception of pleasure included all kinds of positive experiences, including the simple pleasures of sense, wealth, skill, good name, power, piety, benevolence, memory, imagination, expectation, and association.[5] He lists several subcategories for each of these simple pleasures and then goes on to consider complex pleasures. In short, Bentham considers just about any positive experience a pleasure.

Pain is the opposite of pleasure. Whatever is bad is bad because it directly or indirectly deprives people of some form of pleasure or contributes to some form of pain. But again, pain can be any kind of negative experience, such as dread, loneliness, indignation, and poverty—not just physical pain.

Utilitarian reasoning is consequentialist. **Consequentialism** is the view that *what makes actions (laws and policies) right or wrong is not the actions' nature, but their consequences.* All consequences of utilitarian importance concern pleasure and pain, according to hedonistic utilitarianism. An action (law or policy) is right if it produces the greatest total pleasure among available options. Scores for total pleasure, however, must include subtractions for any pain that the action causes, so it is really total *net* pleasure (pleasure minus pain) that (hedonistic) utilitarians think we ought to maximize.

Utilitarianism supports many judgments of common sense. What is wrong with shooting someone in the face, for example, as recounted in Truman Capote's *In Cold Blood*? If there were no bad consequences, we would not consider it any worse than blowing kisses at people. Like good utilitarians, we condemn shooting people in the face because its consequences are generally bad. Herbert Clutter, who was only 47 years old at the time, was killed, eliminating his chances for future happiness. Family and friends suffered the loss of a loved one. Others in society suffer from insecurity when someone is murdered, fearing that they may be next. The problem with shooting people in the face is not the act itself but its consequences,

---

5. Bentham, p. 33.

and all those consequences can be boiled down, (hedonistic) utilitarians claim, to long-term pleasure and pain.

Perhaps the shooter experienced pleasure in the act and continued to experience pleasure whenever he remembered it. This pleasure must be included in any utilitarian calculation of whether the act was right or wrong, because utilitarianism requires that the pleasures and pains of *everyone* affected by an act be counted equally with the pleasures and pains of everyone else involved. However, the act was wrong because the pleasures it eliminated and the pains it introduced are much greater than any pleasure the shooter experienced, so the action lowered overall long-term pleasure and increased overall long-term pain, especially when compared to possible alternatives. The killer could have done any number of other things that would have had better overall consequences, such as going bowling or watching golf on television.

Reconsidering the act of blowing kisses at people supports the utilitarian account of why shooting someone in the face is bad. Usually we approve of blowing kisses because it shows affection and makes people happy without hurting anyone. But imagine a work setting where women who have recently been elevated to managerial positions are resented by some of their male colleagues. These men start blowing kisses at the women to express their view that women should be sexual objects, not managers. This distresses the women and makes the workplace a hostile environment for them, which is exactly what these men intend. Most people think that causing pain (psychological stress) in this way is wrong. Utilitarians agree, claiming it is wrong because the pleasure the men derive is less than the long-term pain they inflict. Besides experiencing stress, the women's work may suffer, harming the company's overall efficiency, productivity, and profit, which detracts from the pleasure of other colleagues and of investors. In addition, the women's careers may be stunted; they may pass up career opportunities to avoid harassment in the future. So according to utilitarians, blowing kisses is good when it promotes maximum long-term pleasure and wrong when it has the opposite effect. Common sense seems to agree.

Insider trading is another example. If it did not harm anyone, utilitarians would favor its legality. In fact, however, when some people trade stocks on the basis of information unavailable to the general public, the few inside traders can usually make better investment decisions and gain profit at the expense of other investors, diminishing their quality of life. If many investors are disappointed, they may curtail investment in stocks, which deprives innovative enterprises of the financial capital they need to produce new or better products that would make consumers happy. Without investment, entrepreneurs also create fewer good jobs for willing workers, which makes potential workers unhappy. Inside traders do not gain enough happiness to offset the amount of unhappiness that they cause to others, so insider trading reduces the sum total of happiness in society—and this is why it is, and should remain, illegal.

According to utilitarians, the vast majority of criminal laws can be justified in the same way. Robbery is illegal because it deprives people of their money or possessions, and this causes suffering. Fraud similarly deprives people of money and possessions. Rape causes physical and psychological suffering. In each case, the pleasure derived by perpetrators is far less than the sum total of pain among victims, and this is why robbery, fraud, insider trading, rape, and murder are illegal, utilitarians claim.

However, there is no utilitarian reason to outlaw using epidurals during delivery to reduce pain. Most people would find a ban on epidurals intolerable. Regardless of any religious justification that might be offered, we consider pain to be bad and want to avoid it if we can. We also gain pleasure from believing that we control our own lives. So utilitarianism can account not only for why we have certain laws, such as laws against murder, sexual harassment, and insider trading but also why we oppose other laws, such as a ban on epidurals during delivery, that interfere with freedoms we enjoy.

The principle of utility also explains why we generally favor law and order. We believe that law enforcement is important to maintain domestic tranquility. The 1992 Los Angeles riots, for example, took 44 lives and caused a billion dollars damage. South Central Los Angeles was left with fewer businesses and jobs and a lower quality of life.

Psychological Egoism and Punishment

Some critics of utilitarianism claim that it is impossibly idealistic. It requires altruism, giving equal importance to the happiness of everyone involved, whereas some critics consider people naturally and inevitably too selfish to care as much about others as they care about themselves. In its extreme form, this view is known as **psychological egoism,** which claims that everyone acts selfishly all the time. *If psychological egoism accurately describes human nature, it seems impossible for anyone to be as altruistic as utilitarianism requires.* What is more, ought implies can. It is unfair to require people to do the impossible. If psychological egoism is correct, utilitarianism seems to be unfair because it says that people ought to act altruistically when they cannot do so.

But is psychological egoism correct? Ironically, the utilitarian Jeremy Bentham thought so. He wrote that pleasure and pain "alone . . . point out what we ought to do, as well as . . . determine what we shall do."[6] If pleasure and pain determine what we shall do, then it seems that we inevitably do what gives us most pleasure without the altruistic regard for the pleasures and pains of others that utilitarianism requires. And it does seem that people sometimes act this way. During the 1992 Los Angeles riot, as already noted, people looted stores in total disregard for anyone's pleasure but their own:

> A yuppie jumped out of his BMW and scrounged through a gutted Radio Shack near Hancock Park. Filipinos in a banged-up old clunker stocked up on baseball mitts and sneakers. . . . Toting a Hefty bag full of electronic calculators, a 13-year-old black kid looked up dizzily and said. "My mom's not gonna believe the stuff I got today."[7]

Psychological egoism claims that everyone naturally behaves this selfishly all the time. The only distinguishing feature of a riot is the absence of law enforcement. Laws backed up by punishment, on this view, stand between normal society and general mayhem. This is the **theory of deterrence.** *People obey the law because they are deterred, scared off, by the prospect of punishment.*

Punishment for law violators makes obeying the law and utilitarian morality compatible with psychological egoism, according to Bentham. People who are likely to be caught and punished severely for stealing baseball mitts and sneakers, for example, act selfishly when they pay for merchandize because the punishment for stealing would causes them much more pain than spending money. If laws are properly designed to forbid behavior that lowers overall happiness in society, and if punishment for violating these laws is probable and severe, completely selfish people will obey the law and act like utilitarians out of fear. Punishment deters antisocial behavior, according to the theory of deterrence, and this is a proper goal of government, according to utilitarianism.

Although deterrence is an important utilitarian reason for punishment, it does not reconcile Bentham's utilitarianism with psychological egoism. If *everyone* is always selfish all the time, then police, prosecutors, judges, and correctional personnel would be, too. They would administer

---

6. Jeremy Bentham, *The Principles of Morals and Legislation* (New York: Hafner Press, 1948), p. 1.
7. "The Siege of L.A." *Newsweek,* Vol. CXIX, No. 19, p. 36.

the criminal justice system merely for the pleasure they could get out of it; they would be completely corrupt. Police would take bribes from criminals and kill witnesses against themselves or their "clients"; prosecutors would not press charges against people who paid them off; judges would not find their friends guilty; correctional officers would allow criminals to escape for a fee. Such things happen occasionally, of course, but if they were the norm, deterrence, which Bentham counts on to reconcile utilitarianism with psychological egoism, would not work. Punishment for breaking the law would not be probable if anyone could pay off police, prosecutors, and judges. Punishment would not be severe if judges and correctional officers could be bribed. But punishment does deter crime in our society, so psychological egoism is false. Everyone does not always act selfishly. Police, prosecutors, judges, and correctional personnel, at least, often do their duty regardless of maximum personal happiness.

Additional evidence against psychological egoism comes from examples of people who act to promote the welfare of others rather than maximize their own pleasure. Consider this true story of a firefighter in New York City on September 11, 2001. Lt. Mickey Kross of Engine 16 was assigned to the World Trade Center's North Tower, the first to be hit by an airplane commandeered by terrorists, but the second to collapse. During the evacuation:

> Lt. Kross went to look for a commander on the 23rd floor, but on the way he encountered a woman who had apparently been left behind in the evacuation; she was elderly and overweight and was having trouble breathing. She told him her name was Josephine. Just then there was a rumble, the sound of the South Tower collapsing. He ordered his men out, but he stayed behind with an officer from Engine One to help the woman down the stairs, one step at a time. They reached the fourth floor at 10:28, when, with "the loudest rumble I ever heard in my life," he said, the building collapsed around them. . . . Somehow, he had landed into a small protected void. . . . Sometime after 1 P.M. Kross crawled out . . . wondering what happened to Josephine and the officer from Engine One.[8]

This story shows that people are not, as psychological egoism claims, always selfish all the time. After the South Tower collapsed and Lt. Kross realized it was too dangerous for his men to stay in the North Tower, he could have left with them. Instead, he stayed behind to help an elderly woman make a painfully slow exit knowing that he was risking his life to

---

8. "Ground Zero," *Newsweek*, Vol. CXXXVIII, No. 13, pp. 81–82.

try to save hers. How can anyone say that this man acted selfishly on this occasion?

Defenders of psychological egoism might say that Lt. Kross probably would have felt guilty if he had not tried to save people at the World Trade Center. So his heroics were selfish after all; he was maximizing his own happiness by avoiding the pain of guilt.

This defense of psychological egoism does not work because it misuses the word "selfish." According to defenders of psychological egoism, people are **selfish** whenever they act to promote their own maximum happiness regardless of the reason for their happiness. But this is not the normal meaning of the word "selfish."

Imagine that you are planning a camping trip and need a fourth person to share expenses. One of your friends proposes Jane, whom he knows but you do not. You ask about Jane before deciding whether or not you want to invite her on the trip. Your friend tells you that she loves the outdoors, canoes well, and is entirely selfish. The bit about selfishness would give you pause. You would fear that if you were paired with her on a canoe trip and you broke your wrist somehow, she would just leave you upstream without a paddle. When you express these fears to the friend who knows Jane he replies that she would never do any such thing. She is extremely conscientious and loyal. Leaving a partner upstream without a paddle would bother her conscience. She is happiest when helping other people and doing more than her share of work.

At this point you would want to have her on the trip but would disagree that Jane is properly described as selfish. Selfish people are those who tend to do less than their share of work, who are not eager to help other people, and who would leave someone upstream without a paddle. In general, *selfish people tend to act with insufficient regard for the welfare of others*. This is why we are wary of undertaking joint projects with them. In this sense of the word, and this is the normal sense, people are not all selfish all the time; psychological egoism is incorrect.

Defenders of psychological egoism have changed the meaning of the word "selfish" to suit their argument. This is called **equivocation.** We assume at the beginning that "selfish" is being used in the normal way to distinguish those who give sufficient regard for the welfare of others from those who do not. But when people such as Lt. Kross are described as "selfish," defenders of psychological egoism employ a new and unusual meaning for the word. They assume that selfishness is acting to maximize one's own happiness, even if that happiness comes primarily from helping others. On this meaning, perhaps everyone is selfish, but this definition is not only unusual, it is unhelpful. It does not allow the word to perform its normal function of helping us decide, for example, who would be an acceptable camping partner and who would not.

Even though psychological egoism is incorrect about selfishness being universal, some people are occasionally selfish in unacceptable ways. Such unacceptably selfish people include murderers, rapists, inside traders, burglars, and others from whom we seek the protection of criminal laws. Punishment for breaking the law aims primarily, according to utilitarianism, to deter criminals and those tempted to imitate them from breaking the law in the future.

Punishment makes criminals unhappy and to this extent reduces happiness in society. But certain crimes reduce happiness more. A shoplifter, for example, may experience 10 units of unhappiness when punished with 30 days in jail. But if that punishment deters or otherwise prevents that thief or others from shoplifting in the future, 20 units of shoplifting-produced unhappiness may be averted, and total happiness in society increased. In general, total happiness is greatest when punishments prevent crimes that would cause more unhappiness than the punishments do.

Besides deterring criminals and would-be criminals, the punishment of law breakers may reduce future crime in two additional ways. It may incapacitate an offender. Someone who is in jail for 30 days, for example, cannot shoplift during the time of her incarceration. Someone guilty of insider trading may be incapable of continuing that activity if he is banned from trading stocks altogether. Such punishments prevent future crime through **incapacitation,** *removing at least temporarily a criminal's ability to commit that type of crime.*

A third way that punishment may reduce crime in the future is through **rehabilitation.** *Rehabilitation occurs when criminals gain skills to be economically and socially successful without recourse to criminal activity and no longer find crime attractive.* Someone who learns to fix computers while serving time for dealing drugs may decide that he would rather earn money legally in the future.

Equality

Utilitarianism is based on equal regard for the welfare of each individual. *The pleasure and pain of each person counts equally in the calculation of pleasure and pain in society.* This is called the **equal consideration of interests.**

Equal consideration may incline utilitarians to favor policies that reduce differences between society's haves and have-nots. The reason for this supposition is **diminishing marginal utility.** In general, many utilitarians claim, *the more a person has of something the less pleasure he derives from getting more.* If I like apples and already have 10 of them, I will probably not get as much pleasure from having an additional apple as will someone who likes apples as much as I do but has none. The marginal utility (extra pleasure) that I get from an additional apple diminishes the more apples I have. Because of this, a utilitarian trying to maximize happiness in society would give the apple to an apple-appreciating person who has none because that person will get more pleasure from it than I will.

The same is generally true, utilitarians often claim, of other material goods and of the money to buy them. The more money I have the less pleasure I get from increased income or wealth. A poor person winning a thousand dollars will be able to experience pleasures that her life might otherwise lack, whereas a thousand dollars will not change my life experiences much. By the same token, if I win a million dollars, my life will be really changed, but if Bill Gates were to win that money his life would go on as before because he is so rich. Utilitarians with money who believe in diminishing marginal utility will therefore tend to give much of their money to the poor, reducing the gap between haves and have-nots, because this, they think, maximizes total happiness.

Utilitarianism, then, seems to justify not only our criminal laws and the system of punishment for their breach but also many tax policies and government programs. Federal income tax, for example, is progressive. It takes a larger percentage and amount of income from rich people than it does from poor people. In 1999, for example, the 20% of taxpayers with the lowest incomes, averaging $8,600 that year, actually received more money from the government than they paid. The middle 20% earned an average of $31,100 and paid 6.096% of that, or about $1,896, in federal income taxes. The top 1%, by contrast, averaged $915,000 income and paid 24.6% of that, or about $225,090, in federal income taxes.[9] This is **progressive taxation.** *Utilitarianism, together with the theory of diminishing marginal utility, justifies progressive taxation because the theory holds that poor people get more pleasure from additional money than do rich people.*

Many government programs can similarly be justified by utilitarian reasoning because they diminish the gap between rich and poor people. Medicaid, for example, provides medical services for poor people who

---

9. "Are Americans Overtaxed?" Citizens for Tax Justice (May 24, 2000), in *Taking Sides: Clashing Views on Controversial Political Issues,* 12th ed., George Mckenna and Stanley Feingold, Eds. (New York: McGraw-Hill, 2001), pp. 323–31, at 326.

may otherwise be unable to afford medical attention needed to avoid life-impairing disabilities. I know of a young woman in Minnesota, whom I have never met personally, who had diabetes. This illness impairs blood circulation in a person's extremities, such as the legs, and makes it hard for the body to fight off infections there. Because this young woman was poor and had no medical insurance she waited too long when she had an infection in her leg. Gangrene set in before she went to a doctor, and the leg had to be amputated. The loss of a limb, most utilitarians assume, diminishes her happiness more than higher taxes to pay for her timely medical attention would have diminished the happiness of a rich person. Medicaid paid for by progressive federal income taxes redistributes benefits and burdens from rich to poor people, which utilitarianism endorses.

Utilitarians do not, however, endorse government programs that enforce complete equality of material welfare. Most utilitarians believe that much inequality is needed to maximize pleasure in society because material rewards motivate people. Most people are not psychological egoists who have no interest in the welfare of others, but they are not completely altruistic either. They tend to favor their own pleasure over the pleasure of others, especially strangers. If they had to give their money and possessions to poor people until they became as poor as the recipients, they would not only be unhappy, but demoralized. They would cease to work hard to become rich. But the hard work of talented people, most utilitarians think, is needed to maximize happiness in society. Talented people invent new products, make manufacture more efficient, and create jobs. Demoralizing such people by enforcing complete equality would lower overall happiness. So utilitarianism supports progressive taxation and government programs like Medicaid that redistribute wealth. But utilitarianism does not support complete material equality.

Hedonism and Preferences

Bentham endorsed hedonism, the view that pleasure is the only good. All other good things are good only insofar as they increase pleasure or decrease pain, according to hedonists. However, most of us do not agree; we value some things even when they do not increase pleasure and decrease pain, such as close personal relationships and justice. Consider Hamlet's situation. He loved his deceased father, the King of Denmark, and suspects that his uncle Claudius was responsible for his father's death. He is tortured by his inability to take revenge on his uncle.

O, what a rogue and peasant slave am I!

. . .

A dull and muddy-mettled rascal, peak,
Like John-a-dreams, unpregnant of my cause,
And can say nothing; no, not for a king
Upon whose property and most dear life
A Damn'd defeat was made. Am I a coward?
Who calls me villain? Breaks my pate across?
Plucks off my beard and blows it in my face?

. . .

Why, what an ass am I? This is most brave,
That I, the son of a dear father murder'd,
Prompted to my revenge by heaven and hell,
Must, like a whore, unpack my heat with words,
And fall a-cursing, like a very drab,
A scullion![10]

Do we think the world would be a better place and Hamlet a better person if, instead of being pained by his father's murder and his own inability to take revenge, he shrugged it off? "Oh well, father bother, what's for lunch?" Most people think that Hamlet's love for his father is admirable even if painful and that seeking justice is worth the trouble even if no one is made happier for it. Such people are not hedonists.

Another way to test the value we place on pleasure is through a thought experiment proposed by philosopher Robert Nozick:

> Suppose there were an experience machine that would give you any experience you desire. Superduper neuropsychologists could stimulate your brain so that you would think and feel you were writing a great novel, or making a friend, or reading an interesting book. All the time you would be floating in a tank, with electrodes attached to your brain. . . . Of course, while in the tank you won't know that you're there; you'll think it's all actually happening.[11]

You can choose to have any experiences you like for the rest of your life. Would you want this kind of life? It does maximize your pleasure and minimize your pain. Suppose that the same option is available to everyone else, so there is no problem of your experience of pleasure causing anyone

---

10. William Shakespeare, "Hamlet, Prince of Denmark," Act II, Scene II, in *The Complete Works of William Shakespeare,* Hardin Craig, Ed. (Fair Lawn, NJ: Scott, Foresman, 1961), pp. 901–943, at 919.
11. Robert Nozick, *Anarchy, State, and Utopia* (New York: Basic Books, 1974), pp. 42–43.

else avoidable pain. If they do not like the fact that you are floating in a vat they can just float in a vat themselves and experience the delusion of a rich friendship with you outside the vat.

Few people would choose life in a vat, even if such a life maximizes happiness. First, Nozick points out, we want not just the experience of doing things but the actuality of doing them. We want our experience to correspond to reality. If I am interested in long-distance running or foreign languages, I do not want to dream that I am completing a marathon or speaking fluent French, I want really to run a marathon or to speak French. In fact, I desire the experience of doing these things precisely because I value actually doing them. Valuing the experience without reality puts the cart before the horse and then, in this thought experiment, kills the horse.

Second, I want to be a certain kind of person, not just think that I am that kind of person. Nozick writes:

> Someone floating in a tank is an indeterminate blob. There is no answer to the question of what a person is like who has long been in the tank. Is he courageous, kind, intelligent, witty, loving? It's not merely that it's difficult to tell; there's no way he is. Plugging into the machine is a kind of suicide.[12]

Again, people who really want to *be* somebody, even if the strains and troubles of real life bring more pain than a fantasy life would, are not hedonists.

Of course, *pleasure is still good and pain is still bad; but they are not the only good and bad in the world.* Other things are also good, such as close personal relationships, justice, real accomplishments, and character formation. If utilitarians claim that proper actions, laws, and public policies maximize the good, they need a conception of what is good that includes more than just good experiences.

Some utilitarians claim that they have such a conception—preference satisfaction. The new utilitarian goal is not to maximize pleasure and minimize pain, which limits the good to good experiences, but to maximize the satisfaction of preferences and minimize the frustration of people's desires. When people prefer pleasure to anything else, as sometimes they do, this form of utilitarianism, called **preference utilitarianism,** endorses the same actions and policies as hedonistic utilitarianism. But when people prefer reality even if that involves unpleasant experiences, then, according to preference utilitarianism, they endorse actions and

---

12. Nozick, p. 43.

policies that maximize the satisfaction of these preferences and minimize the frustration of these desires. The goal is in any case to maximize net preferences—preferences satisfied minus desires frustrated.

Some Preferences Should Not Count

Preference utilitarianism makes no distinctions of quality, importance, or relevance among preferences. Maximizing preference satisfaction requires determining how strong various competing preferences are and how many people have those preferences. Actions, laws, and public policies are then designed to maximize net preference satisfaction. An example of this procedure, however, calls into question whether all preferences should be considered equally important.

"In June 1958," U.S. Supreme Court Justice Earl Warren wrote, "two residents of Virginia, Mildred Jeter, a Negro woman, and Richard Loving, a white man, were married in the District of Columbia. . . ." Upon their return to Virginia they were convicted of violating the state's law against white people marrying anyone of a different race. "The Lovings . . . were sentenced to one year in jail; however, the trial judge suspended the sentence for a period of 25 years on the condition that the Lovings leave the State and not return to Virginia together for 25 years." The trial judge thought that Virginia's law, designed to protect the integrity of the white race, carried out the will of God:

> Almighty God created the races white, black, yellow, malay, and red, and he placed them on separate continents. And but for the interference with his arrangement there would be no cause for such marriages. The fact that he separated the races shows that he did not intend for the races to mix.[13]

This is a natural-law argument for racial segregation; what we find in nature before human "interference" indicates God's will, and our laws should support God's plan.

The Supreme Court of the United States rejected this natural-law argument and decided in 1967 that such laws are unconstitutional because they deny people "due process of law." Utilitarians, however, might reach a different conclusion. Like the Supreme Court, they would ignore religious issues about what God wants. But instead of concentrating on "due process of law," they would ask if the law against interracial marriage maximizes net preferences for all concerned. It may have done so at one time.

---

13. *Loving v. Virginia*, 388 U.S. 1 (1967), at 3.

Imagine a time when most Virginians were so racist that allowing interracial marriage would have distressed them greatly. Suppose, for example, that 2 million Virginians were strongly opposed to interracial marriage, and each would have suffered, on average, 3 units of frustration if such marriages had been allowed; they disliked the thought and sight of mixed-race couples. Suppose also that at the time only 100 interracial couples wanted to get married, but marriage was very important to them; each person in these couples would experience 100 units of frustration if their marriages were not allowed. On this showing, allowing interracial marriage causes 6 million units of frustration whereas disallowing such marriage causes only 20 thousand units of frustration. If this was the situation when Virginia's law was passed, it was justified on utilitarian grounds, and reference to God's natural law was entirely unnecessary.

Utilitarianism might also justify subsequent change in the law. A utilitarian today would note that few Virginians are still so racist as to be greatly frustrated by the presence of interracial couples in their state. Even if racists continue to outnumber those who desire interracial marriage, on average each racist may experience only 1 unit of frustration from the presence in the state of interracial married couples, whereas each of those desiring interracial marriage may suffer 100 units from the denial of a right to marry because marriage is central to their happiness. Suppose there are 1 million racists in Virginia and 20,000 people who now want interracial marriage—and everyone else is indifferent. A law against miscegenation relieves racists of 1 million units of frustration but produces 2 million units among the 20,000 people unable to marry. Reasoning in this way, utilitarians find a law in Virginia against interracial marriage unjustified at this time.

Does this seem like a reasonable way to make public policy? Don't we want to say to racists bothered by interracial marriage, no matter their numbers or the strength of their preferences, that other people's marriages are just none of their business? If this is our view, we endorse neither hedonistic nor preference utilitarianism. We do not want to maximize all preferences whose satisfaction or frustration may be affected by each and every decision. Some preferences should count and others should not. The preferences of busybodies sticking their noses in where they do not belong should not count.

Other preferences that most people would not want to count include those they find repugnant. We currently have laws against cruelty to animals. Such laws restrict behavior and reduce preference satisfaction among people who want to practice animal cruelty. Imagine a woman (equal opportunity repugnance) who wants to trap squirrels that cross her backyard, take them to her completely soundproof basement, and apply what would be thumb screws for people but, given the size of squirrels, are best described as paw screws. There is nothing like a squirming, screaming squirrel to make her day. Suppose that squirrels are plentiful in the area, and no one else need be involved because soundproofing protects others from hearing the squirrels and discreet burial in her garden (great fertilizer!) eliminates visible remains. It would seem that maximizing preference satisfaction calls for repealing any part of the law against cruelty to animals that interferes with this woman's hobby.

Few people think that our laws should accommodate this woman and others like her in People for Animals in Nets (PAIN). But how do we justify denying them their preferences? A utilitarian might say that so many other people are so greatly distressed by the mere thought that any such cruelty should take place that current law maximizes net preference satisfaction. This may be true, but if we are attempting to attain reflective equilibrium, how do we square counting the preferences of people who are not directly involved in animal cruelty when we think it wrong to count the preferences of people not directly involved in interracial marriage?

An alternate utilitarian response may be that people who would do such things to squirrels will turn to hurting human beings someday, so other people are involved, if only indirectly. But until there is solid evidence that cruelty to animals fosters eventual cruelty to people, this objection to animal cruelty rests on pure speculation. If such speculation is allowed to influence utilitarian calculations, people who are left-handed could again be forced to use their right hands if old superstitions about left-handedness are revived. Displays of "gay pride" could be justifiably forbidden on utilitarian grounds if enough people, influenced by their interpretation of the Bible but without secular evidence, fear that God will devastate society if such displays are allowed. *Utilitarian reasoning must be based on real, if not conclusive, evidence, not pure speculation, or else it can justify any restriction on behavior that people imagine to be somehow harmful.*

Another possible utilitarian response is to consider preferences among squirrels as well as among people. Squirrels cannot, of course, express preferences in human language, but they can vote with their feet (paws). Whenever they can, they limp away from this woman and her friends. However, consistent application of utilitarian reasoning that includes animal preferences leads to many puzzles. Here is one.

Consider the hog industry. Commercial hogs, like dogs, are more intelligent and sensitive than squirrels. But to minimize costs, hogs are raised in overcrowded buildings. This creates stress and causes these normally peaceful animals to bite one another's tails. So the United States Department of Agriculture (USDA) recommends tail docking. "Cut tails ¼ to ½ inch from the body with side-cutting pliers or another blunt instrument," the USDA advises.[14] They do not recommend anesthetic. Philosopher Peter Singer quotes a hog farmer about docking: "The pigs just hate it! And I suppose we could probably do without tail-docking if we gave them more room, because they don't get so crazy when they have more space. . . . But we can't afford it. These buildings cost a lot."[15]

Besides being overcrowded, these buildings have concrete floors that are easier to maintain than areas of mud, dirt, and straw that the animals prefer. Concrete floors damage the hogs' feet, but most hogs will be slaughtered before any deformity becomes serious. Breeding sows are the exception because they live longest. Singer writes:

> While pregnant they are usually locked into individual metal stalls two feet wide and six feet long, or scarcely bigger than the sow herself. . . . There they will live for two or three months. During all that time they will be unable to walk more than a single step forward or backward, or to turn around, or to exercise in any other way. . . .[16]

When sows are first put into these stalls, they throw themselves "violently backward, straining against the tether. Sows thrashed their heads about as they twisted and turned in their struggle to free themselves. Often loud screams were emitted and occasionally individuals crashed bodily against the side boards of the tether stalls."[17] While so tethered sows are left continuously hungry, receiving only 60% of a normal diet. This is enough for them to breed successfully so any more feed would waste money.

Gail Eisnitz, an investigator for the Humane Farming Association, reports that transportation from farm to market is horrific. A meatpacking employee told her:

> In the summer they crowd them [hogs] in trucks and run them clear from Canada. They don't stop and spray them to cool them down, so you get a lot of them that die from the heat. . . . In winter after a long

---

14. In Peter Singer, *Animal Liberation*, New Revised Edition (New York, Avon Books, 1990), p. 121.
15. Singer, p. 121.
16. Singer, p. 126.
17. Singer, p. 128.

> run like that, they always got 10 to 15 dead, frozen hogs laying
> around. . . . A lot of times there's live ones in there [with the frozen
> ones]. . . .[18]

Because frozen hogs are ground up for animal feed, unnoticed live hogs among them are sometimes ground up alive, which is really not much worse than what often happens in the slaughterhouse, according to Eisnitz. I spare you the details.

Compare these agricultural practices with squirrel torture. If laws against cruelty to animals are applied to the squirrel torture out of respect for the preferences of squirrels, shouldn't they be applied to cruel hog farming out of respect for the preferences of hogs? This would certainly revolutionize livestock production and raise the price of pork products. Consumers prefer cheap pork, so their desires would be frustrated, but the animal torturer prefers screaming squirrels. How can we in logical consistency allow cruelty to hogs but not to squirrels?

Few people want to abandon all concern for animal welfare, so we are challenged to find consistent policies regarding animals. One approach to the hog/squirrel puzzle, which does not settle many other issues regarding animals, is to deny that all preferences deserve respect. On this view, wanting cheap meat is a respectable preference, whereas wanting to hear squirrels scream is not. This is not the only possibility, but it is attractive because most people want to frustrate rather than satisfy a preference for torturing squirrels. They do not think that satisfying this preference adds to the good. Such people are not preference utilitarians because they do not favor the satisfaction of all preferences.

We have seen two types of cases in which most people disagree with the utilitarian view that positive value be attributed to the satisfaction of all preferences. In some cases (interracial marriage), most people would exclude the preferences of those not directly involved because the matter is none of their business. In other cases (animal cruelty), most people would exclude repugnant preferences that are unworthy of satisfaction.

Criminal Injustice

Even when there is no dispute about which preferences should count, utilitarianism often endorses policies that most people find objectionable. We have seen that utilitarians justify punishment as a means of promoting future social satisfaction; it incapacitates those who might otherwise

---

18. Gail A. Eisnitz, *Slaughterhouse* (Amherst, NY: Prometheus Books, 1997), p. 101.

break the law, (sometimes) reforms people so they no longer want to break the law, and, most important, deters criminal activity.

Some critics of utilitarianism claim that in unusual circumstances pursuing these goals of punishment leads utilitarians to endorse punishing innocent people. Philosopher C. L. Ten presents the following case:

> Suppose that in a particular town . . . a man from one racial group rapes a woman from the other group. Because of existing racial tensions the crime is likely to produce racial violence with many people being injured unless the guilty man is apprehended quickly. Suppose further that the sheriff of the town can prevent the violence by framing an innocent man who was near the scene of the crime, and who will be accepted by the community as the guilty person.[19]

Under these conditions the best consequences may result from framing and punishing an innocent person. If so, utilitarianism would endorse this miscarriage of justice. Critics of utilitarianism point out that most people reject punishing the innocent; they should therefore reject the utilitarian theory that requires such punishment.

There are flaws in this argument against utilitarianism. Framing an innocent man is unlikely to produce the best consequences in the real world (and political philosophies are made for the real world), so utilitarianism does not really endorse it. First, framing an innocent person produces good consequences by relieving racial tensions and avoiding violence only if authorities lie to all concerned and pretend that the man punished is really guilty. But if authorities are so well organized for secrecy and deception that they can get away with such a lie, then they can get away with many other lies and cover-ups as well. They would be law enforcement authorities above the reach of law, and this is dangerous. Although people are not completely selfish, they are too selfish to handle unfettered authority. Without accountability to others, people tend to use their power more selfishly than altruistically, and utilitarian goals are not met.

Second, it is unlikely that authorities would get away with such deception for long. Sooner or later someone would blow the whistle on the practice of framing innocent people to attain maximum preference satisfaction; or new investigative techniques would be developed that expose the practice. The quoted rape example was given before there were DNA tests to determine whose semen is whose. People who were framed in the past could now clear themselves with DNA analysis. No one knows what

---

19. C. L. Ten, *Crime, Guilt, and Punishment* (New York: Oxford University Press, 1987), p. 13.

new forensic tests will become available in the future, so there is never any guarantee that framing innocent people will remain undetected. But if it is eventually exposed, whether through whistle-blowing or new tests, the consequences could be grave. People would lose confidence in the criminal justice system. Juries may be unwilling to convict defendants against whom the evidence is overwhelming if they fear the evidence is not genuine. Suspicion that a racist police officer planted an incriminating glove at the crime scene helped O. J. Simpson win acquittal on charges of double homicide.

In sum, we cannot say that utilitarianism endorses framing innocent people even though in particular cases the best consequences would seem to follow from doing so. **Act utilitarianism** (sometimes called *direct utilitarianism*) concentrates on what is best in individual cases and sometimes leads (as in the hypothetical case about the rape/race riot) to actions that most people find objectionable. **Rule utilitarianism,** by contrast (sometimes called *indirect utilitarianism*), concentrates on rules and principles that will work out best in the long run. Even if act-utilitarians would favor framing an innocent person, rule-utilitarians, for reasons given above, would not. Having chosen a rule against framing innocent people, because that rule promotes the best long-term consequences, they would follow the rule whenever and wherever it applies.

Even rule utilitarianism, however, endorses criminal justice policies that seem morally wrong. On December 12, 2001, actress Winona Ryder was accused of shoplifting about $5,000 of merchandise, designer clothes and purses, from Saks Fifth Avenue in Beverly Hills. Los Angeles District Attorney Steve Cooley pursued four felony counts against Ryder, three related to the shoplifting (second-degree burglary, grand theft, and vandalism) and one related to her possession of a prescription drug for which she had no prescription (possession of a controlled substance). She could have spent nearly four years in prison if convicted on all charges.[20]

"From the get-go, her lawyers have insisted that she is innocent and has merely been singled out for her notoriety," wrote reporter Dahlia Lithwick on the eve of trial in October 2002.[21] Innocence aside, the prosecution was unusually zealous. Consider "the felony drug charge," Lithwick continues. "At the time of her arrest, Ryder was in possession of two tablets—two—of

---

20. Joan Ryan, "Winona's Whine: D.A. Unfair!" (July 15, 2002), www.eonline.com/News/Items/0,1,10245,00.html, accessed April 9, 2003, p. 2 of 2.

21. Dahlia Lithwick, "Justice, Interrupted: Why Winona Ryder Will Do Time for O. J.'s Crimes," October 4, 2002, http://slate.msn.com/?id=2071953, accessed April 10, 2003, p. 1 of 4.

endocet, the generic version of Percocet. She has the prescription for the Percocet, by the way. But the DA's office is pursuing the drug charges because she had the generic version rather than the pricey designer kind." The drug charge, maintained for months, was eventually dropped.

The DA's treatment of the shoplifting charges was truly extraordinary. Independent investigation

> revealed that in court records of all 5,000 grand theft felony cases filed in Los Angeles County last year, not one defendant was facing penalties as harsh as Ryder's. In fact, in all cases involving theft exceeding the amount alleged in Ryder's case, the defendants received standard misdemeanor plea deals. The district attorney's office has refused to accept a plea for anything less than a felony in Ryder's case [and] has refused to accept Saks' own multiple requests to drop the charges against Ryder.[22]

Ryder was eventually convicted after a two-week trial, an unprecedented ordeal on such charges, and sentenced to three years probation, a fine, restitution, and 480 hours of community service.[23] In April 2003 a judge commended Ryder for completing her community service at City of Hope, a cancer treatment center outside Los Angeles. Her lawyer said she would continue her volunteer work there because she had established important relationships with sick children[24] (not to mention her new collection of hospital gowns and surgical equipment—just kidding!).

Was the district attorney justified in treating Ryder's case so much more harshly than other cases of shoplifting? Justice requires treating like cases alike. Relevant likenesses for criminal prosecution concern such matters as the nature and severity of the crime, the harm done, and the defendant's past history of proven criminal behavior. Ryder had never before been charged with any kind of theft, had stolen less than many others, could provide complete restitution, and yet faced felony charges at trial when others could avoid trial by pleading to a misdemeanor. This seems unjust.

Utilitarianism seems to be committed to such injustice. A major reason to punish people is to deter them and others from committing similar offenses in the future. Famous defendants generate publicity and deterrence

---

22. Lithwick, p. 2 of 4.
23. Matt Bean, "Winona Ryder Gets Probation for Shoplifting," December 6, 2002, www.courttv.com/trials/ryder/sentence.html, accessed April 9, 2003, pp. 1–2 of 4.
24. Linda Deutsch, "Ryder Commended for Her Community Service," Associated Press, April 8, 2003, www.oaklandtribune.com/stories/0,1413,82~1865~1309652,00.html, accessed April 9, 2003, p. 1 of 2.

works through publicity, which impresses on people's minds the harsh consequences of illegal behavior. So the district attorney was justified on utilitarian grounds for treating Ryder's case more harshly than others. It will be a lesson to others and reduce future shoplifting. Extraordinarily harsh treatment should be the norm for famous defendants, on this utilitarian reasoning.

In addition, many people seem to assume, perhaps erroneously, that rich and famous people are treated more leniently than others in the criminal justice system. This belief can foster resentment and reduce respect for the law. A utilitarian prosecutor and a utilitarian judge will want to convince the public that celebrity defendants are not treated more leniently than others. They can do this by treating them harshly and publicizing this harsh treatment. Again, utilitarianism seems to endorse treating famous defendants more harshly than others. If it seems unjust to us that Ryder and other famous people should suffer not just for their crimes but also for their fame, we are not thinking like good utilitarians. Perhaps we find utilitarianism a poor guide to justice in these situations.

Social Injustice

Utilitarianism can also endorse injustice in social life. Imagine half of humanity being socialized from birth to think they are less capable and therefore less worthy of well-paid employment than the other half. These are the Downs. Their work is confined to several poorly paid jobs and professions. Because of socialization, the Downs feel uncomfortable competing with members of the other half, the Ups, for better jobs. When they do the same work as Ups they consider it only natural that Ups are paid more. Under these conditions, Downs depend for their livelihood primarily on convincing Ups to support them, and when they are successful in this, they do work for Ups in their homes, receive absolutely no pay at all, and consider themselves lucky.

If this socialization succeeds, half of humanity will be treated unjustly, judged by their group membership, not by their individual talent, ability, and effort. There will be unequal pay for equal work. Promotion will be denied to the best-qualified people if they are members of the wrong group. But utilitarianism would endorse the system because on the whole people are having their preferences satisfied. Ups are happy to avoid competing with half of humanity. They enjoy their elite status and are happy to get cheap labor from Downs at work and free labor from them at home.

Downs are happy, and their preferences are satisfied because they believe that playing their role in this system is the only respectable way to behave. They would be ashamed, as well as scared, to compete directly with Ups. They seek protection from Ups because they think that Ups are naturally better at tasks that earn good incomes.

You might think it unimportant that utilitarianism endorses such injustice. Political philosophies are made for the real world, and the situation described seems like unrealistic science fiction. But it is not. The situation described represents relations between women and men during extended periods in history, including conditions in the United States around 1900. Historian Sheila Rothman writes of that era:

> College graduates ended up as school teachers. . . . Women with less education entered offices; those with still less, retail stores. . . . And no matter what the job, women remained at the lower end of the ladder. In the public schools they were the classroom teachers, not the principals or superintendents; in offices, they made up the ranks of typists and stenographers, not the executives; in the retail stores, they were the clerks and cashiers, not the floorwalkers or managers. In other words, the job that a woman first assumed was generally the one that she kept as long as she worked.
>
> Even the staunchest proponents of women's work wanted [women]—and everyone else—to think of labor essentially as a temporary state (something to do until the right man came along). . . . A woman's job skills were to improve her marital choices . . . and to demonstrate her moral worth through self-support under the most trying circumstances. But a woman was not to work in order to advance a career. In fact, these postulates assumed a self-fulfilling quality. Encouraged to think of themselves in some sense or other as part-time workers, women did not generally expect or press for promotion and equal pay.[25]

Utilitarians, whether rule-utilitarians or act-utilitarians, whether promoting maximum net pleasure or maximum net preference satisfaction, would have no problem with this situation so long as pleasure or preference satisfaction is actually being maximized. Philosopher William Bennett contends that such a system maximized American well-being throughout the 19th century. He quotes the keen observer of American life in the 1830s, Alexis de Tocqueville, who noted that Americans did not think "man and woman have either the duty or the right to perform the

---

25. Sheila M. Rothman, *Woman's Proper Place: A History of Changing Ideals and Practices, 1870 to the Present* (New York: Basic Books, 1978), pp. 47–48.

same offices." But Tocqueville thought America's system of gender bias and exclusion contributed to its prosperity and strength:

> I do not hesitate to avow that although the women of the United States are confined within the narrow circle of domestic life, and their situation is in some respects one of extreme dependence, I have nowhere seen woman occupying a loftier position; and if I were asked . . . to what the singular prosperity and growing strength of that people ought mainly to be attributed, I should reply: To the superiority of their women.[26]

Maybe he was right and gender discrimination maximized the good.

After quoting Tocqueville with approval, Bennett suggests that even in the 21st century equal employment opportunities for women diminish overall good. Bennett argues that nuclear families composed of a father, mother, and children are needed for society to flourish because

> the human family is . . . the arena in which moral understanding is shaped. In the interaction among family members, by example and precept and habit, are forged such qualities as trust, sympathy, and conscience. Without these capacities, which come first and foremost from the home, society itself would be impossible.[27]

Yet, Bennett maintains, "We know that Americans today are simultaneously more concerned with achieving professional and financial success and less willing to invest time, money, and energy in family life."[28] Increasingly, both parents work outside the home, which "means that *both* parents spend less time with their offspring: a combined average of 17 hours per week according to a University of Maryland study, as compared with 30 hours in 1965."[29] Children often go to day care, but according to Bennett, "day care is no substitute for a parent's unqualified love and devotion, patience, empathy, and unhurried attention. . . . Day care cannot measure up to the devotion of a mother, and we are embracing the shadow of a myth if we think otherwise."[30]

The trap is closed with the M-word. Society flourishes when *mothers* stay home to care for children. But if that were the norm, women would not enjoy equal employment opportunity. Employers would reasonably

---

26. In William J. Bennett, *The Broken Hearth: Reversing the Moral Collapse of the American Family* (New York: Doubleday, 2001), pp. 63–64. Bennett does not burden readers with citations.

27. Bennett, p. 44.

28. Bennett, p. 17.

29. Bennett, p. 27. Emphasis in original.

30. Bennett, p. 26.

hire and advance men over women, not wanting people in key roles whose job commitment is unreliable. Educational institutions would reasonably discriminate against women in programs of professional development, not wanting to waste scarce educational resources on people who are less likely to find employment and more likely to interrupt their work for 20 or more years. In sum, Bennett's argument that overall good requires nuclear families with stay-at-home moms presents a utilitarian case for nearly reinstating the unjust gender discrimination of earlier times. Women would return to the "extreme dependence" noted by Tocqueville, whom Bennett quotes with approval.

Although utilitarian calculations have severe problems (our next topic), and some of Bennett's factual assumptions about human needs are open to question, the calculation that gender discrimination maximizes overall preference satisfaction is as good as most. On this basis, a good utilitarian might object not to unjust gender discrimination, but to protest against it. Protest threatens to sow the seeds of discontent, lowering overall happiness and preference satisfaction.

If you think that protest against such injustice is appropriate even if it lowers overall preference satisfaction, then you are not thinking like a good utilitarian.

Utilitarian Calculations

As we have seen, utilitarianism prescribes actions, laws, and policies that maximize pleasure or preference satisfaction for all concerned. But how do we know which actions, laws, and policies will have the best overall consequences? Utilitarians recommend calculation. Consider again the simple case of four people deciding which movie to see together. Suppose there are four possible movies. Utilitarians calculate which movie to see by assigning numbers to the pleasure or preference of each individual regarding each possible movie. For the first movie, for example, person A may have a preference of 2 units (of preference), B might have a preference of 4 units, C of 5 units, and D of negative 3 (hates Stallone). No one else is affected by the choice, so the total score for the group going to the first movie is 8, 11 minus 3. For the second movie the preferences might be 6, minus 2, 5, and 1 for persons A, B, C, and D, yielding a total of 10. The total may be 4 for the third movie and 9 for the fourth. Under these conditions utilitarianism prescribes going to the second movie because it maximizes total preference satisfaction.

Jeremy Bentham, whose utilitarianism was hedonistic because he thought the only good was pleasure and the only bad was pain, called this procedure the **hedonic calculus.** But whether the good is pleasure or preference satisfaction, the same question arises: where did these numbers come from? Consider the reactions of people C and D to the first movie. D hates Stallone, and C really likes Stallone. How could they possibly know that D hates Stallone less (only a minus 3) than C likes Stallone (a positive 5)? What could they possibly say or do to establish these numbers? Do we give C's preference more units than D's aversion because C shouts louder than D, argues longer, or uses more extravagant adjectives? These differences may reflect differences in personal style, persistence, or vocabulary acquisition, not differences in the intensity of preference.

The basic problem is that utilitarian preferences and aversions, like pleasures and pains, are subjective states. They are real, but because they are in our minds and not directly accessible to others except through our behavior, we can never know with precision how different people's preferences compare. We can often guess by their behavior that one person likes a book more than another does, but even if we ask them and they confirm the guess, we have no way of assigning numbers and saying that one person likes the book twice as much as the other. But assigning numbers is essential for the kind of mathematical calculation that utilitarianism requires. The situation is completely hopeless when likes are compared to dislikes. What does it mean to say that one person dislikes the book exactly twice as much as another likes it? It makes no sense.

If act (or direct) utilitarianism is in hot water, as the example above suggests, rule (or indirect) utilitarianism is in a volcano. Indirect utilitarians claim that following certain rules or principles tends to maximize the good in the long run, and this maximization is what justifies society employing those rules or principles. But how do we know what maximizes the good in the long run? For example, most schools have classes in music and art appreciation but not hard rock or tractor-pull appreciation. Society spends tax money to influence people's aesthetic preferences. Does utilitarianism justify the principle that appreciation of the fine arts is better than appreciation of hard rock or tractor pulls? Here is utilitarian R. M. Hare's answer:

> Equal preferences count equally, whatever their content. . . . But it can be argued even so that the "higher pleasures" deserve some protection. To at least a great many people who are able to enjoy them, they afford *more* enjoyment . . . so that the quantity of pleasure in *not* equal. . . . Moreover, if the percentage of such people in the population were to be increased by better education, utility over the foreseeable future would also be increased, on the assumption not only that the better educated people will get more pleasure, minded as

they are, from Bach than from pop music, but that they will get more pleasure from Bach than they would have got if they had never known anything but pop music.[31]

This "calculation" justifies spending tax money to influence people to appreciate Bach.

Note that the "calculation" includes no numbers at all. Even so, Hare claims to know that in general Bach lovers enjoy Bach more than hard rock lovers enjoy hard rock. How does he know that? More important, the policy of educating people to enjoy Bach is justified on utilitarian grounds only if people now enjoying hard rock would enjoy Bach more if only they had been educated properly. How could anyone know that? Hare fails to consider the possibility that he would enjoy hard rock more than he now enjoys Bach if he had been educated properly. He should get out more.

Hare probably enjoys Bach more than popular music, but he presents no evidence supporting a utilitarian argument for current art and music appreciation policies. No one could; there is no way to get the information about preferences that utilitarianism requires. So Hare unwittingly presents his preferences as if utilitarian calculations justified them. But his beliefs about how music education can maximize preference satisfaction are as faith based as any biblical interpretation and, like most such interpretations, probably reflects his particular upbringing. This is no good. We seek secular reasons for laws and public policies so that people can agree that the laws and policies constraining their behavior have some rational basis that all can appreciate. This project is not furthered if public policies reflect legislators' individual preferences or prejudices that others have no reason to share.

Consider another case. We saw that several states had laws against interracial marriage. We imagined how a utilitarian might have argued that such laws maximized preference satisfaction at one time but do so no longer because public sentiment has changed. We imagined that at one time 2 million Virginians would have experienced an average of 3 units of frustration if interracial marriages were allowed, whereas only 100 couples wanted to marry interracially. Although the people in these couples would average 100 units of frustration if their marriages were not allowed, for a total of 20 thousand units, laws against miscegenation were justified on utilitarian grounds because allowing interracial marriage would cause 6 million units of frustration.

---

31. R. M. Hare, *Moral Thinking: Its Levels, Method and Point* (Oxford: Oxford University Press, 1981), p. 145. Emphasis in original.

Where did all these numbers come from? I made them up (it's my book), just as I made up different numbers to show how a utilitarian could argue that changes in public sentiment can justify allowing interracial marriage today. There is no way of justifying such numbers. How can anyone claim to know that each person who wanted to marry interracially was 33 times as frustrated by laws against such marriage as the average person who supported the ban would have been frustrated if the law had been changed? *No controversial law or public policy has ever been justified or rejected on the basis of such calculations, because they are impossible. Again, competing faith-based biblical interpretations are neither better nor worse than competing faith-based utilitarian calculations as justifications for public policy.*

A final point is this. Utilitarianism often puts the cart before the horse. It uses people's preferences to determine which laws and public policies are morally required. However, people often prefer certain laws or public policies because they think that morality requires them. Some people prefer the freedom of interracial marriage because they think it is right that everyone have this freedom; others prefer antimiscegenation laws because they think it is right to keep the races apart. Neither side argues that what they want is right because they want it. Rather, they claim to want it because it *is* right. *When moral principles are at stake, utilitarian reasoning is backward, making morality depend on preferences instead of preferences depend on morality.* We seek the moral principles that justify such preferences.

CONCLUSION

Utilitarianism contains an important observation. *Pleasure and pain, preference satisfaction and frustration of desire, are important. Other things being equal, it is good to have pleasure and bad to have pain, good to be satisfied and bad to be frustrated.* We should include these principles wherever relevant in the moral thinking that justifies laws and public policies. The main reason to allow epidurals during delivery is to reduce pain. Amen. Utilitarian principles help to justify many criminal laws as well as punishment for their violation. Utilitarian reasoning supports the equal consideration of everyone's interests and generally supports laws and policies, such as progressive taxation and health programs for the poor, which reduce gaps between society's haves and have-nots. When promoting pleasure does not seem good, promoting preference satisfaction often seems a viable alternative. None of the later criticisms of utilitarianism negates these findings.

Utilitarianism goes wrong by mistaking utilitarian principles for the whole of moral reasoning, as if no other considerations were morally important. We have found that common morality holds that some preferences, such as the preference for torturing squirrels, are unworthy of satisfaction. Other preferences are suspect because they concern matters beyond the individual's proper sphere of interest, such as the race of the person that someone else should marry. In both cases, our judgments are based on moral principles outside utilitarianism. We appeal to non-utilitarian principles also if we consider it unjust to prosecute famous defendants more diligently than others whose crimes and criminal histories are similar. Again, our principles of justice are non-utilitarian if we object to gender discrimination that satisfies all concerned. In addition, utilitarianism cannot be our sole moral guide, because its arguments require calculations that no one can actually perform. Finally, where matters of moral principles are concerned, moral judgments cannot be based on satisfying preferences, because preferences are based on moral judgments.

We need other principles of morality, alongside or instead of utilitarian principles, which can serve as secular reasons for our laws and public policies.

JUDGMENT CALLS

1. As we have seen, many people think that the race of the person someone marries is no one else's business. How might this relate to the legalization of same-sex marriage, bearing in mind the goal of consistency in reflective equilibrium?

2. Racial profiling exists when police target people of a certain race or ethnicity when trying to enforce certain laws whose violation seems to be most common among people from that group. For example, state police in Illinois may pull over Hispanic-looking people on the interstate if they are trying to interdict drug trafficking from Mexico to Chicago. Is such racial profiling just? How does it relate to utilitarianism and to the extra attention prosecutors pay to famous defendants?

3. Some babies are born with Tay-Sach's disease, "a disorder of the body's metabolism that causes paralysis and blindness; it is invariably fatal in infancy."[32] Such babies never develop distinctively human mental abilities, and attempts to keep them alive

---

32. Jeffery R. M. Kunz and Asher J. Finkel, Eds., *The American Medical Association Family Medical Guide* (New York: Random House, 1987), p. 633.

require frequent hospitalizations and operations. What would utilitarian parents do? Would they try to keep the baby alive as long as possible or refuse to authorize operations, allowing the baby to die sooner rather than later? What are the relevant considerations from a utilitarian perspective?

4. Imagine that the parents of a child with Tay-Sach's disease have decided to let their baby die sooner rather than later. If they are utilitarians, how would they reason when considering the possibility of asking the doctor to give the baby a lethal injection to shorten the dying process?

5. What laws or public policies governing physicians and parents in relation to infants with Tay-Sach's disease would a utilitarian legislator support? Should the law require aggressive treatment to keep babies alive as long as possible? Should the law allow lethal injections?[33]

---

33. See James Rachels, "Active and Passive Euthanasia," in *Biomedical Ethics*, 5th ed., Thomas A. Mappes and Devid DeGrazia, Eds. (New York: McGraw-Hill, 2001), pp. 398–402, and Daniel Callahan, "Killing and Letting Die," for a different view in the same anthology, pp. 402–05.

3 Libertarianism and the Harm Principle

In 1996 California voters passed Proposition 215, which allows doctors to prescribe marijuana for medical use. Cancer survivor James Canter favored the idea:

> Doctors and patients should decide what medicines are best. Ten years ago, I nearly died from testicular cancer that spread into my lungs. Chemotherapy made me sick and nauseous. The standard drugs, like Marinol, didn't help. Marijuana blocked the nausea. As a result, I was able to continue the chemotherapy treatments. Today I've beaten the cancer, and no longer smoke marijuana. I credit marijuana as part of the treatment that saved my life.[1]

Doctors favoring Proposition 215 wrote:

> Marijuana is also effective in: lowering internal eye pressure associated with glaucoma, slowing the onset of blindness; reducing the pain of AIDS patients, and stimulating the appetites of those suffering malnutrition because of AIDS "wasting syndrome"; and alleviating muscle spasticity and chronic pain due to multiple sclerosis, epilepsy, and spinal cord injuries. . . . [Yet] the federal government stopped supplying marijuana to patients in 1991. Now it tells patients to take Marinol, a synthetic substitute . . . that can cost $30,000 a year and is often less reliable and less effective.[2]

Because the federal government bans the use of marijuana for any reason, and federal law overrides state law, Ed Rosenthal, who was licensed by Oakland to grow and distribute marijuana for medical purposes, was convicted in January 2003 of a federal drug violation. Reuters correspondent Todd Zwillich reports:

> The judge in his case prevented Rosenthal's attorney from informing the jury that the action was legal in that state. Marney Craig, who

---

1. www.marijuana.org/ballot%20arg2Hallin.htm, p. 1 of 1.
2. www.marijuana.org/ballot%20arg4Pro.htm, p. 1 of 2.

was a juror in Rosenthal's case, said that she regretted voting to convict him. During the case, jurors were informed only that Rosenthal grew marijuana and not that he had been licensed to do so. "We rendered a verdict that was wrong. We convicted a man who was not a criminal," Craig said.[3]

Libertarians believe that the federal government has overstepped its bounds; it is not the government's job to tell competent adults, doctors, and patients what medications are permissible. **Libertarianism** is the view, in the words of philosopher Jan Narveson, "that *individual liberty is the only proper concern of coercive social institutions.*"[4] The state, a coercive social institution, should protect individual liberty by enforcing laws that protect people from liberty-impairing activities, such as murder, theft, and fraud. It should require that everyone obey these laws and contribute to law enforcement and national defense. These are the only proper functions of government. All additional laws improperly deprive people of liberty.

Libertarians use the **Harm Principle,** proposed by 19th-century philosopher John Stuart Mill, to determine which laws improperly limit individual liberty:

> The only purpose for which power can be rightfully exercised over any member of a civilized community, against his will, is to prevent harm to others. His own good, either physical or moral, is not a sufficient warrant. He cannot rightfully be compelled to do or forbear because it will be better for him to do so, because it will make him happier, because, in the opinions of others, to do so would be wise, or even right.[5]

According to Mill, the state should protect three kinds of freedom for people who are not harming others: "liberty of tastes and pursuits;" "the liberty of expressing and publishing opinions;" and "the freedom to unite, for any purpose. . . ."[6] These are among the **civil liberties** that libertarians champion.

---

3. Todd Zwillich, "Bill Allows Medical Marijuana Defense in Drug Case," *Reuters Health* (April 10, 2003), at www.marijuana.org/reuters4-10-03.htm, p. 1 of 2. On June 4, 2003, Rosenthal was sentenced to only one day in jail and released immediately for time served. He was also fined $1,300. The medical marijuana community considered this an enormous victory; www.hippy.com/php/article.php?sid=6, accessed August 27, 2004.

4. Jan Narveson, *The Libertarian Idea* (Philadelphia: Temple University Press, 1988), p. xi.

5. John Stuart Mill, *On Liberty*, in *On Liberty and Considerations on Representative Government*, R. B. McCallum, Ed. (Oxford: Basil Blackwell, 1946), pp. 1–104, at 8.

6. Mill, p. 11.

This chapter discusses these three kinds of freedom to assess the strengths and limits of the Harm Principle. Mill considered the principle an application of utilitarianism. He thought that governments granting people complete freedom when they are not harming others maximizes utility. However, we have seen that utilitarian moral advice is not always acceptable. Also, we cannot know if the Harm Principle maximizes utility, because the required calculations of utility are impossible. So we consider the Harm Principle independent of any connection to utilitarianism and find that (1) it allows conduct that many people consider abhorrent, and (2) its distinction between conduct that harms others and conduct that does not is problematic.

Medical Paternalism

The Harm Principle opposes **paternalism,** which is *"the overriding or restricting of rights or freedoms of individuals for their own good."*[7] But why not override people's freedom if it is for their own good? Philosopher Alan Goldman gives four reasons: First, people are usually the best judges of their own interests, which may depend on their own particular values that others do not fully appreciate. Suppose, for example, that someone were paternalistically to force me into downhill skiing because he knows that I love thrills (philosophers are wild!) and that skiing provides more thrills than do my usual sports. The skiing busybody does not appreciate that I refrain from downhill skiing to avoid supporting an industry that I find environmentally destructive. Given my values, I am doing what serves my interests best.

Second, according to Goldman, self-determination is a value in itself even when its exercise does not lead to the satisfaction of interests. People should be free to do their own thing even if they hurt themselves. Third, people generally want to be self-determining, so paternalism deprives people of something that most people want. Finally, "maximal freedom for individuals to develop their own projects, to make the pivotal choices that define them, allows for the development of unique creative personalities, who become sources of new value in the goods they create and that they and others enjoy."[8] Paternalism impairs individual uniqueness and stifles social progress.

7. Alan H. Goldman, "The Refutation of Medical Paternalism," *The Moral Foundations of Professional Ethics* (Totowa, NJ: Rowman and Littlefield, 1980), reprinted in part in *Ethical Issues in Modern Medicine*, 6th ed., Bonnie Steinbock, John D. Arras, and Alex John London, Eds. (New York: McGraw-Hill, 2003), pp. 56–64, at 57.
8. Goldman, p. 56.

In medical contexts, *self-determination requires that competent adult patients receive information about, and consent to, medical procedures before they are performed.* This is called **informed consent.** Informed consent applies only to competent adults because children and people with severe mental impairments are believed unable to make proper use of self-determination, or **autonomy,** as it is sometimes called. They may lack settled values or fail to understand which choices serve their interests. For such people, paternalism is appropriate. Everyone else should decide for themselves.

Allowing competent adults to decide for themselves whether to accept medical advice permits people to refuse treatments necessary for survival. We saw in the Introduction that cancer patient Diane refused treatments that provided a 25% probability of complete recovery from her leukemia.[9] From the purely medical point of view, saving Diane's life is most important. A medical paternalist might force Diane to undergo needed therapy. Similarly, a Jehovah's Witness may die as a result of refusing a blood transfusion. Again, medical paternalists want to protect the patient's health regardless of his wishes.

Alan Goldman argues that medical paternalists fail to appreciate that longevity is not our only value. People often eat food they know is bad for their health; they exercise less than they know is healthful; they work too hard on projects they find meaningful. People risk their lives in mountain climbing and other sports. Public policies can also undercut longevity. We design our transportation system around use of the automobile even though nearly 40,000 people die in car accidents in the United States each year. Increased reliance on public transportation and intercity rail would save many lives, but we assume that most Americans prefer cars regardless of risks. It is no surprise that Diane refused treatment for her leukemia so she could deepen personal relationships during the time she had left or that a Jehovah's Witness would refuse treatment he considers sinful.

In sum, health and longevity are only two values among many that people legitimately pursue. Coercing competent adults to undergo medically advised therapies, like coercing them to eat right, exercise, and avoid dangerous sports, disregards the importance of human self-determination and the many other values people cherish. Libertarians believe that individual liberty is paramount; the state should protect people from coercion, even by well-meaning doctors. If people want to risk their lives in

---

9. Timothy E. Quill, "Death and Dignity: A Case of Individualized Decision Making," in Steinbock et al., pp. 77–80.

94 Chapter 3: Libertarianism and the Harm Principle

activities that harm no one but themselves, they should be free to do so. _It is their lives; the only bodies they harm are the ones they own._

Prohibition

Writing in the middle of the 19th century, John Stuart Mill noted, "the people . . . of nearly half the United States have been interdicted by law from making any use whatever of fermented drinks, except for medical purposes. . . ."[10] Mill considered drinking alcohol an individual rather than a social act. So long as it harms no one else, it is none of the law's business. "Selling fermented liquors . . . is trading, and trading is a social act . . ." Mill writes. The injustice of prohibiting the sale of liquor "is not on the liberty of the seller, but on that of the buyer and consumer; since the State might just as well forbid him to drink wine as purposely make it impossible for him to obtain it."[11] In sum, the Harm Principle does not prevent the state from regulating trade except when the regulation's only purpose is depriving consumers of desired products that they can use without harming others. We should have "liberty of tastes and pursuits."

Echoing Mill's views before the Civil War, John A. Andrew, who later became governor of Massachusetts, wrote that it is

> the right of every citizen to determine for himself what he will eat or drink. . . . A law prohibiting him from drinking every kind of alcoholic liquors, universally used in all countries and ages as a beverage, is an arbitrary and unreasonable interference with his rights, and is not justified by the consideration that some men may abuse their rights, and may, therefore, need the counsel and example of good men to lead them to reform.[12]

Yet some Americans favored prohibition and rejected the Harm Principle. For example, the Reverend Josiah Strong wrote in 1914, "'Personal Liberty' is at last an uncrowned, dethroned king, with no one to do him reverence. . . . We are no longer frightened by that ancient bogey—'paternalism in government.' We affirm boldly, it is the business of government to be just that—paternal."[13]

---

10. Mill, p. 79.
11. Mill, p. 80.
12. In Edward Behr, _Prohibition: Thirteen Years That Changed America_ (New York: Arcade Publishing, 1996), p. 31.
13. J. Strong, _The Gospel of the Kingdom_ 8 (July 1914), pp. 97–98, quoted in Thomas Szasz, _Our Right to Drugs: The Case for a Free Market_ (Syracuse: Syracuse University Press, 1992, 1996), p. 47.

But why would Americans need paternal protection against alcohol? According to early 19th-century temperance advocate the Reverend Justin Edwards, liquor "has been among the more constant and fruitful sources of all our woes. Yet such has been its power to deceive men that while evil after evil has rolled in upon them . . . they have continued [to drink]. . . ." Edwards claimed that between 1820 and 1826 "it was realized that if drunkenness was to be done away with, men must abstain not only from abuse but from the use of what intoxicates. . . ."[14] Those who abstain will enjoy better health and longer life because, in the words of Dr. Thomas Sewell of Columbian College, Washington, consuming liquor causes: "dyspepsia, jaundice, emaciation, corpulence, rheumatism, gout, palpitation, lethargy, palsy, apoplexy, melancholy, madness, delirium tremens, [and] premature old age. . . ."[15] In addition, writes historian Edward Behr:

> Physicians . . . began propagating as scientific fact a myth that became accepted, for decades, as verifiable truth: that excessive drinking could lead to the body's spontaneous combustion. Case after case, recorded not only in American but in French and British 19th-century medical journals, involved individuals bursting into flames from close contact with a candle. . . .[16]

In short, liquor is so alluring but harmful to the unwary that the government should paternalistically protect people from themselves.

Protecting drinkers from themselves was not the only goal. Many prohibitionists in America and England believed also that drinking alcohol harms others. Historian Herbert Asbury writes that the saloon, the major outlet for retail sale of alcoholic drinks, promoted many social ills. The saloon

> encouraged drunkenness; few bartenders hesitated to serve children, idiots, and known drunkards. It ignored the law. It corrupted the police, the courts, and the politicians. It was a breeding place of crime and violence, and the hangout of criminals and degenerates of every type. It was the backbone of prostitution. . . . In 1914 the Wisconsin State Vice Committee declared that "the chief cause of the downfall of women and girls is the close connection between alcoholic drinks and commercialized vice."

A Chicago commission came to the same conclusion. It "found that harlots were encouraged to solicit customers in the back rooms of saloons,

---

14. Found in Behr, p. 24.
15. Behr, p. 22.
16. Behr, p. 22.

96 Chapter 3: Libertarianism and the Harm Principle

that they received commissions on drinks sold through their efforts, and that when they were arrested the saloonkeepers usually paid their fines."[17]

The case for prohibition seemed strong. Mill summarized the prohibitionist argument that allowing people to drink alcohol violates the social rights of others:

> It destroys my primary right of security, by constantly creating and stimulating social disorder. It invades my right of equality, by [creating] a misery I am taxed to support. It impedes my right to free moral and intellectual development, by surrounding my path with dangers, and by weakening and demoralizing society, from which I have a right to claim mutual aid and intercourse.[18]

Yet Mill rejects "social rights" because they allow people too much control over one another's behavior. According to the principle of "social rights," Mill complains:

> It is the absolute social right of every individual, that every other individual shall act in every respect exactly as he ought; that whosoever fails thereof in the smallest particular violates my social right, and entitles me to demand from the legislature the removal of the grievance. So monstrous a principle is far more dangerous than any single interference with liberty; there is no violation of liberty which it would not justify. . . .[19]

Mill claims that "social rights" leave people no liberty because almost everything we do affects others. "Perhaps," he writes, "holding opinions in secret, without ever disclosing them," would leave others unaffected, but "the moment an opinion which I consider noxious passes any one's lips, it invades . . . 'social rights' "[20] because it could harm someone. So the Harm Principle means little if freedom exists only when no one else is affected. Instead, the Harm Principle claims, "in things which do not primarily concern others, individuality should assert itself."[21] Secondary effects on others should not limit people's liberty.

This approach means that applying the Harm Principle often requires judging whether effects on others are primary or secondary. Consider again the issue of medical paternalism. Diane's decision to forego therapy for her leukemia affected her family, but the primary effect was on her.

17. Herbert Asbury, *The Great Illusion: An Informal History of Prohibition* (Garden City, NY: Doubleday and Company, 1950), pp. 114–15.

18. Mill, p. 80.

19. Mill, p. 80.

20. Mill, p. 80.

21. Mill, p. 50.

Because *it was her body at stake,* only she would suffer the pain of treatment or the loss of life without treatment. So it was her right to accept or reject treatment, not the right of her husband, children, or employer.

What are the primary effects of someone drinking alcohol? If they included police corruption and increased prostitution, Mill might favor prohibition. However, drinking alcohol is related only remotely and indirectly to these activities. Police corruption and prostitution can exist whether or not people drink socially. If people are to have any freedom at all, such remote and indirect effects cannot justify reduced liberty.

In 1920 prohibition was imposed nationwide in the United States. Utilitarian considerations soon reinforced libertarian arguments for repeal of this encroachment on individual freedom. Prohibition did not reduce drinking very much. (Early 20th-century cowboy-humorist Will Rogers quipped, "Prohibition is better than no liquor at all.")[22] Instead, it promoted crime, police corruption, disrespect for law, and juvenile delinquency. As a special committee of the Wickersham Commission Report on Alcohol Prohibition stated in 1930, the children affected most were those in bootlegging families: "Instead of entering legitimate employment, they help in the family business and tend to acquire a distaste for work with less excitement and smaller returns." Other youths were corrupted as well. The Salvation Army's Colonel William L. Barker reported in 1925, "we have girls in our rescue homes who are 14 and 15 years old, while 10 years ago the youngest was in the early 20s." A hardware merchant in Decatur, Indiana, a small city of 5,000, claimed in 1930 that "every high-school boy has a flask in his hip pocket and an automobile. The drinking among the younger people and the growing disrespect for law are the worst problems we have ever faced."[23]

In sum, prohibition was a disaster. It ran afoul of the Harm Principle and utilitarian reasoning. Still, the consumption of alcohol addicts some drinkers, impairs lives, shortens lives, impoverishes families, and costs taxpayers.

The Right to Drugs

Libertarians view many or all current restrictions on drug use to be the same as prohibition. They acknowledge that drugs can be dangerous. Holly Eitenmiller reports in *Illinois Magazine* on the dangers of abusing methamphetamine. "A sister to crack cocaine in the stimulant class of

---

22. Quoted in Behr, p. 172.
23. Quoted in Asbury, p. 161.

drugs, meth [also called 'crank'] is concocted of man-made chemicals,"[24] she writes.

> According to law enforcement agents, users will stay awake for long stretches of time. They'll go without food and neglect personal hygiene. Long-term abusers end up with heart, liver, and kidney problems, infectious diseases, severely decayed teeth, pneumonia, and hepatitis. In the throes of drug-induced delirium, speeders will often see "crank bugs" creeping over their flesh, a hallucination caused by constricted blood vessels that itch. They'll pick at those areas until they bleed.[25]

Because a typical meth habit costs about $500 per week, some meth-abusing women turn to prostitution. Without meth available, some of these women might be in school or holding down productive employment, advocates of tough drug laws point out.

Libertarians claim, however, that what people choose to eat, snort, or smoke is no one else's business unless they directly put others in harm's way, by driving under the influence, for example. Libertarian psychiatrist Thomas Szasz believes that "a limited government, such as that of the United States, lacks the political legitimacy to deprive competent adults of the right to use whatever substances they choose. The right to chew or smoke a plant that grows wild in nature, such as hemp (marijuana), is anterior to and more basic than the right to vote."[26] This statement accords with Mill's "liberty of tastes and pursuits."

Any other policy deprives people of the right to their own bodies, Szasz reasons. If I seek spiritual comfort or healing, the state allows me to choose any religion whatever to soothe or save my soul because it is *my* soul. To disallow similar liberty with my body implies state ownership; it suggests the state's claim to my body is prior to my own. But, as Mark Twain wrote, "whose property is my body? If I experiment with it, who must be answerable? I, not the State. If I choose injudiciously, does the State die? Oh, no."[27]

Szasz gives this account of why people advocate drug prohibition. They believe that drug use is a disease that causes both crime and additional illness. The disease, they claim, results from

> mental illness, peer pressure, parental neglect, poverty, social injustice, drug pushers, the addictive properties of drugs—anything but

---

24. Holly Eitenmiller, "Methamphetamine Abuse," *Illinois Magazine,* Vol. 2, No. 5 (May 2003), pp. 20–24, at 22.
25. Eitenmiller, p. 23.
26. Szasz, p. xxiv.
27. Mark Twain, "Osteopathy" (1901), quoted in Szasz, p. 5.

the drug user's free will. It is legally just to punish persons who trade in (prohibited) drugs, because they sell a harmful product; and to forcibly treat drug (ab)users, because they are sick (but deny it and refuse to be treated)."[28]

Szasz rejects this logic because *laws prohibiting drugs paternalistically prohibit competent adults from taking drugs voluntarily, thereby impairing personal freedom.* Ethan Nadelmann, director of the Lindesmith Center, a drug-policy research institute in New York City, notes that the vast majority of people who take prohibited drugs are not crazed addicts.

> Only a tiny percentage of the 70 million Americans who have tried marijuana have gone on to have problems with that or any other drug. The same is true of the tens of millions of Americans who have used cocaine or hallucinogens. Most of those who did have a problem at one time or another don't any more. That a few million Americans have serious problems with illicit drugs today . . . is no reason to demonize those drugs and the people who use them.[29]

People use drugs, Szasz maintains, for the same basic reasons that they use many other products of modern civilization, including bicycles, cars, trucks, tractors, ladders, chainsaws, skis, and hang gliders. They make life more productive or pleasant.

> Each year, tens of thousands of people are injured and killed as a result of accidents associated with the use of such artifacts. Why do we not speak of "ski abuse" or a "chain saw problem"? Because we expect people who use such equipment to familiarize themselves with their use and avoid injuring themselves or others. If they hurt themselves, we assume they did so accidentally, and we try to heal their injuries. If they hurt others negligently, we punish them. . . .[30]

Restricting adult access to such items to prevent injury and death would be treating adults paternalistically, like children. The same is true of drugs. Competent adults can use drugs responsibly and safely just as they use skis and chain saws. Accidents will occur, and some adults will act irresponsibly or criminally, but these realities are the price of freedom.

Libertarians also oppose laws requiring prescriptions for certain drugs. People mainly use these drugs without harming others, so prescription-drug laws run afoul of the Harm Principle. Why do we have such laws?

---

28. Szasz, p. 149.
29. Nathan A. Nadelmann, contribution to "The War on Drugs Is Lost," *National Review* (February 12, 1996), pp. 38–40, at 38.
30. Szasz, p. xxiii.

Their goal is generally to protect consumers from themselves on the assumption that most consumers are too ignorant of proper medication to know what to take without professional advice and too lazy or irresponsible to ask a doctor, read, or otherwise inform themselves. In short, prescription drug laws were introduced paternalistically. As a result, Szasz writes,

> virtually all effective medicines were placed beyond the reach of the consumer; the physician, entrusted with the keys to the pharmacopoeia, was interposed between the patient as drug buyer and the pharmacist as drug seller; and the patient was encouraged to distrust his own judgment regarding drugs, deprecate his self-responsibility for the drugs he took, and view the mere act of self-medication as a sort of medical sin.[31]

Dr. Szasz believes that preventing suicide is a major reason why the government denies citizens the right to buy the drugs of their choice. "We view the desire to die as a symptom of mental illness; we interpret virtually all suicide as a tragedy that ought to have been prevented. . . ."[32] Yet, as Szasz sees it, "committing suicide ought to be considered a basic human right, . . . and . . . the expectation or threat of suicide never justifies the coercive control of the (allegedly) suicidal person."[33]

At present, the most reliable method of suicide employs a gun, but many people dislike violence in general or do not want loved ones to see their brains splatted against the wall. Drug legalization would facilitate nonviolent suicide.

> If we had a free market in drugs, we could . . . buy all the chloral hydrate, heroin, and Seconal we wanted and could afford. We would then be free to die easily, comfortably, and surely—without any need for recourse to violent means of suicide or fear of being involuntarily kept alive "dying" in a hospital.[34]

We would not need physician-assisted suicide or a "right to die." People who wanted to die could take responsibility for their act, without involving others, because their lives would be in their own hands, as it should be if we own our own bodies. Szasz concludes:

> Since the most important practical consequence of our loss of the right to bodily self-ownership is the denial of legally unrestricted

---

31. Szasz, p. 53.
32. Szasz, p. 151.
33. Szasz, p. 154.
34. Szasz, p. 151.

access to drugs, the most important symbol of the right to our bodies now resides in our reasserting our right to drugs—to all drugs, not just to one or another so-called recreational drug.[35]

The War on Drugs

Under the administration of President Ronald Reagan (1981–1989), the U.S. government launched a "war on drugs." While libertarians believe this war on drugs violates the right to our bodies, other arguments against the war concern utility, civil rights, family values, and racial justice. Writer and editor William F. Buckley, Jr. makes the utilitarian case:

> More people die every year as a result of the war against drugs than die from what we call, generically, overdosing. These fatalities include, perhaps most prominently, drug merchants who compete for commercial territory but include also people who are robbed and killed by those desperate for money to buy the drug to which they have become addicted.

Robbery for money to buy addictive, illicit drugs would decline dramatically if the drugs were legal because illegality makes the drugs expensive.

> The pharmaceutical cost of cocaine and heroin is approximately 2% of the street price of those drugs. Since a cocaine addict can spend as much as $1,000 per week to sustain his habit, he would need to come up with that $1,000. The approximate fencing cost of stolen goods is 80%, so that to come up with $1,000 can require stealing $5,000 worth of jewels, cars, whatever. We can see that at free-market rates, $20 per week would provide the addict with [drugs].[36]

The illegality that makes drugs expensive makes drug traffickers rich enough to corrupt many law-enforcement officials. Joseph D. McNamara, former chief of police in Kansas City, Missouri, writes, "police scandals are an untallied cost of the drug war. The FBI, the Drug Enforcement Administration, and even the Coast Guard have had to admit to corruption. The gravity of the police crimes [which include murder] is as disturbing as the volume." And when police act conscientiously, "drug enforcement often involves questionable ethical behavior by the police, such as what we did in letting a guilty person go free because he enticed someone else into violating the law."[37] The war on drugs impairs law

---

35. Szasz, p. 154.
36. William F. Buckley, Jr., contribution to "The War on Drugs Is Lost," pp. 35–38, at 36.
37. Joseph D. McNamara, contribution to "The War on Drugs Is Lost," pp. 42–44, at 43.

enforcement also by diverting the attention of about 400,000 police officers from the pursuit of other types of criminals.[38]

Profits from dealing drugs entice young people to drop out of school. Kurt Schmoke, mayor of Baltimore, "visited a high school and asked the students if the high dropout rate was due to kids being hooked on drugs. He was told that the kids were dropping out because they were hooked on drug money, not drugs."[39]

The war against drugs harms family values in three ways. First, when teenagers have illegal means to earn more money than their parents do, parental discipline suffers. Second, many young fathers cannot raise their children owing to drug convictions and incarceration. According to Steven Duke, a professor at Yale Law School, "at least half a million [fathers] are in prison, often for nothing worse than possessing drugs."[40] Third, children are convinced to spy and inform on their parents. Thomas Szasz gives several examples, including this one:

> In August 1986, after listening to an antidrug lecture, Deanna Young, a "blonde, blue-eyed junior high school student [in California] walked into the police station carrying a trash can bag containing an ounce of cocaine . . . [and] small amounts of marijuana and pills. By sunrise, her father and mother had been arrested and jailed." Mrs. Reagan [wife of President Ronald Reagan] rushed to congratulate Ms. Young. "She must have loved her parents a great deal," she told the press.[41]

Szasz reminds readers that breaking down family bonds by encouraging denunciation of family members is a common tactic of totalitarian states.

The United States differs from totalitarian regimes in part by granting rights to criminal defendants. But according to Robert Sweet, formerly Assistant U.S. Attorney and Deputy Mayor of New York, the war on drugs has eroded these rights.

> We have seen the elimination of an accused's right to pretrial release for most charges under the drug laws; heightened restrictions on post-conviction bail; the invasions into the attorney-client relationship through criminal forfeiture. The criteria for securing a search warrant have been relaxed. In drug cases, the Supreme Court has permitted the issuance of search warrants based on anonymous

---

38. Buckley, p. 36.
39. McNamara, p. 43.
40. Steven B. Duke, contribution to "The War on Drugs Is Lost," pp. 47–48, at 48.
41. Szasz, p. 78.

tips and tips from informants known to be corrupt and unreliable; permitted warrantless searches of fields, barns, and private property near a residence; and upheld evidence obtained under defective search warrants. . . .[42]

Blacks suffer most from the war on drugs. A study conducted by *USA Today* showed that in 1988 blacks were disproportionately arrested for drug violations. Blacks constituted 12.7% of the population and 12% of those who regularly used illegal drugs, but constituted 38% of those arrested on drug charges.[43] Other studies showed a worse disproportion, with 44% of those arrested for possession and 57% arrested for sales being black.[44] Professors Alfred McCoy and Alan Block write:

> From the outset, the enforcement emphasis of the Reagan-Bush drug war targeted inner-city street dealing in a way that produced a disproportionate number of black arrests. Federal drug laws require mandatory sentences that are much longer for crack, which is prevalent in minority communities, than cocaine powder, a drug favored by affluent white users. Under Federal law, suspects convicted of selling only 5 grams of the cocaine derivative "crack" worth $125 face the same mandatory five-year sentence as those handling 500 grams of pure cocaine worth $50,000.[45]

Such facts may both result from and contribute to negative racial stereotypes.

The greatest disproportion in the war on drugs is between the treatment of nicotine and other drugs. Cigarettes, the principal source of nicotine consumption and addiction, cause about 400,000 deaths per year in the United States. They remain legal because people realize in the case of cigarettes what should be apparent by now regarding other drugs—that prohibition is impractical and counterproductive. Nor is prohibition necessary. Education efforts have influenced people to give up cigarettes, and new laws now better discourage minors from smoking.[46]

---

42. Robert W. Sweet, contribution to "The War on Drugs Is Lost," pp. 44–45, at 44–45.
43. S. Meddis, "Drug Arrest Rate Is Higher for Blacks," *USA Today,* December 20, 1989, in Szasz, p. 116.
44. "Just the Facts," *FCNL Washington Newsletter* of the Friends Committee on National Legislation (February 1990), in Szasz, p. 116.
45. Alfred W. McCoy and Alan A. Block, "U.S. Narcotics Policy: An Anatomy of Failure," in *War on Drugs,* Alfred W. McCoy and Alan A. Block, Eds. (Boulder: Westview Press, 1992), pp. 1–18, at 7.
46. Steven B. Duke and Albert C. Gross, *America's Longest War: Rethinking Our Tragic Crusade Against Drugs* (New York: Putnam, 1993), pp. 27–32.

104   Chapter 3: Libertarianism and the Harm Principle

This is the proper model for all drugs that are addictive and potentially dangerous.

In sum, libertarian arguments based on the Harm Principle are not alone in favoring drug legalization. They are joined by arguments based on utilitarianism, civil liberties, family values, and racial justice. Such combinations are common. Seldom in politics does one consideration outweigh all others. Typically, political debates feature arguments drawn from several different principles and perspectives.

Libertarians make an important distinction between having a freedom and exercising that freedom. If drug criminalization and the prescription drug system were replaced by a free market that made all drugs available to competent adults who paid for them, adults would have the right to buy and take drugs. The issue of marijuana prescribed for certain medical conditions would disappear because people could legally buy and smoke marijuana for any reason. This does not mean, however, that it would be right for them to do so. Having a right and exercising that right are two different things. Cigarettes are legally available to adults, but starting to smoke is foolish. In a free society people have many rights, including rights to do stupid things. Most libertarians who favor the right to buy drugs do not favor exercising that right.

Other limitations regarding drugs concern harm to others. Drug use that endangers others, such as driving under the influence, should be prohibited. Legalizing certain drugs may also endanger others. If antibiotics were available over the counter, people might use them too much, resulting in the evolution of resistant bacteria that could infect other people who would be harmed by the absence of effective antibiotics.[47]

Finally, people might reasonably reject the libertarian case for drug legalization if they find in reflective equilibrium that incompatible values are more important to them than are individual freedom and the Harm Principle. For example, Szasz would make it legal for someone as young as 18 or 21, whichever is the age of majority, to commit suicide surely and painlessly with easily available drugs. Some people who value human life want neat, painless suicide to remain difficult or uncertain, especially for young adults. To achieve logical consistency, such people would have to reject, or qualify their support for, body self-ownership, the Harm Principle, and the general libertarian "freedom of tastes and pursuits."

---

47. See Laurie Garrett, *The Coming Plague: Newly Emerging Diseases in a World Out of Balance* (New York: Farrar, Straus and Giroux, 1994), especially pp. 411–13.

Freedom of Speech

The First Amendment to the Constitution of the United States guarantees freedoms of speech, press, and assembly to all Americans: "Congress shall make no law . . . abridging the freedom of speech, or of the press; or the right of the people peaceably to assemble, and to petition the Government for a redress of grievances." We take these freedoms seriously because they are foundations of democratic self-government. People who cannot exchange ideas, publish ideas, or petition the government to adopt ideas cannot be free. Free speech, especially political speech, is so important to us that we criticize regimes, such as the former Soviet Union, for denying it. Nobel-Prize-winning Soviet physicist Andrei Sakharov, you may recall from the introductory chapter, was punished for speaking out in support of a boycott of the 1980 Olympic Games held in Moscow. Jaures Medvedev was involuntarily committed to a mental hospital for dissenting from the government's preferred theory of evolution. Our government cannot legally silence dissent.

The Harm Principle supports our First Amendment protections. Although speech affects other people, it is vital to individual liberty. If we cannot exchange ideas, we cannot learn from others what may be helpful in deciding how to live our lives or to conduct national policy. This restriction impairs our self-determination as individuals and societies. J. S. Mill writes, "every age [has] held many opinions which subsequent ages have deemed not only false but absurd."[48] Progress occurs when "wrong opinions and practices gradually yield to fact and argument; but facts and arguments to produce any effect on the mind, must be brought before it."[49] Thus, Mill endorses "the liberty of expressing and publishing opinions."[50]

> Silencing the expression of an opinion . . . is robbing the human race; posterity as well as the existing generation; those who dissent from the opinion, still more than those who hold it. If the opinion is right, they are deprived of the opportunity of exchanging error for truth: if wrong, they lose . . . the clearer perception . . . of truth, produced by its collision with error."[51]

Therefore, "if all mankind minus one were of one opinion, and only one person were of the contrary opinion, mankind would be no more justified

---

48. Mill, p. 15.
49. Mill, p. 16.
50. Mill, p. 11.
51. Mill, pp. 14–15.

in silencing that one person, than he, if he had the power, would be justified in silencing mankind."[52]

Mill recognized that some expressions of opinion may constitute harmful actions. For example, "an opinion that corn-dealers are starvers of the poor . . . ought to be unmolested when simply circulated through the press, but may justly incur punishment when delivered orally to an excited mob assembled before the house of a corn-dealer. . . ."[53] United States Supreme Court Justice Oliver Wendell Holmes, Jr. made the same point when he condemned maliciously shouting fire in a crowded theater. The ensuing panic endangers others, and the state should protect people from such danger.

American law limits speech in many situations in which it constitutes action. For example, if I offer to pay a judge for ruling in my favor, I have attempted bribery. If I tell my boss that I will break his legs if he does not give me a promotion, my speech is a criminal threat. If I say to an employee that she will be promoted only if she dates me, I am guilty of sexual harassment. Many crimes can be completed through speech alone, and the First Amendment does not protect against prosecution.

Even noncriminal speech has limits, according to American law. For example, if my speech constitutes "fighting words," a personal insult normally expected to provoke violence, my speech is not protected. If my speech constitutes a nuisance, such as blaring my opinions to the whole neighborhood night and day so others have no peace and quiet, it is not protected. If my speech exposes the unwary to what they reasonably find horribly distasteful, it is not protected. In all these cases, both criminal and noncriminal, *freedom of speech is curtailed to protect others from harm.*

Some other cases of speech remain controversial. For example, in 1968 the United States was fighting a controversial war in Vietnam. Many soldiers in the war were conscripted through the draft, a system of compelling young men to serve in the armed forces for a minimum of two years. On April 26, 1968 Paul Robert Cohen entered

> the Los Angeles County Courthouse . . . wearing a jacket bearing the words "Fuck the Draft," which were plainly visible. There were women and children present. . . . The defendant was arrested . . . [and] testified that he wore the jacket . . . as a means of informing the public of the depth of his feelings against the Vietnam War and the draft.

---

52. Mill, p. 14.
53. Mill, p. 49.

Is such conduct protected by the guarantee of free speech? The Court of Appeals did not think so because it was "offensive conduct . . . which has the tendency to provoke *others* to acts of violence or to in turn disturb the peace. . . ."[54] Since violence can harm innocent bystanders, such provocative speech seems to run afoul of the Harm Principle.

The United States Supreme Court disagreed. It overturned Cohen's conviction because the writing on the jacket primarily expressed a political opinion. Writing for the court, Justice Harlan noted that emotions are as important to political expression as ideas, so the offensive nature of the word chosen is a protected aspect of political expression. People in the courthouse offended by this expression could have avoided extended exposure by averting their eyes. Cohen's jacket addressed no particular individual, so the "fighting" words exception to free speech is inapplicable, and no one disturbed the peace. Finally, if the state could bar this particular four-letter word, Harlan wrote, "no readily ascertainable general principle exists for stopping short of . . ." cleansing "public debate to the point where it is grammatically palatable to the most squeamish among us. . . ."[55]

Not everyone agreed. Justice Blackmun wrote for a minority of three: "Cohen's absurd and immature antic, in my view, was mainly conduct and little speech." Three justices would have allowed Cohen's prosecution for (potentially) disturbing the peace.

The Supreme Court went farther in protecting speech when it upheld the right of Gregory Lee Johnson to burn the American flag in front of Dallas City Hall during demonstrations protesting President Reagan's policies. Johnson was convicted of desecrating the American flag. We protect the flag from desecration because it symbolizes the country, its values, and its history. Precisely because it is a symbol, however, its desecration during a political demonstration constitutes symbolic speech, Justice Brennan claimed for the Supreme Court majority. No one was personally addressed with "fighting words." No one disturbed the peace. "Federal law designates burning as the preferred means of disposing of a flag" that is too worn for display, so flag burning is not the issue. The only issue is the message Johnson conveyed by burning the flag. However, Brennan pointed out, "if there is a bedrock principle underlying the First Amendment, it is that the Government may not prohibit the expression of an idea

---

54. *Cohen v. California* 408 U.S. 15 (1971), in *Philosophy of Law*, 5ᵗʰ ed., Joel Feinberg and Hyman Gross, Eds. (Belmont, CA: Wadsworth, 1995), pp. 277–81, at 278. Emphasis in original.
55. *Cohen v. California*, p. 280.

simply because society finds the idea itself offensive or disagreeable. . . ."[56] Johnson had a First Amendment right to burn the flag.

Again, not everyone agreed. Chief Justice Rehnquist wrote for a minority of three:

> For more than 200 years, the American flag has occupied a unique position as the symbol of our Nation, a uniqueness that justifies a governmental prohibition against flag burning in the way respondent Johnson did here. . . . Surely one of the high purposes of a democratic society is to legislate against conduct that is regarded as evil and profoundly offensive to the majority of people—whether it be murder, embezzlement, pollution, or flag burning.[57]

Rehnquist pays no attention to the Harm Principle. He puts flag burning, which does no obvious harm, in the same category as murder, embezzlement, and pollution, which typically harm others. The court's majority does observe the Harm Principle.

Hate Speech

The implications of the Harm Principle are less certain in some cases of hate speech. Consider St. Paul, Minnesota's, Bias-Motivated Crime Ordinance:

> Whoever places on public or private property a symbol, object, appellation, characterization or graffiti, including, but not limited to, a burning cross or Nazi swastika, which one knows or has reasonable grounds to know arouses anger, alarm or resentment in others on the basis of race, color, creed, religion or gender commits disorderly conduct and shall be guilty of a misdemeanor. . . .[58]

How does this ordinance relate to the decision in *Johnson v. Texas* that allowed flag burning as a form of symbolic political speech? Flag burning symbolizes contempt for the United States, whereas cross burning symbolizes contempt for African Americans. Like cross burning, burning the flag causes "anger, alarm or resentment," but not on the basis of "race, color, creed, religion or gender." Does the different subject

---

56. *Texas v. Johnson*, 491 U.S. 397, in Feinberg and Gross, pp. 285–93, at 289.
57. *Texas v. Johnson*, pp. 291–92.
58. St. Paul, Minn. Legis. Code Sec. 292.02 (1990). Quoted in *R.A.V. v. St. Paul*, 505 U.S. 377 (1992), majority opinion of Antonin Scalia, and reprinted in *Taking Sides: Clashing Views on Controversial Legal Issues*, 9th ed., M. Ethan Katsh and William Rose, Eds. (Guilford, CT: McGraw-Hill, 2000), pp. 260–66, at 260.

matter make cross burning harmful to others, whereas flag burning is not? It is hard to tell.

St. Paul's ordinance was in effect when,

> in the early morning hours of June 21, 1990, long after they had put their five children to bed, Russ and Laura Jones were awakened by voices outside their house. Russ got up and went to his bedroom window. . . . "I saw a glow," he recalled. There, in the middle of his yard, was a burning cross. The Joneses are black. In the spring of 1990 they had moved into their four-bedroom, three-bathroom dream house on 290 Earl Street in St. Paul, Minnesota. They were the only black family on the block. Two weeks after they had settled into their predominantly white neighborhood, the tires on both their cars were slashed. A few weeks later, one of their cars' windows was shattered, and a group of teenagers had walked past their house and shouted "nigger" at their nine-year-old son. And now this burning cross. Russ Jones did not have to guess at the meaning of this symbol of racial hatred.[59]

Cross burning historically accompanied the vigilante lynching of blacks by whites.

I assume the cross burners were guilty of trespass and liable for any damage to the Jones's property, but these issues were not before the court in *R.A.V v. City of St. Paul.* The issue was whether St. Paul's ordinance violated the First Amendment freedom of speech. It singled out for punishment insults based on "race, color, creed or gender," leaving people free, as Supreme Court Justice Antonin Scalia put it, "to express hostility, for example, on the basis of political affiliation, union membership, or homosexuality. . . ." According to Scalia, "the First Amendment does not permit St. Paul to impose special prohibitions on those speakers who express views on disfavored subjects."[60]

Scalia notes that "according to St. Paul, the ordinance is intended . . . to 'protect against the victimization of a person or persons who are particularly vulnerable because of their membership in a group that historically has been discriminated against.'"[61] This means, Scalia thinks, that St. Paul

---

59. Charles R. Lawrence III, "Crossburning and the Sound of Silence: Antisubordination Theory and the First Amendment," *Villanova Law Review,* Vol. 37, No. 4 (1992), pp. 787–804, in *Taking Sides: Clashing Views on Controversial Political Issues,* 13th ed., George McKenna and Stanley Feingold, Eds. (Guilford, CT: McGraw-Hill, 2003), pp. 200–06, at 200.
60. Scalia in Katsh, p. 264.
61. Scalia in Katsh, p. 265.

is taking sides in a political debate, in violation of the First Amendment. St. Paul would allow people to hold up signs vilifying religious bigots but would prosecute people across the street with signs vilifying Catholics, for example. "St. Paul has no such authority to license one side of a debate to fight freestyle, while requiring the other to follow Marquis of Queensbury Rules."[62]

Justice John Paul Stevens disagreed with Scalia's analysis. "Significantly," he writes, "the St. Paul ordinance regulates speech not on the basis of its subject matter or the viewpoint expressed, but rather on the basis of the *harm* the speech causes."[63] It threatened specific individuals. Legal scholar Charles Lawrence agrees with Stevens.

> The primary intent of the cross burner in R.A.V. was ... to intimidate—to cast fear in the hearts of his victims, to drive them out of the community, to enforce the practice of residential segregation, and to encourage others to join him in the enforcement of that practice. The discriminatory impact of this speech is of even more importance than the speaker's intent.[64]

Lawrence thinks cross burning resembles racist or sexist speech in workplace settings, which courts have held to deny targeted individuals equal access to employment. In this case, equal access to housing is threatened. Such threats do not advance the cause of free speech but impoverish it, Lawrence argues. Russ and Laura Jones brought new experiences and perspectives that they could share with their new neighbors. "A burning cross not only silences people like the Joneses, it impoverishes the democratic process and renders our collective conversation less informed."[65]

But St. Paul's ordinance was not confined to speech that threatened particular individuals; it outlawed all symbolic speech, whether on private or public property, whether directed at particular individuals or the general public, that angers or alarms others on the basis of "race, color, creed, religion or gender." How can all such speech be considered harmful? Jonathan Rauch, a writer for the *Economist*, suggests that many people regard all hate speech as harmful because they mistakenly equate it with violence. They call it "assaultive speech," "words that wound," and "verbal violence." Rauch quotes Toni Morrison, who said, while accepting the

---

62. Scalia in Katsh, p. 264.

63. John Paul Stevens, *R.A.V. v. City of St. Paul*, in Katsh, pp. 267–75, at 273–74. Emphasis in original.

64. Lawrence, pp. 202–03.

65. Lawrence, p. 205.

Nobel Prize for Literature in 1993: "Oppressive language does more than represent violence; it is violence."[66]

Rauch finds this counterproductive. We should welcome speech as an alternative to physical violence because only physical violence does real harm. We do not protect people from physical violence by defining speech as violence and then cracking down on speech. "Every cop or prosecutor chasing words is one fewer chasing criminals. In a world rife with real violence and oppression, full of . . . 11-year-olds spraying bullets at children in Chicago and in turn being executed by gang lords, it is odious of Toni Morrison to say that words are violence."[67] In addition, when words are policed as if they were violent, who will have the right to speak up? Increasingly, only popular views will be allowed and minorities, whom St. Paul was trying to protect, will be hurt most because often their experiences are unique and their views unpopular. Gays, for example, made great strides in the United States in the latter part of the 20th century by speaking up. But their speech offended many. Without the freedom to offend, there is no freedom of speech and without freedom of speech, dissent cannot promote progress.

The Harm Principle is attractive in the abstract, but applying it to particular cases of "the liberty of expressing and publishing opinions" can be difficult. Nevertheless, free speech remains an important civil liberty.

Marriage

Mill endorses the "freedom to unite, for any purpose not involving harm to others. . . ."[68] There are two aspects of this freedom. One is the freedom to form desired relationships; the other is the freedom to keep those relationships exclusive, denying membership to unwanted individuals. We consider first the freedom to form a desired relationship, using marriage as the example.

Although Mill does not discuss it, interracial marriage seems included in the "freedom to unite" because it harms no one else directly. Racists may be offended, but harm to them is indirect and, as we have seen, freedom vanishes when limited by such indirect harm. Unlike utilitarians, libertarians disregard the sensibilities of people not directly involved regardless of their number or the strength of their psychic pain.

---

66. Jonathan Rauch, "In Defense of Prejudice: Why Incendiary Speech Must Be Protected," in McKenna and Feingold, pp. 207–11, at 210.

67. Rauch, pp. 110–11

68. Mill, p. 11.

112 Chapter 3: Libertarianism and the Harm Principle

Mill applies his views explicitly to polygamy, which Mormons practiced when Mill wrote, but in this case American law conflicts with Mill's understanding of the Harm Principle. Mill dislikes polygamy because it conflicts with "the principle of liberty . . . , being a mere riveting of the chains of one half of the community, and an emancipation of the other from reciprocity of obligation towards them." Still, if liberty means anything, it must allow people voluntarily to unite as they choose. "This relation is as much voluntary on the part of the women concerned in it, and who may be deemed the sufferers by it, as is the case with any other form of the marriage institutions."[69] So Mill thinks Mormons and others should be allowed polygamous marriage.

The Mormon case is particularly strong, Mill claims, because "they have left the countries to which their doctrines were unacceptable, and established themselves in a remote corner of the earth, which they have been the first to render habitable to human beings." Under these conditions, "it is difficult to see on what principles but those of tyranny they can be prevented from living there under what laws they please, provided they commit no aggression on other nations, and allow perfect freedom of departure to those who are dissatisfied with their ways." Mill concludes, "I am not aware that any community has a right to force another to be civilized."[70]

However, that "remote corner of the earth" to which Mormons moved was the United States Territory of Utah, governed by Federal law, which made polygamy illegal in 1862. Accordingly, George Reynolds was prosecuted for polygamy after he married a second time knowing that his first wife was living. Mr. Reynolds believed that he was protected from conviction by the First Amendment to the Constitution, which begins: "Congress shall make no law respecting an establishment of religion, or prohibiting the free exercise thereof. . . ." Reynolds claimed that the free exercise of his religion required polygamy, because his Mormon religion prescribed polygamous marriage "when circumstances would admit" and that failure "would be punished, and that the penalty for such failure and refusal would be damnation in the life to come."[71]

The Supreme Court of the United States rejected Reynolds's claim to free exercise of religion when it involves actions that legislatures consider socially harmful. Chief Justice Waite wrote: "Marriage . . . is . . . a civil contract, and usually regulated by law. Upon it society may be said to be built, and out of its fruits spring social relations and social obligations and

---

69. Mill, p. 82.
70. Mill, p. 83.
71. *Reynolds v. United States* [Sup. Ct., Oct. 1878], 145, at 161.

duties, with which government is necessarily required to deal." The court accepted the opinion of a Professor Lieber that <u>polygamy leads to patriarchy</u>, which "fetter the people in stationary despotism," whereas monogamy promotes freedom and progress. So "it is within the power of every civil government to determine whether polygamy or monogamy shall be the law of social life under its dominion."[72]

The trial judge in *Reynolds* instructed the jury before it deliberated to "consider what are to be the consequences to the innocent victims of this delusion," i.e., polygamy.

> As this contest goes on, they multiply, and there are pure-minded women and there are innocent children. . . . These are to be the sufferers; and as jurors fail to do their duty, and as these cases come up in the Territory of Utah, just so do these victims multiply and spread themselves over the land.[73]

The Supreme Court record does not specify the type of suffering these adult women and their children endure, or cite evidence that suffering actually occurs.

In view of the legislature's legitimate aims to protect innocent people from suffering and maintain social institutions that promote freedom and progress, the court found the ban on polygamy to be lawful, regardless of religious objections. The law cannot make exception for all manner of religious practice. The court asks rhetorically, suppose "a wife religiously believed it was her duty to burn herself upon the funeral pile of her dead husband, would it be beyond the power of the civil government to prevent her carrying her belief into practice?"[74] The court assumes this practice should be illegal.

Now consider the issue from Mill's perspective. The suffering of adult women is irrelevant if their plural marriage is voluntary. Many people suffer in monogamous marriage because they choose inappropriate spouses. Surely, it cannot be the law's business to protect adults from marriage mistakes.

As to the children born to polygamous parents, there is no evidence of suffering. But suppose there were. Would the Harm Principle allow states to prohibit polygamy? Not necessarily. It may be that children born to interracial couples suffer compared to other children because society retains some prejudice against their parents' interracial marriage and mixed-race

---

72. *Reynolds,* p. 166.
73. *Reynolds,* pp. 167–68.
74. *Reynolds,* p. 166.

children risk rejection by people of both races. If we think individual freedom is important enough to require states to respect interracial marriage regardless of possible suffering among innocent children, consistency requires similar respect for polygamous marriage even if innocent children suffer, unless the suffering is much greater in one case than another. But if there is a difference in suffering, it may be the interracial child who suffers more. Interracial marriage predominates in few communities, so mixed-race children are almost always a minority among their peers, whereas in a religious community practicing polygamy, children are likely to have peers who also come from polygamous marriages. In such communities many of a child's friends may be siblings.

The court accepts Professor Lieber's opinion that "polygamy leads to the patriarchal principle . . . which, when applied to large communities, fetters the people in stationary despotism, while that principle cannot long exist in connection with monogamy." This is pure speculation. If such speculation were enough to override individual freedom under the Harm Principle, that principle would imply little freedom, because opponents of freedom can always imagine baleful consequences.

Finally, the court rejects polygamy because accepting this religious practice would imply accepting the religious practice of women voluntarily burning to death on the funeral pyre of their dead husbands. But Mill's Harm Principle suggests that adults be allowed to kill themselves with fire no less than with drugs. What good is body self-ownership if you cannot kill yourself on a bonfire? So Mill would not be disturbed that accepting polygamy implies accepting self-immolation, so long as others are not directly harmed. Keep the sparks off the rug.

Freedom of Association

Mill's "freedom to unite, for any purpose not involving harm to others . . ."[75] implies the right to exclude unwanted partners. In American law, competent adults can discriminate and exclude people on any basis when choosing partners for what courts call **intimate association.** This discrimination includes freedom in the choice of whom to invite for dinner and with whom to share a house or a vacation. Justice William Brennan writes:

> The court has concluded that choices to enter into and maintain certain intimate human relationships must be secured against undue intrusion by the State because of the role of such relationships

---

75. Mill, p. 11.

in safeguarding the individual freedom that is central to our constitutional scheme. In this respect, freedom of association receives protection as a fundamental element of personal liberty.[76]

In addition, when people unite to promote an idea, policy, or religion, they can exclude those who disagree with that idea, oppose the policy, or follow a different religion. For example, opponents of abortion rights may exclude abortion rights advocates from their group. This **freedom of expressive association** is needed to allow people to organize for a cause without others subverting their efforts by joining the organization and voting to alter the agenda. Justice Sandra Day O'Connor put the point this way: "Protection of the association's right to define its membership derives from the recognition that the formation of an expressive association is the creation of a voice, and the selection of members is the definition of that voice."[77] If enough proponents of abortion rights were to join a prolife lobbying group, they could change the group's position from prolife to prochoice, effectively denying prolifers an organizational voice in public debate.

These are easy cases. It is harder to know if Mill's Harm Principle and its related freedom of association should allow the Boy Scouts of America to exclude homosexuals. James Dale sought reinstatement after the Scouts expelled him for being homosexual. Dale entered Scouting in 1978 as a Cub Scout and became a Boy Scout in 1981 and an Eagle Scout in 1988. In 1989, at age 18, he became an adult scout and assistant scoutmaster. Supreme Court Chief Justice William Rehnquist tells the rest of the story:

> Dale left home to attend Rutgers University. After arriving at Rutgers, Dale first acknowledged to himself and others that he is gay. He quickly became involved with, and eventually became the copresident of, the Rutgers University Lesbian/Gay Alliance. In 1990, Dale attended a seminar addressing the psychological and health needs of lesbian and gay teenagers. A newspaper covering the event interviewed Dale [and] . . . published the interview and Dale's photograph. . . . Dale received a letter . . . revoking his adult membership. . . . The Boy Scouts "specifically forbids membership to homosexuals."[78]

Did the Boy Scouts violate the Harm Principle? Did they violate the law? Legally, because the Boy Scouts is too large to be an intimate association,

---

76. *Roberts v. United States Jaycees*, 468 U.S. 609, at 617–18 (1984).
77. *Roberts*, p. 633.
78. *Boy Scouts of America v. Dale*, 530 U.S. 640, at 644–45 (2000).

the issue turns on whether they are an expressive association with an anti-homosexual message or a **public accommodation,** which is not allowed to discriminate.

Public accommodations include businesses and clubs that offer goods or services to the public, usually for a fee. *If providers of public accommodations could discriminate at will, racists could exclude blacks from restaurants and buses, returning society to the days when Jim Crow racial exclusions bedeviled the lives of blacks.* Such discrimination is now illegal. New Jersey, for example, where James Dale lived, forbids those who provide public accommodations from discriminating on the basis of "race, creed, color, national origin, ancestry, age, marital status, affectional or sexual orientation, familial status, or sex, subject only to conditions and limitations applicable alike to all persons."[79]

The state outlaws such discrimination to protect individual rights. It believes that discrimination on the basis of color, sex, or sexual orientation, for example, is unjust. Discrimination harms excluded people by impairing their ability to develop their talents and be rewarded for enriching society with their accomplishments. Because it harms individuals, laws against discrimination do not violate the Harm Principle.

Applying antidiscrimination laws can be difficult, however. One problem concerns uncertainty about what counts as a public accommodation rather than a private club. During the Jim Crow era, for example, blacks were excluded from membership and voting in the Jaybird Democratic Association, a supposedly private group of Democrats in Texas. The Jaybirds held a primary for countywide offices in May, before the official Democratic Party primary in July or August. Their stated purpose was to exclude blacks from effective participation in the electoral process. Blacks could vote in the official Democratic Party primary because the Fifteenth Amendment to the Constitution requires that all citizens be granted the right to vote regardless of race or color. But the Jaybirds argued that this applied only to the official vote of the Democratic Party, not to votes taken within a private organization.

However, this supposedly private organization with no official status actually controlled the Democratic Party nominating process in the county. Winners in the Jaybird primaries almost always entered and won the later Democratic Party primary and the general election. The Supreme Court decided in 1953 that even though the Jaybirds were a private association, their goal and function was to choose Democratic Party

---

79. N.J. Stat. Ann. 10:5-5 (West Supp. 2000), in *Boy Scouts of America v. Dale*, p. 662.

candidates through a primary process that excluded blacks, and this violated the Fifteenth Amendment.[80] In sum, *the Supreme Court does not always accept a group's claim that it is not a public accommodation.*

A similar issue arose regarding the United States Jaycees, also known as the Junior Chamber of Commerce, which denied membership to women. Minnesota law disallowed discrimination on the basis of sex. Two possible justifications for excluding women were allowed by law. If the Jaycees were an intimate association, such as a family or a small club held together by mutual acquaintance, it could discriminate at will, just as we can discriminate at will when deciding whom to invite for dinner. However, the Jaycees had about 295,000 members in 7,400 local chapters. It was certainly not exempt from antidiscrimination law by being an intimate association.[81]

The other possibility was that the Jaycees were an expressive association with a message inconsistent with female membership. This is what they claimed. Its bylaws specify that its goal is to "foster . . . in the individual membership . . . a spirit of genuine Americanism and civic interest, and . . . to provide them with opportunity for personal development and achievement and an avenue for intelligent participation by young men in the affairs of their community and nation. . . ."[82] But Justice Brennan found that admitting women to full voting membership "requires no change in the Jaycees' creed of promoting the interests of young men, and it imposes no restriction on the organization's ability to exclude individuals with ideologies or philosophies different from those of its existing members."[83] Justice O'Connor added that much of the Jaycees activity is commercial, even if nonprofit, and the state has good reason to require that predominantly commercial enterprises avoid discrimination based on sex.[84]

The court reached a different conclusion about the decision of the South Boston Allied War Veterans Council to exclude the Irish-American Gay, Lesbian, and Bisexual Group of Boston (GLIB) from its St. Patrick's Day–Evacuation Day Parade. The parade is too large to be an intimate association, so the matter turned on whether it was an essentially expressive activity or a public accommodation. GLIB claimed that the parade was a public accommodation that should be required, as are commercial

---

80. *Terry v. Adams,* 345 U.S. 461 (1953).
81. *Roberts,* p. 613.
82. *Roberts,* pp. 612–13.
83. *Roberts,* p. 627.
84. *Roberts,* pp. 634–40.

establishments, to avoid discrimination on the basis of sexual orientation. The Veterans Council claimed, to the contrary, that parades are essentially expressive and that they had the right to exclude messages that conflicted with their overall viewpoint. Although they seldom rejected applications for this reason, they had rejected the applications of the Ku Klux Klan and of ROAR, a group opposed to bussing children to achieve racial integration. The court agreed with the Veterans.[85] GLIB was not allowed to march.

Given this background, should the Boy Scouts of America (BSA) be able to exclude James Dale and other gays from membership? It is not an intimate association, so either it is an expressive association that can exclude gays because gay membership conflicts with its message, or it is a public accommodation that cannot discriminate against gays. The BSA claimed that in 1978 it adopted the official position that homosexuals cannot occupy leadership positions, including the position of assistant scoutmaster from which Dale was removed. In 1991, after Dale began his lawsuit, the BSA issued a position statement claiming that it promotes the values of being "morally straight" and "clean" and that homosexual conduct conflicts with these values. In 1993 the Scouts' position statement included this:

> The Boy Scouts of America has always reflected the expectations that Scouting families have had for the organization. We do not believe that homosexuals provide a role model consistent with these expectations. Accordingly, we do not allow for the registration of avowed homosexuals as members or as leaders of the BSA.[86]

Chief Justice Rehnquist wrote for the court's majority, "We cannot doubt that the Boy Scouts sincerely holds this view."[87] "A state requirement that the Boy Scouts retain Dale as an assistant scoutmaster would significantly burden the organization's right to oppose or disfavor homosexual conduct."[88] So the BSA is an expressive association that can exclude gays because gay membership conflicts with its message.

Writing in dissent, Justice John Paul Stevens notes several flaws in this reasoning. First, the 1978 official policy banning homosexuals was never published to the general membership, so it could not have been part of the Scouts' basic message.[89] James Dale was unaware of such a policy, and he grew up in scouting.

---

85. *Hurley v. Irish-American Gay, Lesbian, and Bisexual Group of Boston, Inc.,* 515 U.S. 557 (1995).
86. *Boy Scouts of America,* p. 652.
87. *Boy Scouts of America,* p. 653.
88. *Boy Scouts of America,* p. 659.
89. *Boy Scouts of America,* p. 684.

The Scouts' federal charter does not suggest the need to exclude homosexuals. According to the charter, the purpose of the Scouts is "to promote . . . the ability of boys to do things for themselves and others, to train them in scoutcraft, and to teach them patriotism, courage, self-reliance, and kindred values. . . ."[90]

The Scout Oath requires that scouts be "morally straight":

> To be a person of strong character, guide your life with honesty, purity, and justice. Respect and defend the rights of all people. Your relationships with others should be honest and open. Be clean in your speech and actions, and faithful in your religious beliefs. The values you follow as a Scout will help you become virtuous and self-reliant.[91]

There is, again, no obvious conflict between these ideals and homosexuality. The Boy Scout idea of being "clean" is similarly devoid of antigay implications.

Two additional facts explain why we should expect the BSA message to be neutral on the issue of homosexuality. First, it is BSA policy that leaders try to avoid discussing issues of sex and family life.[92] So the BSA purposely avoids a whole group of issues that includes homosexuality. Second, although the Boy Scouts endorses religion, it is completely ecumenical, welcoming boys from religious groups opposed to homosexuality as well as boys from religious groups that oppose discrimination against homosexuals. BSA advises members to consult their respective religious groups about matters of sexuality, undercutting the claim that the BSA's basic message implies opposition to homosexuality.[93] It looks like the Supreme Court majority erred.

In any event, the Boy Scout case illustrates the difficulty of interpreting the Harm Principle's "freedom to unite." Other individuals may be harmed by exclusion.

CONCLUSION

American law seems consistent with the Harm Principle in many areas. It requires informed consent to medical procedures, guarantees the freedoms of speech and association, allows interracial marriage, and generally protects people from discrimination based on race, ethnicity, national

---

90. *Boy Scouts of America*, p. 666.
91. Quoted by Stevens in *Boy Scouts of America*, p. 667.
92. *Boy Scouts of America*, p. 669.
93. *Boy Scouts of America*, p. 670.

origin, and sex. However, it departs from the Harm Principle regarding some matters, for example, the rights to polygamous marriage and to all manner of drugs. Many people side with American law over the Harm Principle on some of these matters, opposing, for example, polygamous marriage and the legal availability of drugs for suicide.

Another problem for the Harm Principle is its presupposition that human activities can be divided between those that directly affect others, which the state can regulate, and those that do not, which the state should not regulate. Some people argue against this distinction, claiming that everything we do and suffer affects others significantly. John Donne gave poetic expression to this view in 1624:

> No man is an Island, entire of it self; every man is a piece of the Continent, a part of the main; if a clod be washed away by the sea, Europe is the less, as well as if a promontory were, as well as if a manor of thy friends or of thine own were; any man's death diminishes me, because I am involved in Mankind; And therefore never send to know for whom the bell tolls; it tolls for thee.[94]

If the fate of others affects everyone so much, state intervention may be more justified than libertarians believe.

JUDGMENT CALLS

1. Imagine that a racist lives across the street from a black family that has just integrated the neighborhood. Instead of burning a cross on the black family's lawn, he burns it on his own and then rings the black family's doorbell so they will be sure to see the burning cross. What reasons are there to consider this protected speech? What reasons are there to consider this an illegal threat?

2. Suppose instead of burning a cross, the neighbor placed a Confederate flag on the black family's lawn? Is this protected speech or a threat? If the answer depends on the symbolic meaning of the Confederate flag, how do we determine what that meaning is? Can the meaning change over time? If so, can the meaning of a burning cross also change?

---

94. John Donne, "Meditation XVII," *Devotions upon Emergent Occasions* (1624), in *The Oxford Dictionary of Quotations*, 5th ed., Elizabeth Knowles, Ed. (New York: Oxford University Press, 1999), p. 275.

3. Many people would object to young adults being able easily and painlessly to kill themselves with drugs that libertarians believe should be made legally available to all adults. Relate this to the ability of young adults to volunteer for dangerous military duty, even "suicide missions," during wartime.

4. Currently, many sports organizations want to diminish the use of performance-enhancing drugs by athletes in international competition. What should the libertarian position be on this issue?

5. Current drug-licensing laws require that medicines be proven safe and effective before they are marketed. Why is proof of effectiveness required for medicines but not for vitamin supplements and weight-loss products? (Burn fat while you sleep!) If there is no significant difference, should proof of effectiveness be required for all these products or not required for any, including medicines?

4 Libertarianism and Property Rights

Libertarians claim that private property rights are indispensable to individual liberty. The sad history of dispossession during the Highland clearances in Scotland illustrates their view. For many generations, Scottish farmers lived in communities growing food, feed, and livestock. "The township held a portion of the glen and a tract of mountain pasture for 30 or 40 black cattle, a small herd of thin and fleshless sheep. The best of the arable land was farmed in . . . strips for which the subtenants periodically drew lots."[1] The farmers, tenants, and subtenants did not own the land they worked but rented it according to custom from the laird. Life was poor and hard, but people were attached to the land. Then they were evicted.

In 1792 a new type of sheep, the Cheviot, was brought to the Highlands by "Sir John Sinclair of Ulbster, a ruddy-faced, hawk-nosed highland gentleman," who noted that the value of wool from the Highlands could be tripled by replacing the current breed of sheep with the new breed.[2] By 1810 plans were underway to clear the majority of Highland Scots from their ancestral homes and glens to make way for a more remunerative mammal. Patrick Sellar, who helped to clear Sutherland, argued

> that the people should be employed in securing the natural riches of the sea-coast, that the mildew of the interior should be allowed to fall upon grass and not upon corn, and that the several hundred miles of alpine plants flourishing in these districts in curious succession at all seasons, should be converted into wool and mutton for English manufacture.[3]

Because the people did not own the land they depended on for subsistence, they were subject to legal eviction, which was announced to the people of Strathnaver in January 1814. "Confused, uneasy, and stubbornly

---

1. John Prebble, *The Highland Clearances* (London: Penguin Books, 1963, 1969), p. 14.
2. Prebble, pp. 26–28.
3. Prebble, p. 63.

reluctant to leave the known for the unknown, the people remained where they were." Forced removals began in June "when most of the Strathnaver men were away in the hills looking for cattle that had strayed. . . ." The people lost their houses and the house-timbers needed to build new ones. "The moss-fir was . . . to be burned when it was torn from the cottages. . . . The burning of the house-timbers began as soon as a cottage was emptied, and even before if the occupants were laggardly. The smoke rolled oily and thick in the moist air." An observer, Angus Mackay, said "he would be a very cruel man who did not mourn for the people. You would have pitied them. . . . Any soft-minded person would have pitied them."[4]

Historian John Prebble tells the story of "Grace Macdonald, a girl of 19 living" in the area. She

> took up shelter up the brae with her family when the township was burnt, and waited there a day and a night, watching Sellar's men sporting about the flames. When a terrified cat sprang from a burning house it was seized and thrown back, and thrown back again until it died there. "There was no mercy or pity shown to young or old," said Grace Macdonald; "all had to clear away, and those who could not get their effects removed in time to a safe distance had it burnt before their eyes. They were happy in Strathnaver, with plenty to take and give, but all are very poor now.[5]

George Macdonald (not related to Grace) recalled that the people

> suffered very much from the want of houses. . . . No compensation was given for the houses burnt, neither any help to build new ones. . . . Some people were removed three or four times, always forced farther down until at last the sea-shore prevented them from being sent any farther unless they took ship for the Colonies, which may of them did."[6]

People bereft of their own property are subject to the will of others. They lack liberty, the freedom to chart their own course in life. Libertarians, who value individual freedom, believe that property rights are essential to liberty.

Libertarian philosopher John Hospers claims that the right to own property is second in importance only to the right to life, and is needed to secure continued life:

> Depriving people of property is *depriving them of the means by which they live*—the freedom of the individual citizen to do what he

---

4. Prebble, pp. 77–78.

5. Prebble, p. 82.

6. Prebble, p. 84.

wishes with his own life and to plan for the future. Indeed, only if property rights are respected is there any point to planning for the future and working to achieve one's goals. *Property rights are what makes* [sic] *long-range planning possible.* . . . Without the right to property, the right to life itself amounts to little: how can you sustain your life if you cannot plan ahead? And how can you plan ahead if the fruits of your labor can at any moment be confiscated. . . .[7]

Other rights also depend on the right to property.

Even the freedom of speech is limited by considerations of property. If a person visiting in your home behaves in a way undesired by you, you have every right to evict him; he can scream or agitate elsewhere if he wishes, but not in your home without your consent. . . . Again, some people seem to assume that the right to free speech (including written speech) means that they can go to a newspaper publisher and demand that he print in his newspaper some propaganda or policy statement for their political party. . . . But of course they have no right to the use of his newspaper. Ownership of the newspaper is the product of his labor, and he has a right to put into his newspaper whatever he wants, for whatever reason.[8]

Libertarian philosopher Jan Narveson makes the more sweeping suggestion that "Liberty is Property." According to Narveson, "the libertarian thesis is really . . . that *a right to our persons as property is the sole fundamental right there is.*"[9] This is the right to body self-ownership discussed in the last chapter. Without the right of body self-ownership we would have no right to do anything, because every action is really an interaction between our bodies and the material world. If we had no right of ownership to control and direct our own bodily movements, all liberty would be lost. Slavery is wrong, according to libertarianism, for precisely this reason. "People, any and all of them, are the fundamental owners of their *own* bodies, and of no one else's."[10]

This chapter explores some reasons to recognize, but also to limit, property rights. *Individual property rights are essential for liberty. However, property rights in the modern world are not natural rights and must be limited. Unlimited property rights can interfere with individual liberty*

---

7. John Hospers, *Libertarianism: A Political Philosophy for Tomorrow* (Los Angeles: Nash Publishing, 1971), p. 62. Emphasis in original.

8. Hospers, pp. 62–63.

9. Jan Narveson, *The Libertarian Idea* (Philadelphia: Temple University Press, 1988), p. 66. Emphasis in original.

10. Narveson, p. 68. Emphasis in original.

and conflict with other important values, including equal opportunity
and material rewards for effort and productivity.

Material Property

Libertarians typically follow John Locke's view that we have **natural
rights** not only to our own bodies but to material goods produced through
the use of our bodies:

> Though the earth and all inferior creature be common to all men, yet
> every man has a property in his own person; this nobody has any
> right to but himself. The labor of his body and the work of his hands,
> we may say, are properly his. Whatsoever then he removes out of the
> state that nature has provided and left it in, he has mixed his labor
> with, and joined to it something that is his own, and thereby makes
> it his property.[11]

One reason that people own the products of their labor is that almost
the entire value of the product results from this labor. In Locke's view,
uncultivated land produces little of what people want and need. Locke
wrote in 1690, "I ask whether in the wild woods and uncultivated waste of
America, left to nature, without any improvement, tillage, or husbandry,
a thousand acres yield the needy and wretched inhabitants as many
conveniences of life as 10 acres of equally fertile land do in Devonshire
[England], where they are well cultivated."[12] Locke thought that human
labor made all the difference, multiplying the value of natural resources
10 or even 100 times. "Whatever bread is more worth than acorns, wine
than water, and cloth or silk than leaves, skins, or moss, that is wholly
owing to labor and industry. . . ."[13]

Locke was sensitive to considerations of equal opportunity, so he
included a proviso that limits claims to ownership. **Locke's proviso** is that
ownership accrues from labor on unowned resources only "where there is
enough and as good left in common for others."[14] This was no longer possible in England, but, he thought, in the wilderness of 17th-century North
America one person's appropriation left equal opportunities for others to

---

11. John Locke, *The Second Treatise of Government* (New York: Bobbs-Merrill, 1952),
     p. 17 (sec. 27).
12. Locke, p. 23 (sec. 37).
13. Locke, p. 25 (sec. 42).
14. Locke, p. 17 (sec. 27).

do the same. In fact, he thought that appropriation improved nature and increased opportunities for others.

> He who appropriates land to himself by his labor does not lessen but increase the common stock of mankind; for the provisions serving to the support of human life produced by one acre of enclosed and cultivated land are . . . 10 times more than those which are yielded by an acre of land of an equal richness lying waste in common. And therefore he that encloses land, and has a greater plenty of the conveniences of life from 10 acres than he could have from 100 left to nature, may truly be said to give 90 acres to mankind.[15]

Someone supplied well by 10 acres instead of 100 can leave the other 90 acres to others, who are thus enriched, not impoverished, by his appropriation of land through his labor.

Some accounts of the Plymouth colony in Massachusetts seem like applications of Locke's views about property. In 1620, Pilgrims crossed the Atlantic on the Mayflower and established a colony at Plymouth. As luck would have it, sickness had killed off almost all the native population in the area, so the Pilgrims came upon truly uninhabited land. At first the colonists started building a common house, but soon "agreed that every man should build his own house, thinking that by that course men would make more haste. . . ."[16] Winter was approaching fast.

This story illustrates Locke's views about acquiring natural property rights. Take something that is not owned or occupied, such as the land and forests around Plymouth, work on the land and forest material to create something of value, such as a house, and one has a natural property right to that house. This property right is natural because it does not depend on any state, law, or government decision. It is just obvious to common sense that the house you build under these conditions is your own. Because this claim to a natural property right depends on common sense, it does not rest on religious beliefs as do the claims about natural law discussed in Chapter 1.

The Pilgrims showed respect for the natural property rights of Indians as well. Robert Cushman, who helped the Pilgrims emigrate, served as their agent in England, and visited the Plymouth colony in 1621, recalls, "We found, traveling abroad, some eight bushels of corn hid up in a cave, and knew no owners of it, yet afterwards hearing of the owners of it, we

---

15. Locke, pp. 22–23 (sec. 37).
16. James Thruslow Adams, *The Founding of New England* (Boston: The Atlantic Monthly Press, 1921), p. 99.

gave them (in their estimation) double the value of it."[17] The bushels of corn were clearly the product of someone's labor, so the Puritans assumed that it had owners, even though there was no law or state to declare or enforce rights of ownership. Again, common sense attributes ownership to those whose labor produces something of value from unowned resources. This is a natural right.

The Entitlement Theory

Libertarian philosopher Robert Nozick incorporates Locke's ideas in his **Entitlement Theory.** According to Nozick, "The subject of justice in holdings consists of three major topics. The first is the *original acquisition of holdings,* the appropriation of unheld things."[18] Nozick raises questions about, but does not offer an alternative to, Locke's ideas about acquisition. The second topic concerns the transfer of holdings from one person to another. The final topic concerns rectification for past injustice when the proper rules for the acquisition or transfer of holdings were violated. Victims of injustice require restitution or compensation.

Nozick offers the following principles of justice:

1. A person who acquires a holding in accordance with the principles of justice in acquisition is entitled to that holding.

2. A person who acquires a holding in accordance with the principles of justice in transfer, from someone else entitled to the holding, is entitled to the holding.

3. No one is entitled to a holding except by (repeated) applications of 1 and 2.[19]

For example, a person who grows apples on his own land is entitled to them. If he sells a bushel to a willing buyer for $10, he gains legitimate claim to the $10 and the buyer to the bushel of apples. If the owner of apples voluntarily gives them away, recipients of this gift also gain legitimate title to some apples.

Like other libertarians, Nozick takes the common sense position that *theft is an unjust method of transferring holdings.* Libertarians stress the value of liberty, which is doing what we want. When people steal property,

---

17. In *Puritans, Indians, and Manifest Destiny,* Charles M. Segal and David C. Stineback, Eds. (New York: G. P. Putnam's Sons, 1977), p. 55.

18. Robert Nozick, *Anarchy, State, and Utopia* (New York: Basic Books, 1974), p. 150. Emphasis in original.

19. Nozick, p. 151.

they take away the liberty of owners to do what they want with their property. *Force and coercion (the threat of force) are also illegitimate bases for property transfer* because they, too, limit property owners' exercise of liberty. People forced by gangsters to sell their house or business, for example, are not doing what they want when making the sale. Finally, *fraud is not a legitimate basis for property transfer* owing to interference with people doing what they want. If I want to buy vitamin C and someone sells me pills that he claims are vitamin C but that are really just sugar pills, I have been denied the liberty of doing what I want with my money.

Note that legitimate transfer of property need not involve the state, laws, or government. *Libertarian ideas about property rights stem from commonsense notions of justice. Locke calls the rights involved "natural" because they exist even when there are no governing institutions,* as cases of ownership in the Plymouth colony illustrate. The state is needed for reasons noted in the Introduction—to protect people's lives, liberty, and property. *According to most libertarians, our rights to life, liberty, and property do not depend on a grant from the state because these are natural rights that preexist any state. The state's foundation and function is the protection of these preexisting rights.*

These preexisting rights do not, however, include **positive rights,** *rights to receive what one needs, from others if necessary, to meet at least minimal levels of some basic human needs, such as food, shelter, clothing, health care, and education.* Libertarians typically deny that people have any positive rights because when the poor are granted (positive) rights to necessities, the government usually meets their needs by raising taxes on financially successful people. Such taxes constitute forced transfers of wealth from the rich to the poor, which libertarians consider little or no better than theft. Libertarians do not object to rich people helping the poor voluntarily, but they believe that all such transfers should be voluntary gifts, not forced taxation.

Many libertarians equate forced taxation with forced labor, such as slavery. According to a 2001 press release from Americans for Tax Reform, "the average American citizen is forced to work 187 uncompensated days a year to pay for government."[20] Nozick says the same. "Taxation of earnings from labor is on a par with forced labor" because "taking the earnings of n hours of labor is like taking n hours from the person; it is like forcing the person to work n hours for another's purpose."[21]

---

20. David Horowitz, *Uncivil Wars: The Controversy over Reparations for Slavery* (San Francisco: Encounter Books, 2002), p. 129, footnote 262.

21. Nozick, p. 169.

> If people force you to do certain work, or unrewarded work, for a cer-
> tain period of time, they decide what you are to do and what pur-
> poses your work is to serve apart from your decisions. This process
> whereby they take this decision from you makes them a *part-owner*
> of you; it gives them a property right in you.[22]

Taxation, in short, violates the principle of body self-ownership. Recognizing positive rights requires raising taxes on some people to pay for the
needs of others, so libertarians reject positive rights in order to protect
everyone from theft and slavery.

Still, few libertarians reject taxes completely because few advocate
anarchism, life without any state at all. Libertarians believe that people
have natural rights that preexist the state, but they usually want a state to
protect those rights. So libertarians advocate a minimal state, one that
protects people's natural rights but does absolutely nothing more. Because
it does no more than protect such rights, its expenses, and therefore the
taxes it must collect to defray expenses, are minimal.

The natural rights that libertarians want the state to protect are called
negative rights. These are *the rights to be left alone to interact with others
on strictly voluntary bases.* These include, for example, rights to the freedoms of speech, press, assembly and association, the right freely to practice the religion of one's choice, the right freely to engage in voluntary
market exchanges of goods and services, and the right to give or lend one's
property to whomever one pleases. The only limit on exercising such negative rights is respect for the equal right of others to exercise these rights.
For example, I cannot practice a religion that requires killing or enslaving
people of a different religion. The word "negative" in the term "negative
rights" refers to the negation of interference with other people's exercise of
freedom. So long as no one interferes with anyone else's rights, including
rights to property, people are free to do as they please. Libertarians champion liberty.

Libertarianism and the Free Market

Because people should be free to do as they wish with their labor and their
property, so long as they leave others equally free by refraining from force
and fraud, libertarians favor a free market. A **free market** exists, according to libertarians, when people are able freely to exchange goods and services with one another without government interference or restriction.

---

22. Nozick, p. 172. Emphasis in original.

So long as force and fraud are excluded, free-market interactions generate wealth and express people's liberty.

A minimal state supports the free market by providing legal protections for people and their market activities. It must have laws that protect property, including laws that specify proper ways of documenting contractual obligations to give contracts legal effect. The state must also have police to protect people's life, liberty, and property against aggression, coercion, theft, and fraud. It must have judges and courts to adjudicate commercial disputes and deal with those accused of crime. It must have prisons to incarcerate criminals and a military to protect people against foreign aggression. By protecting people and free-market activities in these ways, the state does no more than secure the rights to life, liberty, and property that people have by nature.

This libertarian view goes beyond Mill's Harm Principle. Mill wrote: "To individuality should belong the part of life in which it is chiefly the individual that is interested; to society the part which chiefly interests society."[23] Mill believed that "trading is a social act"[24] that is subject to regulation because it "chiefly interests society." More recent libertarians, however, claim that voluntary trading should also be free of government regulation so long as people use their own property, including their own bodies for labor, in voluntary exchanges free of force and fraud.

About 100 years ago the Supreme Court of the United States came close to endorsing this libertarian view. The State of New York had passed a law limiting the working hours of bakers to 60 hours per week and an average of 10 hours per day. Mr. Lochner owned a bakery in New York State that contracted longer hours of work for its bakers. He was convicted of a misdemeanor for this offense and assessed a fine. He appealed his conviction on the ground that the state had no right to interfere with his conduct of business. He and his employees should be free to make and keep any contract they wish, his lawyers argued, so long as no one else is harmed, and neither Lochner nor his employees had harmed anyone.

The U.S. Supreme Court agreed. Mr. Justice Peckham wrote for the majority:

> The statute necessarily interferes with the right of contract between the employer and employees, concerning the number of hours in which the latter may labor in the bakery of the employer. The general right to make a contract in relation to his business is part of the

---

23. John Stuart Mill, *On Liberty*, in *On Liberty and Considerations on Representative Government*, R. B. McCallum, Ed. (Oxford: Basil Blackwell, 1946), p. 66.

24. Mill, p. 80.

liberty of the individual protected by the Fourteenth Amendment of the Federal constitution. . . . Under that provision no State can deprive any person of life, liberty or property without due process of law. The right to purchase or to sell labor is part of the liberty protected by this amendment, unless there are circumstances which exclude the right.[25]

The court went on to point out that the contract in question did not harm the public. "Clean and wholesome bread does not depend upon whether the baker works but 10 hours per day or only 60 hours a week. The limitation of the hours of labor does not come within the police power on that ground."[26] The court considered statutes "limiting the hours in which grown and intelligent men may labor to earn their living . . . mere meddlesome interferences with the rights of the individual. . . ."[27]

Four justices dissented from the majority view. Mr. Justice Harlan, writing for himself and two others, claimed, "It is plain that this statute was enacted in order to protect the physical well-being of those who work in bakery and confectionery establishments."[28] He cited an expert in public health who wrote:

> The constant inhaling of flour dust causes inflammation of the lungs and of the bronchial tubes. The eyes also suffer through this dust, which is responsible for the many cases of running eyes among the bakers. The long hours of toil to which all bakers are subjected produce rheumatism, cramps and swollen legs. . . . [Bakers] seldom live over their 50th year, most of them dying between the ages of 40 and 50. During periods of epidemic diseases the bakers are generally the first to succumb to the disease. . . .[29]

The dissent justifies the statute as a means of protecting bakers from ill health caused by long working hours. But why should the state interfere with the bakers' and their employers' liberty of contract? Why not adopt the **laissez-faire** approach to economics, which *supports free-market transaction unencumbered by government regulations?* Workers should be able to protect their own health in employment contracts.

The legislature may have thought that bakers contract for work in excess of 60 hours per week because they otherwise face unemployment. In a laissez-faire economy where the government protects rights to life,

---

25. *Lochner v. New York,* 198 U.S. 45 (1905), p. 53.
26. *Lochner,* p. 57.
27. *Lochner,* p. 61.
28. *Lochner,* p. 69.
29. *Lochner,* pp. 70–71.

liberty, and property but does not otherwise interfere in the free market there are no positive rights to receive government assistance in case of unemployment. Workers who want to avoid the choice between starvation and uncertain private charity must do whatever it takes to remain employed. Employers know this, so they can drive a hard bargain whenever there is an oversupply of workers; if some workers refuse to work more than 60 hours per week, others will take their place. Workers may thus agree to conditions of employment that jeopardize their health, and New York's statute was designed to protect them.

But is this a proper government activity? Not according to libertarians. They point out that in a free market suppliers compete for customers on the basis of quality, price, and whatever other factors interest customers. Makers of shoes, cars, and beds compete this way, resulting in the production of cheaper and better products. The same situation is true of services. Barbers, carpenters, and gardeners compete for business primarily on the basis of quality, price, and whatever else customers value. The same conditions should prevail, libertarians claim, in the market for labor. The customer is the employer, and potential laborers should compete for jobs on the basis of quality, price, and whatever else employers value. If employers of bakers want bakers to work more than 60 hour per week, then bakers can take bakery jobs under these conditions, move to where bakery employers require fewer hours of work per week, or change their line of work to one with more agreeable conditions of employment. The important point for libertarians is that under these rules everyone has complete liberty to do whatever she wants with her property, whether employer or worker.

Workers may try banding together in a union to get higher pay or better working conditions from employers. This is fine, according to libertarian laissez-faire beliefs, so long as the association is voluntary and uses neither force nor fraud. However, because employers should remain free to hire and fire whomever they please, they can usually fire union organizers and hire only nonunion labor. Under these conditions, unionization is unlikely to improve pay and working conditions when there is an oversupply of workers.

Free-Market Immorality

If people own their bodies and are free to use them to make money in any way not involving force or fraud, prostitution should be legal, libertarians reason. People can rent the houses they own, so why not the bodies they own as well?

Many thinkers, however, object to free-market transactions involving immoral behavior. In its *Lochner* decision, for example, the Supreme Court ruled, "a contract to let one's property for immoral purposes . . . could obtain no protection from the Federal Constitution, as coming under the liberty of person or of free contract."[30] States are permitted to consider prostitution immoral, so renting out your body for sex can be prohibited by law, as is common in America, without any objection from the Supreme Court. Philosopher Jacques Thiroux gives these arguments against legalizing prostitution:

> Prostitution fosters a lack of respect for the prostitute (usually a woman) and for human sexual activity itself, which is supposed to enhance the intimacy of a relationship between partners. . . . Prostitution instead lowers human sexuality to an animalistic act of lust. . . . Prostitution is a big business and is usually managed and run by the criminal element in the United States. Prostitutes are often treated like animals by their pimps and customers; many are beaten, and some are . . . killed. In addition, many prostitutes have been addicted to drugs by their pimps to keep them dependent. . . . There is no faster or more certain way of transmitting social diseases and AIDS than prostitution, for in addition to [AIDS] being transmitted sexually, prostitutes may also become infected by needles as drug abusers. . . .[31]

Libertarians reject these arguments against prostitution's legalization. First, the government should not decide that "human sexual activity . . . is supposed to enhance the intimacy of a relationship between partners. . . ." People should be free to decide for themselves what is important in sexual activity. For some people intimacy may be paramount, but this should not be forced on everyone. If it were, one-night stands would also be illegal. Libertarians are protecting your right to party.

Prostitution can spread diseases, including AIDS, but any adult hiring a prostitute should know that protection is required to avert that danger. Of course, if the prostitute lies about her medical condition, the customer who gets a disease should be able to sue for damages. The libertarian's minimal state has laws that allow people to sue to recover damages that result from fraud. The minimal state would not, however, meddle in the transaction by requiring prostitutes to have regular medical checkups and be licensed. People can protect themselves.

---

30. *Lochner*, pp. 53–54.
31. Jacques Thiroux, *Ethics: Theory and Practice*, 5th ed. (Englewood Cliffs, NJ: Prentice Hall, 1995), p. 359.

Prostitution is, as Thiroux points out, "usually managed and run by the criminal element in the United States." Also, "prostitutes are often treated like animals by their pimps and customers; many are beaten. . . ." But this, the libertarian points out, is all due to the government's meddling in the free market. If prostitution were legal and the government protected everyone against force and fraud, "the criminal element" would not control prostitution any more than they control other legal businesses, such as car rentals. Abuse of prostitutes would no longer be common because prostitutes would enjoy the same kind of police protection against assault as everyone else.

Some people reject libertarianism because it opposes outlawing activities on moral grounds. *Immorality among consenting adults who refrain from force and fraud is not the government's business, according to libertarians. The government's only job is protecting life, liberty, and property, which it does best when it supports free enterprise.*

Equal Opportunity

Some free-market enthusiasts believe that racism naturally disappears in a free market, so there is no need for laws against employment discrimination. Employers who discriminate against blacks, for example, are choosing from a smaller supply of workers than those who do not discriminate. As the supply of an important ingredient decreases, its price increases. So the racist employer who chooses only among white applicants will have to pay higher wages than competitors who offer employment regardless of race. Because he is paying more for labor, the racist employer must either accept lower profits or charge higher prices for his products. If he accepts lower profits, investors will shy away, and he will lack the capital needed to improve products and stay competitive. If he raises prices, he will lose customers to competitors. Thus, the free market eliminates racist employment practices without any government intervention.[32]

Similar considerations eliminate racial discrimination in sales and service. A restaurant, for example, that refuses to serve black customers loses potential profits, which discourages investors and impairs the restaurant's ability to remodel or otherwise remain competitive. Many libertarians conclude that laws against racial or other forms of discrimination constitute unnecessary government meddling in free enterprise.

---

32. See, for example, Mark Michael Lewis, "The Incompatibility of Racism and the Free-Market," at www.choseyourlife.com/ml/docs/ForceRacism.htm. Accessed May 23, 2003.

Experience suggests, however, that racism, sexism, and other forms of discrimination tend to persist in a free market where prejudice is culturally entrenched. In such contexts, people choose goods and services not just on quality, price, convenience, and so forth but also on group association. Consider a restaurant, for example, in the South of the United States during the Jim Crow era. Even if it were entirely legal for the restaurant to serve blacks, free-market considerations would discourage the practice. Due largely to the history of slavery, poor educational opportunities, and persistent racial discrimination, blacks were much poorer than whites. If most whites were so racist that they would boycott a restaurant that served blacks, any restaurant that served blacks would be confining itself to a customer base with relatively little money to spend, which would reduce profits and discourage investors.

The same is true of employment opportunities. If customers were so racist that they would boycott a restaurant with black waiters, but would not mind blacks washing dishes in the back, then restaurant employment opportunities for blacks in that community would be restricted to washing dishes. Such racially based market considerations tend to perpetuate racial stereotypes and keep black income low.

The error of believing that the free market naturally eliminates racism rests on the false assumption that racist customers would choose products and services without regard to race. During the Jim Crow era, however, much segregation rested on custom, not law. Equal employment opportunity in such a racist society requires government intervention to force people to ignore their prejudices or face state-imposed penalties. This role for government goes beyond anything that libertarians would allow.

Whatever applies to race in a racist society applies to gender in a sexist society. If people are so sexist that they will not visit a female physician, medical schools will not waste their time training women to be doctors. If passengers on commercial airlines favor female flight attendants but male pilots, there will be opportunities for women only as flight attendants and never as pilots.

Such stereotypes can be altered. When customers see workers in nontraditional roles, many alter their stereotypes and willingly patronize businesses where blacks are waiters instead of dishwashers and women are pilots instead of flight attendants. But the free market alone will seldom if ever get this process started. Laws mandating equal employment opportunity are required. *Libertarianism will not move a racist or sexist society toward equal opportunity in employment.*

Libertarianism fails also to support equal opportunity in education. A minimal state protects negative rights. Taxes impair the negative right to do with our property and money as we wish, so they should be kept to a minimum. Public education is a tax-supported government program without much justification in a minimal state. People have no positive rights, including a right to education or to equal educational opportunity, according to libertarianism. People should be free to buy whatever educational services they can afford for themselves and their children, but they should not be allowed to force anyone else to contribute money to this effort.

Because some people are much wealthier than others, the result of eliminating public education would be much greater inequality of educational opportunity than at present, and the current situation is far from ideal. In fact, many poor families would not be able to afford to send their children to school at all. Such children may remain completely illiterate. This will impair drastically their ability to compete for good positions in the free-enterprise system.

Equal educational opportunity existed without tax support in the Plymouth Colony because children learned from parents and helpful Indians all the skills they needed for success in colonial life. Matters are different in a complex industrial society. Success requires literacy and formal education. People concerned about equal-employment opportunity, such as those wanting to restrict immoral commercial activities, will reject libertarianism's laissez-faire approach to the economy.

Liberty, Inequality, and Property

Opponents of libertarianism point out that if liberty is the ability to do as one wants, eliminating public education impairs liberty along with equal opportunity. Children of poor, uneducated parents lack the liberty of children from affluent or educated families to develop their talents, should they want to do so. They did nothing wrong to deserve this disadvantage. As most children point out to their parents, usually between the ages of 8 and 12, they did not ask to be born.

Libertarians respond by distinguishing between formal and material liberty. People have **formal liberty** *to do whatever laws and other social rules allow.* If these laws and social rules apply equally to everyone in society, as libertarians generally think they should, then everyone has equal (formal) liberty, regardless of whether or not taxes are levied to support public education.

Opponents of libertarianism object, however, to exclusive attention to formal liberty. Libertarian views are supposed to rest on common sense, and formal liberty is not what common sense finds most important in many situations. A person starving for lack of food and money, for example, has the same formal liberty to eat as a well-fed rich person does, because no law or rule forbids his eating any food available to him. But such formal liberty will not save his life. He needs food. He needs **material liberty,** *the ability actually to do as he likes,* which in this case is to eat, and eating requires that he be provided with some food. Common sense suggests that in situations such as this material liberty is more important than formal liberty.

Regarding education, all people in a libertarian society have the same formal liberty to develop their talents; there is no law or rule against anyone receiving an education. However, in such a society only wealthy people have the material liberty to be educated because they are the only ones with the money to afford it. The material liberty of poor people to be educated requires raising taxes among richer people to pay for high-quality public education available to everyone free of charge. Such taxation reduces the formal and material liberty of richer people to do with their property (their money) as they wish. Insofar as libertarians are committed to promoting liberty, they can achieve reflective equilibrium either by sacrificing the material liberty of the poor (to get an education) or the formal and material liberty of the rich (to do with their money as they wish). *By ignoring material liberty and concentrating exclusively on formal liberty, libertarians rule out state-supported public education funded by forced taxation and sacrifice the material liberty of the poor for the formal and material liberty of the rich.*

People who think that common sense favors attention to material liberty in education may consider the libertarian's opposition to public education an unjustified preference for the (material) liberty of the rich over that of the poor.

The same considerations apply to a variety of positive rights that libertarians reject, such as the right to health care. Wealthy people can purchase health-care services in the marketplace, whereas poor people often cannot. Owing to lack of health care, many poor people suffer disabilities that diminish their material liberty. Libertarians interested in liberty could reach reflective equilibrium by raising taxes to pay for health care for the poor, which reduces the formal and material liberty of rich people, or by sacrificing the material liberty of poor people to be free of treatable diseases and disabilities. *Libertarians who reject positive rights and ignore considerations of material liberty side with the rich against the poor even though liberty could be advanced either way.*

The libertarian position on inheritance also favors the rich over the poor. As we have seen, libertarians typically appeal to people's body

138 Chapter 4: Libertarianism and Property Rights

self-ownership to justify property ownership in material goods. Because you own your body, you naturally own the products of your labor, which you can then use, rent, sell, or give away. Labor is the original justification for property ownership, as it was in the Plymouth colony.

However, when people give their property away, as they do inevitably upon death (you can't take it with you), recipients gain wealth that does not result from their labor. Permitting inheritance undermines the libertarian justification for private property, the connection between property and labor. Disallowing inheritance, however, impairs a key libertarian value, the liberty of owners to do with their property as they desire, which often is to bequeath it to surviving family members. Here is another tension within libertarian thought. Libertarians can achieve reflective equilibrium either by dropping the connection between property and labor, or by disallowing inheritance of unearned wealth.

John Hosper's response to this problem is typical of libertarians:

> What about property which you do not work to earn, but which you *inherit* from someone else? Do you have a right to that . . .? Consider the man who willed it to you: it was his, he had the right to use and dispose of it as *he* saw fit; and if he decided to give it to you, this is a windfall for you, but it was only the exercise of *his* right. Had the property been seized by the government at the man's death . . . , it *would* have been a violation of his rights: for he, who worked to earn and sustain it, would not have been able to dispose of it according to his own judgment. If he doesn't have the right to determine who shall have it, who does?[33]

Hospers chooses to sever the connection between ownership and work by supporting the right of donors to dispose of their property as they see fit. Yet he bows to the connection between ownership and work by supposing that the rich person making the bequest "worked to earn and sustain" the property in question. Of course, after generations of bequests there is no guarantee that the recently deceased did a lick of work to earn the property he is leaving to others.

The choice to favor the right of bequest over the connection of property with labor favors the rich over the poor because it means that the poor must work to earn their living (the minimal state provides no welfare benefits), whereas the rich may not.

Favoring the right of bequest also supports the accumulation of wealth. People who inherit wealth start their role in free-market competition with

---

33. Hospers, p. 71. Emphasis in original.

an advantage over others in addition to advantages derived from better education and health care. It is therefore no surprise that enterprising rich people tend to succeed, often increasing the wealth they inherited and passing even greater wealth to their progeny.

Such concentrations of wealth limit the liberty of others because private property, by its nature, gives owners liberties that others lack. Owners can do as they like with their property. They can decide how their property is used and who may use it. Poor people have the same formal liberty to do as they like with whatever they own, but they often do not own enough for this liberty to be useful. For example, when jobs are in short supply, the material liberty of poor people is at the mercy of rich people who own factories, land, and other capital needed for productive employment. Employers can drive a hard bargain, pay low wages, and fire whomever they want for any reason. This was the situation, described earlier, when Highland Scots were evicted from land they and their forebears had worked for generations. Land was in short supply in Scotland. Inheritance gave this land to a small group of owners who used the formal and material liberty entailed by property rights to evict tenants to increase profits. Tenants were denied the formal and material liberty to continue living on that land.

By favoring the right to bequeath wealth, libertarians side with the (formal and material) liberty of the rich against that of the poor. Again, the value of individual liberty, which is the pole star of libertarianism, does not dictate this choice.

Historical Justifications and Reparations for Slavery

The classic libertarian justification for preferring the liberty of the rich rests on claims about natural property rights and historical continuity. According to most libertarians, people who have money now are entitled to it because they earned or inherited it from people who were entitled to it. In Robert Nozick's words, "a distribution [of property] is just if it arises from another just distribution by legitimate means."[34] So long as currently rich people did not steal or otherwise violate the rules for the transfer of property, they are entitled to all that they possess, assuming that those from whom they gained their property were equally entitled to it. *Historical justifications of concentrated wealth require a history of proper acquisitions and transfers of wealth. Assuming such a history, libertarians could be considered biased not against the poor but for natural rights to property.*

---

34. Nozick, p. 151.

140 Chapter 4: Libertarianism and Property Rights

Unfortunately, history disappoints libertarians. It is filled with invasions, genocide, theft, slavery, and other forms of unjust acquisitions and transfers of wealth. Consider the history of slavery in the United States. Attorney and black activist Randall Robinson advocates reparations to black Americans for slavery and its aftermath. He sees failure of self-confidence to be the primary problem for African Americans today. "The biggest part of our problem is inside us: in how we have come to see ourselves, in our damaged capacity to validate a course for ourselves without outside approval."[35] This failure of self-confidence stems, Robinson claims, ultimately and originally from slavery times when

> with the complicity of the United States government, . . . millions of black people endured unimaginable cruelties—kidnapping, sale as livestock, deaths in the millions during terror-filled sea voyages, backbreaking toil, beatings, rapes, castrations, maimings, murders. . . . Whole peoples lost religions, languages, customs, histories, cultures, children, mothers, fathers. It would make us more forgiving of ourselves, more self-approving, more self-understanding to see, *really see,* that . . . survivors had little choice but to piece together whole new cultures from the rubble shards of what theirs had once been. And they were never made whole. And never compensated. Not one red cent.[36]

Much of the beautiful public architecture of Washington, D.C. was built with slave labor, Robinson claims.[37]

> Black people worked long, hard, killing days, years, centuries—and they were never *paid.* The value of their labor went into others' pockets—plantation owners, northern entrepreneurs, state treasuries, the United States Government.
>
> Where was the money?
>
> Where *is* the money?
>
> There is a debt here.[38]

Robinson thinks we should expect the continuing effects of slavery to be poor self-confidence, lower expectations, and substandard educational achievement.

---

35. Randall Robinson, *The Debt: What America Owes to Blacks* (New York: Plume, 2001), pp. 205–06.
36. Robinson, p. 208. Emphasis in original.
37. Robinson, p. 3.
38. Robinson, p. 207. Emphasis in original.

No nation can enslave a race of people for hundreds of years, set them free bedraggled and penniless, pit them without assistance in a hostile environment, against privileged victimizers, and then reasonably expect the gap between the heirs of the two groups to narrow. Lines, begun parallel and left alone, can never touch.[39]

What is worse, degradation did not end with slavery. Shortly after the Civil War Black Codes were passed in former slave-holding states. These instituted peonage, a form of labor contract for blacks little better than slavery. Destitute former slaves had little choice but to work under these conditions. Historian John Hope Franklin writes:

> Blacks who quit their job could be arrested and imprisoned for breach of contract. They were not allowed to testify in court except in cases involving members of their own race. Numerous fines were imposed for seditious speeches, insulting gestures or acts, absence from work, violating curfew, and the possession of firearms.[40]

Then came the Jim Crow era described in Chapter 1. Legal scholar Boris Bittker writes in *The Case for Black Reparations:*

> Full citizenship was in effect denied by the discriminatory enforcement of state laws governing the right to vote, to serve on juries, and to run for public office. . . . These forms of official discrimination were common in the North as well as the South; the Negro's "place" could be defined by unequal enforcement of the law, even in the absence of a formal system of legal segregation. . . . As late as the eve of World War II, there were segregated lunchrooms and other facilities in many federal buildings, and segregation in the armed forces, with minor exceptions, was the order of the day until well after the war.[41]

Robinson points to the Jim Crow era, too, as promoting feelings of inferiority and low expectations at the root of the present, unenviable state of black America.

Government prejudice also has tangible and quantifiable aspects. Robinson claims, "in the courts of 10 states and the District of Columbia, [a black man] is 10 times more likely to be imprisoned than [is] his white male counterpart for the same offense. . . . While black males constitute

---

39. Robinson, p. 74.
40. John Hope Franklin, *From Slavery to Freedom* (New York: Knopf, 1947), in Robinson, p. 211, without page reference.
41. Boris I. Bittker, *The Case for Black Reparations* (Boston: Beacon Press, 1973, 2003), pp. 15–16.

15% of the nation's drug users, they make up 33% of those arrested for drug use and 57% of those convicted."[42]

Blacks lost money as well as freedom, Bittker notes, owing to the "discriminatory policies of federal agencies administering residential and business loans and guarantees, public housing projects, agricultural extension services, farm-price supports, and other economic and social programs."[43] Robinson quotes a law review article by Robert Westley, "Many Billions Gone:"

> Based on discrimination in home mortgage approval rates, the projected number of credit-worthy home buyers and the median white housing appreciation rate, it is estimated that the current generation of blacks will lose about $82 billion in equity due to institutional discrimination. All things being equal, the next generation of black home owners will lose $93 billion.
>
> As the cardinal means of middle-class wealth accumulation, this missed opportunity for home equity due to private and governmental racial discrimination is devastating to the black community.[44]

Robinson adds:

> Until 1950 the Federal Housing Authority provided subsidies to white mortgage holders who were bound by restrictive covenants to exclude blacks from any future ownership of their real property. This device alone caused blacks to miss out on billions, in home equity wealth accumulation. Since 1950, American residential apartheid and middle-class wealth-building discrimination have been maintained through, among other means, the practice of redlining.[45]

Redlining is the now-illegal banking practice, which may nevertheless persist, of banks refusing to write home mortgage loans for blacks outside certain parts of town where black residents are concentrated.

According to Robinson, this continuing story of discrimination accounts for the fact that "college-educated whites [in 2000] enjoy an average annual income of $38,700, a net worth of $74,922, and net financial assets of $19,823. College-educated blacks, however, earn only $29,440 annually with a net worth of $17,437 and $175 in net financial assets."[46] Robinson concludes, "the racial economic gaps in this country have been locked open

---

42. Robinson, p. 214.

43. Bittker, p. 17.

44. Robert Westley, "Many Billions Gone," *Boston College Law Review* (June 1999), in Robinson, p. 227, without page reference.

45. Robinson, p. 227.

46. Robinson, p. 228.

at constant intervals since the days of slavery. The gaps will not close themselves. To close them will require . . . a [strong] counterforce . . . " that, Robinson believes, must include reparations to black Americans. [47]

Rectification of Injustice

Robert Nozick recognizes that past injustice undermines the validity of current claims to property. There is no natural right to stolen property. He asks:

> What obligations do the performers of injustice have toward those whose position is worse than it would have been had the injustice not been done? Or, than it would have been had compensation been paid promptly? How, if at all, do things change if the beneficiaries and those made worse off are not the direct parties in the act of injustice, but, for example, their descendants? How far back must one go in wiping clean the historical slate of injustices?

Nozick confesses, "I do not know of a thorough or theoretically sophisticated treatment of such issues." He fails to acknowledge that *given serious past injustices in property acquisition and transfer, we cannot claim that anyone has a natural right to the property he owns unless and until we formulate and apply a justifiable theory of rectification.*

Consider my possessions, for example. The house my wife and I own is on land formerly in the domain of Native Americans. Payments on the house depend largely on my hard work as a philosophy professor. (It's tougher than it looks.) But would I have been accepted to graduate school to begin this life if my competition had included as many black people as would have applied and been qualified in the absence of a history of injustice that disadvantaged blacks? We can never know. Would I have outperformed all the women who could have been qualified if they had not been discriminated against in the ways discussed in Chapter 2? Again, we can never know. This is typical. *Almost nothing that anyone owns today meets the libertarian standard of justice in acquisition and transfer.* Under these conditions, Nozick seems committed to acknowledging that we lack natural rights to our property until past injustices have been rectified.

But there are no realistic prospects for rectifying past injustices. Regarding slavery alone, it is impossible to determine the size of the debt, who should pay this debt, in what form it should be paid, and who should

---

47. Robinson, p. 229.

be the beneficiaries. In *The Case against Black Reparation*, Bible Teacher William Banks asks such questions as these about who should pay reparation for slavery: Do current descendants of Africans who sold people into slavery owe part of this reparation? Do current descendants of European traders who profited from the slave trade owe part of it? Do descendants of poor whites who owned no slaves owe anything? What about descendants of Union army soldiers who helped to free the slaves, even if this was not their top priority at the time? What about descendants of white abolitionists who spent years fighting slavery? Do they have any debt? If not, how can we devise a payment plan that excludes them?

Questions also arise about who should receive payment. Should well-off blacks—people such as Bill Cosby, Oprah Winfrey, Michael Jordan, Kobe Bryant and Tiger Woods—receive anything? Should poor African Americans receive payment if their ancestors came to the United States as free immigrants after 1865? Do current black Americans know how many ancestors they may have in this category? Probably not.[48]

What form should the payment be in? Should all beneficiaries receive a lump sum cash payment? Should the payment be the same for everyone? If the worst current effect of slavery is lack of self-confidence among blacks, will a single cash payout help? Perhaps the payment should be in the form of special programs of education and training for black Americans. In that case, however, the message may be conveyed to whites and blacks alike that blacks currently need more help to succeed than do other Americans. This may erode the self-confidence of blacks. Reparation may do more harm than good.

There is no doubt that injustices were done to blacks, American Indians, Asian Americans, and women, to name but a few groups. Debts are certainly owed, but they cannot be measured or assessed. *Libertarians must assume proper original acquisition followed by a chain down to the present of properly based transfers of wealth and restitution where these conditions do not prevail. This is entirely unrealistic, not only in the United States but around the world.* The Duke of Sutherland who asserted property rights and evicted Highland Scots from their farms and homes had ancestors who acquired those rights through force and fraud.[49] History happens. It has been one darn thing after another. We can say of the history

---

48. William L. Banks, *The Case against Black Reparation* (Haverford, PA: Infinity Publishing, 2001), pp. 43-47.

49. See Rosalind Mitchison, *A History of Scotland* (London: Methuen, 1970), especially Chapters 2–4 and R. L. Mackie, *A Short History of Scotland*, Gordon Donaldson, Ed. (New York: Praeger, 1963), especially pp. 73–82 for the background of war and invasions that established property ownership.

of most current wealth what Mae West said in a movie when someone admiring her ring exclaimed, "Goodness, what an enormous diamond you have!" West replied, "Goodness had nothing to do with it."

Property Rights Today

I legitimately own a house, a car, and many other things. I cannot claim a natural right to ownership because I cannot trace my ownership back to anyone's work on unowned resources that conveyed natural rights to property that were transferred without force or fraud down to the present. No one's property rights can be justified in this way. So what do I mean when I say that I legitimately own a car, for example? I mean what common sense tells us. I own it because I paid the previous owner, Saturn of Springfield, the price they asked. I had legitimate title to the money I used to pay for the car because it was drawn from savings on my paycheck from the State of Illinois. Those paychecks were legitimately mine because I have a contract with the University of Illinois at Springfield to do certain kinds of work, and I do that work. I could go on, but you get the point. There is no mystery here. Legitimate property rights stem from work, contracts, gifts, and other sources of income and possession within a system of rules and laws.

We can probably agree with libertarians that because hard work should be rewarded, someone owns what she produces by herself from unowned resources. However, this has little application in modern society. We make few things by ourselves or from unowned resources. No individual made my Saturn, or computer, or desk, or chair, or the books I read, or almost anything else that I use. Almost all products we own and use result from collaborative efforts of many people doing specialized tasks. What is more, the material they used was owned before they worked on it. Someone owned mineral rights that allowed the mining of iron ore that was transformed into the steel that Saturn, Incorporated bought to make the chassis of my car. Thus, the libertarian principle of natural property rights does not apply.

Libertarian defenses of natural property rights fail to accommodate the legal, financial, and commercial complexities of modern industrial life. Our productivity and rewards for that productivity are embedded in a web of commercial relationships defined by contracts and constrained by law. Our legitimate rewards are usually determined by contracts and customers. Contracts sometimes offer rewards for higher quality output but almost never reward people just for hard work. Someone who can write a book more easily than I am writing this one will deserve more income than I will receive if her book sells better and if her contract pays her according to sales. I may have worked harder, but I cannot thereby legitimately claim more income.

People who work in organizations might not receive pay that reflects their productivity, either. If top management at an automobile company misjudges the market and makes small cars when consumers want large ones, assembly line workers may lose their jobs regardless of their productivity. This result is not welcome, but it is legitimate. Companies are usually entitled to fire productive people to downsize when sales decline.

This is all part of the free market, which is central to property ownership in modern industrial societies. But the free market is not, as libertarians claim, the voluntary exchange of goods and services that people own by natural right, because, as we have seen, we cannot claim to own anything by natural right. Instead, *the free market in the modern world is a rule-governed system of production and exchange in which consumer demand is the principal factor determining the nature, quantity, and price of what is produced, as well as the price and conditions of labor involved in production.* The rules come from laws and from contracts and other agreements that conform to law. There can no more be a free market without laws in an industrial society than there can be games without rules. Rules define the nature of the game as laws define the nature of a free market.

Government rules defining who can own property and what counts as property are therefore at the root of all claims to property rights. In 18ᵗʰ-century English law, for example, married women had few rights of property ownership.[50] Today, not only women but corporations can own property. Corporations are legally created "persons." Car companies, movie studios, oil companies, and almost all other large businesses are incorporated, enabling them to outlive all current owners and workers. Ford Motor Company turned 100 in 2003. Incorporation also limits the liability of owners to the amount they invested in the company. But there is nothing natural about corporations or their limited liability. They and their property rights are created entirely by law.

Intellectual property rights, such as J. K. Rowling's property rights in the Harry Potter books, also illustrate that property rights depend on laws. What Rowling owns are strings of words, not the books in which they appear. She owns something literally intangible. Such ownership exists

---

50. Katharine T. Bartlett and Rosanne Kennedy, Eds., *Feminist Legal Theory: Readings in Law and Gender* (Boulder, CO: Westview, 1991), p. 16.

only by law. No one imagines, for example, that Matthew, Mark, Luke, and John owned their accounts of the life of Jesus as Rowling owns Harry Potter. They did not receive or waive royalties on the Gospels, because there were no copyright laws back then and without such laws the Gospels could not be private property. In modern free-market economies, property rights depend on laws. Without property laws there are no property rights.

A major function of government, then, is not just to protect property and property rights but to determine who shall be eligible to own "things" and what kinds of "things" can legally be owned. Political philosophies include justifications for people's views on these matters. For example, the law in the United States generally disallows people owning marijuana. Libertarians argue against this restriction, whereas other political philosophies discussed in later chapters support the current ban on counting marijuana as property. During slavery times, people counted as property. All political philosophies discussed in this book consider slavery immoral and support its current ban.

The rules underlying a free market can change, within limits, while the market remains free, just as the rules of a democracy can change while the government remains democratic. A democracy must, for example, specify a minimum voting age. It used to be 21 in the United States, but now it is 18. It could be 15 or 30. A lower age gives more political power to young people, whereas a higher age has the opposite effect, so the change is significant and could alter who wins an election. But as long as most of the population is allowed to vote, it is still a democracy.

Similarly, the rules of the free market can change and the market can remain free. Copyright protection could last for 17, 57, or 100 years. Longer copyrights improve the chances for authors to earn money from their work, and shorter copyrights improve the public's chances for inexpensive access. There may be good reasons for longer or shorter copyrights, but *the basic system remains a free market in any case so long as consumer demand is the principal factor determining what is produced and how it is produced.*

This fact does not mean that consumer demand is the only factor, however. We do not, for example, allow consumer demand to determine completely the conditions of employment. We have labor laws that generally disallow 8-year-olds working 40 hours per week for a living (unless they are really cute and Disney makes the movie), but the system remains a free market. So long as consumer demand is the main factor affecting production, there is great latitude in the rules that define a given free market.

In addition, a free-market system can survive the exclusion of certain items. We have a free-market system in which possession and sale by private individuals of material to make nuclear weapons is illegal even though there may be significant demand. Maintaining rules designed to thwart meeting this demand does not transform our free market into something else. Nuclear materials are simply outside the free market.

Illegal "markets" in nuclear materials involve possession, not ownership. Possessors cannot summon the police if they lose possession to someone else; they cannot get judges to interpret contracts or sheriffs to enforce judicial decrees. "Markets" with no legal backing are clearly unsuited to current large-scale commercial activity. We need police to protect our legal possessions, judges to decide matters in dispute, and sheriffs to enforce judicial orders. The free market as we know it could not function without such government services. The alternative, anarchism, would be as chaotic and unproductive as the 1992 riot in Los Angeles.

Legitimate Taxation

Taxes are among the rules of the free-market system that define who legitimately owns what property. If we had natural rights to property, as the pilgrims perhaps did to the houses they built alone in the uninhabited wilderness, a property tax would seem like some kind of theft or slavery, as libertarians often claim. However, no one today has a natural right to a house, because no one can trace ownership and the means to purchase ownership back to morally appropriate original acquisitions and proper transfers from then until now. Instead, we trace our ownership to a house to a title gained within a financial system in which the property's origins in the deep past are generally irrelevant. If that financial system is defined and upheld by government rules that attach certain taxes to ownership of the house, taxes are simply part of the deal because they are part of the system without which all such deals are impossible.

In addition, the market value of the house depends on government projects and services that taxes support. Tax money is used, for example, to build roads. A suburban house would lose most of its value quickly if there were no roads to reach it. A more isolated country house would lose even more value. Tax money is used additionally to support military efforts that guarantee not just defense against foreign aggression but also the safe importation of petroleum from overseas. Suburban and country houses would lose market value if an oil shortage made automobile use very expensive. The value of the house on the free market presupposes also such government services as police protection, proper sewerage, adequate public schools, and zoning laws that disallow establishment of a cement factory or a mega-hog farm next door. Taxes are needed to defray the costs of these services. *People cannot legitimately complain that such taxes constitute theft or slavery, taking from them by force what is rightfully theirs, because what is rightfully theirs would not be of much value on the free market without the government services that the taxes make possible.*

Philosophers Liam Murphy and Thomas Nagel put the point this way in *The Myth of Ownership: Taxes and Justice:*

> We are all born into an elaborately structured system governing the acquisition, exchange, and transmission of property rights, and ownership comes to seem the most natural thing in the world. But . . . we cannot start by taking as given . . . what people originally own, what is theirs, prior to government interference. . . . The modern economy in which we earn our salaries, own our homes, bank accounts, retirement savings, and personal possessions, and in which we can use our resources to consume or invest, would be impossible without the framework provided by government supported by taxes.[51]

Government services presupposed by current market values include many that libertarians consider illegitimate. Let us consider just one, state-supported schools. Libertarians advocate eliminating public education in favor of private education because public education is financed by coerced payments, taxes, that require some people to support the education of other people's children. However, eliminating public education threatens to degrade social life and limit economic opportunities for almost everyone. If the state does not provide schools, it cannot require school attendance. But compulsory education is everywhere associated historically with high rates of literacy. *Countries without compulsory education in state-supported schools have high rates of illiteracy.*

Were illiteracy to increase in the United States, many businesses would be hurt. Much of what people do with computers, for example, requires the ability to read and write, so reduced literacy harms computer sales. Also, illiterate people earn little in industrial countries such as the United States. As literacy, income, and purchasing power decline, sales of computers, houses, cars, appliances, clothes, and almost everything else suffer. Increasing illiteracy threatens economic depression.

Of course, in the absence of public education some parents will buy educational services for their children, who will then become literate.

---

51. Liam Murphy and Thomas Nagel, *The Myth of Ownership: Taxes and Justice* (New York: Oxford University Press, 2002), p. 8.

Literate people will be needed in medicine, insurance, engineering, law, science, education, real estate, marketing, accounting, finance, and every other area of commercial life where literacy is essential. These educated people will command high salaries owing to the limited supply of literate people, thus increasing labor costs in all the aforementioned areas. Roads may become more expensive because of increased salaries for road engineers and accountants. Many products will become too expensive for most people to buy, leading to economic depression. American advances in science and technology could decline as the talent pool for scientists diminishes, which could in turn jeopardize American competitiveness in the global market.

Another problem for business concerns social skills among its workers. Much modern work occurs in large organizations where people must be team players. Along with reading, writing, and arithmetic, schools teach children teamwork, fair play, punctuality, patriotism, obedience to authority, and respect for the rights of others. An unschooled labor force may be socially unsuited for work in modern organizations.

Poor people with undeveloped social skills may also be dangerous. It seems that most people who rioted in Los Angeles in 1992 were relatively poor. Imagine that they were also illiterate, so they had no prospects for good jobs, and that they had no formal socialization to be cooperative or patriotic. The challenge for police would be daunting. Yet the talent pool for hiring police officers would be relatively small.

CONCLUSION

Libertarians correctly draw attention to the importance of property rights. Private property is essential to liberty and to the American way of life. Libertarians also remind us of important connections among labor, productivity, and private property. Most Americans consider private property and some accumulation of wealth fitting rewards for hard work and productivity.

Libertarians err, however, when they claim that people in modern industrial societies own property by natural right. This error leads libertarians to subordinate many other moral values, including the value of material liberty, to the importance of property. Private property becomes their primary end or goal, instead of a means for securing liberty.

In addition, many libertarian views seem unrealistic and inapplicable to modern industrial societies. Libertarians would eliminate not only public education but also such government functions as zoning, international trade agreements, safety standards for airlines, food and housing assistance for the poor, and the regulation of banking and financial markets. Like education, however, these government functions are essential to industrial life as we know it. Libertarians perceive correctly that such functions were unnecessary, and therefore taxation to support them would have been illegitimate, in the Plymouth colony and some other rustic societies. But they err when imagining that our society is like them. Political philosophies must be realistic, and libertarian views of property rights unrealistically reject taxes needed to support many government functions.

Nevertheless, several libertarian ideas remain attractive: the self-ownership of one's body; people interacting voluntarily without force or fraud; people reaping material rewards for their hard work and productivity through voluntary free-market exchange; and government being no larger and taxes no higher than necessary. Some of these ideas underlie political philosophies, discussed in Chapters 6 and 7, that justify the foundation of government through a social contract. But before examining those approaches, we first examine a nonlibertarian defense of property rights.

JUDGMENT CALLS

1. Some services currently supported by taxes and performed by the state might be privatized. Private entrepreneurs might build roads that people pay to use, thereby replacing the government's tax-supported roads. People would still have to pay for their use of roads, and property values would still depend on road access, but the government would no longer be involved. The advantage from the libertarian perspective is that all payments for roads would be voluntary rather than coerced. Working out the details would be daunting, however. Road access increases property values of all houses along the road. People who use the road little will pay little for it but still enjoy the full benefits of property value increase. People making greater use of the road will end up supporting a road that enriches neighbors who travel little. How might this be made fair?

2. If you are injured in a libertarian state owing to someone else's negligence, the negligent party can be required to compensate you. What is supposed to happen if the negligent party is poor and will likely never have enough money to pay you? Should the minimal state require that drivers carry liability insurance?

3. Would there be corporations with limited liability in a minimal state? Would it be proper for limits on corporate liability to impair

recovery for damages when the corporation's negligence causes injury or death?

4. What should be done in a minimal state with people who have debilitating drug addictions but who do not commit crimes; they just hang around street corners begging, looking scraggly, and smelling bad?

5. How should the minimal state deal with children who lack food because their parents are hopelessly addicted to drugs?

6. If people lack natural rights to property, how can we account for natural rights to life and liberty?

5   Free-Market Conservatism

property rights = economic prosperity

We saw in the last chapter that property rights today do not rest on people's natural right to benefit from the improvements they make to unowned resources. Yet property rights remain important. This chapter looks at a different basis for property rights: they are needed to generate economic prosperity.

Economic prosperity is widely valued in the United States and elsewhere. People commonly associate their well-being with their "standard of living," usually measured in dollar terms. Those with more money are fortunate because they have a higher standard of living: larger houses, better cars, exotic vacations, designer clothing, and so forth. People generally have more money when they have the high-paying jobs that only a strong and growing economy provides. So, politicians compete with one another in promising, or taking credit for, economic growth. For example, President George W. Bush made economic growth his top priority in his State of the Union Address in 2003.

> Our first goal is clear: we must have an economy that grows fast enough to employ every man and woman who seeks a job. (*Applause.*) After recession, terrorist attacks, corporate scandals, and stock market declines, our economy is recovering—yet it's not growing fast enough, or strongly enough. With unemployment rising, our nation needs more small businesses to open, more companies to invest and expand, more employers to put up the sign that says, "Help Wanted." (*Applause.*)
>
> Jobs are created when the economy grows; the economy grows when Americans have more money to spend and invest; and the best and fairest way to make sure Americans have that money is not to tax it away in the first place. (*Applause.*) Lower taxes and greater investment will help this economy expand. More jobs mean more taxpayers, and higher revenues to our government. . . . A growing economy

and a focus on essential priorities will also be crucial to the future of Social Security. . . .[1]

In short, economic prosperity is essential for the country's well-being. This suggests a justification for property rights different from the libertarian justification. Property rights are needed to promote economic growth and raise people's standard of living. *Property rights provide incentives within a free-market system for people to produce efficiently what human beings need and want and to invent rapidly new technologies that make life longer, healthier, easier, and more interesting.* Free-market conservatism is based on this insight—in addition to supplying security, *a central function of government is to promote prosperity by supporting property rights and the freedom of contract in a free market.* This chapter explores the strengths and limitations of this theory. Major problems concern the theory's concentration on economic growth without sufficient consideration of other values, including justice.

(handwritten margin note: provide incentive for upward mobility)

Property and Prosperity

> "It's like to die," a despairing Xolane Masuko, 18, being deported for the second time in less than a year, said of his homeland. "I don't have money. I don't have food. I don't have everything."
>
> The first time he was deported, Masuko was back inside South Africa within a day, so determined to return that he missed his mother's funeral. This time, he said, he will return, too.[2]

Mr. Masuko was being deported from South Africa to his native land, the neighboring state of Zimbabwe, which has fallen on desperate economic times largely because of the government's failure to respect and protect property rights. Zimbabwe's president, Robert Mugabe, began a campaign in 2000 to reduce white influence in the country by seizing land held by white farmers and giving it to unemployed black, landless peasants. Overriding the property rights of wealthy people to provide food-producing land for the poor may seem good. As self-employed farmers, the poor could grow food for themselves and make money selling additional produce.

---

1. 2003 State of the Union Address, www.whitehouse.gov. *(Please note that the "applause" captions are part of the speech; I did NOT add them.)*
2. Michael Wines, "Zimbabweans on the Night Train to Nowhere," *International Herald Tribune* (September 24, 2003), p.2.

But the fallout has been grievous. By UN estimates, production on large commercial farms is at 10% of its 1990s level, and as many as 900,000 of Zimbabwe's 15 million people have lost their jobs or homes. Unemployment now exceeds 70%.

Production of tobacco, the major cash crop, has collapsed.

Foreign investment has dried up. Shortages of food and outside goods [such as] medicine have fed hyperinflation, now 500% to 700% a year.[3]

These are the conditions that Mr. Masuko and at least 2,500 other Zimbabweans per week try to escape by entering South Africa illegally.

Disrespect for property rights has such dire consequences because *secure property rights under laws that promote free enterprise help to bring prosperity.* Take away those rights, contaminate the law, or interfere with free enterprise, and prosperity declines, claim free-market conservatives.

Llewellyn Rockwell, Jr., president of the Ludwig von Mises Institute, emphasizes the benefits to humanity of free markets and property rights:

> Looking at people's life spans is perhaps the best way to see the hidden history of the rise of economic development. Throughout the first huge period of human history, from the beginning until the birth of our fathers' great-grandfathers, the average lifespan was 20 to 35 years, and a third to half of all children died before reaching the age of 5. . . . As late as the year 1800, the average lifespan was only 40.
>
> But in the last tiny fragment of the history of the world, life spans have more than doubled. . . . By far the largest improvements in these vital statistics have occurred since 1800, at a time when the division of labor expanded dramatically around the world; when property rights were secure; when capital could be accumulated, invested, and a return paid and reinvested; when technological improvements permitted new forms of productivity. What made this possible was the free market.
>
> We take for granted such luxuries as refrigerators, the air conditioner, the internal combustion engine, and electricity, to say nothing of e-mail, the Web, and fiber optics.

These marvels result from understanding "the internal logic of the market economy."[4]

---

3. Michael Wines, "Zimbabweans on the Night Train to Nowhere," *International Herald Tribune* (September 24, 2003), p.2.

4. Llewellyn H. Rockwell, Jr., "The Marvel That Is Capitalism," *The Free Market,* Vol. 20, No. 7 (July 2002), www.mises.org/freemarket, accessed September 24, 2003.

[Margin handwritten note: Free market conservatives → If property rights are unsecure prosperity will decline]

Division of Labor:
Hunters   Shepards

Eighteenth-century Scottish philosopher and economist Adam Smith pioneered this understanding. He advocated the **division of labor** in his masterwork *The Wealth of Nations* (1776). For example:

> In a tribe of hunters or shepherds a particular person makes bows and arrows . . . with more readiness and dexterity than [does] any other. He frequently exchanges them for cattle or for venison with his companions; and he finds at last that he can in this manner get more cattle and venison than if he himself went to the field to catch them. . . . Another excels at making the frames and covers of their little huts. . . . In the same manner a third becomes a smith or a brazier; a fourth, a tanner or dresser of hides or skins, the principal part of [their] clothing. . . . And thus the certainty of being able to exchange . . . the produce of his own labor . . . for . . . the produce of other men's labor . . . encourages every man to apply himself to a particular occupation, and to cultivate and bring to perfection whatever talent or genius he may possess for that particular species of business.[5]

division of labor encourages every man to apply himself to a specialty

When people concentrate on what they do best and trade for everything else they need and want, production is efficient, and society is wealthier than when everyone tries to do everything for themselves after mastering many trades.

What is more, once trading is established, *efficiency and quality improve when suppliers of goods compete with one another for customers.* People who make bows and arrows get everything else they need and want by convincing others to exchange their meat, fish, bread, cloth, and so on for bows and arrows. The better a maker's bows and arrows, the more people will be willing to pay for them and the richer and more comfortable the bow and arrow maker's life. So each maker of bows and arrows has incentive to improve his product. The result is progressive improvement of products available in the market, and the invention of new products that customers are willing to buy. Eventually, for example, people went from hunting with bows and arrows to hunting with rifles.

Methods of production also improve as a result of competition. Makers who discover cheaper, more efficient methods of manufacturing the same product can attract customers and make additional money by selling their products cheaper than the competition can. Early in the 20th century, for example, Henry Ford's Model T made Ford the largest car manufacturer

5. Adam Smith, *The Wealth of Nations*, excerpted in *Property, Profits, and Economic Justice*, Virginia Held, Ed. (Belmont, CA: Wadsworth, 1980), pp. 94–113, at 97.

because efficient production methods made Fords less expensive than other cars of the time. As efficiency improves through competition, society becomes wealthier because its people are producing more and more of what people need and want.

But such economic development and the amazing gains noted by Rockwell depend on establishing and respecting property rights, freedom of contract, and the rule of law. The bow and arrow maker will not concentrate on his craft and trade for everything else if he thinks his equipment, the materials he uses, or his completed products or profits are likely to be stolen. He will not stay in business either if people generally fail to pay as agreed or if, when some people fail to pay, there are no courts and police to help him avoid loss.

"Formal property law enables people to do business with strangers," writes Hernando de Soto in the *Economist*.

> Those who are part of the formal property system have addresses, credit records and identifiable assets. A westerner who does not honour his debts is blacklisted. The bailiffs know where to find him, and what to seize. So he has a powerful incentive to play by the rules.
>
> When you cannot do business with strangers, you have to do everything yourself. This is inefficient. Imagine building your own house. . . . Take Nashon Zimba, a 25-year-old peasant who grows maize, beans and tobacco in . . . [Malawi, Africa]. . . . He digs up mud, shapes it into cuboids, and dries it in the sun to make bricks. He mixes his own cement, also from mud. He cuts branches to make beams, and thatches the roof with sisal or grass. His only industrial input is the metal blade on his axe. . . . Mr. Zimba has erected a house that is dark, cramped, cold in winter, steamy in summer and has running water only when tropical storms come through the roof. An American, by contrast, supported by a network of millions of specialists he has never met, can live in a relative palace without ever needing to learn one end of a hammer from another.[6]

Property rights and free contracts recognized and administered fairly within a free-market system are essential to economic development, technological progress, prosperity, and human flourishing. These are the reasons why a primary function of the state is establishment and maintenance of property rights, freedom of contract, and a free market.

---

6. Hernando de Soto, "Poverty and Property Rights," *The Economist* (March 31, 2001), pp. 21–25, at 22.

158 Chapter 5: Free-Market Conservatism

De Soto explains how failure to establish property rights hampers Third World development. Consider this case:

> Grace and John Tarera slaughter goats for a living . . . in Mtandire, a shanty town near Lilongwe, the capital of Malawi. . . . Demand is brisk: Malawians adore goat stew. The Tareras want to expand their business to meet this demand, but they lack capital. Mrs. Tarera thinks they need about 20,000 kwacha ($250). This may not sound like much, but in Malawi, where the average annual income is only about $200, it can take years to raise such a sum.
>
> But wait: the house where the Tareras live is worth at least 25,000 kwacha. They bought the land five years ago and threw up a brick bungalow, fussily furnished and painted a satisfying shade of light blue. Surely they could borrow using the house as security? No, because they cannot prove they own it.
>
> The Tareras' house, like all the others in Mtadire, is built on "customary" land. That is, the plot's previous owners had no formal title to it. The land was simply part of a field that their family had cultivated for generations. About two-thirds of land in Malawi is owned this way.[7]

Banks will not accept informally owned land and houses as collateral for loans because courts will not recognize such ownership as a genuine property right. From the bank's and court's perspective, the Tareras own no property and therefore have no collateral for a loan. A promising business opportunity and chance for economic development is lost. Again, prosperity requires that states establish, maintain, and enforce property rights.

De Soto notes, "all rich industrialized countries have secure property rights, accessible to more or less all citizens. No poor country has. Better property laws are not the only reason that some countries are richer than others, but they clearly make a difference."[8] A primary function of government, say free-market conservatives, is to establish and maintain secure property rights so people can enjoy prosperity.

Efficiency and Competition: The Microsoft Case

Free-market conservatives agree with libertarians that property rights are very important, but they disagree about the rights' justification and extent. *Libertarians look to the past, tracing property rights to labor that*

[handwritten: Free Market Conservatives + Libertarians agree on importance of property rights → different justification]

---

7. De Soto, p. 21.
8. De Soto, p. 25.

increases the value of unowned resources. Free-market conservatives look to the future, justifying property rights as means to increasing human prosperity and flourishing.

One implication of these different justifications is that free-market conservatives, unlike libertarians, believe that property rights and freedom of contract are not natural and eternal. Instead, governments must alter them to meet the needs of the time. For example, "it is an ancient doctrine," Supreme Court Justice William O. Douglas wrote in 1946, "that at common law ownership of the land extended to the periphery of the universe."[9] Consistent libertarians would consider these rights natural and object to change. But, Justice Douglas claims, such rights are not natural and must now change. He sides with free-market conservatives Milton and Rose Friedman who write: "I own a house. Are you 'trespassing' on my private property if you fly your private airplane 10 feet over my roof? One thousand feet? Thirty thousand feet? There is nothing 'natural' about where my property rights end and yours begin."[10] Similarly, Justice Douglas contends that ownership extending to the periphery of the universe "has no place in the modern world. The air is a public highway, as Congress has declared. Were that not true, every transcontinental flight would subject the operator to countless trespass suits. Common sense revolts at the idea."[11] So do free-market conservatives.

Free-market conservatives also accept restricting property rights and the freedom of contract to prevent monopolies and promote competition. Competition is important for prosperity because when consumers can choose among competing suppliers of goods and services, suppliers must improve their products and methods, finding ever more efficient ways to meet consumers' needs and wants. A monopolist, by contrast, has no incentive to be efficient, to improve products or reduce prices, because consumers are just stuck with whatever she chooses to deliver. Thus, the United States enacted the Sherman Antitrust Act of 1890 making it illegal for any person to "monopolize, or attempt to monopolize, or combine or conspire with any other person or persons, to monopolize any part of the trade or commerce among the several States, or with foreign nations. . . ." Free-market conservative economist Frederick Hayek endorses such laws, writing in the 1940s that the free market needs "a legal system designed both to preserve competition and to make it operate as beneficially as

---

9. *United States v. Causby*, 328 U.S. 256, at 260.
10. Milton and Rose Friedman, *Free to Choose* (New York: Harcourt, Brace, Jovanovich, 1980), p. 30.
11. *Causby*, p. 261.

160 Chapter 5: Free-Market Conservatism

possible. . . . Much depends on the precise definition of the right of property as applied to different things."[12]

Competition-preserving definitions of property rights and freedom of contract can be controversial, however, as the antitrust case against Microsoft Corporation illustrates.[13] By 1998, Microsoft dominated the market in operating systems for personal computers, supplying 97% of systems installed by original equipment manufacturers (OEMs). But, writes former federal judge Robert Bork, "size, even if it confers monopoly power, is not illegal if it is achieved by superior products, service, business acumen, or mere luck."[14] Only anticompetitive behavior, the use of dominant market share to exclude competition, is illegal. Two Microsoft practices that the Justice Department considered anticompetitive were bundling its Internet Explorer (MSIE) with its Windows operating systems and its requiring OEMs to retain a start-up screen that excluded internet rival Netscape.

Consider first the issue of "bundling." In response to the growing importance of the internet to users of its popular Windows operating system, Microsoft added a new browser, Internet Explorer, to Windows at no charge to consumers. Mark Furse writes in *International Review of Law, Computers and Technology:*

> An analogy that has been used by Microsoft staff is to compare the integration of MSIE in the operating system with the integration of a word-check facility in a word processing package: where once a consumer would have been required to buy a stand-alone word-check package they now expect as a matter of course that these are seamlessly integrated with the word processing application."[15]

Receiving free what they want and otherwise would have to buy seems to help consumers. So if "the ultimate purpose of the antitrust laws is to help consumers,"[16] which is the view of Robert Litan, vice president and

[handwritten margin note: size doesn't matter only if the means to get it was not a monopoly]

---

12. Friedrich A. Hayek, *The Road to Serfdom* (Chicago: The University of Chicago Press, 1944), p. 38.
13. I thank my student Michael McDonald for research assistance on this topic.
14. Robert Bork, "White Paper," (July 29, 1998), http://lists.essential.org/1998/am-info/msg03998.html, p. 2 of 15.
15. Mark Furse, "*United States v. Microsoft:* Ill-Considered Antitrust," *International Review of Law, Computers and Technology*, Vol. 12, Issue 1 (March 1998), pp. 99–120, at 109.
16. Thomas Hazlett, Robert Litan, and Edwin Rockefeller, "Legal and Economic Aspects of the Microsoft Case: Antitrust in the Information Age," *Business Economics* (April 2000), pp. 45–53, at 47.

director of Economic Studies at the Brookings Institution, conflict with antitrust law is not obvious.

There is, however, another side to the story. Microsoft faced a major challenge to its dominance in its main business, operating systems. Former judge Bork writes:

> Netscape produced the first browser, the Netscape Navigator, which made searching the internet practicable for the average computer user. Navigator created the possibility of a system that would bypass the Windows operating system. Software applications can be written for the Navigator as they can be for Windows. . . .
>
> A browser with a large number of users can become an alternate platform by, for example, combining with Sun Microsystems' cross-platform programming language, Java, which can run on any operating system. Together, the Navigator and Java could reduce Windows to just one operating system among several as well as provide a route to the internet.[17]

Rather than submit its operating system to such competition, Microsoft used its dominant position in the field to avoid competition, Bork contends. Manufacturers, such as Dell and Gateway, want to include Windows as original equipment on their machines because, given the current dominance of Windows, this is what customers want and expect. When Microsoft bundled its Internet Explorer with its Windows operating system it effectively required that OEMs include Explorer on their machines. Furthermore, it integrated Explorer so completely within Windows that Windows would not operate properly if Explorer were removed. This situation effectively required manufacturers and consumers to keep Explorer on those machines.[18]

Another effect of bundling was to give away free an alternative to what Netscape was selling. Bork writes:

> The number-two man at Microsoft, Steve Ballmer, stated, "we're giving away a pretty good browser as part of the operating system. How long can [Netscape] survive selling it. . . ." The clear intent was not to compete with Netscape on the respective values of the Explorer and the Navigator but to drive Netscape out of the browser market altogether. The effect upon the much smaller Netscape was devastating.[19]
>
> Microsoft's reserves dwarf Netscape's. . . . The market capitalization of Microsoft is approximately $250 billion; that of Netscape is

---

17. Bork, p. 4.
18. Furse, p. 111.
19. Bork, p. 4.

$2.7 billion. . . . The upshot is that Microsoft can easily outlast Netscape in a price war.

Microsoft also makes enormous profits on its monopoly operating system licenses while Netscape has no comparable source of income. As Bill Gates put it, "our business model works even if all Internet software is free. . . . We are still selling operating systems. What does Netscape's business model look like? Not very good."[20]

The antitrust problem is not that Microsoft tried to defeat its competitor, Netscape. In the free market, companies are supposed to try to defeat their rivals. The problem is that Microsoft used its near monopoly to avoid competition with its rival, rather than compete successfully against it. Internal Microsoft memos make this clear. One senior Microsoft official wrote, "it seems clear that it will be very hard to increase browser market share on the merits of IE [Internet Explorer] alone. It will be more important to leverage the OS [operating system] asset to make people use IE instead of Navigator."[21] Bork writes, quoting additional internal Microsoft memos, "Microsoft concluded in late March 1997 that if Windows and the Internet Explorer 'are decoupled, then Navigator has a good chance of winning' and that 'if we take away IE for the OS most nav users will never switch to us.'"[22]

Microsoft also used restrictive licensing agreements with computer manufacturers to avoid competing with Netscape. To put Windows on their machines, OEMs need a license agreement with Microsoft, which holds copyrights on Windows. Microsoft insisted that "licenses for Windows 98 prohibit manufacturers from modifying the screen first seen when users turn on their personal computers," Bork observes.

> This enforced uniformity prevents computer manufacturers from offering customers a choice of first screens. But the restriction also has another anticompetitive result. The Windows first screen is a platform from which software applications, such as word processing programs, are launched. Netscape's Navigator can also serve as such a platform. If consumers prefer the Netscape platform to the Windows platform, computer manufacturers will configure their machines so that the first screen to appear is that generated by Netscape's browser. If a significant number of computers had the Netscape first screen, software developers would write programs for it, and competition would flourish in the operating system market.

---

20. Bork, p. 10.
21. Found in Bork, p. 4.
22. Bork, p. 5.

Microsoft's first-screen restriction squelches that. This effectively blocks Netscape from the most important channel for getting its browser to consumers.[23]

Besides outward actions and internal memos regarding corporate intentions, pricing and profit indicate Microsoft's anticompetitive behavior. Robert Litan notes that federal judge Robert Penfield Jackson, who heard the Microsoft case, focused on an internal Microsoft memo about pricing. The memo

> said that while the company could charge 49 dollars for their operating system and make a decent profit, they might as well go ahead and charge 89 dollars. The judge inferred that there was a 40-dollar overcharge, and that it was a consequence of the activities that Microsoft engaged in—exclusive contracts, threats, and so forth. . . . If it is true, it is evidence of consumer harm.[24]

In addition, former judge Bork observed, Microsoft's "own financial statements show a profit margin of about 47%. Though profit levels are viewed by some as ambiguous indicators of monopoly power, this profit margin is so high that many commentators would think it raises a strong inference of monopolistic pricing."[25] It also suggests consumer harm, because consumers are paying more than they would have to if genuine competition existed.

In the end, Judge Jackson determined that Microsoft had violated the Sherman Antitrust Act. On appeal his remedy of breaking up the corporation was rejected. Microsoft can keep its property, but its freedom of contract is limited by court order. It must now allow manufacturers who install Windows to alter the initial screen so as to promote alternate operating systems; it must enable Internet Explorer to be deleted easily from Windows without harm to the operating system; and it must cease "its efforts to contain and subvert Java technologies from developing as a cross-platform threat to Windows."[26] In short, Microsoft can keep its property but not use it anticompetitively.

This result conforms to free-market conservatism. Competition is essential for improved efficiency, so corporations must be required to compete, even if this means altering their property rights or limiting their

---

23. Bork, p. 6.
24. Hazlett et. al., p. 47.
25. Bork, p. 2.
26. Neal R. Stoll and Shepard Goldfein, "Antitrust Trade and Practice: *Government v. Microsoft*, 1991–2002?" *New York Law Journal*, News, Vol. 228 (December 17, 2002), p. 3, col. 1.

freedom of contract. Libertarians, by contrast, think that if Microsoft did not use force, the threat of force, or fraud to achieve its unusually high profits, it did no wrong. The Sherman Antitrust Act, according to libertarians, unjustly limits property rights and the freedom of contract.

The Tragedy of the Commons

Economist Garrett Hardin maintains that, whatever one's views about competition, private property rights promote efficiency by avoiding what he calls **the tragedy of the commons.** Hardin gives this parable to illustrate the tragedy. Imagine families who make their living raising cattle on a common pasture no one owns.

> The tragedy of the commons develops in this way. . . . It is to be expected that each herdsman will try to keep as many cattle as possible on the commons . . . [because] as a rational being each herdsman seeks to maximize his gain. Explicitly or implicitly, more or less consciously, he asks, "What is the utility *to me* of adding one more animal to my herd?"[27]

Suppose that each herdsman has 10 head of cattle and that 10 herdsmen share the commons. If any one adds an additional two cattle, the total number of cattle grazing on the common pasture will go from 100 to 102. Even if the pasture cannot stay in its best condition when more than 100 head graze on it—each animal suffers a bit because overgrazing reduces available nutrition—the herdsman who adds two extra head will benefit greatly. His income will increase 20%, minus the slight decline in yield per head owing to overgrazing. Hardin continues:

> The rational herdsman concludes that the only sensible course for him to pursue is to add another animal to his herd. And another; and another. . . . But this is the conclusion reached by each and every rational herdsman sharing the commons. Therein is the tragedy. Each man is locked into a system that compels him to increase his herd without limit—in a world that is limited. Ruin is the destination toward which all men rush. . . .[28]

---

27. Garrett Hardin, "The Tragedy of the Commons," *Science*, Vol. 162 (December 1968), pp. 1243–48. It is widely reprinted. The quote here is taken from *Population and Ethics*, Michael D. Bayles, Ed. (Cambridge, MA: Schenkman Publishing, 1976), pp. 3–18, at 7. Emphasis in original.
28. Hardin, pp. 7–8.

The pasture is eventually ruined by overgrazing and can no longer support a dozen, much less the original 100, head of cattle. The herdsmen ruin their own source of income. This is a tragedy because it results inevitably from self-seeking behavior. It is also inefficient.

Economists use the concept of **externality** to explain what happens in these situations. Each herdsman initially benefits from extra cattle much more than he is harmed because he shares the harms equally with nine other herdsmen. Economists say that he has externalized nine-tenths of the harm that his extra cattle do to the commons. Nine-tenths of the harm is external to this herdsman's private economic calculations; it harms others, not him, so he does not take it into economic account. He takes into account only the harm that he has to suffer personally, which is only one-tenth of the total harm. So long as that one-tenth is less than he gains from adding extra cattle, he will continue to add cattle. Others will do the same, and the commons will be ruined.

Avoiding the tragedy requires establishing a system whereby herdsmen automatically take into account the total harm they do; they *internalize* the total cost they create. When they internalize what was previously an externality, they include this harm in their calculations of private advantage and avoid actions that reduce overall productivity.

Privatization often aids the internalization of externalities. If the common pasture were divided into 10 sections, each capable of supporting 10 head of cattle, and each of the 10 herdsmen were given one of these 10 portions as his private property, the tragedy would be averted. *An important aspect of private property is the ability to exclude others.* If each herdsman owns a part of the pasture as private property, he can exclude the cattle of other herders. Those who bring extra cattle onto their parts of the pasture will hurt only themselves. They will not externalize any of the cost of their behavior, so they will not add extra cattle if costs exceed benefits. Self-interest now promotes efficiency. In general, free-market conservatives claim, *the selfish behavior of private property owners operating in a free market tends, as if, to use Adam Smith's phrase, by an "invisible hand," to improve and enrich society in general.*

[Margin note: Selfish behavior benefits private property owners]

The Dilemma of Selfishness

[Margin note: "invisible hand" doesn't always work]

Unfortunately, this principle does not always work. *In some contexts, selfish attempts to maximize individual returns leave everyone worse off than cooperative behavior does. This reality contradicts Adam Smith's theory of the invisible hand.* One story that illustrates the counterproductivity of selfishness concerns prisoners, so the dilemma is often called the **Prisoner's Dilemma,** but the plot of the opera *Tosca* illustrates this **dilemma of selfishness** as well. Tosca was beautiful (well, a soprano anyway) and in love with Mario (a tenor, of course). Scarpia, the chief of police who lusted after Tosca, had Mario arrested and was planning to execute him (unjustifiably) for treason. Scarpia figured that with Mario out of the way, Tosca would be his. To avoid Mario's execution, Tosca goes to Scarpia and offers him a deal. She will sleep with him once in return for Mario's arranged escape from execution. Scarpia agrees.

This deal would give everyone much, but not all, of what they want. Scarpia would get to sleep with Tosca; Mario would get to live; and Tosca would be able to live happily ever after with Mario. But Scarpia would prefer to have Tosca forever, not just for one night; Mario would prefer that his lover not sleep with another man; and Tosca would prefer avoiding a night with Scarpia. The dilemma is this: According to the theory of the invisible hand, overall results should be best if people try selfishly to get as much as possible of what they want; yet we find that selfish actions by Tosca and Scarpia (Mario is out of action in prison) produce tragedy for all concerned.

Scarpia arranges a meeting with Tosca during which he pretends to send a note telling the guards to save Mario's life by putting blanks in the firing squad's guns; the guards will then allow Mario to escape. Had he actually sent such a note, however, Scarpia would have had only one night with Tosca, after which she would go off with Mario. To get what he wants most, Tosca forever, Scarpia actually writes to the guards that they should be sure that Mario is dead as a doornail (a rough translation of the Italian).

Tosca's part of the deal is to sleep with Scarpia after he sends the note. However, she would prefer to have the note sent without having to sleep with Scarpia later. So she sneaks a knife into their meeting and, after Scarpia has sent the note, kills him. The result of Tosca and Scarpia each selfishly trying to get as much as possible of what they want is that Scarpia gets killed instead of lucky, Mario is killed, and Tosca loses Mario. If only Tosca and Scarpia had both stuck with the deal, they would have both been much better off.

Cooperation would have averted the tragedy, but cooperation requires trust. If Tosca had been cooperative and Scarpia totally selfish, she would have voluntarily slept with Scarpia only to have Mario killed by the firing squad anyway. This would have been the worst outcome from her perspective. Similarly, if Scarpia had been cooperative and Tosca totally selfish, he would have sent a note that saved Mario's life and then been killed by Tosca. This would have been the worst outcome from his perspective.

If neither trusts the other to be cooperative, that is, if each assumes the other will be totally selfish, the only way to avoid the worst outcome is to act selfishly oneself, which is exactly what each did. Scarpia secured Mario's death, and Tosca avoided sleeping with Scarpia, but the overall results were still tragic. In many situations, where trust is absent, rationally selfish people act in ultimately self-destructive ways. *In many situations, no invisible hand converts selfish behavior into general benefit.*

Public Goods and Government Regulation

Such situations are common because they arise often regarding **public goods.** *A public good is something good that no one can benefit from unless many others benefit as well.* The classic example is national defense. If the nation is defended against foreign enemies, then just about everyone in the nation is defended. Another common example is clean (outside) air. If the air is clean for some people, many others will also enjoy it. The key here is the inability to target the benefit to some people and exclude all others. *Public goods cannot be privatized. An important aspect of private property is the ability to exclude others, and this ability is reduced where public goods are concerned.*

Selfish people have little incentive to provide or voluntarily contribute to public goods. This is another dilemma of selfishness. Suppose that I voluntarily contribute money to national defense. The country will not be well defended by my contribution alone; millions must contribute many billions of dollars. So I may as well forget my voluntary contribution until millions of others make their contributions. But if millions of others make their contributions, it still makes no sense for me voluntarily to contribute to national defense because it is already taken care of; I am well defended whether I contribute or not. From my selfish perspective, my best course is to enjoy national defense at other people's expense. Selfishness, in other words, suggests that I become a **free rider,** a person who benefits from a public good paid for by others yet available to all, including me.

Of course, everyone reasons the same way, so no one pays for national defense. The country may be overrun by enemies who enslave us and reduce us to poverty. We would all have been better off from a purely selfish perspective if we had a national defense, but everyone who was rationally selfish tried to be a free rider. You may think this shows free riding to be irrational, but it does not. It is the only rational position unless you trust that others will give enough to national defense to keep foreign enemies at bay. After all, the worst outcome from your perspective is that you

168 Chapter 5: Free-Market Conservatism

contribute to national defense, forgoing the enjoyment of spending money on yourself, but not enough others do the same, so you are eventually enslaved anyway. Attempted free riding rationally avoids this worst outcome but fails to provide the necessary public good.

The dilemma of selfishness helps to explain why we do not use voluntary, noncoercive means, such as bake sales, to fund national defense and other public goods. If no one has a private incentive to provide for public goods, they will not be provided by private initiative, and so the government must step in to provide them. It must do just the opposite of privatization. It must take what has been privately owned, some citizen wealth and income, and make it public property so the government can use the money to provide national defense.

private goods must sometimes become public to benefit all

In sum, according to free-market conservatism, individualistic, self-serving, competitive behavior generally tends to increase social wealth and improve human lives by providing people what they need and want. However, public goods are the exception. Free-market conservative Friedrich Hayek writes:

> Where . . . it is impracticable to make the enjoyment of certain services dependent on the payment of a price, competition will not produce the services; and the price system becomes similarly ineffective when the damage caused to others by certain uses of property cannot be effectively charged to the owner of that property. . . . Thus neither the provision of signposts on the roads nor, in most circumstances, that of the roads themselves can be paid for by every individual user. Nor can certain harmful effects of deforestation, of some methods of farming, or of the smoke and noise of factories be confined to the owner of the property in question or to those who are willing to submit to the damage for an agreed compensation. In such instances we must find some substitute for the regulation by the price mechanism.[29]

Public goods ARE EXCEPTION to FMC

Government must intervene with taxes or regulations to promote efficiency.

Cost-Benefit Analysis

But if efficiency is our goal, government intervention is dangerous because governments tend to monopolize instead of compete within their fields of operation. In general, the government alone provides national defense and protects environmental quality by setting standards for

---

29. Hayek, pp. 38–39.

smoke and noise from factories. Government monopoly is justified, according to Hayek, because competition does not promote the efficient use and protection of public goods. But monopoly, as we have seen, also tends to be inefficient. We need measures of efficiency applicable to government activity so we can hold the government accountable for the efficiency of its laws and regulations.

Free markets promote efficiency through pricing goods and services. Human satisfactions from limited resources are maximized, free-market conservatives maintain, when people use their typically limited funds to buy as much as possible of what they need and want. This usually involves trade-offs. People may forego some luxury features in their car, for example, to afford an upgrade of their home entertainment system. *Government decisions regarding public goods can maximize efficiency only if they employ similar trade-offs that provide people with the greatest sum total of benefits as measured by people's willingness to pay for things.*

Economists use **cost-benefit analysis** (**CBA**) for this purpose. CBA simulates free-market decision making by assigning monetary values to all aspects of a situation and determining by these values what government action is most efficient. Those *monetary values should reflect, as do monetary values in a free market, what people are willing to pay for various items and outcomes, given that they have many other uses for their money as well.* Government actions guided by people's (simulated or hypothetical) willingness to pay will satisfy as many needs and wants as possible. Because needs and wants are expressed in monetary terms, these actions will maximize the dollar value of society's resources or, in other words, maximize social wealth.

Consider, for example, air pollution from cars. Such pollution is a major ingredient in smog, which is unsightly, harms people's health, and causes premature death. But clean air, like national defense, is a public good which individualistic, self-serving, competitive behavior will not produce or maintain. Everyone would like the air to be made clean by other people driving less or installing expensive pollution abatement equipment on their cars. But most self-interested people prefer to be free riders who benefit from, without contributing to, the reduction of car-related air pollution.

From an efficiency perspective, however, government regulations aimed at reducing air pollution are justified only if benefits outweigh costs, that is, only when reducing air pollution is cheaper than leaving it alone. For example, imagine that the air pollution from cars in the United States costs $10 billion per year as a result of building corrosion, lost work days because of illness, the health care and insurance costs of illness, lost

[handwritten margin note: Governments must use "trade-offs" to better designate resources + provide more benefits]

earnings owing to premature death, and increased life-insurance premiums. Suppose that 1 million new cars are sold in the United States each year and that for $500 per car a pollution device could be installed that reduced car-related pollution by 70% and saved $6 billion in car-pollution-related expenses. CBA may recommend that the government require installation of this device on all new cars because the savings to society (when these cars eventually dominate the roadways) are $6 billion per year and the cost only one-half billion dollars per year ($500 per car for 1 million cars). Here protecting the public good by lowering air pollution improves overall efficiency and increases national wealth by $5.5 billion. Free-market conservatism endorses this kind of government intervention, government monopoly notwithstanding, because it is efficient.

Suppose now that before the first pollution-control device is installed on any cars someone invents a much better device. It can reduce car-related air pollution by 95% and related costs by 90%. Costs would go down from $10 billion to only $1 billion per year. However, this device costs $5,000 per car, for a total of $5 billion each year for the 1 million cars sold. This may also seem efficient, because what costs $5 billion yields $9 billion in benefits, a net gain of $4 billion. But it is not the most efficient method of pollution control. The first, cheaper and less powerful pollution-control device costs only one-half billion dollars and saves $6 billion, for a net gain of $5.5 billion.

In sum, public goods are important, but there are many other important things as well. Efficiency results when trade-offs are made that give people maximum satisfaction of their needs and wants as measured by their willingness to pay for things. CBA enables government decision makers to approximate the efficiency of free markets.

CBA is not just an economist's perspective on the role of government. Given its promise to promote prosperity, politicians often endorse its use. The most sweeping endorsement was President Reagan's. On February 19, 1981, he issued Executive Order 12,291, which required all executive department orders and federal agency regulations to be supported by CBA.[30] Even where it is not strictly required, government agencies commonly use CBA to justify their orders and regulations. The National Environmental Policy Act of 1969, for example, requires that an environmental impact statement accompany all "major Federal actions significantly affecting the quality of the human environment."[31] These impact statements often use CBA. The Nuclear Regulatory Commission uses CBA as well.

---

30. 46 Federal Register 13,193 (1981).
31. 42 U.S.C. Paragraph 4332 (2) (B) (1976).

Human Lives and Future Generations

CBA remains controversial. *As we have seen, to simulate the free market's promotion of efficient trade-offs that maximize social wealth, every variable must be put in monetary terms, including "items" normally excluded from market transactions, such as human lives.* Economists find **shadow prices** for such items by using market values to infer the prices of things outside the market. The monetary worth of a human life, for example, may be inferred from the extra pay people get for doing dangerous work, jury awards for wrongful death, lost earnings owing to premature death, the amount of life insurance people buy, and responses to questionnaires. But there are problems.

First, some people object to assigning a monetary value to human life. They consider human life too precious for monetary value to be appropriate. Second, the worth of a human life varies enormously in different surveys within the United States. In the early 1970s, for example, when actual wage differentials were used, the inferred value of a human life varied from $136,000 to $2.6 million. When hypothetical questions were asked, variation was even greater, from $28,000 to $5 million.[32] The economic rationality of a proposal that affects human lives is uncertain when the worth of a life remains uncertain. How much money should we spend to putting up better road signs or redesigning highways to save lives? CBA will not tell us unless we have a justified dollar estimate of a life's worth. In 2003, the Environmental Protection Agency used the figure of $6.1 million per human life.[33]

A third problem is that CBA assigns less worth to the lives of people in poor Third World countries than to those in rich industrial countries. Consider what happened after people were poisoned by an accidental gas leak at a Union Carbide plant in Bhopal, India, in 1984. About 10,000 people were killed and hundreds of thousands injured. After a four-year legal battle, the Indian Supreme Court ordered Union Carbide Corporation to pay a total of $470 million dollars to compensate victims. This may seem like a lot of money but, as Ward Morehouse reports in the *Ecologist,*

> this sum, equivalent to only $793 for each of the 592,000 who had then filed claims, was not even sufficient to cover health care and monitoring of the gas-exposed population, which had been conservatively estimated at $600 million over the next 20 to 30 years. The

CBA requires assignment of values

---

32. A. Myrick Freeman, III, Robert H. Haveman, and Allen V. Kneese, *The Economics of Environmental Policy* (New York: John Wiley and Sons, Inc., 1973), pp. 187–89.

33. National Public Radio, *Morning Edition* with Bob Edwards, Joseph Shapiro reporting, May 5, 2003.

settlement was so favorable for Union Carbide that its stock price rose $2 a share on the New York Stock Exchange the day it was announced.[34]

Some Americans get more compensation for a strained back than Indians got for life-impairing injuries from toxic gases.

International disparity in the worth of a human life is the logical outcome of using CBA. While he worked for the World Bank, Lawrence Summers, now president of Harvard University, suggested in a memo "encouraging *more* migration of the dirty industries to the LDCs [least developed countries]." His first reason was this:

> The measurement of the costs of health-impairing pollution depends on the forgone earnings from increased morbidity and mortality. From this point of view a given amount of health-impairing pollution should be done in the country with the lowest cost, which will be the country with the lowest wages. I think the economic logic behind dumping a load of toxic waste in the lowest-wage country is impeccable and we should face up to that.[35]

Although he was widely criticized for being politically incorrect, the *Economist* agreed with his economic logic, "pollution had lower costs in poor countries than in rich ones."[36] The reason is that the dollar value of a human life is less in such countries.

Some who do not object to assigning dollar values to human lives may object to assigning different values to people in different countries. They may think such assignments violate the principle that all human beings have an equal right to life.

A fourth problem is that *future generations are also assigned less value than present people in CBA, and some thinkers find this objectionable.* In banking and economics, money (in constant dollars) that will be received in the future is worth less than money available now. If I have $100 dollars now, I can put it into a secure savings account at 3% interest and have $103 dollars next year. At the same interest rate, in order to have $100 next year, I need only a little more than $97 dollars now. So the present worth of next year's $100 is a little more than $97. The present worth of $100 that I will not receive for two years is even less, because I have to put

---

34. Ward Morehouse, "Unfinished Business: Bhopal Ten Years After," *The Ecologist*, Vol. 24, No. 5 (September/October 1994), pp. 164–68, at 167.

35. *The Guardian*, 14 February 1992, p. 29. Emphasis in original. Reprinted in Steven Yearly, *Sociology, Environmentalism, Globalization* (Thousand Oaks, CA: Sage Publications, 1996), p. 75.

36. *The Economist* (11–17 March 1995), p. 73. Reprinted in Yearly, p. 76.

less money in the bank today to get $100 at compound interest two years from now. Interest rates make the present worth of money that you will receive in the future less than its eventual future worth. This is why a $100 savings bond may cost only $50 at present. Economists say that the present worth is discounted, and the percentage rate of discounting, which in this example is the interest rate, is called the **discount rate.**

Whatever dollar figure represents a human life in CBA, that figure and that life must be discounted like all other items. A group of energy economists headed by Sam Schurr do this in *Energy in America's Future: The Choices before Us* when arguing for nuclear power. Operating nuclear power plants results in some radiation-induced deaths. Wanting to minimize the importance of those deaths, they write:

> If all the predicted deaths over all future years were to be added up, the totals would be very large, 100 to 800 per [nuclear power] plant. [We] propose discounting these effects to yield their present-day equivalents, just as future incomes are discounted to represent the smaller value of future events in present-day calculations. If these effects are discounted at reasonable rates, such as 5%, contributions for each plant-year would be between 0.07 and .3 fatality.[37]

These economists are not trying to hurt people. They are just taking seriously the implications of CBA. All variables must have monetary equivalents, and all dollars must be considered equal for CBA to indicate policies that maximize national wealth. Thinkers who do not want people treated like money cannot use CBA and cannot know which policies move the country toward its greatest prosperity as measured by market value.

CBA nearly discounts out of consideration the lives of people living hundreds of years in the future because discounting at compound interest becomes overwhelming. Here is how. Generally speaking, we can determine when a sum of money doubles in dollar value at a given compound interest rate by dividing the interest rate into 72. At a 3% interest rate, for example, money doubles in value every 24 years. By the same logic, an amount of money that will not be available for 24 years is presently worth only one-half of its eventual worth if the discount rate is 3%. If it will not be available for 48 years its current worth is only one-fourth of its eventual worth. By this logic, at a 3% discount rate, the present value of $3 trillion dollars that will not be available for 1,000 years is less than $1.

---

37. Sam Schurr et al., *Energy in America's Future: The Choices before Us* (Baltimore: Johns Hopkins University Press, 1979), p. 355, in Herman E. Daly and John B. Cobb, Jr., *For the Common Good* (Boston: Beacon Press, 1994), p. 153.

Therefore, whatever value we place on a human life, 3 trillion human lives 1,000 years from now are worth less than one human life today at a 3% discount rate.

Consider the policy implications of the 3% rate on the burial of high-level nuclear waste. The present plan is to bury most high-level nuclear waste in Yucca Mountain, Nevada. Nevadans complain that thousands of years from now the burial site may be flooded by rising groundwater, causing an explosion that will spread still-dangerous radiation far and wide. Millions of people could be killed. The analyst conscientiously using CBA must reply: so what? Assuming the site will be secure for at least 1,000 years, a later explosion could kill all of humanity, 10 or 20 billion people, and still the loss would be equal to less than one-half of 1% of a human life today.

This has important implications for the amount of money we spend to protect people of the distant future. If we can save some money cutting corners in the way we bury nuclear waste, for example, and still have burial that is safe for 1,000 years, we should certainly do so. We can use that money for AIDS prevention and save human lives in the short term. Poisoning all of humanity 1,000 years from now is worth much less than a single human life saved in this decade. Yet the United States Environmental Protection Agency, which uses CBA regularly and assigns a dollar value to human lives, requires the Department of Energy try to protect people from nuclear waste's radiation for at least 10,000 years.[38] According to CBA, however, spending a dime on people who will live thousands of years from now is totally irrational. Many people think that *CBA is a poor guide to policies affecting humans who will live in the distant future.*

Equal Consideration of Interests

A fifth problem with CBA concerns its bias in favor of rich people over the poor. Most people think the government should have equal concern for the well-being of all citizens. All (adult) citizens have the right to vote so they can equally influence government to serve their needs and wants. Of course rich individuals and some special interests may have more influence than most citizens because of their campaign contributions, business

---

38. James Flynn, Paul Slovic, Roger E. Kasperson, and Howard Kunreuther, "The High-Level Nuclear Waste Program Is Misguided, *Nuclear and Toxic Waste*, Thomas Streissguth, Ed. (San Diego, CA: Greenhaven Press, 2001), pp. 71–83, at 76. Originally appeared as "Overcoming Tunnel Vision: Redirecting the U.S. High-Level Nuclear Waste Program," *Environment*, April 1997.

equal consideration of interests: gov. shows equal concern for needs & wants of all individuals (no matter what)

connections, and personal ties to government leaders, but this is usually considered an imperfection. The ideal is that the government shows equal concern for the needs and wants of all individuals, regardless of race, religion, national origin, or income. This is the principle of **equal consideration of interests,** which CBA violates.

CBA recommends policies that maximize the dollar value of national wealth. Dollar values are determined by market values or approximations of market values through shadow pricing. These dollar values reflect how much people are willing to pay for goods and services. Other things being equal, the more money people have, the more they can be willing to pay, and the greater their influence on prices. If the government tries to maximize national wealth as measured by dollar values (prices) and those dollar values reflect disproportionately the needs and wants of rich people, the government will automatically and inevitably favor the needs and wants of the rich over the poor. Economist A. Myrick Freeman, III writes:

> Willingness to pay for a good is constrained by ability to pay. Economic theory shows that an individual's willingness to pay for a good depends on his income and that for most goods, higher income means higher willingness to pay, other things equal. As a consequence, [CBA] has a tendency to give greater weight to the preferences of those individuals with higher incomes.[39]

This tendency simply reflects the fact that CBA simulates economic activity in private sector free markets so that government decisions, like those in the free market, will be efficient. Car dealerships, hair salons, restaurants, hardware stores, and other businesses in the free market properly cater to the needs and wants of potential customers, people willing to pay for their goods and services. BMW dealers therefore properly ignore the transportation needs of people who cannot pay $50,000 for a car.

The problem with CBA is that it recommends that the government similarly attend to the needs and wants of people proportionate to their willingness to pay. Each dollar is given equal consideration with every other dollar, but each person is not; people with more dollars have a greater impact on the dollar value of the nation's wealth and therefore on the policies needed to maximize national wealth.

Consider this hypothetical example. Imagine that the government needs to bury some low-level nuclear waste and must choose between two sites that are geologically suitable. One site is a few miles outside an

---

39. A. Myrick Freeman, III, "The Ethical Basis of the Economic View of the Environment," in *The Environmental Ethics and Policy Book,* 3rd ed., Donald VanDeVeer and Christine Pierce, Eds. (Belmont, CA: Wadsworth, 2003), pp. 318–26, at 321.

176 Chapter 5: Free-Market Conservatism

up-market community of 5,000 people where the average house is worth $1 million. The other is a few miles outside a down-and-out town of 20,000 people where the average house is worth $50,000. In both cases, location of a low-level nuclear waste facility a few miles from town will lower property values 50% (owing to fear of radiation, whether rational or not). If there are 2,000 homes in the small, wealthy community and each loses half its 1 million dollar value, the total loss is $1 billion. If there are 10,000 homes in the poor community and each loses half its $50,000 value, the total loss is only one-quarter billion dollars. CBA recommends placing the low-level nuclear waste facility near the down-and-out community because that maximizes the dollar value of national wealth.

This recommendation does not reflect undue political influence by the rich or any underhanded activity. *It is a logical consequence of policies designed to maximize national wealth that government caters to the needs and wants of rich people over poor people.* CBA thus justifies many common government actions that harm the poor more than the rich people. For example, freeways in large cities are typically sited to disrupt or destroy poor, not rich, neighborhoods.

Scarcity

Free-market conservatism suffers from problems deeper than the inadequacies of CBA. The biggest problem is that maximizing economic growth and social wealth sometimes harms people more than it helps them.

Adam Smith noted in *The Wealth of Nations* that the monetary value of items, which is their "value in exchange," often does not reflect their usefulness. "Nothing is more useful than water," he notes, "but it will purchase scarcely anything; scarcely anything can be had in exchange for it."[40] The reason is that, at Smith's time and place, clean water was plentiful. People could have all they wanted at the local stream. There was no scarcity; no one had to buy water from anyone else, so it had little or no exchange value. People seldom buy what they can have free.

Now potable water is increasingly scarce in many places because of increases in the human population, water-intensive methods of agriculture, and water pollution stemming from industrial and consumer activity.[41] In most parts of the world today, because water is increasingly scarce, people

---

40. Smith in Held, p. 99.
41. David Bollier, *Silent Theft: The Private Plunder of Our Public Wealth* (New York: Routledge, 2002), p. 70.

have to pay for it. Given the law of supply and demand, as scarcity increases, other things being equal, so does price. If a country's wealth is measured by the dollar value of all it contains, as free-market conservatism and CBA propose, then, other things being equal, an increase in the price of water increases national wealth. But this is not good; it harms most people by straining their budgets. Consider this case from David Bollier's *Silent Theft*.

> In Bolivia, the World Bank engineered a private takeover of the water supplies in 1998, allowing a subsidiary of the Bechtel conglomerate to sell permits for access to water. Prices rose from 35 to 300%, forcing many people to spend nearly half of their monthly budgets for water. After a general strike . . . protesters forced the government to rescind . . . water privatization. . . .[42]

Concentrating exclusively on national wealth as measured in dollar terms, free-market conservatism cannot explain why higher water prices are not good. The problem is that increased national wealth may not reflect greater efficiency and productivity to meet human needs and wants, which most people consider worthy goals. Instead, *increased national wealth may reflect scarcity, sometimes contrived scarcity, that harms human well-being.* Thus, increased national wealth, the pole star of CBA and free-market conservatism, is an unreliable guide to human improvement. We need to look at *how* the nation's wealth is increased before we know whether or not to approve.[43]

Selling Babies

Another problem for free-market conservatism is that it endorses the sale of some items that many people think should be excluded from free-market transactions. Babies are a prime example. Elisabeth Landes and Richard Posner argue for laws establishing a market in babies put up for adoption. Posner is a major advocate of the **economic theory of law,** which *says that laws should be designed to promote economic efficiency, the essential claim of free-market conservatism.* If Landes and Posner are correct, free-market conservatives should support laws that legalize selling babies for adoption.

---

42. Bollier, p. 72.

43. This point was made first by economist James M. Lauderdale, *An Inquiry into the Nature and Origin of Public Wealth and into the Means and Causes of Its Increase,* 2nd ed. (Edinburgh: Constable, 1819). I found it in Daly and Cobb, pp. 147–48.

Writing in 1978, Landes and Posner claim, "students of adoption agree on two things. The first is that there is a shortage of white babies for adoption; the second is that there is a glut . . . of children who are no longer babies, for adoption."[44] One symptom of shortage is long waiting lists for adoption. Another is that "many childless couples undergo extensive, costly, and often futile methods of fertility treatment in order to increase their chances of bearing a child."[45] These conditions persist into the 21st century. Current law forbids natural parents selling babies for adoption.[46] Landes and Posner claim that this restriction "has created a baby shortage . . . by preventing a free market from equilibrating the demand for and supply of babies for adoption, and . . . has contributed to a glut of unadopted children maintained in foster homes. . . ."[47]

The supply problem is due primarily, they say, to contraception, abortion, and the fact that "a larger proportion of parents of illegitimate children are keeping them." However, if women could sell children for adoption, they would be less likely to keep them. "At a higher price for babies, the incidence of abortion, the reluctance to part with an illegitimate child, and even the incentive to use contraceptives would diminish because the costs of unwanted pregnancy would be lower while the (opportunity) costs to the natural mother of retaining her illegitimate child would rise."[48] Payment would be justified because natural mothers do work that adoptive mothers avoid.

> Adoption is a process by which the adoptive mother in effect contracts out one of the steps in the process of child production and rearing, namely, the actual pregnancy and childbirth. The anxieties and inconveniences of pregnancy are a cost to the biological mother but a cost saving to the adoptive mother.[49]

It is only reasonable that adoptive mothers pay for this service, the authors suggest.

"Just as a buyer's queue is a symptom of a shortage, a seller's queue is a symptom of a glut," they argue. "The thousands of children in foster care . . . are comparable to an unsold inventory stored in a warehouse."[50]

---

44. Elisabeth M. Landes and Richard A. Posner, "The Economics of the Baby Shortage," *The Journal of Legal Studies,* Vol. 7 (1978), pp. 323–48, at 324–25.
45. Landes and Posner, p. 346.
46. Landes and Posner, p. 328.
47. Landes and Posner, p. 324.
48. Landes and Posner, p. 325.
49. Landes and Posner, p. 340.
50. Landes and Posner, p. 327.

Allowing people to sell babies could lessen the glut problem too, because it results partly from the inability to sell babies.

> Since the natural parents have no financial incentive to place a child for adoption, often they will decide to place it in foster care instead. This is proper so long as they seriously intend to reacquire custody of the child at some later date. But when they do not the consequence of their decision to place the child in foster care may be to render the child unadoptable, for by the time the parents relinquish their parental rights the child may be too old to be placed for adoption. This would happen less often if parents had a financial incentive to relinquish their rights at a time when the child was still young enough to be adoptable.[51]

A market in children for adoption will help prospective adoptive parents by increasing the supply. Landes and Posner reject the criticism that such a market will favor only wealthy people, because increased supply tends to bring the price down. Compared to the current system, they claim, "prices for children of *equivalent quality* would be much lower . . . perhaps no more than the cost of an automobile. . . ."[52]

The authors are not worried either that sold babies will be abused. First, "the logical approach . . . is to require every prospective baby buyer to undergo some minimal background investigation. This approach would be analogous to licensing automobile drivers. . . ." Second, "abuse is not the normal motive for adopting a child. And once we put abuse aside, willingness to pay money for a baby would seem on the whole a reassuring factor from the standpoint of child welfare. Few people buy a car or a television set in order to smash it. In general, the more costly a purchase, the more care the purchaser will lavish on it."[53]

The only major concern that Landes and Posner have is that a legal market in babies for adoption will expose racism in society. "Were baby prices quoted as prices of soybean futures are quoted, a racial ranking of these prices would be evident, with white baby prices higher than non-white baby prices."[54] The authors worry that "bringing this fact out into the open would exacerbate racial tensions in our society."[55] Even so, they think, the overall effect of a legal market in babies is positive. More babies will be available for adoption, the price for quality babies will decline,

---

51. Landes and Posner, p. 338.
52. Landes and Posner, p. 339 and 340. Emphasis in original.
53. Landes and Posner, p. 343.
54. Landes and Posner, p. 344.
55. Landes and Posner, p. 345.

natural mothers will receive the money they deserve for their work, adoptive couples will find the children they seek, fewer fetuses will be aborted, and fewer children will end up in foster care.

Landes and Posner recognize what they call "symbolic objections to baby sale. . . ."[56] Some people think it disrespectful to human dignity for a person to be sold. But the rights of children would be protected. No one would be sold for slavery, and child abuse would remain illegal.

The logic of their argument is strong. Some readers may favor baby selling as an excellent case of private-property and free-market-activity-producing efficiencies and human satisfaction. Others may object to free-market conservatism if it requires treating children as commodities.

Comparison with Utilitarianism

In some respect, free-market conservatism resembles utilitarianism. Both views advocate maximizing something, happiness or preference satisfaction for utilitarianism and social wealth for free-market conservatism. But their different targets for maximization make them vulnerable to different objections.

Objections to free-market conservatism stem from concerns about material prosperity, justice, and other values. Although economic growth generally promotes prosperity, the connection between economic growth and prosperity is not universal. If the dollar value of goods and services in society increases owing to increased scarcity, economic growth may not improve prosperity. Concentration on happiness or preference satisfaction makes utilitarianism immune to this objection. Material scarcity usually impairs happiness or satisfaction, so utilitarians will seldom endorse increased scarcity.

When CBA is used by governments to protect public goods, as efficiency requires, poorer people are automatically given less consideration by the government than richer people are. Government's unequal consideration of interests is usually considered unjust. CBA also requires that a price be put on human lives. Some people find it inappropriate for the government to assign a dollar value to human lives even when the same value is assigned to everyone in the country. Worse than this, CBA raises issues of justice by assigning less value to the lives of people in poor countries and by virtually ignoring the value of people, regardless of country, who will live in the distant future.

---

56. Landes and Posner, p. 346.

Utilitarianism avoids all objections that stem from assigning dollar values to lives. It gives equal consideration to everyone's interests and never considers some lives more important than others. Nevertheless, as we have seen, it too has problems with justice. Because its goal is to maximize happiness or preference satisfaction, utilitarianism can advocate policies that treat individuals unjustly in order to maximize total good.

Free-market conservatism ignores a host of values that are important for human flourishing because it assigns value only to what money can buy in actual or simulated markets. Free markets enable people to interact productively with strangers, but some needs cannot be filled by strangers. It is a commonplace observation that money cannot buy happiness and, as the Beatles sang, "Can't Buy Me Love." Human beings are a social species, so human flourishing requires that people care for one another in personal relationships, for example, in religious and other communities. People also need intimate relationships in families, hence the importance of family values.

People also flourish through personal accomplishments that money cannot buy, such as knitting a sweater, making a cabinet, learning a foreign language, or learning to play an instrument. Such accomplishments typically require some purchases that stimulate the economy, but the time devoted to these pursuits usually exceeds monetary values. People would generally promote economic growth more by working longer hours at what they do professionally and buying finished products instead of knitting sweaters and making cabinets. Such a division of labor was Adam Smith's prescription for economic prosperity. The value of personal accomplishment in hobbies is lost.

Utilitarianism is again immune to these objections. Because its goal is maximum happiness or preference satisfaction, it can include the values of friendship, love, family, community, personal accomplishments and other good things that money cannot buy. Assuming that these good things contribute to happiness or preference satisfaction, utilitarians would tend to support public policies that promote them.

The crucial weakness of utilitarianism, however, besides problems concerning justice, is its inability to specify how to measure what it believes society should maximize, happiness or preference satisfaction. As we have seen, these are essentially subjective phenomena inaccessible to direct observation. It is hard to imagine any method of calculation that accurately compares one person's happiness or unhappiness, satisfaction or dissatisfaction, with another's. Free-market conservatives solve this problem by using willingness to pay money as a substitute for unobservable psychological states. In this respect, free-market conservatism is superior to utilitarianism, but the cost of superiority on this point is all the problems associated with assigning dollar values to everything.

CONCLUSION

Most people consider economic growth important and good because it generally leads to prosperity and higher standards of living. In addition to security, a concern of all political philosophies, free-market conservatism favors private property rights, freedom of contract, and free markets because they promote efficiencies needed for economic growth and prosperity. These principles represent its strength. Like happiness and preference satisfaction, economic prosperity is a good that no political philosophy can ignore. The weakness of free-market conservatism stems from its exclusive attention to what money can buy. Governments must promote many other values as well if people are to flourish: community, family values, personal accomplishments, and justice. John Rawls's theory, considered in the next chapter, concentrates on justice.

JUDGMENT CALLS

1. If we do not assign monetary values to human lives, how do we decide how much money to spend on better road signs and roads in order to save human lives?

2. In the spring of 2003, the United States Environmental Protection Agency, which assigned the value of $6.1 million to each American life, proposed discounting the lives of older Americans. They suggested that the lives of people over 65 should be valued at 63% or less of the normal value.[57] How might you argue for or against this proposal? What might a free-market conservative say?

3. Many couples who are infertile and want children contract with a woman to bear a child for them. In a typical arrangement, that woman, called a *surrogate*, is paid a fee exceeding her expenses to be artificially inseminated with the sperm of the man in the couple. She must, according to the contract, give the child to the couple when it is born. How does this compare to selling babies? How do such surrogacy arrangements relate to the freedom of contract? Should surrogacy contracts be legally binding?

4. What might free-market conservatives say about legalizing prostitution?

---

57. National Public Radio, Morning Edition with Bob Edwards, Joseph Shapiro reporting, May 5, 2003.

5. What might free-market conservatives say about legalizing the international market in the sale of kidneys from live donors?[58]

6. Economist Richard Titmuss argues that in the 1960s the British system of disallowing payment for human blood needed in transfusions was more efficient than the American free-market system that allowed the sale of blood. Costs, infection rates, and mortality were all lower in the British system. In addition, according to Titmuss, Britain's National Blood Transfusion Service "has allowed and encouraged sentiments of altruism, reciprocity, and societal duty to express themselves; to be made explicit . . . by all social groups and classes."[59] Assuming Titmuss is correct, why, do you think, is commercialization of blood donations inefficient? Are there other goods or services that can be provided more efficiently outside the market? How much effort should governments put into "encouraging sentiments of altruism, reciprocity and societal duty?" How important are such sentiments to human well-being? Why, how, and to what extent, if at all, do market transactions erode or interfere with such sentiments?

---

58. See Sheila M. and David J. Rothman, "The Organ Market," *The New York Review of Books*, Vol. L, No. 16 (October 23, 2003), pp. 49–51.

59. Richard Titmuss, *The Gift Relationship: From Human Blood to Social Policy* (New York: Pantheon, 1971), p. 225, in Bollier, p. 34.

6   Rawls's Liberal Contractarianism

We have seen that libertarianism and free-market conservatism defend property rights, which are needed to respect individual freedom and promote general prosperity. But property rights can also promote inequalities that many people find unjust. Consider this headline in the *International Herald Tribune* in fall 2003: "U.S. rich get richer, and poor poorer, data shows." The article goes on to explain:

> The gap between rich and poor in the United States has widened into an even deeper gulf in which the richest 1% of Americans, or 2.8 million people, had more after-tax money in 2000 than did the bottom 40%, or 110 million. By contrast, in 1979 the wealthiest 1% had less than half the total economic pie of the poorest 40%, according to new data from the Congressional Budget Office. . . . The figures show 2000 as the period of greatest economic disparity between rich and poor for any year covered by the budget office data, 1979 through 2000. . . .
>
> The National Bureau of Economic Research, a nonpartisan research organization . . . , found that in 2000, the wealthiest 1% had the largest share of before-tax income for any year since 1929 . . . [and] a greater share of the nation's total after-tax prosperity since at least 1936.
>
> [Adjusted for inflation,] the wealthiest 1% had on average $862,700 after taxes in 2000, triple 1979's level. . . . By contrast, the poorest one-fifth of households had $13,700, only 9% more than in 1979. . . .[1]

Is this a problem? The issue makes headlines in part because some people believe it is unjust for the richest 1% to have a 300% increase in income over a 21-year period while the poorest 20% of the population gained only 9%.

Libertarians would not see this as unjust so long as no force or fraud was used to increase disparities between rich and poor. Free-market

---

1. Linnley Browning, "U.S. Rich Get Richer, and Poor Poorer, Data Shows," *International Herald Tribune* (September 25, 2003), p. 5.

conservatives would not condemn increased disparities if this maximized the entire economic pie. The pie grew a lot between 1979 and 2000, although it may not have been maximized. Utilitarians would not complain unless data showed that total happiness or preference satisfaction in the population could have been higher, and there is no such data in these figures. On what grounds, then, can anyone complain? *The assumptions, concepts, and history of the social contract tradition in political philosophy, culminating in the 20th-century view of John Rawls, justify concern about disparities between rich and poor. This tradition may influence many people to condemn increasing inequalities of wealth and income.*

The **social contract tradition** in political philosophy holds that *legitimate governments are founded on the consent of the governed. Justice results when people follow rules that they have approved, or rules established by authorities they have agreed to obey.* This conforms to common sense in our society.

The Pilgrims provided a model for the social contract view in the Mayflower Compact that they signed before occupying land in North America. [We],

> having undertaken for the Glory of God, and Advancement of the Christian Faith, and the Honour of our King and Country, a voyage to plant the first colony in the northern Parts of Virginia; do by these Presents, solemnly and mutually in the Presence of God and one another, covenant and combine ourselves together into a civil Body Politic, for our better Ordering and Preservation, and Furtherance of the Ends aforesaid; and by Virtue hereof to enact, constitute, and frame, such just and equal Laws and Ordinances, Acts, Constitutions and Offices, from time to time, as shall be thought most meet and convenient for the General good of the Colony; unto which we promise due submission and Obedience.

Some of what they agreed to would not suit modern conditions. For example, they were religious people who agreed to exclude from their colony anyone who did not profess and practice Puritanism. This would not work in our religiously pluralistic society.

Less than a generation after the Pilgrims, the Englishman Thomas Hobbes maintained that all governments, not just the Plymouth Colony's, derive legitimacy from the consent of the governed. As we saw in the Introduction, Hobbes believed that without a state to maintain law and order, "the life of man is solitary, poor, nasty, brutish, and short."[2] To achieve security, Hobbes thought, people would agree to establish a single

---

2. Thomas Hobbes, *Leviathan* (Indianapolis: The Bobbs-Merrill Company, 1958), p. 107.

-Hobbes:
-Law & Order
- Locke:
Tyranny

authority with absolute power, the Leviathan. Hobbes believed the rationality of consenting to the Leviathan's rule conferred legitimacy on that rule. However, we saw that because power tends to corrupt, it would not be rational for people to give absolute power to any person or group. They would be subjecting themselves to tyranny.

A generation after Hobbes, John Locke was more worried about tyranny than about law and order and therefore set limits on state power.[3] He thought that people have natural rights to life, liberty, and property and that they establish the state through a social contract primarily to protect these rights. The state must not, therefore, violate these rights. Locke's view supports current libertarian defenses of property rights and shares both the strengths and limitations of libertarian views on these matters.

In sum, Locke, Hobbes, and the Pilgrims advocated founding the state on a social contract, but the regimes they had in mind would not satisfy most people today. We explore in this chapter the 20th-century liberal contractarianism of John Rawls, who attempts to overcome the defects of previous social contract views. Rawls's view explains disquiet at increasing disparities between rich and poor and justifies social programs aimed at reducing those disparities. It claims to be neutral among different visions of the good life, which some people consider liberating but others find troubling if, as suggested below, it allows using state money for religious proselytizing in parochial schools. In addition, some people question the neutrality of liberal contractarianism because it favors individualistic decision making over permanent commitment to a group or community. Finally, the liberal contractarian emphasis on individual rights over group membership could jeopardize programs that some people favor, such as racial profiling to reduce crime and affirmative action to promote diversity at educational institutions.

The Original Position and the Veil of Ignorance

In most commercial contexts, people agree to contracts that they think will benefit them. The roofer signs a contract with the homeowner to put a new roof on a house for $6,000 because the roofer would prefer spending time and money to fix the homeowner's roof for $6,000 than to

---

3. John Locke, *The Second Treatise of Government* (Indianapolis: Bobbs-Merrill, 1952), paragraph 94, pp. 53–54 and paragraph 131, p. 73.

remain idle. The homeowner prefers a fixed roof to retaining that $6,000. It is the kind of win-win situation that is common in a free market. Self-centered, law-abiding behavior by both parties produces a good and just result.

When it comes to setting up a state by contract, however, self-centered behavior may not produce such a good and just result. If the parties to the contract have very different ideas about what constitutes a good society, they may not be able to agree at all. For example, some may want a religiously oriented government, as the Pilgrims had, whereas others may want a separation of church and state. In addition, there may be irreconcilable differences between people depending on wealth and occupation. Wealthy people may want low taxes so they can keep as much of their money as possible. Poorer people may want government services that help the poor, such as good state-supported schools, parks, and day care, paid for by high taxes on the rich. Aspiring entrepreneurs may want strong antitrust laws that give them the chance to defeat established businesses in competition for customers. Many established businesses may want laws relatively tolerant of monopolies. In short, given the diversity of people's beliefs, aspirations, and interests, it is hard to see how they can agree on a contract that establishes a state that all will consider legitimate; a state to which all will "promise due submission and Obedience." Unanimous agreement seems highly unlikely.

Yet a state established by majority, rather than unanimous, agreement may be unjust. For example, majority agreement may result from threat, bribery, bias, or fraud. If people with a lot of money hire enough thugs, they may intimidate a majority to agree to a state whose rules favor the rich, a state that considers property rights to be natural rights and rules out taxation for public education. On the other hand, some power-hungry, talented demagogue may incite the majority of people to demand the confiscation of rich people's property. Or religious zealots may convince a majority to require all citizens to join and support their church. If a state established by social contract may be unjust, how can anyone use a social contract to justify the state's legitimacy?

Imagination is the key. John Rawls suggests that the state's foundation and legitimacy do not rest on the actual agreement of real people to a real contract. Instead, he wants us to imagine fictional people agreeing to a contract under conditions that he calls the **original position.** Here is Rawls's thought experiment. People in the original position are behind what Rawls calls a **veil of ignorance.** These people do not know their own identities. They do not know if they are male or female, tall or short, religiously, musically, or athletically inclined, old or young, and so forth. They do know that they have been called together to decide what principles of justice should govern a modern industrial state such as the United States.

The parties to the contract know also some basic things about the world, human nature, and politics. They know, for example, that many people want more goods and services than are actually available to them; that many people have a tendency to be selfish; that material rewards often motivate people to work hard; that people have very different likes, values, and religious commitments from one another; that people want to be treated by their government as equals and without prejudice; and that equal voting rights help people secure such treatment from the government.

Rawls claims that because people in the original position are behind the veil of ignorance and do not know their personal identities, they will agree to general principles governing the state that rule out favoritism and runaway inequality in order to be fair to everyone. If the state is unfair or unjust to anyone, a contracting party will reason, she may be among those treated unjustly. For example, if the contract allows the hard-earned money of rich people to be confiscated for no good reason but jealousy and spite, she may feel unjustly dispossessed when the veil is lifted because she discovers she is rich. If the contract requires everyone to pay for and attend a particular church, she may find that she is pleased when the veil is lifted because she discovers herself to be a devout member of this church. However, she may find, instead, that she is the member of a rival church, or an atheist. *The safest course is to make a contract that provides justice for everyone, regardless of religion, sex, race, wealth, occupation, or national origin.*

[handwritten margin note: w/ veil of ignorance, bias is eliminated]

In effect, Rawls believes the veil serves to motivate self-interested contractors to establish a government that gives equal consideration to the interests of all members of society. According to contractarians, libertarianism and free-market conservatism fail to do this; they tend to endorse policies that serve the interests of the rich at the expense of the poor. In addition, the veil motivates self-interested contractors to disallow unfairly sacrificing some members of society for the overall public good. If anyone is so sacrificed, a contractor reasons behind the veil, I may be among those sacrificed. To avoid this possibility, I will agree to a government only if it disallows any such practice. Thus, for example, utilitarian reasons for unfairly prosecuting famous people like Winona Ryder more vigorously than most other people would be disallowed. In this respect, contractarianism differs from utilitarianism.

[handwritten margin note: they do not take into account the struggle of poorer people]

The Principles of Justice

Rawls believes that people in the original position will agree to the following two principles of justice:

a. Each person has the same indefeasible claim to a fully adequate scheme of equal basic liberties, which scheme is compatible with the same scheme of liberties for all; and

b. Social and economic inequalities are to satisfy two conditions: first, they are to be attached to offices and positions open to all under conditions of fair equality of opportunity; and second, they are to be to the greatest benefit of the least-advantaged members of society (the difference principle).[4]

The first principle guarantees equal basic civil and political liberties, which Rawls specifies as follows:

> Freedom of thought and liberty of conscience; political liberties (for example, the right to vote and to participate in politics) and freedom of association, as well as the rights and liberties specified by the liberty and integrity (physical and psychological) of the person; and finally, the rights and liberties covered by the rule of law.[5]

The freedoms of conscience and association, for example, would give everyone an equal right to freedom of religion, but that freedom would be limited by the basic civil and political liberties of others. Religious freedom does not give anyone the right to attack members of other religious groups or intimidate them to give up their religious beliefs or practices. Nor would religious freedom justify anyone denying others the right to vote because they belong to a different religion. Religious freedom extends only so far as it is compatible with a like freedom, and all the other basic freedoms, for everyone else. This is the view Rawls thinks people would have in the original position because, in that position, no one knows if, when the veil is lifted, she will discover herself to be in a religious group subject to attack or prejudice if such attacks or prejudice are allowed.

The second principle is in two parts. It concerns inequalities that must exist in any industrial society if it is to prosper. Free-market conservatism is based on the idea that selfish people operating in a free market will enrich not only themselves but society in general by competing with one another to supply ever better goods and services to willing customers. We have seen that there are some exceptions to this, especially regarding

---

4. John Rawls, *Justice as Fairness: A Restatement*, Erin Kelly, Ed. (Cambridge, MA: Harvard University Press, 2001), pp. 42–43.

5. Rawls (2001), p. 44.

public goods, but the general idea seems correct, and Rawls supposes that people in the original position know this and prefer a richer to a poorer society. So they must *allow some people who provide better goods and services to become richer than others.* But inequalities can become so extreme as to be unjust. Rawls's second principle is designed to assure that inequalities do not involve such injustice.

The first part of the second principle requires that the better positions in society be "open to all under conditions of fair equality of opportunity." Mere **equality of opportunity** is *the equal legal right of everyone to compete for good positions.* Such equality of opportunity is good, but not good enough because it may be unfair. If some people, through no fault of their own, lack the childhood nutrition or basic education in literacy needed to compete on equal terms with others, everyone has an equal legal right to compete, but the competition is unfair. The first part of Rawls's second principle is meant to rule out such unfairness. He thinks that people in the original position will want to be sure they have a fair shot at the better positions, so they will require **fair equality of opportunity.** *Everyone must have some minimal level of nutrition, health care, and education supplied by the state when no other source is available.*

The second part of the second principle grows out of the original reason for allowing inequalities in the first place, namely, to encourage talented people to gain education and use their talents to create social wealth. If I am behind the veil of ignorance in the original position, I do not know whether, when the veil is lifted, I will be among society's talented people. I will want to be sure that, whether I am talented or not, I will gain from the social wealth created by talented people who are motivated by the prospect of becoming richer than others. If the rich are allowed to get richer only on condition that the poor benefit, then even if I am poor, I have reason to support letting talented people be richer than the rest. Rawls argues that *people behind the veil would want the condition of the worst off to be not only improved, but improved as much as possible.* This is the idea behind **maximin,** which requires maximizing the minimum level of welfare in society. Assuming that bringing up the bottom (maximizing the minimum) tends to raise the average for everyone else, I will benefit wherever I discover myself to be (when the veil is lifted) on the talent or income spectrum.[6] This reasoning yields the **difference principle:** "Social and economic inequalities are . . . to be to the greatest benefit of the least-advantaged members of society. . . ."

---

6. See John Rawls, *A Theory of Justice* (Cambridge, MA: Harvard University Press, 1971), pp. 80–82.

Rawls claims that people in the original position who know that they are choosing principles of justice for an industrial society such as the United States will value their equal basic civil and political liberties so much that they will not trade off any of these liberties for "the social and economic advantages regulated by the difference principle. For example, the equal political liberties cannot be denied to certain groups on the grounds that their having these liberties" interferes with efficiency and economic growth.[7] Rawls calls this "the priority of the first principle over the second. . . ."[8] He thinks people behind the veil will reason this way: An industrial society has the wherewithal to feed, clothe, house, medically treat, and educate everyone. Additional riches are fine, but not essential. Basic civil and political liberties, by contrast, are essential to a decent life. If I am denied the equal protection of the law to be free of unjustified physical assault, for example, additional affluence helps me little if it turns out, when the veil is lifted, that I belong to a minority subject to unjustified assault. Similarly, if I were to trade away my equal rights to assemble and vote I may be unable to defend myself against political intrigues that dispossess me. So, *people in the original position will not trade their basic civil and political liberties in order to promote increased efficiency and social wealth.*

Much of the political debate concerning inequality in the United States reflects views similar to Rawls's. Free-market conservatives often counter complaints about inequality with the claim that the prospect of great wealth is needed to motivate talented people to help the economy grow, and that when the economy grows, everyone benefits. A common phrase is "A rising tide lifts all boats." Free-market conservatives seem to agree with Rawls's view that differences in income and wealth require a justification and that benefiting the poor through a growing economy supplies that justification.

Many critics of free-market conservatism agree that increasing gaps between rich and poor would be acceptable if *everyone* really benefited, but, they contend, economic growth making some people rich is not really helping the poor and middle class. Kevin Phillips, a former advisor to President Ronald Reagan and now a critic of concentrated wealth, writes in *Wealth and Democracy:*

> With federal taxes as well as inflation allowed for, the average income of the median fifth of families actually declined by 1% between 1977 and 1994.

---

7. Rawls (2001), p. 47.
8. Rawls (2001), p. 46.

> Ordinary families gained amid the late 90s boom, but even in 1999, analysts found that the average real after-tax income of the middle 60% of the population was lower than in 1977—an extraordinary contrast with the huge gains of the top 1%.[9]

Worse yet, most Americans lost ground financially even though they worked more hours.

> Ordinary families pressed to maintain their purchasing power sent new waves of women into the labor markets. This gave the United States the world's highest ratio of two-income households, with its hidden, de facto tax on time and families. Whereas back in 1960 only 19% of married women with children under six had worked, by 1995 fully 64% did, exceeding the other industrial nations.

Americans in general work more than they used to and more than people elsewhere. The work year for average Americans increased 184 hours between 1989 and 1999, Phillips notes. "The Bureau of Labor Statistics reported that the typical American worked 350 hours more per year than [did] the typical European, the equivalent of nine work weeks."[10]

Phillips' objection to increasing gaps between rich and poor accords with Rawls's expectations about choices made in the original position. Both would object to the rich getting richer while the income and welfare of the poor and the middle class stagnate.

Let us now critically examine Rawls's principles of justice in reverse order of Rawls's presentation, starting with the difference principle.

The Difference Principle and Welfare

Rawls's principle that "social and economic inequalities are to . . . be to the greatest benefit of the least-advantaged members of society (the difference principle)"[11] has drawn criticism from libertarians and free-market conservatives. The libertarian Robert Nozick calls it "a patterned end-state principle."[12] With patterned end-state principles, justice does not emerge naturally from the free choices people make. Instead, justice requires a certain pattern of results, such as that specified by the difference principle. The least-advantaged members of society, according to the

9. Kevin Phillips, *Wealth and Democracy* (New York: Broadway Books, 2002), p. 111.
10. Phillips, p. 113.
11. Rawls (2001), p. 42–43.
12. Robert Nozick, *Anarchy, State, and Utopia* (New York: Basic Books, 1974), p. 209.

difference principle, must end up with the greatest advantages from any inequalities in society.

Libertarians object that such principles interfere with individual liberty and require repeated government intervention in the economy. Nozick gives this example: Suppose a famous athlete decides to come out of retirement on condition that fans at the games he plays in pay an extra dollar for their tickets and that he receives this additional dollar as a supplement to his salary. Imagine that many fans agree to this willingly, so team management agrees. Everyone is exercising individual liberty. But the result of this exercise of freedom is that if the famous player's income and wealth were previously in keeping with a pattern of income and wealth that Rawls would consider just, it is now far removed from that pattern because the famous player makes an extra $20,000 per game. Someone has gotten richer with no obvious benefit to society's poorest members. The only way to maintain the kind of pattern required by the difference principle, Nozick remarks wryly, is for the state "to forbid capitalist acts between consenting adults,"[13] or to take from some people and give to others whenever capitalist acts mess up the pattern.

Rawls can reply, however, that his difference principle does not limit or negate freedom by requiring repeated government intervention to reestablish a just pattern of income and wealth. Instead, legislators guided by the difference principle can pass laws that have the effect of reducing disparities in income and wealth between rich and poor. Such laws form the background conditions within which capitalist acts take place. In the United States, for example, federal income taxes are progressive; the federal government takes a larger percentage of income from rich than from poor people. Relatively rich people must give the federal government about 30% of each extra dollar they earn, whereas lower-income people may be required to give only 15% of each additional dollar, and the poorest pay no federal income tax at all. The effect is to reduce disparities in after-tax income between rich and poor. This is the kind of government policy that the difference principle promotes. It does not require repeated government interventions in the economy to meet a pattern of income distribution because the tax code is part of the relatively stable context within which economic transactions take place. In addition, widespread (although not universal) acceptance of progressive taxation suggests that the difference principle, or something like it, strikes most Americans as just.

---

13. Nozick, p. 163. Nozick's original example on pp. 161–63 concerns former basketball great Wilt Chamberlain. I have adapted that example.

194 Chapter 6: Rawls's Liberal Contractarianism

The difference principle would apply to government expenditures as well as taxes. Welfare laws, among others, fall into this category. They are predictable elements in the economic and social order that need change no more often than do other laws. They neither reverse economic decisions that individuals make nor interfere with capitalist acts between consenting adults, proponents claim. Welfare laws simply redistribute income and other benefits in a reasonably predictable way to help the least-advantaged members of society, as the difference principle suggests they should. Such laws have included Aid to Families with Dependant Children (AFDC) which gave cash to poor families with children; food stamps, which could be used to purchase inexpensive, healthful food; and Medicaid, which gives poor families a card they can use for free medical care.

Yet the relationship between the difference principle and **traditional welfare programs** is problematic. Many libertarians and free-market conservatives object that such programs, especially as they existed before 1996, divorced income from work. The programs divided the economic pie without due regard for the work needed to generate wealth in the first place. *Libertarians and free-market conservatives stress the importance of tying income and ownership to work.* Should the difference principle be interpreted to require work from the least advantaged who are able to work?

Self-respect is an important consideration. Welfare divorced from work deprives poor people of the dignity and self-respect that comes from work, earning money, and paying bills with earned money. For example, welfare critic James Payne writes, "Douglas Besharov of the American Enterprise Institute found that in 1992 the average unwed mother on welfare obtained a total of $17,434 a year in benefits, while the same woman working full-time (and also receiving some welfare benefits) ended up with $15,583."[14] Researchers Kathryn Edin and Laura Lein interviewed 214 welfare-reliant mothers. They found that most wanted to work, but low wages, job insecurity, and the loss of welfare benefits most often made working impractical. The following statement from a welfare-reliant mother in 1992 is typical, they claim:

> When you go get a job, you lose everything, just about. For every nickle you make, they take a dime from you. [I have been] on and off welfare. Like when I [tried] working at a nursing home, I was making $4.50 an hour, and they felt like I ma[de] too much money. Then

---

14. James L. Payne, "The High Value of Welfare Benefits Keeps the Poor on Welfare," excerpted from James L. Payne, *Overcoming Welfare: Expecting More from the Poor—and from Ourselves* (New York: BasicBooks, 1998), in *Welfare: Opposing Viewpoints,* James Haley, Ed. (Farmington Hills, MI: Greenhaven Press, 2003), pp. 20–28, at 24.

they cut me off. And I just couldn't make ends meet with $4.50 an hour, because I was paying for day care too. So I [had] to quit my job to get back on it. It took me forever to get back on, and meanwhile I had to starve and beg from friends. . . .[15]

This is a bad situation resulting from a divorce between work and benefits.

Rawls emphasizes the importance of self-respect. One type of primary good that he thinks all people need from society is "the social bases of self-respect, understood as those aspects of basic institutions normally essential if citizens are to have a lively sense of their worth as persons and to be able to advance their ends with self-confidence."[16] If work aids self-respect, traditional welfare programs were "aspects of basic institutions" that deprived the worst-off people of an essential component of the good life.

In addition, the difference principle's rationale depends on tying work to rewards. Some people are allowed to become richer than others so they will have the incentive of extra wealth and position to motivate hard work. *Poor people, too, can be expected to work harder when their work yields individual rewards.* So Rawls's difference principle suggests tying benefits to work wherever possible, and traditional welfare failed to do this.

The **earned income tax credit** is the type of program that Rawls could endorse. It ties government benefits to work and still helps the poor. People whose earnings fall below a certain level receive extra money from the government to supplement their income. Suppose, for example, that someone earning $8,000 per year does not have enough money to live decently, which requires $16,000 per year. The government could give a tax return of the additional $8,000 to this person when she files her income tax. As her income increases, the government could share the increase equally with her. If she earns $10,000 in a year, an additional $2,000, the government would reduce the $8,000 they were giving her by only $1,000, so her total income would go from $16,000 to $17,000. This would give her incentive to try to earn more money. On this schedule of reduced government payments, she would cease to get a check back when she earns $24,000 per year.

There are limitations to this approach, however. First, it does not take care of the truly disabled, who cannot work. In addition, many poor people cannot find jobs when the economy is slow. But if these people are

---

15. Kathryn Edin and Laura Lein, *Making Ends Meet: How Single Mothers Survive Welfare and Low-Wage Work* (New York: Russell Sage Foundation, 1997), excerpted in Haley, Ed., pp. 29–37, at 34.
16. Rawls (2001), p. 59.

simply given money without the need to work, the work ethic and self-respect may suffer. Third, earned income tax credits do not assure that society's worst-off members will gain whenever the rich get richer. If the rich get richer by keeping salaries low, such as through increased immigration, someone earning $8,000 per year may just continue earning that amount, or earning even less, and end up, when the earned income tax credit is figured in, with the same $16,000 as before. This problem could be remedied by tying the minimum total to the overall size of the economy, so when the economy grows by 5%, for example, the $16,000 minimum is raised 5%. However the details are worked out, *Rawls's difference principle supports government programs that help the worst-off group and tie benefits to work whenever possible.* This principle may be what people would consider just in the original position when, not knowing their positions in society, they want to protect themselves from bad outcomes.

Unequal Educational Opportunities

Rawls believes that people behind the veil of ignorance find inequalities acceptable only if each individual has a fair shot at attaining the more desirable positions. He writes, "social and economic inequalities are to . . . be attached to offices and positions open to all under conditions of fair equality of opportunity. . . ."[17] Such equality of opportunity requires many things. *Here we concentrate on the requirement that every child receive an education adequate to enable her to compete with all others. This ideal is far from realized in the United States.* Consider this story from the Associated Press about competition for slots in New York City's premier preschools. Yes, preschools!

> The race begins at 9 A.M. the day after Labor Day, as parents speed-dial the city's elite nursery schools in hopes of just getting an application. . . .
>
> Reports last week that former Wall Street analyst Jack Grubman may have elevated his rating of AT&T stock so Citigroup chief Sanford Weill would help Grubman's twins get into a top nursery school show how cutthroat admissions can be among the City's privileged.
>
> The prize—admission to the 10 or so best schools in the city for 2- and 3-year-olds—is perceived as the first step to the best kindergarten, the best college, the best connections.
>
> The children are "really with New York's best and brightest," said Victoria Goldman, author of *The Manhattan Directory to Private Nursery Schools.* . . . "It never hurts to rub elbows with the right ones."

---

17. Rawls (2001), p. 42.

> Some speak up to three languages already and are taught by teachers with master's degrees in early childhood education. . . . Annual tuitions can top $15,000.[18]

Compare this with the story Randall Robinson tells about 28-year-old Anna, a single parent with two children, and her 12-year-old daughter Sarah. They lived in

> a Boston public housing tenement. . . . The foyer, which smelled of urine, had two rows of mailboxes, all long ago rifled and mangled so far out of alignment that the metal doors would no longer lock. . . .
>
> Anna rose every day at 5:30 A.M., . . . ate toast made of day-old bread, roused her two children, and leaving them to fend for themselves, headed out in darkness by 6:30 A.M. to catch a train and two buses in order to arrive on time at her place of work.

In winter, Anna would arrive home after dark.

> It would be seven o'clock before she would ask both [children] about their homework assignments. Her questions were perfunctory. Having left school at 16, Anna had little if any capacity to help her children with schoolwork they couldn't understand. . . .
>
> By nine o'clock, Anna would climb into bed and lie sleepless with nameless worry. . . . She was . . . concerned . . . about whether Sarah would become pregnant in high school as Anna had, and lose what small chance she had of getting *out*.
>
> Anna was very tired. . . . She wanted her children, above all, to get an "education," though for her the word was little more than a mantra. . . .
>
> Anna did not own a car. She did not own a clothes washer or a dryer or a vacuum cleaner or a dishwasher. . . . Every necessary ordinary little task required a trip. A trip required a bus. A bus took time. Time she did not have. Her building had no washing machines, so she had to take a bus to the Laundromat.[19]

Sarah was falling behind in her reading, so school officials and people monitoring **Title I,** *a federal program designed to help poor children having problems in reading and math,* wanted to meet with Anna to see how, together, they could help Sarah succeed.

---

18. Amy Westfeldt, "It's Not What the Kids Know, It's Who the Parents Know," *The State Journal-Register* (Springfield, Illinois), (November 17, 2002), p. 42.
19. Randall Robinson, *The Debt: What America Owes to Blacks* (New York: Plume, 2000), pp. 63–65. Emphasis in original.

198 Chapter 6: Rawls's Liberal Contractarianism

Title I regulations required . . . the active involvement of parents in programs assisting their children. The people in Washington who wrote the laws had time to spend in their children's schools. They must have thought that Anna too could make time to spend in her children's. But, as was the case with the vast majority of the working poor, time was not Anna's to make. It was her supervisor's, and he was not sympathetic.

Anna finally met with school officials on a Saturday. Robinson continues the story:

"How many times have you been able to come to the Title I parent meetings at school in the last year, Mrs. Brown?" asked one of the white lawyers. . . .

"Well, I come when I can." This was an evasion. . . .

"But just how many times?"

"I have never been to one."

Anna told them about her life, in the idiom of her world, with no embarrassed fakery. She told them about the long hours spent on her job and at the Laundromat and cooking. . . . She told them about struggling to make it on a minimum-wage paycheck. . . .

"Do you read with Sarah at home?" asked the other white lawyer.

"Yes, as often as I can," answered Anna wearily. *Are these people Crazy? Have they listened to nothing I've said?* Anna looked at Ms. Cooper [Sarah's teacher]. . . .

Anna did not know that Sarah had been assigned to Ms. Cooper's class by computer. She also did not know that the school's principal considered Ms. Cooper to be one of his weakest teachers and that, computer assignments notwithstanding, students with parents likely to complain were never assigned to teachers like Ms. Cooper.[20]

Robinson concludes:

Give a black or white child the tools (nurture, nutrition, material necessities, a home/school milieu of intellectual stimulation, high expectation, pride of self) that a child needs to learn and the child *will* learn. . . .

Sarah was failing. She was failing when she should not have been. . . . Sarah was not failing because she was black. She was failing for the same reasons that Appalachian white children fail. Grinding, disabling poverty.[21]

---

20. Robinson, pp. 69–72. Emphasis in original.
21. Robinson, p. 78. Emphasis in original.

In sum, fair equality of opportunity does not exist in the United States, according to Robinson, because some people are so much poorer than others. Nevertheless, educational institutions can attempt to help children from poor backgrounds. Title I is such an attempt. Another attempt involves **school vouchers.**

Fair Equality of Opportunity and School Vouchers

The basic idea behind vouchers is to give parents choices regarding the schools their children attend. Parental choice requires schools to compete for students, and competition improves efficiency. Writing in 1979, Milton and Rose Friedman, free-market conservatives, believe that public schools show increasing inefficiency.

> In the five years from school year 1971–72 to school year 1976–77, total professional staff in all U.S. public schools went up 8%, costs per pupil went up . . . 11% after correction for inflation. *Input clearly up.*
>
> The number of students went *down* 4%, the number of schools went *down* 4%. And . . . the quality of schooling went *down* even more drastically. . . . That is certainly the story told by the declining grades recorded on standardized examinations. *Output clearly down.*[22]

Major reasons for the problem, they think, are lack of parental control and school accountability. "Excellent public schools" do exist, they point out, but they

> tend to be concentrated in the wealthier suburbs of the larger cities, where parent control remains very real. The situation is worst in the inner cities of the larger metropolises—New York, Chicago, Los Angeles, Boston. . . . Expenditures on schooling per pupil are often as high in the inner cities as in even the wealthy suburbs, but the quality of schooling is vastly lower. In the suburbs almost all of the money goes for education; in the inner cities much of it must go to preserving discipline, preventing vandalism, or repairing its effects.[23]

The Friedmans advocate encouraging parents of children in failing schools to transfer their children to more successful schools. Parents

---

22. Milton and Rose Friedman, *Free to Choose* (New York: Harcourt, Brace, Jovanovich, 1979), p. 156. Emphasis in original.
23. Friedmans, p. 158.

already have the right to seek admission for their children in private or parochial (religiously oriented) schools, but they must usually pay tuition because such schools are not supported by taxes. This discourages parents from transferring their children out of failing schools and into schools of parental choice where children tend to learn better.

> One example at the elementary level is a parochial school, St. John Chrysostom's, that we visited in one of the poorest neighborhoods in New York City's Bronx. . . . The youngsters are at the school because their parents chose it. Almost all are from poor families, yet their parents are all paying at least some of the costs. The children are well behaved, eager to learn. The teachers are dedicated. The atmosphere is quiet and serene.
>
> The cost per pupil is far less than in public schools. . . . Yet on the average, the children are two grades ahead of their peers in public school. That's because teachers and parents are free to choose how the children shall be taught. . . .
>
> Another example, this one at the secondary level, is . . . Harlem Prep, designed to appeal to youngsters for whom conventional education had failed. . . .
>
> The school was phenomenally successful. Many of its students went to college, including some of the leading colleges. But unfortunately . . . , the school ran short of cash.[24]

To reduce the financial difficulties of private and parochial schools, encourage competition among schools, and help parents choose their children's schools, the Friedmans propose that the state give parents vouchers that they can use to pay for their children's education at any accredited public, private, or parochial school.

Such voucher programs have since been tried. One such program was started in Cleveland, Ohio, because the inner-city schools were inadequately educating some of Ohio's poorest residents. Participating private (which here includes parochial) schools must cap their tuition at $2,500 per year. The poorest families are required to pay 10% of this sum, or do some work for the school, so the voucher from state funds is worth $2,250. Parents with higher incomes are required to pay up to 25% of the $2,500 per-year cost of private education from schools participating in the program.[25]

---

24. Friedmans, p. 159.
25. Brief for respondents in *Zelman v. Simmons-Harris* (December 14, 2001), 2001 WL 1636765, at westlaw.com, accessed October 14, 2002, p. 4 of 34.

The rationale for the program follows the Friedmans' reasoning. The idea is to help the poor attain fair equality of opportunity. According to a legal brief filed in November 2001 by the American Civil Rights Union (ACRU) defending Cleveland's program against legal challenge, the problems of poor education

> are most acute in our nation's lowest income areas, particularly among minority students. The most recent national test results show that over half of black and Hispanic 4th graders in the U.S. cannot read at the most basic level. Moreover, the gap in achievement between black and white students has been widening for almost 10 years. Low income and minority schools are also often plagued by violence, physical deterioration, high drop-out rates, and drug and alcohol abuse.[26]

The Cleveland public schools exemplified the problem. "Because of the disastrous educational performance of the Cleveland public schools, the court transferred control of the school district to the state of Ohio under a mandate to reform the system to improve performance. The school voucher program was part of the response of the state to this mandate."[27] The intention of the voucher program is to improve education in Cleveland by giving parents a choice of schools for their children.

> The point of school choice is to improve education performance in part by creating competition for public schools, forcing them to improve or lose students. Choice in any event would allow parents and students to gravitate to the schools that performed the best, improving overall education results. Most importantly, low-income and minority students would be able to choose schools that offered a sound education, enabling them to escape a life of poverty.[28]

Under this description, it seems that anyone who, like John Rawls, favors fair equality of opportunity should favor school voucher programs like the one in Cleveland.

There is another side, however. Opponents of voucher programs worry that the poorest of the poor will be left behind by such programs. First, they may be least able to pay $250 per child per year (or do work at the school instead) to take advantage of the voucher. Second, vouchers will not address the problems of physical violence and drug and alcohol abuse

---

26. Brief of Amicus Curiae American Civil Rights Union in Support of Petitioners, in *Zelman v. Simmons-Harris*, 2001 WL 1480652, at westlaw.com, accessed October 14, 2002, p. 8 of 14.

27. Brief of ACRU, p. 12 of 14.

28. Brief of ACRU, p. 6 of 14.

in public schools. Instead, vouchers may concentrate those problems in such schools. Private schools accepting vouchers do not have the public schools' mandate to serve the educational needs of all children. They can refuse to admit children with severe behavior problems and can expel students more easily and quickly than can public schools—and expel them permanently. As a result, children with the greatest behavior disorders, voucher opponents fear, will be concentrated in public schools. Those schools will become more dangerous and less functional, and children from the poorest families will be stuck in those schools because their parents cannot afford fees to send them elsewhere, even with the help of a voucher.

Third, many voucher proponents, such as Milton and Rose Friedman, advocate allowing parents to combine the voucher with money of their own to purchase a more expensive private education for their children than either the state provides through vouchers or the parents could afford without vouchers. This was not part of Cleveland's plan, which limited parental contributions and the total that any voucher-accepting school could charge in tuition. But allowing unlimited parental add-ons is a major issue in most voucher plans. The result of allowing unlimited parental add-ons would be financial segregation among students using vouchers to attend private schools. John Coons and Stephen Sugarman support vouchers but oppose allowing parental add-ons.

> Families unable to add extra dollars would patronize those schools that charged no tuition above the voucher, while the wealthier would be free to distribute themselves among the more expensive schools. What is today merely a personal choice of the wealthy, secured entirely with private funds [private education], would become an invidious privilege assisted by government. . . . This offends a fundamental value commitment—that any choice plan must secure equal family opportunity to attend any participating school.[29]

The Friedmans reject this criticism of add-ons with the observation that "public financing for hardship cases might remain," which they suppose would apply to 5 or 10% of school children. Apparently, they do not see a problem regarding equal opportunity if some parents can add $10,000 per year so their child can attend a school with a $12,000 tuition, whereas others, not in the hardship category, can add only $2,000 for an education that costs only $4,500 per year. Further, would hardship cases

---

29. John E. Coons and Stephen Sugarman, *Education by Choice: The Case for Family Control* (Berkeley: University of California Press, 1978), p. 191. Found in Friedmans, p. 167.

receive extra money so they could attend, say, schools that charge $4,500 per year instead of those charging only $2,500? Taxpayers would have to vote for this extra money to help the poorest children escape failing public schools and join their children in better schools. Will taxpayers adding a considerable sum to the voucher amount so their children can attend schools that are better than both the public schools and the poorer voucher schools want to spend more money just so their children can rub elbows with the children of society's poorest members? Opponents of add-ons think they will not. But without additional public help, the poorest of the poor may receive inexpensive, inferior instruction, whether in public schools (where children with discipline problems will be concentrated) or in the cheapest voucher schools.

Proponents of vouchers counter these speculations with evidence of success in pilot voucher programs.

> In-depth follow-up studies of the pioneering Milwaukee Parental Choice Program (MPCP) conclude, for example, that choice-program parents are more satisfied in every respect with their chosen private schools than with their former public schools. . . . Milwaukee parents are . . . much more likely to become involved in their child's education. . . . Like their parents, choice-program students are generally more involved in their schools. . . . And a mountain of evidence demonstrates that classrooms in school-choice programs are, on average, significantly more racially integrated than [are] their public school counterparts. . . . And three separate studies of the Milwaukee program conclude that MPCP students' performance is as good as or better than that of their public school counterparts.[30]

This sounds good, but are the poorest of the poor included, and are behavior problems increasingly concentrated in the public schools? There is still much we do not know.

Separation of Church and State

Cleveland's voucher plan was challenged in federal court, not on grounds that it fails to help the poorest children, because that is not a constitutional issue, but on grounds that it breaches the separation of church and state. *Through vouchers state money supports religious schools in Cleveland.* In the 1999–2000 school year, 82% of the participating schools were religiously oriented, and 96% of voucher students attended these

---

30. Reply Brief of State Petitioners in *Zelman v. Simmons-Harris*, January 22, 2002, 2002 WL 206360, at westlaw.com, accessed October 14, 2002.

schools. Some voucher opponents claimed that this violates the Establishment Clause in the First Amendment of the United States Constitution which says: "Congress shall make no law respecting the establishment of religion. . . ."

The Establishment Clause was added to the Constitution in 1791 to prevent the federal government from levying taxes to pay for some politically favored religion, as was the case in England where taxes supported the Anglican Church. Establishment Clause proponents wanted to disallow government sponsorship of religion so that religion would remain a matter of private individual or family decision. The Establishment Clause is now commonly interpreted to mean that no government entity, federal, state, or local, may show preference for one religion over others, nor may it show preference for religious over secular outlooks and pursuits. In 1971 the Supreme Court ruled that the Establishment Clause disallows state aid to church-affiliated schools.[31]

Opponents of Cleveland's voucher plan claimed that *the ability of parents to sign over state money to church-affiliated schools amounts to state aid to such schools in violation of the Establishment Clause.* Voucher schools are not allowed to discriminate against students based on religious affiliation, but they are free to use voucher money "not only to indoctrinate children of families belonging to the schools' respective religions but also to proselytize among the majority of the voucher students whose families are of religions other than the sponsors of the schools they attend."[32]

Many schools in the program are not shy about their religious mission. Here are some examples that opponents claim to be typical. "The Cleveland Diocese says in its District Plan for Catholic Schools: 'Our CATHOLIC IDENTITY will permeate every aspect of the school climate and program.'" A Lutheran school's statement of purpose includes this:

> The primary focus . . . is on our Lord and Savior, Jesus Christ. In all of our goals, Jesus Christ must be preeminent. Because of our commitment to that focus and to our beliefs and philosophy, it is highly inconsistent for any parents to send a child to this school if they: are not a Christian and/or are not interested in learning about Jesus Christ; are not living a Christian life or willing to learn how to lead such a life; are not a supporting part of a Christian congregation through worship and sharing of time and talents.

The handbook at Saint Francis School says: "We are a Catholic School which promotes Catholic values, traditions and morals. . . . Students are

---

31. See *Lemon v. Kurtzman*, 403 U.S. 602, especially 612–13 (1971).
32. Brief for Respondent, p. 6 of 34.

required to participate in religion classes, prayer, and worship held during the school day." The West Park Lutheran School Parent Handbook for 1999–2000 goes farther: "Children will be expected to attend church and Sunday School at least 75% of the Sundays during the school year. Church and Sunday School attendance will be taken in the classroom each Monday and noted on the child's report card."[33] The voucher plan clearly allows state money to support religiously sectarian goals. How can this be constitutional?

The answer, in a phrase, is parental choice. *The state is not choosing to support religious over secular education; the parents are choosing religious education for 96% of the children in the voucher program through their choice of religious schools.*

Program opponents say that this is not a free choice because the voucher program caps total school tuition, including parental contributions, at $2,500 per student per year. Religious organizations, which can draw on other contributions to the church, are best able to provide an education at such low tuition.

This reasoning seems to put voucher programs in a bind. If a program allows tuitions to increase through parental add-ons, it segregates voucher students financially, failing to provide them with fair equality of opportunity. But voucher programs that keep tuition rates low may bias voucher schools toward religious education, in violation of the Establishment Clause. Some people may conclude that voucher opponents are determined to be dissatisfied no matter what, whereas others may conclude that these unpalatable alternatives show that vouchers are a bad idea from the start.

In any case, voucher programs are relevant to a study of Rawls's political philosophy because they address an issue raised by the first part of Rawls's second principle of justice, the requirement that all people have fair equality of opportunity.

Liberal Neutrality, the Two Moral Powers, and Unencumbered Selves

The Establishment Clause concern about vouchers is relevant to Rawls's political philosophy in additional ways, all related to the heart of what Rawls thinks is essential about his and other liberal political philosophies. Liberals, according to Rawls, believe that *the state must remain*

---

33. Brief for Respondent, pp. 8–9 of 34. Capitalizations in original.

neutral about different values, goals, and plans of life. Because there is no one way of life, no one goal or set of shared values that can be shown superior to all others, Rawls believes that there is a **reasonable pluralism** of goals, values, and ways of life in liberal political societies. Such societies should welcome all of these in their diversity so long as they are compatible with the political conception of justice outlined in the two principles of justice.

People who share a particular outlook, goal, value, or way of life tend to form communities where they share the expression of their common views. Membership in communities requires commitment to specific values. Such communities include "churches and scientific societies, . . . but universities and other cultural institutions are also communities."[34] A community may exclude people who reject the community's view about values and ways of life, but a democratic political society must include everyone and remain neutral among the specific values and ideals of different communities the way the U.S. Supreme Court thinks the government should remain neutral regarding different religions and religious versus secular outlooks.

Given this background, what would Rawls say about the state providing vouchers that parents can use to support accredited schools that have different values and goals? Would Rawls think it reasonable for the state to support in this way a school dedicated to promoting salvation through Jesus of Nazareth? Would it matter if the school taught that all non-Christians are condemned by God to eternal damnation? What about a fundamentalist school that denies the theory of biological evolution, a Boy Scout school that teaches that homosexuality is morally evil, an all-girls science-oriented school, or a Black Panther school that advocates black self-help and withdrawal from, but not violence against, mainstream white society?

Unlike the Supreme Court, Rawls would be guided by his theory of justice, not by the U.S. Constitution. He would exclude only those approaches incompatible with his two principles of justice. He believes that promoting these principles requires cultivating people's **two moral powers.** These are, first, "the capacity for a sense of justice," which is "the capacity to understand, to apply, and to act from . . . the principles of political justice that specify the fair terms of social cooperation. . . ." People have to be willing and able to understand and abide by the two principles of justice. The second moral power is "a capacity for a conception of the good," which is "the capacity to have, to revise, and rationally to pursue a

---

34. Rawls (2001), p. 20.

conception of the good, . . . which specifies . . . what is of value in human life or, alternatively, . . . what is regarded as a fully worthwhile life."[35]

If a school taught children to hate and harm homosexuals, it would be working against the first of these two moral powers. It would be teaching people to violate "fair terms of social cooperation," which require, according to the first principle of justice, respect for "the equal basic liberties" of everyone. Aggression against homosexuals violates their equal basic liberties. But if a Boy Scout school teaching that homosexuality is evil advocates converting homosexuals peacefully, Rawls may have to condone the school even if he disagrees with its stand on sexual orientation. Its stand would express the values of that particular group, without endangering societywide cooperation. Rawls would analyze other possible voucher-supported schools in a similar way to test for compatibility with the first of the two moral powers. Some people may reject Rawls's account of public neutrality between different values and ways of life if it entails equal public funding for schools that oppose and schools that support interfaith marriage, coeducation of girls and boys, or nontraditional roles for women.

The second of the moral powers raises different problems. The second power includes, according to Rawls, "the capacity to have, to revise, and rationally to pursue a conception of the good."[36] It is Rawls's insistence that people be educated for the capacity *to revise* their conception of the good that raises difficulties. *Many communities persist by convincing young people to identify so closely with the community's values and way of life that breaking away is unimaginable.* Community membership, values, and life styles constitute part of who these people are, not just what they believe. Rawls seems committed to rejecting this kind of enculturation, whether the public pays for it or not. Rawls wants all people to be able rationally to revise their conception of the good and their ideas about what makes life worthwhile.

The first problem with Rawls's second moral power is that it seems to rule out many educational efforts that are currently considered acceptable. For example, most Catholic schools do not educate people to be intellectually flexible so they can revise their ideas about the impermissibility of divorce and contraception, to name but two matters central to human happiness and fulfillment. Catholic schools generally educate people to oppose divorce and contraception throughout their lives. Orthodox Jews do not educate their young to be flexible about the need to find a

---

35. Rawls (2001), pp. 18–19.
36. Rawls (2001), p. 19.

Jewish mate and avoid homosexuality. Fundamentalist schools do not want students ever to revise their belief that salvation comes only from Jesus Christ. It is hard to imagine these groups maintaining their integrity while educating people as Rawls seems to require.

The second problem, a corollary of the first, is that Rawls's state is not as neutral as he claims. Rawls thinks the best life is one in which people remain continuously open to new ideas, to considering different ways of life based on new information about worthy goals. Rawls thinks the state is neutral when it promotes cultivation of this flexibility, which is part of the second of the two moral powers. The problem is that this may be an attractive model for many people, but it is not neutral among competing conceptions of the good life, because many other people think that single-minded, lifelong commitment to certain unquestioned values makes the best life.

Finally, Michael Sandel argues that Rawls's conception of the good is really not possible anyway. Rawls imagines that people are who they are and then *have* certain commitments or values that they have taken on and can later alter or remove, rather like coats and gloves. But people relating in this way to their commitments and values would have to be people whose individuality exists without the encumbrance of fixed commitments and values. Sandel claims that such free-floating, dissociated people do not really exist.[37]

As people mature from infancy through childhood to adulthood, they increasingly become able to decide for themselves what is good and important. By the time they can decide most matters of great importance, however, they have already developed certain values and goals, committed themselves to some relationships, and accepted particular obligations. When I was 20 years old, for example, I had not yet decided to study and teach philosophy. I could have studied law or economics. Raised in a liberal Jewish tradition, I could have become a Quaker or a Unitarian. But my realistic options were limited by my being already socialized to be a certain kind of person. I was not a blank slate; I already had certain fixed obligations, values, and tastes that were part of my identity. There is no way that I would abandon my family if they needed me. I could not possibly have become a fundamentalist Christian or studied medicine (the-sight-of-blood thing), and my sexual preference was fixed. *People of an age to make important decisions already have identities that limit their options.* Rawls seems to ignore this when he suggests, through the second

---

37. See Michael J. Sandel, *Liberalism and the Limits of Justice* (Cambridge: Cambridge University Press, 1982), especially pp. 62–64 and 178–79.

moral power, that people should have unlimited openness to revising their "conception of the good," their "final ends and aims," and what they regard as "a fully worthwhile life."[38] (Rawls may just mean that people should be open to limited revisions; but he does not say so, and the first two objections given above would still apply.)

Equal Basic Liberties and Racial Profiling

One of Rawls's goals in his theory of justice is to overcome the difficulty that utilitarianism has regarding justice. We saw in Chapter 2 that utilitarian attempts to maximize the good (pleasure or preference satisfaction) may require treating some people unjustly. For example, utility may be maximized by punishing celebrity defendants more harshly than other lawbreakers and by socializing half the population to want to serve the other half without just compensation. *Rawls's first principle of justice guarantees that "each person has the same indefeasible claim to a fully adequate scheme of equal basic liberties, which scheme is compatible with the same scheme of liberties for all."*[39] This guarantee takes precedence in democratic societies (Rawls calls this "lexical priority") over any program of economic improvement. In other words, each individual has rights that the government should not violate no matter how much the common economic good may be advanced by such violations. To this extent, unlike utilitarianism, Rawls advocates respecting individual rights over advancing the good of the group.

Let us see how this might work out regarding some current controversies—racial profiling and affirmative action. We will only touch the surface of these complex matters to illustrate some uncertainties about Rawls's defense of individual rights.

Consider this account of racial profiling: A "well-dressed young African American man driving his Ford Explorer" is stopped by the highway patrol.

> He is on his way to Atlanta for a job interview. The stop, ostensibly for speeding, should not take long, he reasons. . . . But instead of simply asking for a driver's license and writing a speeding ticket, the trooper calls for backup. . . .
>
> The young man is told to leave the vehicle, as the troopers announce their intention to search it. "Hey, where did you get the money for something like this?" one trooper asks mockingly while he

---

38. Rawls (2001), p. 19.
39. Rawls (2001), p. 42. Emphasis added.

starts the process of going through every door panel. More disman-
tling of the vehicle follows. They say they are looking for drugs, but
in the end find nothing. After ticketing the driver for speeding, the
two officers casually drive off. Sitting in his now-trashed SUV, the
young man weeps in his anger and humiliation.[40]

Here a person's car is trashed by law-enforcement officials simply because
he is black. This seems unjust.

Defenders of racial profiling claim that law-enforcement officials tar-
geting blacks for special scrutiny are simply using their resources in the
most efficient way possible to deter and detect serious criminal activity.
John Derbyshire writes in the *National Review,* "in Department of Justice
figures for 1997, victims reported 60% of robberies as having been committed by black persons. In that same year, a black American was eight
times more likely than a nonblack to commit homicide. . . ."[41] Derbyshire
also quotes the black political activist Jesse Jackson's 1993 statement:
"There is nothing more painful to me at this stage in my life than to walk
down the street and hear footsteps and start thinking about robbery, then
look around and see somebody white and feel relieved."[42] Derbyshire
agrees with African-American Bernard Parks, former chief of the Los
Angeles Police Department, who said in 1999 that racial profiling is just
common sense.

Would Rawls approve? Unlike utilitarians, Rawls wants to protect
individuals from injustices perpetrated in the cause of promoting the overall best outcome for society in general. Racial profiling seems to be such
an injustice, because even if blacks as a group commit a disproportionate
number of violent crimes, the vast majority of blacks are as law-abiding as
anyone else. Yet police using racial profiling stop them, detain them,
search them, trash their cars, and make them late for appointments when
they have done nothing wrong or suspicious as individuals. Suspicion falls
on them merely because of race. Rawls suggests that any society with the
"economic means . . . , education . . . , [and] the many skills needed to run
a democratic regime" should avoid infringing the basic rights and liberties

40. Gene Callahan and William Anderson, "Racial Profiling Should Be Eliminated," in
     Discrimination: Opposing Viewpoints, Mary E. Williams, Ed. (Farmington Hills, MI:
     Greenhaven Press, 2003), pp. 160–69, at 161. Excerpted from Gene Callahan and
     William Anderson, "The Roots of Racial Profiling," *Reason,* August 2001.
41. John Derbyshire, "Racial Profiling Should Not Be Banned," in Williams, Ed.,
     pp. 170–79, at 178. Excerpted from "In Defense of Racial Profiling: Where Is Our
     Common Sense?" in *National Review,* February 19, 2001.
42. Derbyshire, pp. 174–75.

included in the first principle of justice. The only exception would be for "the defense of these equal liberties themselves."[43]

Is increased efficiency in the prevention and detection of violent crime, assuming for the moment that racial profiling is more efficient than the alternatives, adequate justification for infringing the basic rights and liberties of racial minorities? If race-neutral policing simply costs more money for the same level of safety, Rawls might oppose racial profiling. On this assumption, racial profiling improves economic efficiency at the expense of basic rights. The priority of the first principle of justice to the second forbids this. In any case, Rawls's response to racial profiling reveals the degree of difference between his views and those of the utilitarians he criticizes. If the difference is great, the issue of racial profiling can help people choose between Rawls's views and utilitarianism.

Equal Basic Liberties and Affirmative Action

Consider the relationship between equal basic liberties and affirmative action. Affirmative action has many forms, and there are many arguments pro and con that cannot be included here. We consider just one argument for one program. The University of Michigan Law School was sued by a rejected candidate, Barbara Grutter, who claimed that the school's affirmative action program violated her right to equal protection of the laws. The school's admissions policies took race into account. As a result, race could be the determining factor that results in one candidate's admission and another's rejection. The law school is a state institution. The state's unequal treatment based on race seems inconsistent with the Fourteenth Amendment's guarantee of equal protection of the laws. In at least one respect this is like racial profiling; the *state treats people differently merely because of race or ethnicity*.

The law school claimed that it needed to include race as one element in a complex set of considerations in order to promote diversity in the student body. Such diversity, they claimed, improves the general educational climate and overall educational opportunities at the school. The admissions policy includes preference for diversity of many kinds, but only preferences promoting racial diversity were challenged in court. Professor Richard Lempert, who chaired the committee that drafted the school's admissions policy, claimed that taking race into account served, as expressed by Justice Sandra Day O'Connor, "to bring to the Law School a perspective

---

43. Rawls (2001), p. 47.

different from that of members of groups which have not been the victims of such discrimination."[44] One can imagine that minority members currently targeted by racial profiling may have different perspectives on a range of issues than do other students. Unfortunately, without some racial preference in the admissions process, too few such minority-group members would be admitted most years to form "a number that encourages [them] to participate in the classroom and not feel isolated."[45] So, race-conscious admissions are justified, according to the law school, to provide the best education for all students. The Supreme Court accepted this rationale and approved the school's race conscious admissions standard.

How does this compare with racial profiling? In both cases, race is used as a factor to discriminate among people. But there are some important differences between racial profiling and affirmative action. Racial profiling relates to the provision of basic security and may therefore seem more justified than an affirmative action program designed merely to improve a school's educational climate.

On the other hand, racial profiling impairs the basic liberty rights of minorities, and the security it promotes may be provided, even if less efficiently, without any racial profiling. Admission to an elite law school, by contrast, does not affect anyone's basic liberties, and law schools cannot avoid discriminating among candidates for admission. The University of Michigan Law School receives about 3,500 applications to fill only 350 slots.

Second, elite institutions that must turn away most applicants typically use several criteria for admission, some of which have nothing to do with promoting diversity or with academic performance or potential. Such nonacademic criteria include the fact that the applicant is a celebrated college athlete or his parent is an alumnus. Some of these candidates may have less academic potential than Ms. Grutter, but no one objects.

Third, the diversity rationale for racial preference remains unchallenged regarding geographic preferences to promote a diverse student body that improves educational opportunities for everyone. No one objects if preference is given on the diversity rationale to a candidate because she is a Montana rancher with rodeo experience. But race attracts objections.

Justice Clarence Thomas, the only African-American member of the Supreme Court hearing Ms. Grutter's complaint, argued in dissent that race should be treated differently from other factors, such as geographic diversity. "The Constitution abhors classifications based on race, Thomas

---

44. *Grutter v. Bollinger,* 539 U.S. 306 (2003), at 319.
45. *Grutter,* O'Connor at 318.

claims. "Purchased at the price of immeasurable human suffering [i.e., slavery], the equal protection principle reflects our Nation's understanding that such classifications ultimately have a destructive impact on the individual and our society." To avoid repeating such destructiveness, the law should be color blind; race should not be used to classify people except when racial classifications are needed "to provide a bulwark against anarchy, or to prevent violence. . . ."[46] Classifications by geography are not similarly associated with gross injustice, were not the focus of the Fourteenth Amendment, and therefore are not constitutionally suspect.

In affirmative action contexts, however, the implications of this reasoning seem ironic. *Benefits based on racial membership are disallowed precisely because past racism was so unjust. Prior, uncompensated victimization of one's ancestors justifies denial of group-related benefits available to people on different group-related grounds, such as geographic origin. This is like reverse reparations; prior injustice justifies current deprivation of group-related benefits available to other groups.*

Justice Thomas has additional arguments, however. He claims that *racial preferences harm their intended beneficiaries who are often unprepared to compete well at the institutions that racial preferences enable them to attend.* They therefore fail in disproportionate numbers. Even when they graduate, Thomas believes, "there is no evidence that they have received a qualitatively better legal education (or become better lawyers) than if they had gone to a less 'elite' law school for which they were better prepared."[47] Racial preferences harm minority group members also by leaving the impression in the general population that people in the preferred group are incapable of succeeding without special preferences. This perpetuates racism and denies to those minority-group members who can and do succeed without preferences the recognition they deserve for their abilities and accomplishments.[48]

Finally, preferences in higher education, especially at elite schools, do not help the worst-off members of society, or the worst-off people in those preferred racial groups. Thomas writes, "it must be remembered that the Law School's racial discrimination does nothing for those too poor or uneducated to participate in elite higher education and therefore presents only an illusory solution to the challenges facing our nation."[49] This point would be of interest to Rawls, who thinks social institutions should be

---

46. *Grutter,* Thomas (dissent) at 353.

47. *Grutter,* Thomas (dissent) at 372.

48. *Grutter,* Thomas (dissent) at 373.

49. *Grutter,* Thomas (dissent) at 354, in footnote #3.

structured to benefit members of the worst-off group. Thomas is saying that blacks are not the worst-off group. He may concede that some blacks, disproportionate to their numbers in the American population, are in that group. But his point remains that these people are not the ones helped by affirmative action at the University of Michigan's law school.

Others may disagree, claiming that although most of the direct beneficiaries of Michigan's affirmative action program are relatively privileged, their preferment eventually helps all blacks indirectly. For example, as Justice O'Connor points out in her opinion for the court, "individuals with law degrees occupy roughly half the state governorships, more than half the seats in the United States Senate, and more than a third of the seats in the United States House of Representatives."[50] Additional representatives who understand the particular concerns of African Americans can help all black people, even the least advantaged. That is a plausible speculation, but it is just a speculation.

Some political liberals favor affirmative action because they think it generally helps disadvantaged people, whether directly or indirectly, and promotes overall, long-term social well-being. But even if they are correct about disadvantaged people and overall social well-being, is affirmative action consistent with giving priority, as Rawls says we should, to individual human rights? It seems to sacrifice the individual rights of people excluded from favorable positions merely on account of race.

If we take individual rights as seriously as Rawls, however, can we endorse racial profiling? *It seems that some people would sacrifice individual rights (consider people more as group members than as individuals) to promote social welfare through law enforcement, but not through affirmative actions. Others take exactly the opposite stand, wanting to consider people as group members, rather than as individuals, in the context of affirmative action, but not in the context of law enforcement. Both sides need to explain why individual rights are overriding in one context but not the other.* It is not clear that either side agrees with Rawls about the priority of individual rights.

CONCLUSION

Rawls's liberal contractarianism is attractive to many people for several reasons. It bases state legitimacy on the consent of the governed, even if it is only hypothetical consent in the original position. It associates consent with contractual agreement, which is attractive because contracts are familiar forms of consent in commercial contexts, usually meant to promote

---

50. *Grutter*, O'Connor at 332.

mutual benefit. The idea that the state governs for mutual benefit is attractive. Protections for individual rights in Rawls's first principle of justice resonate with the individual rights tradition strong in the United States and embodied in the Constitution's Bill of Rights. The idea that the state should generally be neutral among different ideals of life is also attractive to most Americans who want to be able to join groups of their own choosing or just go their own way with minimal government interference. Economically, most people favor equal opportunity and resent an economic elite benefiting in society much more than others. They therefore welcome Rawls's second principle of justice, which endorses fair equality of opportunity and the difference principle.

Rawls's liberal contractarianism, however, does not please everyone. Some people are not content to have the state neutral among different, competing visions of the good life, as Rawls proposes. If some societies are better than others, they think, the state should foster social change in the direction of social improvement. Proponents of communitarianism, moral conservatism, multiculturalism, feminism, and environmentalism, as we shall see in coming chapters, criticize liberalism on this ground. It seems, in addition, that Rawls's proposal fosters a society that is not actually neutral anyway; his society favors individualism and flexibility over community and group commitments. Communitarianism, as we shall see in the next chapter, faults liberalism for being overly individualistic.

JUDGMENT CALLS

1. Rawls's principles apply only to relationships among people. How might a liberal contractarian justify opposition to the cruel treatment of animals?

2. If the government provides vouchers for education, should public money be used for a Christian school that teaches girls that women should be subordinate to men? What about a Jewish school that promotes arranged marriages among traditional Jews or an all-girls school that promotes scientific achievement among women? How can people justify on liberal contractarian grounds favoring some options over others?

3. Is racial profiling justified in the war against terrorism? Relate this to Rawls's belief that the first principle of justice has priority over the second.

4. How might a school voucher program help or hurt Sarah, the 12-year-old daughter of Anna, whose plight was described by Randall Robinson?

Reflective Equilibrium: where principles of
justice are provisionally settled upon
↳ both open to revisions

216 Chapter 6: Rawls's Liberal Contractarianism

5. Consider this voucher proposal. In any given year, the voucher is worth exactly as much as the school district spends on public education per child. Voucher schools would have to be accredited, but they could be religious or secular. No parental or other add-on money would be allowed, so a church or a foundation, for example, would not be able to make one school richer than others. Voucher schools would have to include children on the same basis as the public schools, including those with disabilities and behavior disorders. Parents may avoid both public and voucher schools only by home schooling or sending their children to private (or parochial) school with no state aid at all. How does this relate to the free-market conservative ideal of school improvement through competition? What might Rawls and other liberals think?

6. Should state-supported universities be forbidden to consider any nonacademic qualifications of applicants, such as their athletic ability, the geographic area where they were raised, or their relationship to alumni or major benefactors? Consider the views of utilitarians, free-market conservatives, and contractarians.

2 Principles of
Justice:
1.

Obligatory vs. Superogatory
↓
- Obligations of justice   - Obligations of beneficience
↳wrong not to fulfill   - obligations desirable to fulfill
- Linked to institutions
        (political)
            * priority of right to the good
            * maximin principle
Social Contract
    - Justify the state → link liberty to rightful rule by
                        mutual obligations b/w citizens & state

    - Hobbes: one authority of people reflected in one rule
    - Locke: one authority of people reflected in multiple
                                        instit.
        - Rousseau: one authority → rule by themselves
        - Kant: one authority → "Right Justice" (people + institutions)
? * - Rawls: one authority →

7 Communitarianism and Moral Conservatism

[Handwritten annotations:]
Libertarianism, Free-Market Conservatism + Liberal contractarianism
- Individualism: individual rights, freedoms, liberties + opp.
  ↳ primary goal of state → protect rights & promote situations that foster that
- Political liberalism: states should remain neutral regarding values, goals, & actions that don't interfere w/ autonomy

In spite of their differences concerning competition and equal opportunity, libertarianism, free-market conservatism, and liberal contractarianism have much in common. All three advocate **individualism** and **political liberalism.** Individualism emphasizes individual rights, liberties, and opportunities. The state's primary goal is to protect individual rights and promote development of social and economic conditions in which people can flourish through pursuit of their individually chosen goals. Political liberalism adds the corollary that the state should remain neutral regarding values, goals, and actions that do not directly interfere with anyone's **autonomy** (or self-determination).

[Handwritten annotation:] ✱ Individualist obligations ✱

Individualist obligations are of only two kinds. First, there are universal obligations, obligations owed to everyone—to obey the law, tell the truth, and generally respect the rights and autonomy of others. Second, there are special obligations that people incur voluntarily through individually agreed contracts, promises, and the like.

[Handwritten annotation:] communitarians & moral conservatives believe state must play a role

Rejecting such individualism, communitarians and moral conservatives believe that people have additional obligations based on community commitments and traditions. Some of these obligations are inherited, rather than chosen, and are specific to individuals or groups, rather than universal. What is more, communitarians and moral conservatives reject political liberalism; the state cannot be, and should not try to be, neutral among competing goals. Some individually chosen goals that do not directly interfere with anyone's autonomy may degrade community life. Instead of trying to accommodate all individual preferences, the state should limit individual choice and guide people toward morally preferred paths. The belief that the state should sponsor a particular vision of virtue and the good life is called **perfectionism.** *[Handwritten:]* Sponsor particular vision of virtue

(The terminology above may be confusing because it includes free-market conservatives among political liberals. I am sorry about this, but these terms developed historically. In the 19th century, the view we now call (free-market) conservatism was called "liberal" because *free-market*

217

conservatives advocate (nearly) maximum *individual liberty,* and it was considered liberal to promote liberty. *Moral* conservatives, by contrast, are not political liberals because they would restrict liberty to promote morality.)

We will find that communitarians and moral conservatives introduce several helpful concepts. They correctly claim that political liberalism is not really morally neutral and that attempting neutrality ties political liberals to some questionable policies. But moral conservatives seem committed to some questionable policies of their own, especially regarding women. Also, communitarian programs imply more radical changes in social policies and goals than communitarians acknowledge.

The Benefits of Community Orientation

The story of football star Pat Tillman illustrates the devotion to community over individual pursuits that communitarians and moral conservatives advocate. Tillman starred at Arizona State University, where he earned a 3.84 grade point average, and was in the middle of a successful professional career with the Arizona Cardinals of the National Football League when he and his brother joined the military. They did so in Denver to avoid publicity, wrote Dirk Johnson and Andrew Murr in *Newsweek:*

> Tillman gave up a $3.6 million contract to join the harrowing world of life as an Army Ranger.... Rangers are sent to places where the danger is the worst. That's where Tillman was on Thursday [April 22, 2004]. Dusk was falling and the new moon hadn't risen yet—the darkest time of the night for eyes still smarting from the blinding mountain sun and daytime temperatures of 105 degrees. Military officials say that Tillman's unit was ambushed in a region [of Afghanistan] where [al] Qaeda forces sneak across from Pakistan.
>
> Tillman wanted no attention, no glory, for joining the rank and file. He "didn't want to be singled out from his brothers and sisters in the military," says former Cardinals coach Dave McGinnis. Tillman apparently made a pact with his family to stay silent about his service, a promise they have kept.[1]

So why did he do it? It seems that after the terrorist attacks of September 11, 2001, Tillman felt he had a duty to his community, past and present, to join the fight against terrorism. He told a team camera crew, almost in shame, six months before he enlisted: "You know, my

---

1. Dirk Johnson and Andrews Murr, "A Heroic Life," *Newsweek,* Vol. CXLIII, No. 18 (May 3, 2004), pp. 27–28, at 28.

great-grandfather was at Pearl Harbor, and a lot of my family have . . . fought in wars. . . . I haven't done a damn thing as far as laying myself on the line like that."[2] Apparently, Tillman's conception of the good life placed community service ahead of individual reward.

Contrast this with events of March 13, 1963, in Kew Gardens, a mostly residential section of Queens in New York City. About 3:20 A.M. Kitty Genovese was returning home and parked her car near her apartment. *New York Times* reporter Marty Ganzberg picks up the story from there:

> Miss Genovese noticed a man at the far end of the [parking] lot. . . . She halted. Then, nervously, she headed up Austin Street toward Lefferts Boulevard, where there is a call box to the 102nd Police Precinct in nearby Richmond Hill.
>
> She got as far as a street light in front of a bookstore before the man grabbed her. She screamed. Lights went on in the 10-story apartment house at 82-67 Austin Street, which faces the bookstore. Windows slid open and voices punctured the early-morning stillness.
>
> Miss Genovese screamed: "Oh, my God, he stabbed me! Please help me! Please help me!"
>
> From one of the upper windows in the apartment house, a man called down: "Let that girl alone!"
>
> The assailant looked up at him, shrugged and walked down Austin Street toward a white sedan parked a short distance away. Miss Genovese struggled to her feet.
>
> Lights went out. The killer returned to Miss Genovese, now trying to make her way around the side of the building by the parking lot to get to her apartment. The assailant stabbed her again.
>
> "I'm dying!" she shrieked. "I'm dying!"
>
> Windows were opened again, and lights went on in many apartments. The assailant got into his car and drove away. . . . It was 3:35 A.M.
>
> The assailant returned. By then Miss Genovese had crawled [inside the outer door of her apartment building]. The killer tried the first door; she wasn't there. At the second door, 82-62 Austin Street, he saw her slumped on the floor at the foot of the stairs. He stabbed her a third time—fatally.[3]

It was not until 3:50 A.M. that a neighbor called the police; they arrived in just two minutes. Had that neighbor or any one of the 38 people who

---

2. Johnson and Murr, p. 27.

3. Quoted in A. M. Rosenthal, *Thirty-Eight Witnesses* (New York: McGraw-Hill, 1964), pp. 33–36.

heard the screams called the police after the first, or even after the second attack, Miss Genovese would likely have survived. Why did no one call? Ganzberg reports:

> The police said most persons had told them they had been afraid to call, but had given meaningless answers when asked what they had feared. . . . Lieutenant Jacobs said . . . , "where they are in their homes, near phones, why should they be afraid to call the police?[4]
>
> A housewife . . . said, "We thought it was a lover's quarrel." A husband and wife both said, "Frankly, we were afraid. . . ." A distraught woman, wiping her hand in her apron, said, "I didn't want my husband to get involved."
>
> A man peeked out from a slight opening in the doorway to his apartment and rattled off an account of the killer's second attack. Why hadn't he called the police at that time? "I was tired," he said without emotion. "I went back to bed."[5]

In a politically liberal society that champions individual freedom, people are legally free to mind their own business. None of the 38 witnesses had broken the law. But is this the kind of society we want? Communitarians think not. Preoccupation with our individual lives and goals should be balanced by attention to the public good, not primarily through legal imposition of additional duties but through actions undertaken freely in a spirit of public participation, like Pat Tillman's decision to join the military.

[handwritten: Communitarians → must be balance b/w Individual lives + goals + community]

Encumbered Individuals and Living Traditions

Communitarians claim that political liberals favor individual autonomy over communal good because liberals view the individual as essentially unencumbered. An **unencumbered self** is *an individual whose identity makes no essential reference to other people.* **Encumbered selves,** by contrast, *have attachments and obligations to particular individuals and groups that partly constitute their identity.* Pat Tillman, for example, acted as an encumbered person because his self-concept included reference to relatives who helped to defend the country. He felt constrained in his individual choices by their example. The 38 witnesses to Kitty Genovese's murder, however, felt unencumbered by community ties, so they avoided "getting involved" and failed to call the police.

[handwritten: Unencumbered vs. Encumbered / unattached vs attached]

---

4. In Rosenthal, p. 42.
5. In Rosenthal, pp. 44–45.

Communitarian Michael Sandel[6] argues that no entirely unencumbered selves really exist. We all have "loyalties and convictions whose moral force consists partly in the fact that living by them is inseparable from understanding ourselves as the particular persons we are—as members of this family or community or nation or people, as bearers of this history, as sons and daughters of that revolution, as citizens of this republic."[7] As an American, for example, I probably feel more connection to the 19th-century treatment of Native Americans than many Germans feel, whereas many Germans feel more connected to the holocaust, even if they were born after World War II. The reason is that I am part of the American nation whose current size and composition reflects, among many other factors, past genocide of Native Americans. Current Germans are part of a nation and culture that included the holocaust. As human beings, we all inherit this kind of baggage. But it is not all bad. As an American I take pride in my country's invention of jazz, although it took place before my birth, and Germans properly take pride in the poets, philosophers, and musicians who make German culture beautiful and profound.

The encumbrances of loyalty to community, nation, or religion do not eliminate individual autonomy, communitarians maintain. I am free to influence the kind of person I become. However, because of encumbrances not of my choosing, my goal is not to become just any kind of person that I might autonomously want. Instead, my goal is **authenticity.** The authentic individual recognizes that her choices help to shape who she is, but they do not entirely constitute her identity. Instead, *she starts out with historical baggage, both good and bad, from family, country, culture, and so forth that give her life story some fixed elements and direction. She must choose how to extend this story into the future as she faces opportunities for decision. Her goal is to be her own best self.*

Communitarian Alasdair MacIntyre[8] emphasizes that *the narrative element in human decision making is communal, not just individual. We decide what to do, how to continue our particular stories, on the basis of the stories told in our culture.*

6. Sandel was associated with philosophical communitarianism during its formative period in the 1980s, when it concentrated on criticizing Rawls's political liberalism. Sandel's classification as a communitarian since that time has been contested.

7. Michael J. Sandel, *Liberalism and the Limits of Justice* (New York: Cambridge University Press, 1982), p. 179.

8. MacIntyre was associated with philosophical communitarianism during its formative period in the 1980s, when it concentrated on criticizing Rawls's political liberalism. MacIntyre's classification as a communitarian since that time has been contested.

> I can only answer the question "What am I to do?" if I can answer the prior question "Of what story or stories do I find myself a part?" We enter human society, that is, with one or more imputed characters—roles into which we have been drafted—and we have to learn what they are in order to be able to understand how others respond to us and how our responses to them are apt to be construed. It is through hearing stories about wicked stepmothers, lost children, good but misguided kings . . . that children learn or mislearn both what a child and what a parent is, what the cast of characters may be in the drama into which they have been born, and what the ways of the world are.[9]

A culture's stories reflect its particular conception of the good life. "What the good life is for a 5th-century Athenian general will not be the same as what it was for a medieval nun or a 17th-century farmer,"[10] MacIntyre writes. I must fit my story into my society's historically continuous narrative or **tradition,** which legal philosopher Michael Perry defines as "a history or narrative in which the central motif is an aspiration to a particular form of life, to certain projects, goals, [and] ideals. . . ." A **community,** Perry adds, is "a group of persons united principally by their identification of themselves as the present bearers of, and participants in, a tradition."[11]

Traditions are not static and do not dictate how people should behave. Instead, they form the context within which people debate the good for themselves individually and collectively. MacIntyre writes:

> So when an institution—a university, say, or a farm, or a hospital—is the bearer of a tradition . . . , its common life will be partly, but in a centrally important way, constituted by a continuous argument as to what a university is and ought to be or what good farming is or what good medicine is. Traditions, when vital, embody continuities of conflict. . . . A living tradition then is an historically extended, socially embodied argument, and an argument precisely in part about the goods which constitute the tradition.[12]

The 38 witnesses to Kitty Genovese's murder were criticized for their inaction. Typical letters to the Editor of the *New York Times* included this one:

> I feel it is the duty of the *New York Times* to try to obtain the names of the witnesses involved and to publish the list. . . . These people

9. Alasdair MacIntyre, *After Virtue* (Notre Dame, IN: University of Notre Dame Press, 1981), p. 201.
10. MacIntyre, p. 204.
11. Michael J. Perry, *Morality, Politics, and Law* (New York: Oxford University Press, 1988), p. 137.
12. MacIntyre, pp. 206–07.

should be held up for public ridicule, since they cannot be held [legally] responsible. . . .

Apparently these 37 people [one of the 38 eventually called the police, when it was too late] feel no moral obligation to their fellow men. Therefore constant reminders in the newspapers are necessary to show them the contempt in which other morally responsible citizens hold them.[13]

MacIntyre might interpret this letter as part of the ongoing argument in our cultural tradition about what neighbors owe to one another simply because they are neighbors, regardless of any other social relationship between them. Individual autonomy, which allows people to ignore the needs of neighbors whom they have not specifically agreed to help, is part of our political tradition, as political liberals correctly point out. But it is not the entirety of that tradition, as negative reactions to the 38 witnesses attest.

Sandel believes that glorification of autonomy is unrealistic because we all have essential attachments and obligations to others without specific agreement. No one is entirely unencumbered. We must therefore decide which encumbrances we want to acknowledge or emphasize. This often involves legislation as well as personal decision.

Unencumbered Selves and No-Fault Divorce

The communitarian concept of encumbered selves helps to explain why some people object to no-fault divorce. Moral conservative William Bennett believes that "the stunning separation between megastar Meg Ryan and actor Dennis Quaid after nine years of marriage" illustrates what is lacking in marital commitment today. Following the July 17, 2000 account in *People* magazine, Bennett notes,

By all accounts, Ryan and Quaid were one of Hollywood's "golden couples," happily married and devoted parents of an eight-year-old son, Jack. "I loved him [when I married him], and love him now," Ryan said of Quaid only . . . months earlier. . . . Quaid told reporters . . . , "For me, family is most important."

But then came the filming of *Proof of Life,* and Meg Ryan met the New Zealand actor Russell Crowe. In June, the two flew to London to shoot extra scenes, and rumors emerged. . . . On June 28 came the announcement of a separation. . . .

---

13. Rosenthal, pp. 53–54.

Associates say Quaid was deeply shaken . . . [and] very concerned about the effects on his son. But Meg Ryan's mother, Susan Jordan, told reporters . . . "I think Russell is exciting and is giving her something that was clearly lacking in her marriage." Six months later it was over.[14]

Communitarian Michael Sandel ties casual attitudes toward marriage and changes in American divorce law to the increasing influence of the liberal idea that people are essentially unencumbered individuals. "For over a century," Sandel writes,

> divorce law reflected and enforced a particular ideal of marriage. . . . This ideal included duties of lifelong mutual responsibility and fidelity, tied to traditional gender-based roles. The husband had the duty of economic support; the wife, the duty of domestic service. . . . Only a serious breach of moral duties, such as adultery, cruelty, or desertion, provided grounds for divorce. The obligations of marriage could persist long after divorce, in the form of alimony payments by the husband to his former wife.[15]

Then, starting in 1970, no-fault divorce became the norm. People can dissolve their marriages to promote individual self-fulfillment, regardless of moral fault. Marital assets and future incomes are divided to provide for everyone's economic needs without reference to any moral failings that may have precipitated the divorce. Alimony, once owed for a lifetime, became a transitional means of helping the poorer partner establish her own means of support. "By 1978," Sandel notes, "only 17% of divorced women were awarded any alimony at all."[16]

Sandel relates these developments to political liberalism's promotion of unencumbered selves and neutrality among competing visions of the good life.

> First, the rejection of fault as grounds for divorce and property settlements reflects the liberal resolve to bracket moral judgments, to make law neutral among competing conceptions of the good. As in liberal theories of distributive justice, so now in divorce settlements, distributive shares are not intended to reward virtue but simply to meet the economic needs of the parties. . . .

---

14. William J. Bennett, *The Broken Hearth: Reversing the Moral Collapse of the American Family* (New York: Doubleday, 2001), pp. 89–90.

15. Michael J. Sandel, *Democracy's Discontent: America in Search of a Public Philosophy* (Cambridge, MA: Harvard University Press, 1996), pp. 108–09.

16. Sandel (1996), p. 109.

Second, the provision for divorce as a unilateral decision without mutual consent, the rejection of marital roles tied to lifelong obligations, and the emphasis on self-sufficiency after divorce all reflect the liberal conception of persons as unencumbered selves independent of their roles and unbound by moral ties they choose to reject. The old law treated persons as situated selves, whose identity as legal persons was tied to their roles as husbands, wives, and parents.[17]

Sandel claims that no-fault divorce is not as neutral as its proponents claim because it requires prudent women to develop careers even if they would prefer to remain home raising children. Their partner may end the marriage and leave them impoverished if they have not developed a career of their own. This has happened to many women, Sandel reports: "For men, divorce brings a 42% increase in standard of living, while divorced women and their children suffer a 73% decline."[18] Divorce is now a major cause of poverty among women and their children. However, when both marriage partners develop careers to avoid poverty in case of divorce, family life suffers as people "invest less in the family than in their individual lives and careers."[19]

Communitarian sociologist Amitai Etzioni suggests changes in current divorce law to make divorce more difficult and to send a symbolic message about the importance of marriage. He writes:

> When we changed the laws that apply to divorce to make it "no fault," far from being viewed as a technical change or as [a] way to make divorce less costly, many considered the new law to be one more indication that the community was less troubled by easy divorce than it had been. For much the same reason, if we were now to enact somewhat stricter divorce requirements, it would signal that we were restoring our respect for the family.[20]

One idea for divorce reform comes from Britain's Law Commission. A couple would have to wait nine months from the time they first declare their intention to divorce to the time of actual divorce. "The idea is that this would encourage parents to concentrate on the results of a family breakup [especially the effects on children] and possibly discourage the divorce."[21] Divorce tends to harm children not only financially

---

17. Sandel (1996), pp. 111–12.
18. Sandel (1996), p. 111.
19. Sandel (1996), p. 115.
20. Amitai Etzioni, *The Spirit of the Community: Rights, Responsibilities, and the Communitarian Agenda* (New York: Crown Publishers, 1993), p. 48.
21. Etzioni, p. 81.

but emotionally and socially as well. The University of Chicago's Jean Bethke Elshtain notes:

> There is a high correlation between broken homes and a whole range of troubles for children. Three out of four teenage suicides occur in households where a parent has been absent. Eighty percent of adolescents in psychiatric hospitals come from broken homes. Tracking studies report that five out of six adolescents caught up in the criminal justice system come from families where a parent (usually the father) is absent.[22]

In sum, "according to the National Commission on Children, those growing up in single-parent households are at greater risk than those in two-parent households for poverty, substance abuse, adolescent childbearing, criminality, suicide, mental illness, and dropping out of school."[23] A communitarian or moral conservative critic of Rawls could justifiably complain that his liberal support for fair equality of opportunity is hollow if it does not include measures to discourage the divorce of couples with children.

Legal Prostitution vs. the Practice of Marriage

Lifelong marriage is clearly a valuable social institution. Yet political liberals, whether libertarians, free-market conservatives, or liberal contractarians, find it hard to justify opposing legalized prostitution, even if it damages the institution of marriage. The communitarian concept of a *practice*, in contrast, allows communitarians to make powerful arguments against legalizing prostitution.

Let us consider first why political liberals seem committed to supporting legalization. Legalizing prostitution expands the scope for the legal expression of individual autonomy and provides economic opportunities that can aid economic growth. Columnist George Will expresses a libertarian position that stresses increased freedom.

> The reasons for decriminalizing prostitution ... [involve] respect for privacy, liberty, [and] the Constitution.... Prostitution is immoral, but it is not a threat to the fabric of society. Because prostitution is private sexual conduct between consenting adults the state

---

22. Jean Bethke Elshtain, "Society's Well-Being Depends upon the Traditional Family," in *American Values: Opposing Viewpoints*, Jennifer A. Hurley, Ed. (San Diego: Greenhaven Press, 2000), pp. 54–62, at 55.

23. Elshtain, p. 60.

should not proscribe it unless the state can demonstrate that it involves substantial harmful public consequences. But the harmful public consequences associated with prostitution are either unaffected by attempts to proscribe it or are produced by those attempts. . . .

The evils of prostitution include the mistreatment of prostitutes by employers and clients. Legalization would allow prostitutes recourse to police protection, thereby reducing this evil. Another evil concerns the spread of sexually transmitted diseases. Legalization would allow licensing prostitutes and requiring periodic health exams to reduce the transmission of disease. Finally, Will argues, "anti-prostitution laws invariably violate the right to privacy. . . . Usually in their words and invariably in their application [they also] violate the equal protection provisions of the Constitution by discriminating against women."[24]

These libertarian (politically liberal) considerations can be joined by considerations of economic growth that free-market conservatives emphasize. With less likelihood of contracting disease, more people may be willing to frequent prostitutes. With less likelihood of being subjected to illegal violence, more people may be willing to serve as prostitutes. Prostitution would likely increase. It is a business that helps the economy grow, and legal prostitution would be taxed, thereby reducing the tax burden on other people who would then have more money to spend on consumer items.

Liberal contractarians could agree with all the preceding points and add that legalization would tend to help some of the poorest members of society, as few people enter the profession from positions of privilege. Besides getting police protection, legal prostitutes could form unions and bargain for better pay and working conditions.

Opponents of prostitution often concentrate on its tendency to weaken the institution of marriage. Philosopher Gerald Runkle, for example, opposes prostitution because it involves sex outside marriage. He writes:

> We must ask ourselves whether the institution of marriage is good. For if it is, then anything that corrupts or weakens it is bad. The family is a partnership between the husband and wife, economic and social as well as sexual. . . . Each has chosen a person whom he or she loves in a way no other can be loved. While benevolence and friendship may go out to others, conjugal love is unique. What is shared

---

24. George F. Will, "Prostitution Should Be Decriminalized," *The Washington Post* (August 26, 1974). Reprinted in Robert Baum, Ed., *Ethical Arguments for Analysis*, 2nd ed. (New York: Holt, Rinehart and Winston, 1976), p. 80.

228 Chapter 7: Communitarianism and Moral Conservatism

with people outside the union is no longer unique and special when accorded to the spouse. . . . In choosing a spouse, we give up certain familiarities with others. Adultery . . . is destructive of that special and unique relationship.[25]

If legalizing prostitution makes it safer and easier for married people to have sex outside marriage, Runkle would oppose it.

We have seen that, at least for child rearing, lifelong marriage is a valuable social institution. Communitarian Alasdair MacIntyre might call it a **practice,** which is *a socially defined, complex activity with internal goods whose achievement requires development of skills or virtues that are specific to that kind of activity.* MacIntyre's initial example of a practice is the game of chess. It is a practice because it requires development of "a certain highly particular kind of analytical skill, strategic imagination, and competitive intensity. . . ."[26] These qualities are **internal goods** related to the game of chess. Someone who loves the game will value improving her skills, imagination, and competitiveness simply because they make her better at chess. Of course, if she gets good enough she may also win fame and fortune, which are **external goods** in relation to chess because they can be obtained through success in any number of activities; they are not peculiar to chess. Similarly, portrait painting is a practice with both internal and external goods. The external goods are mostly the same as with chess—fame and fortune—but the internal goods are completely different. A successful portrait displays a subject's true personality through depiction of her outward appearance.

There are many other practices in society, including farming, architecture, politics, business management, and the writing of poetry, drama, history, and novels. Each practice calls for development of particular skills or virtues, which are the goods internal to the practice that help to define it. Like traditions, practices evolve through regular consideration of possible improvements, but so long as the practice promotes human excellence and meets important human needs, it should not be destroyed.

Marriage, as Runkle and other proponents describe it, is a valuable practice. It contains its own, particular kind and combination of love, commitment, closeness, vulnerability, security, and common purpose unobtainable in other relationships. It requires development of skills and virtues to make it work, such as patience, tolerance, forgiveness, and sexual fidelity. Most of these can be transferred to other pursuits, but their

---

25. Gerald Runkle, *Ethics: An Examination of Contemporary Moral Problems* (New York: Holt, Rinehart and Winston, 1982), pp. 72–73.
26. MacIntye, pp. 175–76.

combination in marriage is unique.[27] Like other practices, marriage can bring external rewards, such as money or career advancement, but these are distinct from the goods internal to marriage.

The practice of marriage has evolved over the years. At one time it involved relatively fixed gender-role differentiation (men go to work for money and women stay home with the children). Now husband and wife are freer to determine for themselves how roles should be divided. But sexual exclusivity remains central to the practice, communitarians and moral conservatives might reasonably claim, so legalizing prostitution is a bad idea if it jeopardizes such exclusivity.

Legal Prostitution and Spheres of Justice

Communitarian Michael Walzer's "spheres of justice" idea suggests that prostitution inserts money where it does not belong.[28] Walzer believes that different rewards are appropriate to different spheres of activity and that money is an appropriate reward for some activities, but not others.

Walzer claims that what people recognize as a reward, and therefore as good, is a social invention. A million dollars means nothing outside a society that allows people to exchange money for goods. A congressional medal of honor is meaningless outside the context of a nation with a military that honors soldiers with medals. Election to office in a democracy presupposes a socially established democracy. Chairmanship of a corporation's board of directors presupposes legislation that allows for the establishment of corporations, a corporate charter, and corporate bylaws. Admission to elite schools presupposes social recognition of the schools' excellence and socially accepted criteria of scholarly potential. The love of family presupposes shared social understandings about who is a member of my family (which has differed widely from society to society) as well as what kind of behavior is appropriate to which kinds of family relationships.

---

27. In a society in which marriage is a practice, people may choose to mimic marriage without actually getting married. Even if all the goods and virtues internal to the practice of marriage can be obtained in this way, which is uncertain, the availability of this option is parasitic on society's regular practice of marriage.

28. Walzer was associated with philosophical communitarianism during its formative period in the 1980s, when it concentrated on criticizing Rawls's political liberalism. Walzer's classification as a communitarian since that time has been contested. We shall see in the next chapter that he shares much with political liberals and that he is also a multiculturalist.

230 Chapter 7: Communitarianism and Moral Conservatism

Walzer maintains also that the type of reward appropriate in one sphere differs from the type appropriate in a different sphere. "Social goods have social meanings, and we find our way to distributive justice through an interpretation of those meanings. We search for principles internal to each distributive sphere."[29] Military honors appropriately reward military heroism; admission to an elite school appropriately rewards academic potential or excellence; acquittal appropriately rewards innocence at criminal trial; political influence appropriately rewards success in elective politics in democratic countries; familial gratitude and love appropriately reward meeting social expectation regarding family obligations; money and selection as corporate CEO appropriately reward success in business, and so forth. Walzer writes:

> When [social] meanings are distinct, distributions must be autonomous. Every social good or set of goods constitutes, as it were, a distributive sphere within which only certain criteria and arrangements are appropriate. Money is inappropriate in the sphere of ecclesiastical office; it is an intrusion from another sphere. And piety should make for no advantage in the marketplace, as the marketplace has commonly been understood.[30]

Walzer calls a "good" dominant "if the individuals who have it, because they have it, can command a wide range of other goods. . . . Dominance describes a way of using social goods that isn't limited by their intrinsic meanings. . . ."[31] Such dominance breeds injustice because it allows people to appropriate goods for which they lack appropriate entitlement. In our society, money is, or threatens to be, such a dominant good. Many people in our society worry that the rich can use their money to "buy" elective office through expensive media campaigns, or that they can buy their way out of criminal trouble by hiring extraordinarily talented attorneys, or buy their way into elite schools without appropriate academic credentials. Most people consider this unjust, and communitarians agree. Walzer notes with approval the wide range of goods, in addition to the ones above, that we commonly think it inappropriate to buy or sell. These include "exemptions from military service, from jury duty and from any other form of communally imposed work . . . , basic welfare services like police protection . . . , prizes and honors of many sorts, [such as] the

29. Michael Walzer, *Spheres of Justice: A Defense of Pluralism and Equality* (New York: Basic Books, 1983), p. 19.
30. Walzer, p. 10.
31. Walzer, pp. 10–11.

Congressional Medal of Honor [or] the Pulitzer Prize or the Most Valuable Player Award . . . , divine grace . . . , and love and friendship. . . .ʺ[32]

It is obvious from this list that Walzer might object to legalizing prostitution because prostitution allows the purchase of sex, which should not be bought and sold. More generally, legalizing prostitution favors money as a dominant good, which allows the rich inappropriate power in many areas, such as politics, education, and religion. Finally, the prostitution example suggests that political liberalism is not morally neutral. It favors legalizing prostitution, which many Americans consider immoral.

Economic Growth and Bourgeois Values

Contractarians and some moral conservatives object on other grounds as well to the goal, shared by free-market conservatives and liberal contractarians, of maximizing economic growth in order to satisfy as many consumer preferences as possible. Economic growth requires increasing consumer demand, as Victor Lebow, an American retailing analyst, made clear shortly after World War II.

> Our enormously productive economy . . . demands that we make consumption our way of life, that we convert the buying and use of goods into rituals, that we seek our spiritual satisfaction, our ego satisfaction, in consumption. . . . We need things consumed, burned up, worn out, replaced, and discarded at an ever-increasing rate.[33]

But people typically increase consumption when they are discontented with what they have. Radio talk show host Dave Ramsay writes in *More Than Enough* that the principal object of marketing is to create discontent.

> Professional marketers and advertisers understand that they have to point out a need to you so you will recognize a need you didn't know you had. When you recognize that need, [a] process . . . has started [that] will end in frustration and finally purchase. . . . If you are a good marketer or advertiser your job is to bring dissonance or a disturbance to the person receiving your message. . . . That is the essence of marketing, to create an emotional disturbance.[34]

---

32. Walzer, pp. 101–02,

33. Quoted in Vicki Robin and Joe Dominguez, *Your Money or Your Life* (New York: Penguin Books, 1992), p. 17.

34. Dave Ramsey, *More Than Enough* (New York: Viking Penguin, 1999), p. 234.

232   Chapter 7: Communitarianism and Moral Conservatism

Thus, the goal of maximizing economic growth requires turning citizens into discontented consumers seeking satisfaction. Communitarian Amitai Etzioni complains, "citizens and community members need self-control so that they will not demand ever more services and handouts while being unwilling to pay taxes and make contributions to the commons, a form of citizen infantilism."[35] Consumerism and economic growth thrive on exactly the message that you "need" more than you already have, so the state should lower taxes and increase services. Here is another example of "infantile" individualism:

> A study has shown that young Americans expect to be tried before a jury of their peers but are rather reluctant to serve on one. This paradox highlights a major aspect of contemporary American civic culture: a strong sense of entitlement—that is, a demand that the community provide more services and strongly uphold rights—coupled with a rather weak sense of obligation to the local and national community.[36]

Of course, political liberals also want people to be community-minded, hard-working, and fair, but they tend to take these virtues for granted, failing to see the disruptive effects of consumerism and the pursuit of maximum economic growth. Communitarians and some moral conservatives, by contrast, believe that essential virtues are hard to establish and easy to lose. Moral conservative Irving Kristol notes that the founders of the American republic who wrote *The Federalist Papers*

> talk about the frailties of human nature and the necessity for a political system to take such frailties into account. . . . They understood that republican self-government could not exist if humanity did not possess—at some moments, and to a fair degree—the traditional "republican virtues" of self-control, self-reliance, and disinterested concern for the public good. They also understood that these virtues did not exist everywhere, at all times, and that there was no guarantee of their "natural" preponderance.[37]

Kristol worries that a

> people of firm moral convictions, a people of self-reliance and self-discipline, a people who do not expect the universe to be offering

35. Amitai Etzioni, *The Spirit of Community: Rights, Responsibilities, and the Communitarian Agenda* (New York: Crown Publishers, 1993), p. 91.

36. Etzioni, p. 3.

37. Irving Kristol, "The American Revolution as a Successful Revolution," in *Neo-Conservatism: The Autobiography of an Idea* (New York: The Free Press, 1995), pp. 235–52, at 238–39.

them something for nothing—in short . . . the *bourgeois citizen* . . . is now on the verge of becoming an extinct species. He has been killed off by bourgeois prosperity, which has corrupted his character from that of *citizen* to that of a *consumer*. . . . When I was very young, it was understood that the only people who would buy things on the installment plan were the irresponsibles, the wastrels, those whose characters were too weak to control their appetites. "Save now, buy later" is what the work ethic used to prescribe. To buy now and pay later was a sign of moral corruption. . . . A people who have mortgaged themselves to the hilt are a dependent people, and ultimately they will look to the state to save them from bankruptcy.[38]

Free-market conservatism, Kristol believes, tends to undermine the prerequisite moral qualities needed to maintain a free society. In the free market, the private vice of individual selfishness is supposed to produce public benefits because market competition motivates selfish people to improve products and lower prices. Kristol counters:

In the end, you can maintain the belief that private vices, freely exercised, will lead to public benefits only if you are further persuaded that human nature cannot be utterly corrupted by these vices, but rather will always transcend them. The idea of bourgeois virtue has been eliminated from [Milton] Friedman's conception of bourgeois society and has been replaced by the idea of individual liberty, [as if] in "the nature of things," the latter will certainly lead to the former.[39]

Kristol challenges this assumption. He maintains that the same lack of self-control that fosters unlimited economic growth by encouraging people to live on credit leads also to welfare dependency and the expectation that the state will relieve individuals of responsibility for their lives. In short, without rigorous training in virtue, people tend to be corrupt because, "in every society, the overwhelming majority of the people lead lives of considerable frustration, and if society is to endure, it needs to be able to rely on a goodly measure of stoical resignation."[40] Such resignation comes only from rigorous moral training, which communitarians and moral conservatives endorse but political liberals tend to ignore because they take bourgeois virtue for granted.

---

38. Kristol, "Utopianism, Ancient and Modern," pp. 184–99, at 195. Emphasis in original.
39. Kristol, "Capitalism, Socialism, and Nihilism," pp. 92–105, at 102.
40. Kristol, p. 99.

Social Capital and the Good Society

Robert Putnam, professor of Public Policy at Harvard University, claims that communities are better when they have a lot of what he calls **social capital:**

> Whereas physical capital refers to physical objects and human capital refers to properties of individuals, *social capital refers to connections among individuals—social networks and the norms of reciprocity and trustworthiness that arise from them.* In that sense social capital is closely related to what some have called "civic virtue."[41]
>
> Members of a community that follows the principle of generalized reciprocity—raking your leaves before they blow onto your neighbors' yard, lending a dime to a stranger for a parking meter, buying a round of drinks the week you earn overtime, keeping an eye on a friend's house, taking turns bringing snacks to Sunday school, caring for the child of the crack-head one flight down—find that their self-interest is served. . . .[42]

Putnam quotes Yogi Berra on the advantages of reciprocity: "If you don't go to somebody's funeral, they won't come to yours."[43]

Honesty and trust are also important in good communities and have measurable economic advantages. Without trust, people protect themselves with lawyer-drawn contracts before productive work can begin. Without honesty, people do not pay as agreed and must be sued. Complex contracts and lawsuits take up time and money, which economists call "transaction costs," that are saved where generalized trust and honesty prevail.

> Generalized trust also improves civic involvement, Putnam notes: Other things being equal, people who trust their fellow citizens volunteer more often, contribute more to charity, participate more often in politics and community organizations, serve more readily on juries, give blood more frequently, comply more fully with their tax obligations, are more tolerant of minority views, and display many other forms of civic virtue. . . .
>
> In short, people who trust others are all-round good citizens. . . . Conversely, the civically disengaged believe themselves to be surrounded by miscreants and feel less constrained to be honest

---

41. Robert D. Putnam, *Bowling Alone* (New York: Simon and Schuster, 2000), p. 19. Emphasis added.
42. Putnam, p. 135.
43. Putnam, p. 20.

themselves. The causal arrows among civic involvement, reciprocity, honesty, and social trust are as tangled as well-tossed spaghetti.[44]

Putnam notes some surprising advantages of a community with a lot of social capital. He compared educational achievements in different states to the amount of formal and informal social capital in those states.

> Unexpectedly, the level of *informal* social capital in the state is a stronger predictor of student achievement than is the level of *formal* institutionalized social capital. In other words, level of social trust in a state and the frequency with which people connected informally with one another (in card games, visiting with friends, and the like) were even more closely correlated with educational performance than was the amount of time state residents devoted to club meetings, church attendance, and community projects. That is not to say that formal activities were unimportant. Rather, . . . there is something about communities where people connect with one another— over and above how rich or poor they are materially, how well educated the adults themselves are, what race or religion they are— that positively affects the education of children.[45]

Another strong correlation concerns health. "Statistically speaking, the evidence for the health consequences of social connectedness is as strong today as was the evidence for the health consequences of smoking at the time of the first surgeon general's report on smoking."[46]

Marriage is a form of social connectedness that is generally more important for happiness than a lot of money. Putnam writes:

> Generally speaking, as one rises up the income hierarchy, life contentment increases. So money can buy happiness after all. But not as much as marriage. Controlling for education, age, gender, marital status, income, and civic engagement, the marginal "effect" of marriage on life contentment is equivalent to . . . quadrupling your annual income.[47]

Clearly, *social capital—trust, honesty, civic involvement, and personal connectedness—are important aspects of "the good society." Liberal neutrality seems out of place if the state can promote increased social capital.*

Unfortunately, the level of social capital declined in the United States from 1960 through the end of the century. One result is that people are

---

44. Putnam, pp. 136–37.
45. Putnam, pp. 300–01. Emphasis in original.
46. Putnam, p. 327.
47. Putnam, p. 333.

sicker and more depressed. "The younger you are, the worse things have gotten over the last decades of the 20th century in terms of headaches, indigestion, sleeplessness, as well as general satisfaction with life and even likelihood of taking your own life."[48]

Two factors that tend to degrade social capital are television viewing and financial anxiety. "Most studies estimate that the average American now watches roughly four hours per day, very nearly the highest viewership anywhere in the world."[49] As a result, people have less time for civic involvement and personal connectedness.

> People who say that TV is their "primary form of entertainment" volunteer and work on community projects less often, attend fewer dinner parties, . . . picnic less, are less interested in politics, give blood less often, write friends less regularly, make fewer long-distance calls, send fewer greeting cards and less email, and express more road rage than demographically matched people who differ only in saying that TV is *not* their primary form of entertainment.[50]

At one time most families had only one television, but increasingly families have one for each member of the household, which encourages isolation of family members from one another. Putnam writes:

> The fraction of sixth-graders with a TV set in their bedroom grew from 6% in 1970 to 77% in 1999. (Two kids in three aged 8–18 say that TV is usually on during meals in their home.) At the same time, during the 1980s the rapid diffusion of videocassette players and video games into American households added yet other forms of "screen time."[51]

Family members see less of one another and interact less frequently.

The other major cause of decline in social capital is financial anxiety, which is

> associated . . . with less time spent with friends, less card playing, less home entertaining, less frequent attendance at church, less volunteering, and less interest in politics. Even social activities with little or no financial cost are inhibited by financial distress. . . . It is not low income per se, but the financial worry that it engenders, that inhibits social engagement. Even among the well-to-do, a sense of financial vulnerability dampens community involvement.[52]

---

48. Putnam, p. 263.
49. Putnam, p. 222.
50. Putnam, p. 231. Emphasis in original.
51. Putnam, p. 223.
52. Putnam, p. 193.

These two causes of decline are related to each other and to the goal of maximizing economic growth. Consumer spending is the main engine of economic growth but is also a major cause of consumer debt and financial anxiety. Watching TV promotes consumer spending and indebtedness. Dave Ramsey cites these figures:

> Juliet B. Schor, in her book *The Overspent American,* states that her research shows that each added hour of television viewing increases a consumer's spending by roughly $200 per year. So an average level of TV watching of 15 hours per week equals nearly $3,000 extra spent per year. When you consider a study by A. C. Nielsen Co. that says that in 1996 Americans watched 250 billion hours of TV, the overspending as a culture is incredible.[53]

These facts reinforce Kristol's relatively intuitive reflection that overemphasis on economic growth can undermine the civic society that political liberals take for granted.

Some Concerns about Moral Conservatism

I have so far presented moral conservatives and communitarians together because they have much in common. They both reject political liberalism's devotion to individual autonomy. Both reject state neutrality in matters of value and favor some nonneutral, perfectionist goals because they think societies are sometimes better when they do not carry autonomy too far. For example, a society is better when divorce is rare and social capital is high. Both believe that the hard-working, compassionate, honest, law-abiding, self-restrained people needed for society to flourish are made, not born and that the state must promote family life and other social structures conducive to their nurture. Yet the views are different enough to justify retaining their different labels and considering their limitations separately. I begin with the limits of moral conservatism.

Moral conservatives tend to look with favor on traditional roles. In addition, like free-market conservatives, they are wary of government intervention in the economy. These ideas combine to create some problematic views regarding women and families.

Consistent with his general distrust of government economic programs, William Bennett thinks Aid to Families with Dependent Children (AFDC) promoted out-of-wedlock births. "What welfare has done is to

---

53. Ramsey, pp. 234–35.

make illegitimacy economically viable," Bennett claims, so he would phase out government benefits for women who have illegitimate children.[54] He applauds the repeal of AFDC and its replacement with Temporary Assistance to Needy Families (TANF), which "made it easier to incorporate rigorous new work requirements and performance standards for welfare recipients."[55] In Oklahoma, he notes, TANF funds are being used "to promote a culture of marriage. . . . Some of the specific actions include working with religious leaders to help develop community-based, marriage-strengthening programs; training workers to teach marriage skill courses; and documenting divorce trends." Bennett would also like to see programs aimed at "expanding group homes for pregnant single women; promoting adoption; and enforcing already existing laws that allow the state to protect neglected and abused children."[56]

There are some problems of internal coherence here. Bennett rejoices that "since 1994 (the peak year), welfare rolls have been cut in half." However, he notes, "During the same period when welfare rolls were being reduced by 50%, the percentage of births out of wedlock was growing."[57] This seems inconsistent with his continuing to blame government welfare for unmarried women having children.

Other problems concern the role of mothers in children's lives. Bennett claims, as we saw in Chapter 2, that children do best when mothers stay home from work to care for them. "Day care cannot measure up to the devotion of a mother," he writes.[58] "One emerging trend [that Bennett seems to favor] is for mothers to stay at home while their children are very young and then reenter the labor force once they enroll in school."[59] So on the one hand, Bennett favors child care by mothers. On the other hand, however, he also favors denying welfare benefits to future unwed mothers so they will have to go to work. The result may be that many illegitimate children, as Bennett calls them, will be neglected or relegated to the kind of day care that Bennett considers inadequate.

Bennett's views are consistent only on the assumption that if poor women know beforehand that they will get no government assistance, they will either refrain from having children out of wedlock or allow such children to be adopted. Recognizing that this will not work in all cases, however, Bennett would strengthen laws against abuse and neglect,

---

54. Bennett, p. 96.
55. Bennett, p. 95.
56. Bennett, p. 98.
57. Bennett, p. 95.
58. Bennett, p. 26.
59. Bennett, p. 27.

threatening poor, single women with loss of their children to state child protective agencies if poverty results in substandard care. But if day care is bad, even though children see their mothers most days after work, is foster care better when children may not see parents for months on end?

Bennett's views may not please women and their friends also because he seems to envision a reduced role for women in the marketplace. Bennett does not advocate "going back . . . to a time when . . . women were subjugated and demeaned, or denied participation in the labor force."[60] Still, he notes that

> in general, and whatever the income level, two full-time working spouses are much more likely to divorce. Moreover, women who work outside the home are more likely to divorce than those who do not, and highly educated career women (but not men) show a higher rate of divorce than women of lower educational and career level.[61]

He points out, in this connection, that "the rise of women's work has devalued the breadwinning contribution of men, leading some wives to believe that if they divorce, they will not be giving up all that much financially.[62] It seems that women's economic success is a problem because it encourages divorce. Bennett's suggestion that women interrupt their careers to stay home with preschool children also encourages women to avoid careerism. They should be content with less pay and prestige.

Bennett's criticism of no-fault divorce, like Sandel's similar criticism, implies the same. "Thanks to no-fault divorce," he writes, "many more women are in the labor force than would otherwise be the case. Such women are in a double bind. Under our no-fault regime a wife has less confidence than ever that her marriage will last, and she cannot hope to gain a favorable settlement should it end." Society would be better, and women would gain, he implies, if divorce were more difficult so more women, confident in lifelong marriage, could stay out of the workforce. Those who envision the good society as encouraging and eventually achieving gender parity in money, power, and prestige outside the home will not agree with Bennett.

Another problem is Bennett's concentration on women as the focal point for improvement. He writes that he concentrates on women because "our leverage with men is limited."[63] Communitarians, we shall see below, think otherwise.

---

60. Bennett, p. 67.
61. Bennett, p. 148.
62. Bennett, p. 150.
63. Bennett, p. 99.

Finally, Bennett fails to consider consumerism and the goal of maximum economic growth as primary factors creating the problems he properly decries. He mentions consumerism only once in his book on family values, but never discusses it. Instead, his recommendations seem designed for compatibility with the free-market conservative view that promoting economic growth is a primary function of government. Fellow moral conservative Irving Kristol, as we have seen, does object to the consumerist orientation of free-market conservatism, but he suggests no government interventions in the economy to address the problems it creates.

Some Concerns about Communitarianism

Communitarian Amitai Etzioni stresses the importance of gender equality. He acknowledges that

> few people who advocated equal rights for women favored a society in which sexual equality would mean a society in which all adults would act like men, who in the past were relatively inattentive to children. . . . Women were to be free to work any place they wanted, and men would be free to show emotion, care, and domestic commitment.

Recognizing that so far gender-equality has impoverished family life and jeopardized children, Etzioni does not suggest return to the traditional family. Instead, he writes, "parents in a Communitarian family, in the 'age of we,' are entitled not just to equal pay for equal work, equal credit and housing opportunities, and the right to choose a last name, they also must bear equal responsibilities—above all, for their children."[64]

Unfortunately, no one has yet specified how to inaugurate the "age of we" regarding parental time investment. In this respect Bennett seems correct that we have little leverage. However, Etzioni endorses a realistic plan, first advanced by Harvard University's David Ellwood, for extracting money from both parents:

> Both parents' Social Security numbers should be registered on a child's birth certificate, so that it would be possible to find either parent if he or she left the child. He further suggests that all absent parents be required to allot a portion of their income to the support of their children and that these payments be withheld from their

---

64. Etzioni, p. 63.

paychecks [as is] Social Security. . . . In this way the responsibility of absent parents would be clearly expressed and enforced.[65]

Men who know they will be financially responsible for children they produce may take greater care to avoid getting women pregnant outside of committed relationships. An additional state resource exists, not mentioned by either author, to discourage out-of-wedlock births to underage women. Police could use DNA evidence to identify the men who fathered these children and then prosecute them for statutory rape. Men who see a child as incriminating evidence will figure out how to avoid "unwanted pregnancies."

Etzioni envisions state-mandated maternity leave for working women so they can spend at least two years with a newborn.

> A bare minimum of two years of intensive parenting is essential. . . . Corporations should provide six months of paid leave and another year and a half (18 months) of unpaid leave. (The costs should be shared by the employers of the father and the mother.) Of the 18 months, the government should cover six months from public funds (many European countries do at least this much), and the rest should be absorbed by the family.[66]

Moral conservatives would probably oppose such a government mandate on two grounds. First, they agree with free-market conservatives that the government should minimize its intervention in the economy, and this is a massive intervention. Second, they want women to avoid the conflict of work and mothering by quitting work and depending on husbands for financial support. Conservatives may worry that programs designed to help working mothers keep their jobs will encourage what they see as a generally harmful trend, mothers working full-time outside of home.

Political liberals may object that Etzioni's proposal could disadvantage women in the job market. Employers may covertly, illegally, but effectively discriminate against women of childbearing potential, fearing that an employee's pregnancy will result not only in contribution to maternity leave (shared equally with the father's employer) but in a six-month to two-year absence. Prudent employers, especially in smaller companies, may be reluctant to give young women positions of responsibility. This could harm their career potential.

---

65. Etzioni, p. 83. See David T. Ellwood, *Poor Support: Poverty in the American Family* (New York: Basic Books, 1988), especially Chapter 5.
66. Etzioni, pp. 71–72.

Communitarians and moral conservatives generally agree, however, that many parents should spend more time with their children and that work outside of home interferes with family time. Communitarians are more apt to point out that much of this work is tied to financial pressures resulting from unnecessary consumer spending. Etzioni points out that

> people need rather little: shelter, liquids, a certain amount of calories and vitamins a day, and a few other such things that can be bought quite cheaply. Most of what people *feel* that they "must have"—from VCRs to shoes that match their pocketbooks to $150 Nike sneakers to designer frames for their sunglasses—is socially conditioned.

Etzioni is "arguing not that people should lead a life of denial and poverty, but that . . . in the long run parents will find more satisfaction and will contribute more to the community if they heed their children more and their social status less."[67]

There are two problems here. First, as we have seen, increasing consumer demand is required to drive the American economy forward. People choosing voluntary simplicity (deliberately working less and spending less) in sufficient numbers to affect the general quality of parenting in society may cause massive unemployment owing to lack of consumer demand. Second, two parents working full-time, minimum-wage jobs to support themselves and two children have a household income so low that they qualify for the Earned Income Tax Credit discussed in Chapter 6. Without a considerable restructuring of wage rates, it is hard to imagine how such people could afford to cut back on work to spend more time with their children. Put together, these two problems suggest that, like moral conservatives, communitarians do an excellent job of pointing out deficiencies in our society. But they do not acknowledge that radical change would be required to seriously address the issues they raise.

Theocrats and Moral Conservatives

Moral conservatives in the United States stress the importance of religion in a good society. Irving Kristol writes: "The three pillars of modern conservatism are religion, nationalism, and economic growth. Of these, religion is easily the most important because it is the only power that, in the longer term, can shape people's characters and regulate their

---

67. Etzioni, pp. 65–66. Emphasis in original.

motivation."[68] As noted earlier, Kristol believes that life for most people is disappointing and frustrating, so most citizens must cultivate a high level of stoical resignation. He writes,

> in theory, this could be philosophical rather than religious; in fact, philosophical stoicism has never been found suitable for mass consumption. Philosophical stoicism . . . has never been able to give an acceptable rationale of "one's station and one's duties" to those whose stations are low and whose duties are onerous.[69]

Philosophy fails because people philosophize only as they mature, whereas, Kristol claims, "it is not possible to motivate people to do the right thing, and avoid doing the wrong thing, unless people are told, from childhood on, what the right things and the wrong things are."[70] Philosophy starts too late, so it is not "going to convince anyone that it makes sense for him to die for his country."[71] In sum, "religion, and a moral philosophy associated with religion, is far more important politically than the philosophy of liberal individualism admits."[72]

In spite of the importance they place on religion and religious education, moral conservatives are not necessarily theocrats, whose views were discussed in Chapter 1. Theocrats believe that moral truths about socially contentious matters can be derived from the true religion; that they adhere to this religion; that they understand the religion's moral truths; and that state law should reflect these truths. For example, theocratic Muslims who believe as religious truth that women should be dressed modestly in public would impose state laws requiring modest dress of all women, regardless of their religion. Theocratic Christians who believe as religious truth that God hates homosexuality would have the state ban homosexual conduct.

Some moral conservatives may also be theocrats, but Irving Kristol's promotion of religion is very different. He supports any religious tradition that teaches children from an early age the basics of human decency. Thus, moral conservatives want the state to promote religion in general, which includes versions of all the world's great religious traditions, not any one religion, much less any one version of that religion.

The issue of school vouchers discussed in Chapter 6 brings out differences among theocrats, moral conservatives, and free-market

68. Kristol, "The Coming 'Conservative Century,'" pp. 364–68, at 365.
69. Kristol, p. 99.
70. Kristol, p. 365.
71. Kristol, p. 100.
72. Kristol, p. 101.

conservatives. All could favor state-provided school vouchers that can be used in religiously oriented schools, but for different reasons. Theocrats would support vouchers if they thought that the religiously oriented schools in question would, at least in most cases, teach the true religion. Theocratic Christians, for example, may want state support for religious schools in the United States, but oppose it in Muslim Iraq. Moral conservatives, by contrast, would favor vouchers for religious education regardless of the religion taught so long as the religion inculcates universal moral truths and respect for everyone. Free-market conservatives favor vouchers to promote competition that improves efficiency in education. They do not care if voucher schools are religiously oriented or not. They want religious schools in voucher plans to generate as much competition as possible.

CONCLUSION

Communitarians and moral conservatives claim to find pressing problems in society that political liberalism cannot adequately address because liberals attempt to be neutral among competing conceptions of the good life and the good society. Liberals believe that increasing individual freedom increases human welfare. They want to protect individual rights, promote economic growth, and, in the case of contractarians, foster distributive justice, without any further specification of values. One result is that, absent negative effects on individual rights, economic growth, or social and economic equality, political liberals cannot identify the breakdown of the family, related failures of child care, self-centered citizens, and reduced social capital as political problems.

Communitarians and moral conservatives, by contrast, reject value neutrality in favor of perfectionist goals. They claim to identify some traits of good societies, including a high rate of lifelong, child-centered marriages and lots of social capital. They claim further that political liberalism, far from being value neutral, promotes individual autonomy and related, self-centered values, which are inferior. No-fault divorce, for example, punishes women who fail to develop careers, and the legalization of prostitution trivializes sex.

Communitarians and moral conservatives make some telling points against political liberalism, but some implications of their views, especially regarding women, remain controversial. Also, the communitarian road to the "age of we" seems uncharted. A more fundamental problem is that some values that communitarians and moral conservatives would have us promote require a more thorough rethinking of our society's basic premises than they have acknowledged. Consumerism and economic growth are basic to American society, yet many of the goods that communitarians and moral conservatives champion require increasing frugality and giving priority to family, leisure, and informal, "unproductive" socializing over wage-earning productivity. It is not clear how this could possibly come about, much less, as moral conservatives would like, with little government involvement.

In sum, communitarians and moral conservatives certainly show that excessive individualism can harm society and that value neutrality is a myth. However, their own vision of the good society requires clarification and may be controversial. We must move on to compare their views with some others not yet considered.

JUDGMENT CALLS

1. Consider the pros and cons of so-called Good Samaritan laws. Such laws require people to help others in distress when this can be done with no personal danger and only minimal inconvenience. A Good Samaritan law would have made the 38 witnesses to Kitty Genovese's murder guilty of a crime because they failed to call the police.

2. If no-fault divorce poses problems, as communitarians and moral conservatives say, consider laws that would allow divorce only in cases in which certain inappropriate behaviors, such as adultery, desertion, or domestic abuse, were proven in court. What results should we expect from such a law?

3. If marriage is better than people just living together, even in stable relationships, how can moral conservatives argue against same-sex marriage?

4. Some married couples are infertile due to the wife's lack of viable eggs (ova). In some cases the couple contracts with a woman, called a *surrogate*, who agrees to be artificially inseminated with the sperm of the man in the couple. When the child is born the surrogate relinquishes all rights, allowing the couple to raise the child as their own, in exchange for payment of living expenses, medical bills, and a fee of between $10,000 and $20,000. How does this relate to the family values that communitarians and moral conservatives support? How does it relate to Walzer's "spheres of justice?" What considerations count for or against making surrogacy contracts legal?

5. Communitarians and political conservatives think that political liberals overemphasize the importance of individual rights. Accordingly, to reduce alcohol-related traffic accidents and death, Amitai Etzioni proposes sobriety checkpoints, announced in advance, where police check every driver's alcohol level. Etzioni also supports strict campaign finance laws to reduce the influence of money in politics. How are the impositions on individual rights in these proposals the same, and how are they different? What would moral conservatives say about these proposals? How might political liberals in reflective equilibrium favor one of these proposals more than the other? Which one?

6. If two parents working full-time who earn the minimum wage cannot adequately support two children without the Earned Income Tax Credit, perhaps the minimum wage is too low. Consider the possibility of establishing a minimum wage that provides adequate income for a family of four when the parents work a total of only one and one-half full-time jobs (so one parent can be home when children arrive from school). What are the pros and cons? What would the wage have to be?

8 Deliberative Democracy, Multiculturalism, and the Limits of Tolerance

Darlene Miller had worked at the Kitty Kat Lounge in South Bend, Indiana, for about two years making good money dancing in a G-string with pasties over her nipples. Dancers received no hourly wage but were given a 100% commission on the first $60 of drinks sold while they were dancing. Ms. Miller believed she could make more money dancing entirely nude, but Kitty Kat's owners were prevented from allowing nude dancing by an Indiana statute forbidding public nudity.[1] Because only willing, adult patrons would be exposed to this nudity, libertarians would support Ms. Miller. But proponents of majority-rule **democracy** may not. The Indiana legislators who passed the law were democratically elected, so we assume their judgment reflects the will of the majority. It seems that a "tyranny of the majority" may deprive people of the individual rights that libertarians champion.

Democracy has its defenders, however. *People commonly think that the legitimacy of a government, its right to rule, rests on the consent of the governed. Democracies incorporate this consent by regularly allowing most adults a significant voice in determining state laws and policies.* A common form of democracy is majority rule, also called **aggregative democracy,** which uses voting to determine popular will. This is the form of democracy that allowed public opinion to frustrate Ms. Miller.

In Michigan, Joy Rzeznik's former husband disputed her custody of their eight-year-old son, Calen, because Ms. Rzeznik, who works for Detroit Edison and owns an occult bookstore, took Calen to Florida for initiation into the Santeria religion. "The child later said he had taken part in rites involving the sacrifice of chickens, goats, a dog, pigeons, and a fawn. . . ."[2] Susan Borovich, head of the county agency investigating the

---

1. *Barnes v. Glen Theatre, Inc.* 501 U.S. 560, at 563.
2. Detroit News, "Mother Wins Custody of Son, Even Though She Practices Animal Sacrifice," (January 20, 1994), www.menweb.org/throop/custody-divorce/cases/santa-ria.html, accessed March 2, 2004.

case, recommended to the court that Ms. Rzeznik retain custody, but only so long as she refrains from allowing animals to be sacrificed in front of Calen.

This case raises issues of **multiculturalism.** Multiculturalism in political philosophy is motivated by respect for cultural diversity, which reflects belief that *no single culture, including our own, has a monopoly on insights or practices that promote human flourishing. Just as reasonable people have different religions and religious practices, different philosophies of life and lifestyles, so they have different cultural beliefs and practices.* Philosophers refer to this diversity of reasonable religions, lifestyles, and cultures as **reasonable pluralism.** Reasonable people, according to this politically liberal perspective, favor state rules that everyone can find acceptable. In the light of reasonable pluralism, many people will not be able to accept rules that tolerate only one or a few religions, lifestyles, or cultures, so political liberals believe that toleration should expand to include great variety.

At issue in the custody case was full toleration of the Santeria religion. Michigan law bans all religious animal sacrifice in the state. But animal sacrifice is reasonable, the Santeria argue, because it does not hurt anyone or interfere with other people's lifestyles or religions. In this case, multiculturalism suggests allowing the practice and, assuming that Michigan law reflects majority sentiment in the state, aggregative democracy suggests banning it. Aggregative democracy, it seems, supports policies that oppose multiculturalism on this issue as it allowed public opinion to oppose individual rights on the issue of nude dancing.

Deliberative democracy, by contrast, may yield a different result. According to John Dryzek, a leading proponent of deliberative democracy, people who deliberate with one another "are amenable to changing their judgments, preferences, and views during the course of their interactions, which involve persuasion rather than coercion, manipulation, or deception. The essence of democracy itself is . . . deliberation, as opposed to voting [or] aggregation. . . ."[3] Deliberation among proponents and opponents of nude dancing or animal sacrifice may yield government policies acceptable to all.

This chapter explores the value and limits of deliberative democracy and cultural (including religious) diversity. We find that multiculturalism can promote self-respect and democracy and that deliberative democracy can support individual rights and cultural diversity. But multiculturalism

3. John S. Dryzek, *Deliberative Democracy and Beyond: Liberals, Critics, Contestations* (New York: Oxford University Press, 2000), p. 1.

can jeopardize individual rights, and extremes of poverty and wealth can jeopardize democracy.

The Deliberative Ideal

According to the deliberative model of democracy, the legitimacy of state policies depends not on rational grounds but on the processes by which they are determined. A policy is legitimate only if it, in the words of philosopher Seyla Benhabib, "results from processes of collective deliberation conducted rationally and fairly among free and equal individuals."[4] Everyone affected by the outcome of deliberations must have an equal chance to participate, to set or change the agenda, and to call into question the results of previous deliberations. Participants must advance good reasons for their point of view, which means "what would count as a good reason for all others involved."[5] *Political legitimacy requires that people have good reasons to accept laws that affect them.*

This view of political legitimacy reflects philosopher T. M. Scanlon's version of liberal contractarianism. "Thinking about right and wrong is, at the most basic level," Scanlon writes, "thinking about what could be justified to others on grounds that they, if appropriately motivated, could not reasonably reject."[6] The ability of others to appreciate one's justifications is particularly important where political principles justifying state action are concerned, philosopher Charles Larmore adds:

> In general, political principles are precisely those principles which we believe may be enforced by coercion, if need be. The idea that such principles must be rationally acceptable to those who are to be subject to them rests on a moral view about the conditions under which norms may be backed up by force. This underlying moral commitment is that no one should be made by force to comply with a norm of action when it is not possible for him to recognize through reason the validity of that norm. . . . This is, at root, a norm of equal respect.[7]

---

4. Seyla Benhabib, "Toward a Deliberative Model of Democratic Legitimacy," in *Justice: Alternative Political Perspectives*, 4th ed., James P. Sterba, Ed. (Belmont, CA: Wadsworth, 2003), pp. 172–85, at 174.

5. Benhabib, p. 175.

6. T. M. Scanlon, *What We Owe to Each Other* (Cambridge, MA: Harvard University Press, 1998), p. 5.

7. Charles Larmore, "The Foundations of Modern Democracy," in Sterba, pp. 163–71, at 170.

Deliberative democracy rests on equal respect, not on one's own self-interest. Political scientist Joshua Cohen maintains that one's own self-interest

> carries no weight in public deliberation of the relevant kind, because others, concerned with their advantage . . . , will not accept it as a reason; moreover, it is reasonable for them not to accept it, in part because they can dismiss it while at the same time treating me as an equal and giving my good the same weight in their deliberations that they insist I give to theirs.[8]

Acceptable reasons must concern the public good and show equal respect for everyone.

But how can deliberations be conducted in a modern state that may contain tens or hundreds of millions of people? Such populations cannot assemble for discussion, and with so many people, time constraints would allow only a small percentage to speak. Benhabib recognizes these difficulties and replies:

> A deliberative . . . model of democracy does not need to operate with the fiction of a general deliberative assembly [because] the procedural specifications of this model privilege a *plurality of modes of association* in which all affected can have the right to articulate their point of view. These can range from political parties, to citizens' initiatives, to social movements, to voluntary associations, to consciousness-raising groups, and the like. *It is through the interlocking net of these multiple forms of associations, networks, and organizations that an anonymous "public conversation" results.*[9]

These multiple associations exist in **civil society,** which Dryzek defines as "all social interaction not subsumed by the state or the economy."[10] Civil society thus includes diverse organizations, such as Little League, Girl Scouts, the YMCA, churches, the American Civil Liberties Union (ACLU), Operation Rescue, and Common Cause. Some of these organizations, such as Little League and Girl Scouts, do not seek political influence, whereas others, such as the ACLU and Operation Rescue, have political and/or legal action as their primary focus. They institute lawsuits, conduct campaigns to rally public support, advertise their views in the media,

---

8. Joshua Cohen, "Democracy and Liberty," in *Deliberative Democracy,* Jon Elster, Ed. (Cambridge: Cambridge University Press, 1998), pp. 185–231, at 197.
9. Benhabib, p. 176. Emphasis in original.
10. Dryzek, p. 23.

and/or engage in public protest. Dryzek gives several examples of effective political action by such groups.

> First, political action in civil society can change the terms of political discourse and so affect the content of public policy. The rhetorical achievements of Martin Luther King are exemplary here. . . .
>
> Second . . . , social movements can produce lasting effects in political culture by legitimating particular forms of collective action such as the sit-in, and by establishing a permanent place for issues on the public agenda.
>
> Third, policy-oriented deliberative fora can be constituted within civil society. A good example is the Global Forum, which assembled as the civil society counterpart to the 1992 United Nations Conference on Environment and Development in Rio. Composed of nongovern-mental activists from all over the world, the Global Forum influenced what transpired in the official proceedings of the Conference, in part by shaming . . . some of the official participants. . . .
>
> Fourth, protest in civil society can create fear of political instabil-ity and so draw forth a governmental response. . . .
>
> These four civil society activities involve the more or less democ-ratic exercise of power *over* the state. . . . In addition, civil society can reclaim power *from* the state—and from the economy. . . . When feminists and others speak of "empowerment" they do not mean in-fluence over government, but rather control of their own lives, facil-itated by support groups and the like. . . . Citizens can exercise power directly over economic actors through means such as boycotts of cor-porations or products. Thus in 1995 Greenpeace organized [success-ful] protests against the Shell Oil Corporation's plan to dispose of the redundant Brent Spar oil platform in the North Atlantic. . . .

In sum, "civil society can itself feature problem solving, not merely cheap talk."[11]

The democratic aspect of such activity in civil society stems from the facts that participation is open to everyone, that the activities involve con-veying information and expressing opinions, and that intended results in-clude altering laws and public policies through changing people's minds.

Deliberative Democracy and Nude Dancing

Joshua Cohen finds a better rationale for individual liberty, perhaps including nude dancing, in deliberative democracy than in the prevailing libertarian rationale. As we saw in Chapter 3, libertarians, stressing the

---

11. Dryzek, pp. 101–02. Emphasis in original.

value of individual autonomy or self-determination, reject government restrictions on behavior that does not directly harm anyone else. Libertarians would see no harm in nude dancing among consenting adults.

One problem with this defense of individual liberty, as we saw in Chapter 6 regarding John Rawls's philosophy, is that not everyone agrees that autonomy, individual flexibility, and life experimentation are good. Some people think that lifelong commitment to an unexamined tradition makes the best life. It is not obvious why the state should favor autonomous nude dancing over traditional modesty when reasonable people differ on the relative merits of autonomy and tradition.

Cohen's argument for individual freedom rests not on the superior value of autonomy but on reasonable pluralism. Deliberative democracy requires equal respect for everyone. When neither side in a debate is supported by convincing evidence that appeals to values shared by almost everyone, equal respect requires toleration of differences. Darlene Miller went to court because she and her customers disagree with the majority about the value of modesty. Such disagreements, Cohen argues,

> are fundamental and deeply rooted in reasonable differences of outlook, associated with, among other things, different views about our bodies [and] about the role of our embodiment and the pleasures associated with it in the conduct of our lives. . . . Some citizens find the law of sin in our members: they see in the body an obstacle to our highest purposes. . . . Others think, not unreasonably, that embodiment is essential to our nature, that bodily pleasures provide ways to break free of conventional constraints, and that our capacity to transcend such constraints is fundamental to our nature as free agents. . . .

Cohen sees an impasse here. "The constraints of shared evidence and conceptual precision required for agreement are simply not in view. Law has no place here, not in a democracy committed to treating its members as equals."[12]

In sum, according to Cohen, people should be permitted to dance nude among consenting adults not because autonomy is more important than tradition but because reasonable people disagree about the relative importance of autonomy and tradition. *The state should avoid areas of reasonable disagreement to avoid illegitimately imposing debatable, even if majority, views on a reasonable minority.* Unlike aggregative democracy, deliberative democracy protects minorities.

---

12. Cohen, pp. 219–20.

In the end, however, Cohen concedes, "should regulations not impinge very deeply—should the reasons supporting the conduct be less substantial—then the case against enforcement is less compelling, even if the reasons come from conventional ethics."[13] Majority rule may reasonably prevail when "regulations do not . . . cover conduct rooted in fundamental obligations or supported in other ways by substantial reasons."[14] It is not obvious whether this covers, or uncovers, Ms. Miller. She wanted to take off her G-string and pasties just to make more money. But everybody's got to eat.

Deliberative Democracy and Multiculturalism

Deliberative democracy supports cultural minorities just as it protects individual rights. For example, the City of Hialeah, Florida outlawed the Santeria practice of animal sacrifice, claiming it endangered public health and violated Florida's anticruelty statute. The Santeria invoked the First Amendment: "Congress shall make no law respecting an establishment of religion, or prohibiting the free exercise thereof." The Santeria religion requires animal sacrifice "to mark significant events such as birth, marriage and death, or when new members or priests are initiated. . . . The animals are killed in a ritual manner. . . . The sacrificed animal may be cooked and eaten, except when used in healing and death rituals."[15]

But what about Florida's anticruelty law? It states: "Whoever unnecessarily overloads, overdrives, tortures, torments, deprives of necessary sustenance or mutilates or kills any animal, or causes the same to be done . . . shall be guilty of a misdemeanor of the first degree." The words "torture," "torment," and "cruelty" include "every act, omission, or neglect whereby unnecessary or unjustifiable pain or suffering is caused, except when done in the interest of medical science. . . ."[16] It seems that aggregative democracy opposes Santeria animal sacrifice. How can deliberative democracy support it?

Let us consider only three matters in this complex case, the pain inflicted by the Santeria method of killing, the necessity of the killing, and the protection of public health. Gary Francione represented People for the Ethical Treatment of Animals (PETA), which filed a brief supporting the city's ban. He argued that the Santeria method of killing is more painful

---

13. Cohen, p. 220.
14. Cohen, p. 221.
15. Animal Rights Law, "Introduction to Santeria and Animal Sacrifice," www.animal-law.org/sacrifice/sacrfc.htm, p. 1 of 2.
16. # 828.12, Florida Statutes.

than methods allowed by the Humane Slaughter Act. The Supreme Court of the United States, however, eventually ruled that Santeria slaughter resembles the legal religious methods of traditional Jews and Muslims "whereby the animal suffers loss of consciousness caused by the simultaneous and instantaneous severance of the carotid arteries with a sharp instrument. . . ."[17]

Even if the slaughter is humane, the anticruelty statute forbids killing animals unnecessarily. Are these Santeria killings necessary? The City of Hialeah claimed that the killings are unnecessary, but a brief in the case supporting the Santeria contends, "the faith could not survive without animal sacrifice, because sacrifice is essential to the initiation of new priests."[18] Some church members also find it helpful. Reuters news service covered a congress of Santeria worshipers in Havana, Cuba in 2003, and spoke with "Iya Osunyemi Ifanike, a teacher from New York in Cuba for the congress." She

> said she turned to the faith three years ago when she was ill and having trouble at work. "I went to seven Christian churches and the pastors laid their hands on me and prayed but nothing happened, until I was introduced to a babalao who pinpointed my problem right away," she said. He told her that three jealous colleagues were using witchcraft against her and the remedy was an animal sacrifice. "I gave a goat to Oggun," said the Antigua native who moved to New York 35 years ago and has three master's degrees in Education.[19]

Some people may be skeptical, but the Free Exercise Clause bars the state from judging matters of religious doctrine. The state cannot decide what is religiously necessary.

In addition, we saw in Chapter 6 (regarding school vouchers) that the state must be neutral between religious and secular views. Many lethal secular uses of animals are considered necessary, the Brief for the Santeria points out:

> City and state law obviously assume that it is "necessary" to kill fish and game animals for recreation, that it is "necessary" to kill unwanted pets for human convenience, and so on. . . . Petitioners have found no successful prosecution in Florida for the "unnecessary" killing of an animal.[20]

---

17. 7 U.S.C 1902 (1988). Cited in Gary L. Francione, "Brief in *Church of the Lukumi Babalu Aye, Inc. v. City of Hialeah*," www.animal-law.org/sacrifice/hialbrf.htm, p. 7 of 11.

18. Steven R. Shapiro et. al., Petitioner's Brief, No. 91–948, May 22, 1992, p. 2.

19. Reuters, July 9, 2003.

20. Shapiro et. al., p. 23.

The only case in Florida questioning the necessity, and therefore cruelty, of animal killing concerned the use of rabbits to train greyhounds for racing. According to court records, trainers "release live rabbits in an enclosure from which they cannot escape. Greyhounds are then turned into the enclosure where they run the rabbits down and chew them to pieces." A Florida appeals court found this use necessary.[21] The Santeria argue that if this secular use is considered necessary, only unconstitutional prejudice against religion could explain a contrary judgment about Santeria animal sacrifice.

Finally, the City of Hialeah claimed their ban on Santeria animal sacrifice was needed to protect public health from pollution created by the improper disposal of dead animals. However, Justice Kennedy noted for the U.S. Supreme Court, "if improper disposal, not the sacrifice itself, is the harm to be prevented, the city could have imposed a general regulation on the disposal of organic garbage. It did not do so."[22] In the end, the court protected religious diversity, concluding that animal sacrifice is included in the Santeria's constitutional right to free exercise of religion.

Deliberative democracy generally supports this decision. As we have seen, the state's equal respect for everyone is integral to deliberative democracy's ideal. This requires the state to give justifications for its laws that all people affected can find reasonable. A law forbidding Santeria animal sacrifice would lack a justification that the Santeria could recognize as reasonable when the state allows animals to be killed for human convenience and even to train greyhounds.

This line of thinking leads philosopher Joshua Cohen to claim that deliberative democracy generally favors religious freedom. People deliberate, rather than simply vote, in order to understand the perspectives of others and find solutions to social problems acceptable to everyone. "Religious views," Cohen writes, "set demands of an especially high order—perhaps transcendent obligations—on their adherents. Moreover, if we see these requirements from the believer's standpoint, we cannot see them as *self-imposed*—chosen by the agent."[23] So it is difficult for religious believers to find restrictions on their religious practices to be reasonable.

Political theorist John Dryzek adds that deliberative democracy promotes multiculturalism also by supporting creative problem solving

---

21. *Kiper v. State*, 310 So2nd 42. The quote is from the dissenting opinion of Judge McCord, at 44.
22. *Church of Lukumi Babalu Aye, Inc. v. Hialeah,* at 538.
23. Cohen, p. 203. Emphasis in original.

to reach solutions acceptable to all sides. He gives the example of the (so far) successful resolution of conflicts in Northern Ireland. The underlying issues included socioeconomic inequality between Protestants and Catholics, voting and welfare bias that favored Protestants over Catholics, continued integration of Northern Ireland in the United Kingdom, and illegal violence by Catholic and Protestant militants. Dryzek writes, "if the issue is framed as 'Protestant versus Catholic' or 'Unionist versus Republican,' then we have an intractable conflict with no conceivable solution that can conceivably satisfy the two communities in Northern Ireland as well as the governments of the United Kingdom and Irish Republic." But when people deliberated, attempting to find solutions acceptable to all concerned, common ground emerged related to

> respect for identity, guarantees of civil rights, and forgiveness of past politically motivated crimes (which turns out to unite the gunmen on both sides). Aspirations short of full sovereignty gain purchase; mixed forms of multilevel and cross-national political control and power sharing surface as options; ways of recognizing and affirming community identity without intercommunal conflict are explored. The process is not exactly a paragon of deliberation, as threats of violence linger in the background . . . . But the deliberative element is also undeniable, and . . . traditionally hostile actors began to learn how to live together despite continuing deep divisions.[24]

On this account, deliberative democracy supports religious and cultural diversity, in a word, multiculturalism. We now consider the merits of multiculturalism.

The Value of Multiculturalism

Some political liberals, such as philosopher Will Kymlicka, support cultural diversity because they agree with communitarians that membership in a cultural community is needed for individual development. Cultural identification gives people a reference point for their own decisions, criteria for evaluating life's possibilities and goals. Even when people reject much of what their original culture offers, the culture helps them by raising appropriate issues.[25] Philosopher Michael Walzer agrees:

---

24. Dryzek, p. 41.
25. See Will Kymlicka, *Multicultural Citizenship* (New York: Oxford University Press, 1995), p. 89.

American society...is perhaps the most individualist society in human history.... We are free to "do our own thing...." Nonetheless, many Americans lack the means and the power to "do their own thing" or even to find their own thing to do. Empowerment is more often a familial, class, or communal achievement than an individual one....[26] [So] the real alternative to multicultural toleration is... an empty or randomly filled individualism, a great drift of human flotsam and jetsam away from every creative center.[27]

Specific cultural identity, Kymlica adds, helps individuals also by giving them a sense of self-worth. Cultural identity rests on belonging, not accomplishment, so it is seldom threatened by individual shortcomings. Unless the cultural group is despised by society at large, this effortless identity with a group gives people the sense of security needed to face life's challenges with confidence.[28]

Cultural identity also deepens the meaning of personal accomplishments by incorporating them into a continuing tradition or pursuit that extends to future generations. People benefit emotionally from identification with some large and valuable movement or whole that transcends their individual lives.[29]

These benefits of cultural identification are implied, Kymlicka notes, by "the leaders of racist and oppressive regimes around the world, who have tried to destroy and degrade the cultural heritage of the people they oppress in order to undermine their sense of personal efficacy." A black South African writes that whites who ruled the country under apartheid "tried to make us believe that our people had no history.... They wanted us to carry an image of ourselves as pathetic, utterly defeated, dependent, incapable and powerless." Kymlicka comments, "this strategy only makes sense if one's sense of personal agency is tied to one's cultural heritage. Why else would telling an individual that her *people* had no history have the effect of giving the individual an image of *herself* as powerless?"[30]

If continuing cultural self-identification is needed for self-respect and self-efficacy, one goal of a liberal state should be to help such cultures

---

26. Michael Walzer, *On Toleration* (New Haven: Yale University Press, 1997), p. 100.

27. Walzer, p. 102.

28. Kymlicka (1995), p. 89.

29. See Kymlicka (1995), pp. 89–91.

30. Will Kymlicka, *Liberalism, Community, and Culture* (New York: Oxford University Press, 1989), pp. 175–76. Emphasis in original.

survive. Kymlicka relates this to Rawls's liberal contractarianism. Rawls imagines people behind a veil of ignorance, where they do not know their personal identities or desires, agreeing to the basic rules that will govern society. Rawls thinks they will all want to maximize their primary goods, all-purpose goods they can use to secure whatever particular goods they will find attractive when the veil is lifted. Rawls writes,

> perhaps the most important primary good is that of self-respect, [which] includes [first] a person's sense of his own value, his secure conviction that his conception of his good, his plan of life, is worth carrying out, and second . . . , a confidence in one's ability . . . to fulfill one's intentions. . . . It is clear then why self-respect is a primary good. Without it nothing may seem worth doing, or if some things have value for us, we lack the will to strive for them. . . .[31]

Kymlicka adds, "the relationship between cultural membership and self-respect gives the parties to the original position a strong incentive to give cultural membership status as a primary good."[32] *Whereas the Supreme Court supported Santeria animal sacrifice to protect religious freedom, liberal contractarians should support it to protect the multicultural diversity that is needed for self-respect.*

According to Michael Walzer, *multiculturalism is valuable also because it supports deliberative democracy.* Walzer argues that, deprived of cultural membership and facing the world as mere individuals, people tend to be insecure, which breeds intolerance because insecure people perceive difference as a threat. For this reason, Walzer writes, "many . . . dissociated individuals are available for far-right, ultranationalist, fundamentalist, or xenophobic mobilizations of the sort that democracies ought to avoid. . . ."[33] Democracy cannot thrive among extremists.

In addition, Walzer observes, cultural associations foster development of citizen skills needed in democracies:

> For it is only in the context of associational activity that individuals learn to deliberate, argue, make decisions, and take responsibility. This is an old argument, first made on behalf of Protestant congregations . . . , which served, so we are told, as schools of democracy in 19th-century Great Britain.[34]

---

31. John Rawls, *A Theory of Justice* (Cambridge, MA: Harvard University Press, 1971), p. 440.

32. Kymlicka (1989), p. 166.

33. Walzer, p. 104.

34. Walzer, p. 104.

In sum, multiculturalism fosters the tolerance and disposition to negotiate needed in democracies for the peaceful resolution of conflicts.

Because multiculturalism furthers democracy, Walzer supports government programs that promote diversity. Writing in 1997, he applauds

> the current set of federal programs—including tax exemptions, matching grants, subsidies, and entitlements—that enable religious communities to run their own hospitals, old age homes, schools, day care centers, and family services. . . . Tax money is used to second charitable contributions in ways that reinforce the patterns of mutual assistance and cultural reproduction that arise spontaneously within civil society. But these patterns need to be greatly extended, because coverage at present is radically unequal. And more groups must be brought into the business of welfare provision: racial and ethnic as well as religious groups.[35]

Walzer wants schools to become involved "by recognizing the plurality of cultures and by teaching something about the different groups. . . ." The state's second aim in this regard should be "to produce hyphenated citizens, [such as Polish-Americans, Jewish-Americans, and African-Americans], men and women who will defend toleration within their different communities while still valuing and reproducing (and rethinking and revising) the differences."[36]

Some people object to any special government support, whether in school or elsewhere, for minority religions and cultures, claiming that justice requires treating everyone the same, regardless of religion, ethnicity, or culture. *The state should not be hostile to minorities; it should simply ignore them, treat them with benign neglect.*

Kymlicka disagrees, arguing that a policy of benign neglect is impossible because states regularly make decisions favoring people within the majority religion and culture and disadvantaging minorities. Consider, for example, public holidays:

> Some people object to legislation that exempts Jews and Muslims from Sunday closing legislation, on the ground that this violates the separation of state and ethnicity. But almost any decision on public holidays will do so. . . . Decisions about government holidays were made when there was far less religious diversity, and people just took it for granted that the government work week should accommodate Christian beliefs about days of rest and religious celebration. . . . Muslims [and] Jews . . . are simply asking that their religious needs

---

35. Walzer, p. 106.
36. Walzer, p. 110.

be taken into consideration in the same way that the needs of Christians have always been taken into account.[37]

The benign neglect view fails to address other inequities as well, such as those concerning official uniforms for government service. Regulations often disallow wearing a turban, as the Sikh religion requires of all adult males, whereas they do not disallow any dress that is common among Christians. For example, Kymlicka writes:

> It is virtually inconceivable that designers of government dress codes would have ever considered designing a uniform that prevented people from wearing wedding rings, unless this was strictly necessary for the job. . . . This should not be seen as a deliberate attempt to promote Christianity. It [was] simply . . . taken for granted that uniforms should not unnecessarily conflict with Christian religious beliefs.[38]

So when Sikhs ask permission to wear turbans while working as police officers, which requires exemption from government dress-code regulations, they are not asking for anything that the majority does not already have, a dress code consistent with their religious beliefs. Accommodating their religious beliefs is therefore only fair.

Kymlicka concludes that the state should often give minority groups **external protection** against policies regarding such matters as public holidays and official dress codes that disadvantage minority-group members, encourage defection from the group, and jeopardize the group's continued existence.

He has a different view, however, regarding, internal dissent, which may also endanger a group's existence. When people within a group decide to quit and join some other group, those interested in group preservation may want to impose **internal restrictions** to discourage defection.[39] In the Canadian case of *Hofer v. Hofer*, for example, two lifelong members of a rural Hutterite community were expelled for apostasy. The community holds its resources in common, not as individual shares. The individuals expelled had contributed many years of hard work to help create the common wealth and wanted to have their portion when they left the community. Church rules that disallow sharing out the common wealth discourage people from leaving. Kymlicka considers this an unjustified internal restriction on individual decision making. The church is

---

37. Kymlicka (1995), p. 114.
38. Kymlicka (1995), p. 115.
39. Kymlicka (1995), pp. 35–38.

protecting itself not from the outside world (external protection) but from its own members (internal restriction). This impairs the members' individual freedom. But the Canadian Supreme Court sided with the church, accepting their claim that holding property in common was integral to their religion.[40]

Amish School Attendance and Internal Restrictions

The distinction between external protection and internal restriction breaks down regarding education. Through education the state promotes patriotism, fosters a common sense of history and purpose, imparts skills needed in the workplace, and provides (usually imperfect) equality of opportunity. Yet, like dress codes and official holidays, state education requirements applied equally to everyone can harm minorities. The compulsory school attendance law in Wisconsin, for example, requires that children attend school (public, private, or approved home schooling) until age 16. Some members of the Amish community, Supreme Court Chief Justice Warren Burger wrote in 1972, "declined to send their children, ages 14 and 15, to public school after they completed the eighth grade. The children were not enrolled in any private school, or within any recognized exception to the compulsory-attendance law. . . ."[41] The state prosecuted the parents for violating the school attendance law.

The Supreme Court ruled in *Wisconsin v. Yoder* that Wisconsin's law denied these Amish parents the free exercise of their religion. Burger writes,

> Old Order Amish communities today are characterized by a fundamental belief that salvation requires life in a church community separate and apart from the world and worldly influences.[42]
>
> Formal high school education beyond the eighth grade is contrary to Amish beliefs, not only because it places Amish children in an environment hostile to Amish beliefs with increasing emphasis on competition in class work and sports and with pressure to conform to the styles, manners, and ways of the peer group, but also because it takes them away from their community, physically and emotionally, during the crucial and formative adolescent period of life. During this period, the children must acquire Amish attitudes favoring manual work and self-reliance and the specific skills needed

---

40. Kymlicka (1995), p. 161.
41. *Wisconsin v. Yoder*, 406 U.S. 205, at 207.
42. *Yoder*, p. 210.

to perform the adult role of an Amish farmer or housewife. They must learn to enjoy physical labor.[43]

> On the basis of such considerations, Dr. Hostetler [an expert on Amish society] testified that compulsory high school attendance . . . would . . . ultimately result in the destruction of the Old Order Amish church community as it exists in the United States today.[44]

The state properly views education as necessary to prepare future citizens and workers for adult responsibilities, but the Amish do this successfully without formal education past the eighth grade, as indicated by the community's prosperity and peace. Therefore, the court ruled, the state's interest in two additional years of education for Amish children is less important than the Amish interest in religious freedom. Using Kymlicka's terminology, the court provided the Amish with external protection against government rules that could destroy the group.

Justice William O. Douglas, by contrast, concentrated on what Kymlicka might consider an internal restriction that the Amish were imposing on their young members. Douglas objected to the court majority ignoring the views of the children affected. They will miss high school owing to parental religious beliefs.

> If the parents in this case are allowed a religious exemption, the inevitable effect is to impose the parents' notions of religious duty upon their children. Where the child is mature enough to express potentially conflicting desires, it would be an invasion of the child's rights to permit such an imposition without canvassing his views.[45] Children far younger than the 14- and 15-year-olds involved here are regularly permitted to testify in custody and other proceedings.[46]

Affected children who decide to leave the Amish community as adults may be disadvantaged by lack of formal education after the eighth grade.

Chief Justice Burger replied, "the same argument could, of course, be made with respect to all church schools short of college. There is nothing in the record or in the ordinary course of human experience to suggest that non-Amish parents generally consult with children of ages 14–16 if they are placed in a church school of the parents' faith."[47]

Although Justice Douglas lost the argument at the Supreme Court, he raised an issue of general concern for multiculturalists. Educating the

---

43. *Yoder*, p. 211.
44. *Yoder*, p. 212.
45. *Yoder*, p. 242.
46. *Yoder*, p. 245, footnote 3.
47. *Yoder*, p. 232.

next generation is typically necessary for group survival because few cultures can maintain membership based solely on adult recruits. However, whether it is religious training and attendance, religious schools, the language spoken in the home, or summer camps, attempts to perpetuate the culture through enculturation of the young commonly impose values and perspectives, sometimes at odds with mainstream society, on children too young to make membership decisions for themselves. Defection is not forbidden these people when they become adults, but early training discourages it.

Multiculturalism and Other Isms Compared

Moral Conservatism

Some of Walzer's ideas resemble those of moral conservatives. Like Walzer, moral conservatives emphasize the importance of religious communities and favor their support by government. A few years after Walzer published his views, U.S. President George W. Bush proposed "faith-based initiatives," welcomed by moral conservatives, designed to increase public support for religious groups. Also like moral conservatives, Walzer includes single parenthood, a high divorce rate, and declining church membership among America's problems.[48]

However, Walzer differs from moral conservatives in wanting government support not only for faith-based groups but for others as well, including ethnic, racial, and occupational groups. In addition, as we have seen, Walzer wants schools to expose children to different cultures and encourage multicultural identification. Many moral conservatives, by contrast, support school vouchers so that more students can receive monocultural religious messages throughout their school days and years.

Communitarianism

Walzer is considered a communitarian as well as a multiculturalist because of his belief that individuals require community identification in order to flourish. And like communitarians who decry the loss of social capital in the United States, Walzer decries increasing "disengagement from cultural association and identity for the sake of the private pursuit of happiness. . . ." However, whereas some communitarians, such as Amitai Etzioni, emphasize the country or nation as the community for primary

---

48. Walzer, p. 103.

personal identification, Walzer emphasizes smaller groups, including those based on religion, race, ethnicity, and occupation. Because there are many such groups, and each can be a locus of personal cultural identification, Walzer is a multiculturalist, not just a communitarian. For example, Walzer wants schools to encourage students to think of themselves as hyphenated Americans, whereas most communitarians favor educational programs that emphasize what students share simply as Americans.

Political Liberalism

Walzer and Kymlicka are in some respects political liberals (individualists) as well as multiculturalists. They support the flourishing of many cultures in large part to aid individual self-respect and self-efficacy, which, in agreement with Rawls's political liberalism, they consider fundamentally important. Kymlicka, as we have seen, thinks the state should promote cultural diversity but not at the expense of individuals. He wants the external protection of cultures but opposes internal restrictions that cultures place on individual members to discourage defection. Walzer similarly advocates both multiculturalism and individualism. He writes:

> Despite appearances, the critical conflict in American life today is not between multiculturalism and some kind of cultural hegemony or singularity. . . . We live instead with the . . . conflict of manyness of groups and of individuals. And this is a conflict in which we have no choice except to affirm the value of both sides. The two pluralisms [of groups and of individuals] make America what it is or sometimes is and set the pattern for what it should be. Taken together, but only together, they are entirely consistent with a common democratic citizenship.[49]

However, as we saw regarding Amish education and Hutterite property rules, it is sometimes hard to know the proper balance between individual rights and cultural needs.

Feminism

Because many cultures disadvantage women, political scientist Susan Moller Okin supports individual rights over multiculturalism on feminist grounds. She defines feminism as "the belief that women should not be disadvantaged by their sex" and multiculturalism as the view that "minority cultures . . . are not sufficiently protected by . . . individual rights, and

---

49. Walzer, p. 102.

as a consequence . . . should be protected through special *group* rights or privileges."[50] She writes:

> Most cultures are suffused with practices and ideologies concerning gender. Suppose, then, that a culture endorses and facilitates the control of men over women in various ways. . . . Suppose, too, that there are fairly clear disparities in power between the sexes, such that the more powerful, male members are those who are generally in a position to determine and articulate the group's beliefs, practices, and interests. Under such conditions, group rights are potentially, and in many cases actually, antifeminist.[51]

Okin notes, for example, that "the overwhelming majority of 'cultural defenses' that are increasingly being invoked in U.S. criminal cases involving members of cultural minorities are connected with gender—in particular with male control over women and children."[52] Let us look into that.

The Cultural Defense and Hmong Marriage-by-Capture

Consider the case of *People v. Moua.*[53] Law professor Doriane Lambelet Coleman writes, "the defendant, a Laotian Hmong man, forcibly abducted a Laotian woman from the Fresno City College campus and forced her to engage in sexual intercourse. The woman subsequently called the police and accused the defendant of kidnapping and rape." The case seemed easy to prosecute until the issue of cultural difference was raised, whereupon "the State declined to pursue kidnapping charges and instead accepted Moua's plea of guilty to a false imprisonment charge. The judge . . . sentenced him to a 120-day jail term and a $1,000 fine, $900 of which was paid to the victim as 'reparations.'"[54] Moua received no punishment for kidnapping or rape.

Strictly speaking, the result in *Moua* was not dictated by a **cultural defense,** because no such defense is officially recognized in American law. Nevertheless, cultural factors greatly influenced the disposition of the case. The prosecutor in *People v. Moua* was aware of a case in Minnesota

---

50. Susan Moller Okin, *Is Multiculturalism Bad for Women?* (Princeton: Princeton University Press, 1999), pp. 10–11. Emphasis in original.
51. Okin, p. 12.
52. Okin, p. 18.
53. Record of Court Proceedings, No. 315972-0 (Super. Ct. Fresno County Feb. 7, 1985).
54. Doriane Lambelet Coleman, "Individualizing Justice through Multiculturalism: The Liberals' Dilemma," *Columbia Law Review,* Vol. 96, No. 5 (June 1996), pp. 1093–1167, at 1106.

of a Hmong man raping a girl not yet 12 years old and receiving little punishment. Here is a newspaper account of that case:

> With the help of St. Paul's Southeast Asian Refugee Study Project, [the prosecutor] learned that in the Hmong "marriage by capture," the woman or girl, often under 15 years of age, must protest her capture by insisting "No, no, I am not ready" to be considered virtuous and desirable. If the man does not . . . lead her off to his own home, he is considered too weak to be a husband.
>
> The prosecutor decided that it would be almost impossible to convince a jury that the girl really meant "no" and had been taken away against her will and raped. So he opted for a plea bargain.
>
> "I went to the victim's family and said, 'How would you resolve this in the old country'" [the prosecutor] said.
>
> "The victim's aunt, who spoke English, told me $3,000 and no jail, $2,000 and 60 days, or $1,000 and 90 days to restore the family honor and pride. . . ."
>
> The defendant was allowed to plead guilty to sexual intercourse with a child under the age of 12, and fined $1,000 with no jail time.[55]

Coleman notes, "the prosecutor did not charge the man either with kidnapping or rape, turning instead to Hmong culture to craft a plea bargain."[56] Cultural considerations let a man virtually get away with what we would call, from our cultural perspective, kidnapping and raping a child.

Yet a formal cultural defense has some proponents. In 1986, an Unsigned Note in the *Harvard Law Review* argued that at present cultural factors enter the criminal justice system, as in *Moua*, unsystematically. Their use depends primarily on prosecutorial discretion in filing charges and striking plea bargains and on judicial discretion in sentencing. One problem with such discretionary procedures, the Note argues, is "the opportunity for officials to exercise prejudice against cultural minorities. Statistics on the sentencing of criminals, for example, indicates the existence of systematic discrimination against minorities." In addition, "unlike excuses such as the cultural defense, these procedures do not subject cultural factors to scrutiny before a public forum, thus making it more difficult for the legal system to evaluate how justly and effectively it is dealing with cultural factors."[57]

---

55. Quoted in Coleman, pp. 1106–07.
56. Coleman, p. 1107.
57. Unsigned Note, "The Cultural Defense in the Criminal Law," in *Philosophical Problems in the Law*, 2nd ed., David M. Adams, Ed. (Belmont, CA: Wadsworth, 1996), pp. 391–98, at 393.

But why should the criminal law be sensitive to cultural factors in the first place, whether through discretionary procedures or a formal defense? One reason is to individualize justice. Normally, for example, ignorance of the law is no excuse because it is fair to assume that people raised in the country have been socialized to know its laws, whereas it may not be fair to impute the same knowledge to someone socialized abroad. Second, "laws are more effective in commanding obedience when individuals internalize the underlying norms to the point where they believe that the law embodies morally correct values. . . . An ordinarily law-abiding person raised in a foreign culture may have committed a criminal act solely because the values of her native culture compelled her to do so." Finally, all the reasons considered so far in support of multiculturalism favor a formal cultural defense. Such a defense shows respect for a plurality of cultures and for individuals who adhere to those cultures.

> Repudiation of a cultural defense may send out a broader message that an ethnic group must trade in its cultural values for that of the mainstream if it is to be accepted as an equal by the majority. It is hard to imagine a system more likely to convince a person that the majority regards her culture as inferior than one that punishes her for following the dictates of her culture.[58]
>
> When an ethnic group's cultural values are ignored by the mainstream society, the group is likely to become alienated from the majority culture. Alienation could, in turn, engender hostility and intergroup conflict that disrupt social order.[59]

In addition, perceived disdain for a culture's values may impair law abidance by weakening the culture in the minds of it members.

> Cultural values provide norms of conduct to fill the gaps in the criminal codes: such values serve independently from legal sanctions as a check on undesirable behavior. Recognition of a cultural defense is one way of preserving this nucleus of values that, although leading to undesirable behavior in some contexts, is conducive to law-abiding conduct in many others.[60]

Of course, the Note acknowledges, "if each person were required to adhere to the law only to the extent that it was consistent with her own values, societies would tend toward anarchy."[61] So the Note suggests a

---

58. Unsigned Note, p. 394.
59. Unsigned Note, p. 396.
60. Unsigned Note, p. 396.
61. Unsigned Note, p. 395.

cultural defense weighing in individual cases "the degree of the defendant's assimilation into the mainstream culture" against such considerations as "the likelihood of recurrence of the proscribed conduct . . . , whether the crime is victimless . . . , [and] whether serious bodily or emotional harm was inflicted."[62]

Kidnapping and rape seriously harm victims, so the Note may not condone light punishment for Hmong marriage-by-capture. Another important factor is "the likelihood of recurrence." Will a $1,000 fine deter Hmong men or suggest to them that Americans do not really object to their marital customs? Cultural differences may bedevil attempts to predict recidivism rates.

Other problems associated with the cultural defense in serious criminal cases concern racism and sexism. Okin seems correct that the defense is used most often, as in *Moua,* to excuse otherwise unacceptable behavior toward women and girls. Katha Pollitt, a columnist for the *Nation* writes:

> How far would an Algerian immigrant get, I wonder, if he refused to pay the interest on his Visa bill on the grounds that Islam forbids interest on borrowed money? Or a Russian who argued that the cradle-to-grave social security provided by the former Soviet Union was part of his cultural tradition and should be extended to him in Brooklyn as well? Everyone understands that money is much too important to be handed out in this whimsical fashion. Women and children are another story.[63]

Legal scholar Daina Chiu suggests accordingly that the lenient treatment of Moua, although ostensibly based on differences between the Hmong and American cultures, actually reveals their similar acceptance of men dominating women.[64]

Race is another factor. The woman in *Moua* and the girl in Minnesota were Hmong. Would cases involving white victims be handled differently? Coleman draws attention to the "selective process of sympathy and indifference that is sometimes at play in . . . prosecutorial decisions" by quoting the popular press regarding two homicides.

> He was a white 10-year-old who disappeared from a riverbank. She was a black 13-year-old suspected of running away from home.

---

62. Unsigned Note, p. 397.
63. Katha Pollitt, "Whose Culture?" in Okin, pp. 27–30, at 29.
64. Daina C. Chiu, "The Cultural Defense: Beyond Exclusion, Assimilation, and Guilty Liberalism," 82 Calif. L. Rev. 1053, http://web.lexis-nexis.com/universe, p. 33 of 75. Accessed March 2, 2004.

Different race, different families, same fate: both ended up on the police blotter as young murder victims.

Christopher Meyer's case riveted the region for two weeks, prompting an extensive search and relentless news coverage. Ophelia Williams's death barely raised a cry.

In a candid assessment, Police Chief William Doster said his community is simply "numb" when it comes to black victims.

"Christopher was white, and Ophelia was black. . . . The disease of racism has brought about the cancer of indifference."[65]

Perhaps prosecutors and judges are similarly less concerned about Hmong women and girls than about white Americans.

In sum, *although multiculturalism has its merits, it also has its limits. When serious crime is at issue many people think that individual rights are more important than multicultural rights.*

Money and Elective Politics

Having explored the strengths and limits of multiculturalism, we return now to our account of deliberative democracy. We have already found it better suited than aggregative democracy to accommodate the needs of cultural minorities. Another claim, explored now, is that deliberative practices offer the potential of greater political influence by ordinary people because voting and elections tend to favor the rich. *If the legitimacy of government rests on the consent of the governed, and democratic processes are meant to guarantee that consent, processes that limit access to a small segment of the population impair legitimacy.* Let us explore the claim that American elective politics is dominated by rich people through political advertisements and campaign contributions.

Compared to the enormous wealth of the country, Americans do not spend lavishly on political advertisements and campaigns. Total candidate expenditures for all federal offices in a presidential election year may amount to only $3 to $5 billion. This amount includes candidate expenditures in primaries and general elections for 435 seats in the House of Representatives and 33 or 34 places in the Senate, as well as for president and vice-president. This is small compared to the federal budget and may be less than consumers spend yearly on antacids.[66]

---

65. Coleman, p. 1135, note 207.
66. Kevin Phillips, *Wealth and Democracy* (New York: Broadway Books, 2002), p. 419.

What is more, the candidate with the most money does not always win. In the March 2004 primary for the U.S. Senate seat in Illinois, for example, a political newcomer, Democrat Blair Hull, spent about $40 million of his own money and was roundly defeated for the Democratic nomination by State Senator Barack Obama who spent much less. The Republican nomination was won by Jack Ryan who seems to have been among the poorer multimillionaires in the Republican race.

Nevertheless, elective politics generally confirms one of my mother's favorite sayings: "Rich or poor it's nice to have money." Political analyst Kevin Phillips writes:

> Reports by the Center for Responsive Politics and Citizen Action contended that in the 1996 congressional races, the candidates who raised the most money won 92% of the time in the House and 88% of the time in the Senate. In the 60 House districts identified before the election as toss-ups, Republicans had an average of 42% more money to spend.[67]

Republicans retained their slim margin of control in the House.

Campaign expenditures have increased, Phillips notes: "In 1976, winning Senate incumbents laid out an average of $610,000 on their races. By 1986, the figure had grown to $3 million. By 2000, the average figure for all Senate incumbents was $4.4 million, while the average winner in all races raised $7.3 million."[68] What is chump change in the economy at large, and in some industries, is unattainable by many individuals who want to run for public office, so they must appeal to political donors. For millions of dollars donors representing major industries gain influence over government taxes and regulations worth billions of dollars to the industry.

The situation provoked the following satire during the 2000 election campaign. The group calling itself "billionairesforbushorgore.com" used real facts and figures:

> While you may be familiar with stocks and bonds, currency speculation, IPOs and all the rest, there's a new investment arena you should be aware of: *legislation*. If a mutual fund returns 20% a year, that's considered quite good, but in the low-risk, high-return world of legislation, a 20% return is positively lousy. There's no reason why your investment dollar can't return 100,000% or more.
>
> Too good to be true? Don't worry, it's completely legal. With the help of a professional legislation broker (called a Lobbyist), you place

---

67. Phillips, pp. 323–24.
68. Phillips, p. 323.

your investment (called a Campaign Contribution) with a carefully selected list of legislation manufacturers (called Members of Congress). These manufacturers then go to work, crafting industry-specific subsidies, inserting tax breaks into the code, extending patents or giving away public property for free.

Just check out these results. The Timber Industry spent $8 million in campaign contributions to preserve the logging road subsidy, worth $458 million—the return on their investment was 5,725%. Glaxo Wellcome invested $1.2 million in campaign contributions to get a 19-month patent extension on Zantac worth $1 billion—their net return: 83,333%. The Tobacco Industry spent $30 million in contributions for a tax break worth $50 billion—a return on their investment: 167,000%. For a paltry $5 million in campaign contributions, the Broadcasting Industry was able to secure free digital TV licenses, a give-away of public property worth $70 billion—that's an incredible 1,400,000% return on their investment.

Phillips adds: "Some three-quarters of the individual [as opposed to industry] money that fueled turn-of-the-century presidential and congressional races came from donors with incomes over $200,000 a year (in essence, the top 1–1.5%)."[69] Perhaps as a result, tax cuts in 2001 benefited these individuals most, whereas reduced government revenues required scaling back government services of greatest benefit to the poor and middle class, such as subsidies for food, schools, and college tuition.

In sum, electoral politics (aggregative democracy) in the United States seems to be not entirely, but disproportionately, by the rich and for the rich. If democracy, by definition, regularly allows most adults in the country a significant voice in establishing and altering state laws and government policies, it seems that current electoral politics is a seriously flawed form of democracy. But is deliberative democracy any better?

Money and Civil Society

Concentrated wealth impairs deliberative democracy as it does elective politics. Deliberative democracy depends on ordinary people having access to information so they can discuss matters they consider important. Concentrated wealth allows some people to short-circuit the process at the start with misinformation.

The image that many people have of the news is shaped by the story of Woodward and Bernstein uncovering the Watergate scandal and toppling

---

69. Phillips, p. 326. Emphasis in original.

President Nixon. Few people wonder why only two reporters were on the case and why the original break-in, which occurred in April in a presidential election year, was not widely investigated before the November election. "According to Project Censored," write John Stauber and Sheldon Rampton in *Toxic Sludge Is Good for You*, "a phone call from the Nixon Whitehouse was all it took to persuade CBS chair William Paley to scale back Walter Cronkite's attempt to do an extraordinary two-part series about Watergate on the *CBS Evening News* before the election."[70]

Another example concerns news coverage of the war in El Salvador in the 1980s. Lance Bennett writes in *News: The Politics of Illusion:*

> The *New York Times* sent a bright young reporter named Ray Bonner to cover [the war]. Unfortunately, Bonner was inexperienced in the fine points of press-government cooperation and had the audacity to develop contacts among rebel leaders fighting the U.S.-backed government. Some of Bonner's early stories suggested that the rebels had considerable popular support, while the regime proclaimed "democratic" by U.S. officials had engaged repeatedly in terrorism, torture, intimidation, and massacre of its own people. . . . According to a "well-placed" reporter on the *Times,* [the U.S. ambassador in El Salvador] "became hysterical" about Bonner's critical reporting. . . .

The *Times* Executive Editor Abe Rosenthal visited El Salvador, met with the ambassador, replaced Bonner with a new reporter, and "*Times* coverage swung clearly toward the official definition of the situation with the story of the day making the headlines of the day. . . . After the war ended, teams of United Nations investigators discovered mass graves" that confirmed much of what Bonner had reported.[71] But this information was too late to affect American public opinion or foreign policy.

Money is at the root of the problem. Investigative reporting costs much more money than simply reporting on staged political events and quoting "official sources." *Large corporations increasingly own news media and want to increase profit. Cost-cutting involves reducing the staff of reporters, which makes news organizations increasingly dependent on government officials for information. Under these conditions, the media dare not offend such officials with challenging stories* on a political break-in or a controversial war.

---

70. John Stauber and Sheldon Rampton, *Toxic Sludge Is Good for You* (Monroe, ME: Common Courage Press, 1995), p. 180.

71. W. Lance Bennett, *News: The Politics of Illusion,* 5th ed., (Addison Wesley Longman, Inc., 2003), pp. 154–55.

Money is involved also when politicians take their cues from industry leaders and the press follows the politicians. In 1994, when President Clinton unveiled his plan to cover all Americans with health insurance, the health insurance industry, which stood to lose a lot of money, began running ads featuring a fictitious couple, Harry and Louise, who expressed doubts about the Clinton plan, Lance Bennett writes.

> Meanwhile, behind the scenes the health care industry was spending widely on lobbying and campaign contributions to key members of Congress to pry their support away for the president's plan. Not surprisingly, the authoritative opposition voices from Congress that were heard in the news echoed the same elements of doubt raised in the advertising. . . .[72]
>
> After more than a year of concerted news and advertising information blitzes, a strong majority of 74% favored the idea of universal coverage, a cornerstone of the Clinton plan. At the same time, only 33% backed the Clinton plan. . . . Perhaps most telling of all was the discovery made by the White House polling team led by Stanley Greenberg that after all the sides had weighed in, the public actually understood less about the Clinton plan than they did at the time it was first unveiled.[73]

Concentrated wealth undermined public debate from the start, precluding meaningful deliberation.

Perhaps more surprising is the fact that much of what appears as news originates in corporate public relations departments. Due to cost-cutting in the news department, there are now fewer reporters than PR people. According to Jeff and Marie Blyskal, authors of *PR: How the Public Relations Industry Writes the News*,

> whole sections of the news are virtually owned by PR. . . . Unfortunately, "news" hatched by a PR person and journalists working together looks much like real news dug up by enterprising journalists working independently. The public thus does not know which news stories and journalists are playing servant to PR.[74]

Stauber and Rampton add:

> The North American Precis Syndicate . . . sends camera-ready stories on behalf of most of the top PR firms and most Fortune 500

---

72. Bennett, p. 227.
73. Bennett, p. 228.
74. Found in Stauber and Rampton, p. 183.

companies to 10,000 newspapers, almost all of whom reprint some of the material. The stories are designed to promote products, or serve clients' political agendas. . . .[75]

A similar business, RadioUSA, "supplies broadcast quality news scripts to 5,000 radio stations throughout the country. . . . We'll write, typeset, print, and distribute broadcast quality scripts. . . ." Hard-pressed radio journalists greet these canned scripts with relief rather than suspicion.

Video news releases, known as VNRs, typically come packaged with two versions of the story the PR firm is trying to promote. The first version is fully edited, with voiceovers already included. . . . The second version is known as a "B-roll" and consists of the raw footage that was used to produce the fully edited version. The receiving station can edit the B-roll footage itself, or combine it with other footage received from other sources.[76]

In short, in civil society involving deliberative democracy, as in elective politics involving aggregative democracy, wealthy individuals and corporations exercise influence disproportionate to their numbers. This degrades political legitimacy if legitimacy rests on the democratic principle of government by the people.

Democracy and Distributive Justice

We saw in Chapter 6 that John Rawls argued for what he called the difference principle, which requires that economic inequality benefit society's poorest members most. *The importance of democracy in creating and sustaining political legitimacy and the degree to which concentrated wealth degrades legitimacy are additional reasons for the state to ensure the wide distribution of income and wealth.*

Rawls distinguishes between political liberty, which is the formal right to participate in political decisions, and the *value* of that political liberty, which is the ability genuinely to affect political outcomes. He writes:

> The liberties protected by the principle of participation lose much of their value whenever those who have greater private means are permitted to use their advantages to control the course of public debate. For eventually these inequalities will enable those better situated to

---

75. Stauber and Rampton, p. 183.
76. Stauber and Rampton, p. 184.

exercise a larger influence over the development of legislation. In due time they are likely to acquire a preponderant weight in settling social questions, at least in regard . . . to those things that support their favored circumstance.[77]

Kevin Phillips notes some effects of wealthy people using their power. National economic policy is made increasingly in Western democracies by unelected officials in central banks, such as Alan Greenspan of the United States Federal Reserve System. Crucial decisions are taken out of voters' hands and left up to influence by "boundaryless international—and equally self-serving—networks of bankers, securities firms, hedge funds, [and] economists . . . [who] collectively shape money supplies, stock markets, growth patterns, and recessions. . . ."[78] Greenspan's "choice to protect accumulated wealth through slow growth, which requires minimizing wage increases, has been a formula for favoring holders of financial assets and accepting a concomitant steady increase in economic inequality and polarization."[79]

Public discussions of wages and immigration show bias toward the rich. Both Democratic and Republican administrations work to keep wages low to avoid inflation, but then favor legal immigration to fill low-paying jobs. The idea of dramatically raising the minimum wage to attract Americans to these jobs is not even on the public agenda because that would be costly to big business and lower the value of investors' financial assets. Also off the political agenda is the enormous income increase of the top 1% of Americans. Only the poor earning more is considered an economic problem. Would such priorities continue if poor people influenced economic policy commensurate with their numbers in the population, as democracy suggests they should? It seems that the entire process of economic deliberation is dominated by the rich and serves to further their advantage, which further entrenches their domination, and so on.

Tax policy is another example. "By now," writes Nobel Prize-winning economist Joseph Stiglitz,

it is well known how [President] Bush's tax package [which was being debated in 2003] favors the rich. . . . While 50% of all tax filers would receive $100 or less, and two thirds $500 or less, Bush

---

77. John Rawls, *A Theory of Justice* (Cambridge, MA: Harvard University Press, 1971), p. 225.

78. Phillips, pp. 414–15.

79. Phillips, p. 416.

himself, according to Bloomberg News, would have saved $44,500 on his 2001 tax returns, and [Vice-President] Cheney $326,555.... The calculations of the Brookings Institution Tax Policy Center show that more than half of the benefits of exempting corporate dividends from the individual income tax would flow to the top 5% of the population. All the taxpayers in that group earn more than $140,000, and they have an average income of $350,000. The 226,000 richest tax filers, those with incomes over $1 million, will receive a benefit roughly equal in size to the 120 million tax filers with incomes below $100,000.[80]

Would anyone in a democracy where the middle-class majority has political power commensurate with their numbers have proposed such lopsided tax reductions? The weakness of popular protest reflects the power of moneyed interests to dominate debate.

Examples of this abound. Great controversy arose early in the new century about what was called "the death tax." Since death is inevitable, this sounds like a tax that applies to everyone. However, "the death tax" turns out to be an inheritance tax applied only to large estates. Only the wealthiest 2% of the population receives enough inheritance to be required to pay this tax. Is this system fair? If moneyed interests did not dominate debate, the answer would be obvious to 98% of the population because, at the same time, government programs needed for fair equality of opportunity were being cut. For example, owing primarily to budget problems at the state level, tuition at many state universities was increasing by double-digit percentages most years.[81] Because the federal government had enormous budget deficits caused partly by tax reductions for rich people, it was unable to increase help for middle-class families sending children to college.

The point here is not to advocate particular tax policies but to note that *what is taken seriously in public conversation tends to favor the rich.* Other views are expressed but tend to be marginalized. *This marginalization impairs both aggregative and deliberative democracy and degrades political legitimacy.*

---

80. Joseph E. Stiglitz, "Bush's Tax Plan—The Dangers," *The New York Review of Books* (March 13, 2003), pp. 13–15, at 14.

81. National Public Radio's "Morning Edition" reported on March 25, 2004 that the average increase of tuition and fees at all state universities between 2002 and 2003 was 14%.

CONCLUSION

According to T. M Scanlon, as we have seen, right and wrong are determined by "what could be justified to others on grounds that they, if appropriately motivated, could not reasonably reject."[82] The appropriate motivation is their desire also to live by rules that others could not reasonably reject.

Subjecting legal rules to the test of reasonable rejection supports both multiculturalism and democracy. Cultures are foundational for self-development, self-efficacy, self-respect, and democratic participation, and they should be protected for these reasons. The test of reasonable rejection supplies an additional rationale for their protection. Minority-group members can reasonably reject legal rules, such as laws against sacrificing animals in religious rituals, that interfere with their culture if the rules are designed to avert harms, such as pain to animals, that the majority culture generally allows, such as in rodeos.

Yet limits to tolerance exist. Sacrificing children instead of animals, for example, even naughty children of church members, is intolerable because the harm is extraordinary. Society allows no comparable violation of a child's right to life. Between these extremes, however, lie many issues, some regarding education, where the reasonableness of rejecting state laws is uncertain.

Scanlon's test of reasonable rejection also supports the democratic ideal of giving the majority of people the opportunity to influence state laws and policies. People are less likely to be subject to laws they can reasonably reject if they participate as equals in the political process that generates those laws. However, aggregative democracy can result in a tyranny of the majority, so deliberative democracy is needed to promote multicultural understanding of minority perspectives and to protect individuals in the majority culture, such as would-be nude dancer Darlene Miller, who seek reasonable deviation from social norms. Aggregation and deliberation are not mutually exclusive alternatives because deliberations ultimately, although indirectly, influence elections and legislation. Both are needed for state legitimacy, if legitimacy rests in some sense on the consent of the governed.

Finally, *if the foundation of state legitimacy is democracy, rule by the people, enormous disparities between have and have-nots and growing gaps between the rich and the middle class compromise that foundation*

---

82. Scanlon, p. 5.

whether democracy is aggregative or deliberative. The state must include moderating such disparities and gaps among its functions if it is to avoid jeopardizing its foundation.

JUDGMENT CALLS

1. The Indiana statute against all public nudity, even in nightclubs frequented by willing adults, also makes public "sexual intercourse" and "deviate sexual conduct" illegal. What considerations, if any, beyond those that apply to simple nudity, might justify outlawing public sexual intercourse and public deviate sexual conduct even in nightclubs frequented by willing adults? How might deliberative democratic discussions deal with these considerations?

2. What does the ideal of deliberative democracy suggest about including in the deliberative process people with strong racial, religious, or ethnic prejudice? For example, should a student who hates African Americans be allowed to hang a Confederate battle flag outside his dorm window to indicate his belief that the South should have won the Civil War and blacks should still be slaves? In other words, how should reasonable people view legal proscriptions of hate speech?

3. If the *Yoder* decision made an exception to Wisconsin's school attendance law to accommodate the Amish, what reasons, if any, justify refusal to accommodate Mormons, if there are any, who want to practice polygamy? Consider arguments needed to reach reflective equilibrium.

4. Headscarves (worn by many Muslim women), kipas (scull caps worn by Orthodox Jewish men), conspicuous crosses worn by Christians, and all other visible symbols of religious affiliation were banned from public (secular) schools in France in 2004. What does this tell us about multiculturalism in France? How might deliberative democratic processes produce this result or its opposite?

5. Fumiko Kimura, a Japanese-American, killed her two children and almost killed herself after learning that her husband was having an affair. The defense at her trial said that her behavior conformed to a Japanese custom that called for mother-child suicide in such circumstances.[83] How might feminists view this use of a cultural

---

83. See Coleman, pp. 1109–11.

defense differently than they view it in the Hmong marriage-by-capture case? Is a different view justified? Tune in to the next chapter for more discussion of this case and its relationship to feminism.

6. Money is not the only problem besetting democracy. In addition, many citizens seem unwilling or unable to accept unexpected or unwelcome information. Historian and political commentator Garry Wills wrote shortly after the 2004 presidential election: "A poll taken just before the elections showed that 75% of Mr. Bush's supporters believe Iraq either worked closely with Al Qaeda or was directly involved in the attacks of 9/11."[84] All available evidence contradicts this view, and Democrats, who spend roughly the same amount of money in their campaign as Republicans, stressed the irrelevance of Iraq to the 9/11 attacks. Citizen aversion to relevant information impairs both aggregative and deliberative democracy. What can be done?

---

84. Gary Wills, "The Day the Enlightenment Went Out," *New York Times,* November 4, 2004, www.nytimes.com/2004/11/04/wills.html?th, p. 2 of 2. Retrieved November 5, 2004.

9 Feminism

Political scientist Susan Moller Okin defines **feminism** as "the belief that women should not be disadvantaged by their sex, that they should be recognized as having human dignity equal to that of men, and that they should have the opportunity to live as fulfilling and as freely chosen lives as men can."[1] Compare such feminism with the ideal of femininity advocated in 1965 by actress Arlene Dahl in *Always Ask a Man: Arlene Dahl's Key to Femininity*. Dahl believes that any woman's highest fulfillment is in a loving relationship with a man. To achieve this goal women should try to please men, and the best way to know what pleases them is to always ask a man.

> By listening to men you learn what qualities every Adam looks for in his Eve, and this should be used as a guide to help you become a more appealing female. Incidentally, while you are gathering this important data you are already making a great impression because all men love to be listened to! See how it works?[2]

In her own research Dahl has found that flattery is very helpful:

> Let him know that you think he's wonderful. . . . Stop trying to prove that anything he can do you can do better. The truth of the matter is that even if you could, it wouldn't be much fun. . . .
>
> NEVER upstage a man. Don't top his joke, even if you have to bite your tongue to keep from doing it. Never launch loudly into your own opinions on a subject—whether it's petunias or politics. Instead, draw out his ideas to which you can gracefully add your footnotes from time to time. You may be well equipped to steal the spotlight, but most females would rather sing a duet than a solo.[3]

---

1. Susan Moller Okin, *Is Multiculturalism Bad for Women?* (Princeton, NJ: Princeton University Press, 1999), p. 10.
2. Arlene Dahl, *Always Ask a Man: Arlene Dahl's Key to Femininity* (Englewood Cliffs, NJ: Prentice Hall, 1965), Preface.
3. Dahl, p. 12.

> In a restaurant, let your mate or date do the ordering. It's more fun to eat hot dogs with a man than caviar by yourself. You may know more about vintage wines than the wine steward, but if you're smart you'll let your man do the choosing and be ecstatic over his selection, even if it tastes like shampoo.[4]

Deference to men should last a lifetime, according to Dahl. To keep their marriages vital, women should center their lives around their husbands:

> Never let your own interests override your husband's. Let *his* job, *his* hobbies, *his* interests come first.
>
> There should be nothing that takes precedence in your day's schedule over making yourself attractive and appealing for the man in your life, [including] . . . children's activities.[5]

Okin's feminism and Dahl's femininity appear at odds. It does not seem that women can have "human dignity equal to that of men" and "live . . . freely chosen lives," as feminism requires, if they are dedicated to praising and pleasing men. This chapter explores several views about appropriate relationships between women and men. Some moral conservatives believe that women do best when they emphasize traditional female roles that include femininity. Liberal feminists, by contrast, believe that women should have equality with men, but they often differ with one another about what this requires. Some liberals believe that equality requires applying the same state laws and policies to men and women, whereas others believe that differences between the sexes justify different treatment in certain situations, such as when a battered woman kills her abuser.

Radical feminists claim that subordinating women is at the heart of our culture and that the distinction between private and public spheres of activity often masks this fact. They advocate new social practices and massive government programs to give women equal power with men. These include state-supported day care for the children of working women and a crackdown on sexual harassment. Finally, cultural feminists believe that women and men have by nature or socialization different virtues and that the virtues of women are superior. Character traits traditionally associated with women should be promoted for everyone, and people with these traits should increasingly be in positions of power.

---

4. Dahl, p. 13.
5. Dahl, p. 175. Emphasis in original.

All the thinkers considered here make some good points, but even collectively they do not exhaust feminist (or antifeminist) thought because they are white scholars discussing issues of concern primarily to white people in industrial societies, especially the United States. Some problems discussed in the last chapter regarding multiculturalism, by contrast, are of greatest direct concern to people of color in the United States, and some issues of moral relativism discussed in Chapter 11 are of greatest direct concern to women of color in Third World countries. So, although this is the book's only chapter devoted to feminism, it is not the only chapter to address feminist concerns.

Classical Liberal Feminism

In the 19th century, women in the United States were prohibited by law from entering professions for which they were considered naturally unsuited, including law. Thus, the State of Illinois prevented Myra Bradwell, who had all requisite qualifications, from receiving a license to practice law. In 1872 the United States Supreme Court upheld Illinois' statute. In his concurring opinion, Justice Bradley wrote:

> Man is, or should be, woman's protector and defender. The natural and proper timidity and delicacy which belongs to the female sex evidently unfits it for many of the occupations of civil life. The constitution of the family organization, which is founded in the divine ordinance, as well as the nature of things, indicates the domestic sphere as that which properly belongs to the domain and functions of womanhood, [fulfilling there] the noble and benign offices of wife and mother.[6]

Few people today defend such blanket discrimination against women. Christina Hoff Sommers applauds classical liberal feminism for effecting this change. She writes in her 1994 book *Who Stole Feminism? How Women Have Betrayed Women*:

> The traditional, classically liberal, humanistic feminism that was initiated more than 150 years ago . . . had a specific agenda, demanding for women the same rights before the law that men enjoyed. The suffrage had to be won, and the laws regarding property, marriage, divorce, and child custody had to be made equitable. More recently, abortion rights had to be protected.

---

6. *Bradwell v. The State* 16 Wall. 130, at 141.

Most American women subscribe philosophically to that older "First Wave" kind of feminism whose main goal is equity. . . . "We ask no better laws than those you have made for yourselves. We need no other protection than that which your present laws secure to you," said Elizabeth Cady Stanton . . . , addressing the New York State Legislature in 1854.[7]

Classical liberal feminists do not question the basic liberal ideals of individual autonomy, civil rights, political equality, and equal opportunity. They just want women to be included along with men on equitable terms because it is the individual, whether male or female, not the family or social group, who is ultimately important to liberals.

Classical liberal feminism has been successful. In 1920 women began to vote. In 1963 Congress passed the Equal Pay Act, which disallows pay discrimination "on the basis of sex."[8] Title VII of the 1964 Civil Rights Act outlaws employment discrimination on the basis of "race, color, religion, sex, or national origin."[9] Liberal feminists favor abortion rights in part because a woman lacks equal opportunity when an unwanted pregnancy can disrupt her career and impair her fair competition with men. If abortion rights damage the nuclear family, as many moral conservatives claim, they do so only through choices made by individual women, and such decisions must be respected.

Sommers recommends also changing the typical university tenure system to accommodate

> the growing number of females entering academic careers. Since all new professors are required to "publish or perish" in the first six years of their career, the tenure clock ticks away at exactly the same rate as young women's biological clocks. Adjustments are called for since this state of affairs seriously affects equality of opportunity.[10]

In sum, *classical liberal feminists such as Sommers are basically free-market conservatives whose feminism consists in demanding that women be treated the same as men except in rare cases when different treatment promotes equal opportunity.*

Such feminists are generally wary of rules designed to accommodate women's child-bearing potential because such rules often impair equal

---

7. Christina Hoff Sommers, *Who Stole Feminism: How Women Have Betrayed Women* (New York: Simon and Schuster), p. 22.

8. 29 U.S.C. (d) 1.

9. Public Law 88-352, 78 STAT 241.

10. Sommers, p. 242.

opportunity. A case in point, not discussed by Sommers, is *International Union, UAW v. Johnson Controls, Inc.* Johnson Controls makes batteries, exposing workers to lead in the manufacturing process. High lead levels in a person's blood can harm any child that may be conceived. In 1982 Johnson Controls instituted a policy allowing only men to have the better-paying jobs making batteries, supposedly to protect the fetuses of women who might get pregnant with too much lead in their blood. Johnson Controls relegated all women, regardless of their intention to have a child, to predominantly lower-paid positions in the office, "except those whose inability to bear children is medically documented" because "eight employees [became] pregnant while maintaining blood lead levels in excess of 30 micrograms per deciliter."[11]

The court found Johnson Controls' policy in violation of Title VII of the Civil Rights Act because it discriminates against women employees.

> Despite evidence in the record about the debilitating effect of lead exposure on the male reproductive system, Johnson Controls is concerned only with the harms that may befall the unborn offspring of its female employees. . . . Johnson Controls' policy is facially discriminatory because it requires only a female employee to produce proof that she is not capable of reproducing.

The court saw illegal discrimination in the fact that research shows danger to children conceived by anyone, male or female, with high lead levels. The company's restriction of women only violated Title VII because it relegated women to lower-paid positions.

Moral Conservative Arguments against Feminism

Mainstream moral conservatives today do not oppose Title VII, but they claim that *natural and permanent differences between men and women dictate that women and society flourish only when most women are wives and mothers in traditional families.* They therefore decry such social and legal developments as: "sexual liberation" and easily available birth control and abortion to help women, like men, dissociate sex from pregnancy and marriage; no-fault divorce to help women exit unwanted marriages; affirmative action to help women enter traditionally male-dominated,

---

11. *International Union, UAW v. Johnson Controls, Inc.* 499 U.S. 187 (1991), abbreviated in *Philosophical Problems in the Law,* 2nd ed., David M. Adams, Ed. (Belmont, CA: Wadsworth, 1996), pp. 315–18, at 316.

and often high-paying, jobs; and government-supported day care to meet parental responsibilities when women work outside the home. Such changes, moral conservatives claim, harm the nuclear family, frustrate women who naturally flourish as wives and mothers, increase out-of-wedlock births, and impoverish women and children.

Moral conservative Irving Kristol challenges the value to women of "sexual liberation."

> The agenda of a candid, casual attitude toward sex was vigorously sponsored by feminists who mistakenly perceived it as a step toward "equality. . . ." [But it] has turned out to be—as it was destined to be— a male scam. Easy, available sex is pleasing to men and debasing to women, who are used and abused in the process. . . . True equality between men and women can only be achieved by a moral code that offers women some protection against male predators—and all men are, to one degree or another, natural predators when it comes to sex.[12]
>
> It is a fact of our human nature that . . . for men, the sexual act can represent a neat combination of power and pleasure, with the woman an agreeable "sex object." For women, it tends to be suffused with more generalized human emotions. . . .
>
> Our media, trapped in a progressive mode of thinking about sex, keep desperately trying to pretend that this difference does not exist. So do our universities, as they blithely crowd their students into mixed dorms, even mixed shower rooms. In both cases, we are presented with the myth of modern, liberated women, usually pursuing a professional career, who can "handle" sex as easily, as calmly, as confidently as their male counterparts are presumed to do. It is a myth that has ruined countless lives.[13]

Victorian morality is better for women, Kristol claims, than sexual liberation.

Conservative political activist Phyllis Schlafly agrees with Kristol and notes that no-fault divorce, like sexual liberation, helps men but harms women: "We saw the victims of the easy divorce laws so eagerly promoted by the feminist movement in the 1970s. In truth, those easy divorce laws liberated husbands to trade in a faithful wife of 20 years and enjoy a younger woman."[14] The ideal of equal independence for men and women hurts women because the sexes are naturally and importantly different.

---

12. Irving Kristol, *Neo-Conservatism: The Autobiography of an Idea* (New York: Free Press, 1995), p. 56.
13. Kristol, pp. 60–61.
14. Phyllis Schlafly, *Feminist Fantasies* (Dallas, TX: Spence Publishing, 2003), p. 19.

Schlafly points out that *children display gender-related differences despite parental efforts at gender neutrality.*

> A case in point is a hilarious article in the *Washington Post* called "Boys Just Want to Have Guns." The *Post* writer admitted that her three-year-old son, and the sons of all her pacifist-feminist-yuppie friends, despite their parents' persistent efforts to bring them up sex-neutral (without toy guns . . .) nevertheless are naturally, irrepressibly male: boyish, aggressive, and fascinated by guns.
>
> In addition, she moaned, the daughters . . . , given trucks and airplanes, still go for dolls and dress-up jewelry. "The boys slug each other and the girls paint their fingernails. Where are they getting this stuff?" she asks.[15]

Owing to innate and ineradicable differences of this kind, Schlafly contends, we should not expect equal employment opportunity to produce equal participation of men and women in every line of work.

> Since 1964, federal laws have guaranteed women open access to every type of job, but 99% of plumbers are still men. Are we prisoners of obsolete stereotypes? Hardly. Even high wages can't lure many women to this most essential trade. On the other hand, 97% of day-care workers are women. No one dares admit there is a biological maternal instinct, but the statistics can't be disputed.[16]

Schlafly assumes that individual choice guided by innate propensities, rather than illegal gender discrimination for which affirmative action might be an appropriate legal remedy, produces these results. Her own children's career choices bolster this assumption. Ms. Schlafly's engineer husband tried to talk all six of their children into studying engineering, but only their sons followed this advice. Their two daughters freely chose to study liberal arts, where pay tends to be low.

One fundamental difference between men and women that justifies their different treatment in law and social custom is that "women have babies and men don't," Schlafly writes. This difference justifies the traditional nuclear family and the desire of most women to be wives and mothers.

> Our Judeo-Christian civilization has developed the law and custom that, since women bear the physical consequences of the sex act, men must be required to pay in other ways. These laws and customs decree that a man must carry his share by physical protection and

---

15. Schlafly, p. 13.
16. Schlafly, p. 132.

financial support of his children and of the woman who bears his children, and also by a code of behavior that benefits and protects both the woman and the children.

This is accomplished by the institution of the family. Our respect for the family as the basic unit of society . . . is the greatest single achievement in the history of women's rights. It assures a woman the most precious and important right of all—the right to keep her own baby and to be supported and protected. . . .

The institution of the family is advantageous for women for many reasons. After all, what do we want out of life? To love and be loved? Mankind has not discovered a better nest for a lifetime of reciprocal love. A sense of achievement? A man may search 30 to 40 years for accomplishment in his profession. A woman can enjoy real achievement when she is young by having a baby.[17]

Women are emotionally harmed when deprived of marriage and family, Schlafly adds. In 1986 *Ms. Magazine,* a tribune of feminism, reported the continuing desire of many professional women for marriage and family. Schlafly writes:

The first article that caught my eye, "Learning to Flirt at 37," was the confession of a mature feminist with a good job and an apartment of her own, who grew up in the 1960s believing that flirting was "Victorian in the midst of the sexual revolution." After all those years of buying her own flowers, opening her own doors, and cooking dinners for herself after going to the movies alone, she actually answered an ad in the local newspaper headlined "Learn to Flirt."[18]

Another article confessed that the main topic of conversation among brainy, successful women is the "man shortage."[19]

In 1997 Schlafly found that disappointment with feminism continued. "Now we are starting to see acute bitterness from the generation that believed the liberationist lies and have discovered that, contrary to feminist ideology, women, indeed, have a biological clock." The Independent Women's Forum's *Women's Quarterly* reported in August of that year on women who built impressive careers but

are angry because they discovered too late that "the window for getting married and having children is way smaller than one can possibly foresee at age 25."

---

17. Schlafly, pp. 89–90. Emphasis added.
18. Schlafly, p. 16
19. Schlafly, p. 17.

> So, we hear the anguish of babyless 40ish women frustrated by their inability to get pregnant, spending their money and tears on chemicals and on clinics dispensing procedures with high failure rates.[20]

The television series "Sex and the City" often refers to professional women's desire for marriage and family, although the characters seem unaware of Arlene Dahl's advice.

The Feminization of Poverty

The "sexual revolution" of the 1960s and 1970s harmed women financially as well as emotionally, moral conservative William Bennett claims. Sex was no longer "conditioned on a promise of marriage if pregnancy resulted," producing "a huge increase in out-of-wedlock births." What is worse, "as pregnancy and childbirth increasingly became the choice of the woman alone, men felt less duty bound either to marry or to provide for the welfare of the child."[21]

In 2002 Andrew Hacker reported in the *New York Review of Books* some consequences for women and children. "One American child in three is now born to unmarried parents, whereas in 1960 the figure was one in 20. . . . In the early 1970s, half of premarital pregnancies led to marriage. By the 1990s, fewer than a quarter did." This tends to impoverish women and children, Hacker continues:

> The most recent census figures show that the median income for all married couples with children is $60,168. It is $45,315 when only the father works but rises to $72,773 when both parents are employed full-time. In contrast, the median income for women raising children on their own is $19,934, and for those who have never married it is a poverty-level 13,048.[22]

Some unmarried parents live together, but this is little help, Hacker writes. "The median income for unmarried couples is $39,838, well under that of their married counterparts, although some of the difference may be caused by their being younger." However, "the average

---

20. Schlafly, p. 80.

21. William J. Bennett, *The Broken Hearth: Reversing the Moral Collapse of the American Family* (New York: Doubleday, 2001), p. 19.

22. Andrew Hacker, "How Are Women Doing?" *The New York Review of Books*, April 11, 2002, pp. 63–66, at 64.

duration of cohabiting unions remains relatively short. . . . Only about half last more than 18 months."[23] In most cases, the immediate result of breakup is a single woman raising one or two children at or near the poverty line.

Classical liberal feminist Christina Sommers is more positive. Writing in the early 1990s, she does not worry about the feminization of poverty, claiming instead that "by most measures, the 80s were a time of rather spectacular gains by American women—in education, in wages, and in such traditionally male professions as business, law and medicine." Consider, for example, education:

> Today more than ever, economic position is a function of education. In 1970, 41% of college students were women; in 1979, 50% were women; and in 1992, 55% were women. In 1970, 5% of law degrees were granted to women. In 1989, the figure was 41%; by 1991 it was 43%, and it has since gone up. In 1970, women earned 8% of medical degrees. This rose to 33% in 1989; by 1991 it was 36%.[24]

Women's earnings compared to men's have increased as well. Instead of earning only 59 cents for every dollar earned by a man, as they did in the 1970s, women in the 1990s earned about 72 cents for every dollar a man earned. When only younger women are considered, the figure is 80 cents. Most of the remaining differences in earnings, Sommers claims, "reflect such prosaic matters as shorter work weeks and lesser workplace experience. For example, the average work week for full-time, year-round females is shorter than for males. When economists compare men's and women's *hourly* earnings instead of their *yearly* earnings, the wage gap narrows even more.[25]

Sommers challenges the view that there is a "glass ceiling" that prevents women from entry into the highest echelons of pay, power, and prestige.

> Promotion in high-powered professional jobs often goes to those who have put in long hours in evenings and on weekends. Husbands may be more likely to do so than wives, for a variety of reasons, including unequal division of responsibilities at home, in which case the source of the difficulty is at home, not in the marketplace.
>
> Obviously, the experience gap also reflects the fact that many women choose to move into and out of the work force during

---

23. Hacker, p. 65.
24. Sommers, p. 238.
25. Sommers, pp. 240–41. Emphasis in original.

childbearing and child-rearing years. This reduces the amount of experience they acquire . . . and naturally results in lower earnings, quite apart from any possible discrimination.[26]

According to Sommers, then, most remaining differences in pay between younger men and women reflect choices women make favoring family over career. As a liberal (primarily a free-market conservative on these matters), Sommers respects such choices. Just as she rejects laws and social policies that restrict women's choices in order to maintain the traditional nuclear family, she rejects government intervention aimed at getting women to choose career over family. If women choose to marry or have children and this reduces their earning potential, there is no problem. Absent gender discrimination, women are getting what they deserve.

Sommers's free-market conservative views lead many feminists to reject her claim to represent feminism, as she fails to acknowledge and address continuing discrimination against women and the feminization of poverty. Moral conservatives are not troubled by discrimination and poverty if it leads women to embrace traditional roles and institutions. Radical feminists, by contrast, believe that more radical change is needed to promote freedom and combat discrimination and poverty.

Radical Feminism

Sommers is a political liberal. Whether libertarian, free-market conservative, or liberal contractarian, liberals carve out a sphere of activity that they deem private, that the state should largely ignore. The nature and extent of this private realm has changed over time, opening private family relationships to increasing public regulation. Some parental punishments formerly considered private are now treated as criminal child abuse. A husband's nonconsensual sex with his wife used to be a private matter, but we now call it rape. Still, political liberals, including traditional liberal feminists such as Sommers, uphold a distinction between public and private realms and oppose state intervention in truly private matters.

Radical feminists reject the public/private distinction and claim that the personal is political. They agree on this point with moral conservatives who also want the state to intervene in personal matters and facilitate beneficial private relationships. However, as we have seen, moral conservatives believe that women and society in general fare best when people

---

26. Sommers, p. 241.

occupy traditional roles in their personal lives, so they advocate state policies designed to support traditional nuclear families. Radical feminists, by contrast, claim that the personal is political because "private" relationships contribute to the general subordination of women to men, which they call **patriarchy.**

"In order to qualify as a radical feminist," writes philosopher Rosemarie Tong, "a feminist must insist the sex/gender system is the fundamental cause of women's oppression."[27] The **sex/gender system** associates biological sex with gender roles. It contributes to women's oppression by assigning women dependent, subordinate positions in "private" life. The "private" nuclear family is a perfect example. The husband works outside the home to earn the vast majority, if not all, of the income the family needs. This gives him predominant power in the family, according to the new golden rule: whoever has the gold rules. In addition, in a society in which personal worth is often measured by financial attainment, the fact that women in such families are not paid for the work expected of them— cleaning house, doing laundry, preparing meals, tending to children, and so on—results in women, more than men, being personally as well as financially insecure. Thus, the private nuclear family promotes patriarchy, the social and political domination of women by men. Arlene Dahl's advice that women should fawn over men manifests patriarchy. If women had equal power, they would not need to hide their talents and pretend that mediocre men are wonderful.

When the norm of the nuclear family prevails in private life, women lack equal employment opportunity at work because, even if they work outside the home, they are expected to skip work whenever a child is sick, to leave work early to attend a parent-teacher conference, to leave the office on time to make the evening meal at home, and to quit their jobs when a husband's job, which typically brings in more money, requires relocation. For any political philosophy that espouses equal opportunity for men and women, these private arrangements are political because they incline reasonable employers to hire men rather than women for key positions. Equality for women requires cultural change regarding private life.

Alternatively, women's equality requires changes in the workplace to accommodate family needs. Most highly paid jobs have been designed with the assumption that workers are men who have wives at home taking care of the house and children. Fair equality of opportunity for women

---

27. Rosemarie Putnam Tong, *Feminist Thought: A More Comprehensive Introduction,* 2nd ed. (Boulder: Westview, 1997), p. 46.

requires redefinitions of what counts as reasonable commitments of time and energy at work. Philosopher Janet Radcliffe-Richards writes, "I am firmly convinced that if women had been fully involved in the running of society from the start they would have *found* a way of arranging work and children to fit each other. Men have had no such motivations, and we can see the result."[28] Because men had power, they designed work schedules that help them keep power. Women, much more often than men, must choose between family and career. Again, the liberal separation of public and private life is unrealistic.

Many aspects of our culture's sex/gender system reinforce patriarchy. In general, getting ahead in society requires people to be active, assertive, smart, and strong. Sex/gender stereotypes attribute these characteristic mostly to men, making a woman with these traits seem odd to herself and others. Philosopher Alison Jaggar writes:

> Male-dominant culture, as all feminists have observed, defines masculinity and femininity as contrasting forms. In contemporary society, men are defined as active, women as passive; men are intellectual, women are intuitive; men are inexpressive, women emotional; men are strong, women weak; men are dominant, women submissive, etc.; ad nauseam.[29]

These contrasts keep women down. Radcliffe-Richards adds:

> Taking the lead, one of the strongest status indicators of all, nearly always falls by convention to men. The man gives orders, drives the car, makes the advances in courtship. In couples where these roles are reversed there is a tendency for social disapproval or mockery; the man is henpecked, the woman wears the trousers. In courtship, a woman who does what men are expected to do is forward, or desperate, or a slut. The present institutions bring about nothing like equality . . . , men have the advantage.[30]

If you think these cultural peculiarities are unimportant, consider the ways that our culture is clearly biased against women. These biases are so pervasive and long-standing that most people do not notice them. We saw

---

28. Janet Radcliffe-Richards, *The Skeptical Feminist: A Philosophical Inquiry* (London: Routledge and Kegan Paul, 1980), p. 114, in Will Kymlicka, *Contemporary Political Philosophy: An Introduction* (New York: Oxford University Press, 2002), p. 381.

29. Alison M. Jaggar, *Feminist Politics and Human Nature* (Lanham, MD: Rowman and Littlefield, 1983), p. 316.

30. Janet Radcliffe-Richards, "The Unpersuaded," in *Justice: Alternative Political Perspectives*, 2nd ed., James P. Sterba, Ed. (Belmont, CA: Wadsworth, 1992), pp. 326–45, at 333.

in the last chapter, for example, that the cultural defense is used to honor a foreign cultural practice that disadvantages women, Hmong marriage-by-capture. This would be rape but for the cultural defense.[31] Another example of the cultural defense is the practice of a man killing his adulterous wife. Honoring this Chinese custom has allowed some men to avoid serious prosecution for homicide.[32] Women receive no such benefit. When a man is adulterous, no cultural defense protects a wife who murders him. Instead, we have a cultural defense for the wife only if she tries conveniently to disappear by killing herself and her children, thereby leaving the adulterous husband free of unwanted family burdens.[33]

We saw that no cultural defense is available for shirking financial obligations, but our society, which lives by commercial transactions, has somehow failed to figure out how to get men reliably to pay child support. Most of these men pay federal income tax, but women and children suffer poverty because the government does not use the internal revenue service to collect child support along with taxes. The political is personal.

In April 2004 some bishops of the Catholic Church, which opposes abortion, suggested that priests deny Holy Communion to political candidates who differ on this matter. No one in the church suggested denying communion to candidates who differ with the church's equally firm stand against the death penalty. These bishops targeted only those candidates whose differences with the church are aimed at helping women.

In sum, cultural changes are need for equality because current culturally accepted views almost invariably favor men, Catherine MacKinnon writes:

> Men's physiology defines most sports, their needs define auto and health insurance coverage, their socially designed biographies define workplace expectations and successful career patterns, their perspectives and concerns define quality in scholarship, their experiences and obsessions define merit, their objectification of life defines art, their military service defines citizenship, their inability to get along with each other—their wars and rulerships—define history, [and] their image defines god. . . .[34]

---

31. *People v. Moua*, Record of Court Proceedings, No. 315972-0 (Super. Ct. Fresno County Feb. 7, 1985).

32 *People v. Chen*, No. 87-774 (Super. Ct. N.Y. County Dec. 2, 1988).

33. *People v. Kimura*, Record of Court Proceedings, No. A-091133 (Super. Ct. S.A. County Nov. 21, 1985) and *People v. Wu*, 286 Cal. Rptr. 868 (1991).

34. Catherine MacKinnon, *Feminism Unmodified: Discourses on Life and Law* (Cambridge, MA: Harvard University Press), p. 36, in Kymlicka, pp. 381–82.

Sexual Harassment

One barrier to women's equal employment opportunity is **sexual harassment.** Consider this example given by freelance writer Sarah Glazer:

> Peggy Kimzey, a Wal-Mart shipping clerk in Warsaw, Mo., was bending over a package when she heard the store manager and another male employee snickering behind her. Kimzey stood up and asked what they were doing. "Well," the manager smirked, "I just found someplace to put my screwdriver." When Kimzey asked him to stop the crude remarks, he replied, "You don't know, you might like it."[35]

According to the Equal Employment Opportunity Commission (EEOC), which monitors compliance with Title VII of the Civil Rights Act, "unwelcome sexual advances, requests for sexual favors, and other verbal or physical conduct of a sexual nature" constitute sexual harassment whenever "submission to or rejection of such conduct by an individual is used as the basis for employment decisions affecting the individual, or . . . such conduct has the purpose or effect of unreasonably interfering with an individual's work performance or creating an intimidating, hostile, or offensive working environment."[36] Thus, there are two kinds of sexual harassment. *Quid pro quo* harassment exists when an employee's response to unwelcome sexual advances affects personnel decisions. Hostile environment sexual harassment exists when, as at Wal-Mart, unwelcome conduct of a sexual nature interferes with employees' performance by poisoning the work atmosphere.

Sexual harassment has been common in the American workplace. Philosopher James Sterba quotes these figures:

> According to the U.S. Merit Systems Protection Board, within the federal government, 56% of 8,500 female workers surveyed claimed to have experienced sexual harassment. According to the *National Law Journal*, 64% of women in "pink-collar" jobs [support positions primarily held by women] reported being sexually harassed, and 60% of 3,000 women lawyers at 250 top law firms said that they had been harassed at some point in their careers. In a . . . survey by *Working Women* magazine, 60% of high-ranking corporate women said they have been harassed; 33% more knew of others who had been.[37]

---

35. Sarah Glazer, "Sexual Harassment: An Overview," in *Sexual Harassment*, Louise I. Gerdes, Ed. (San Diego, CA: Greenhaven Press, 1999), pp. 16–26, at 16.

36. James P. Sterba, "Sexual Equality in the Workplace Would Reduce Sexual Harassment," in Gerdes, Ed., pp. 123–30, at 125–26.

37. Sterba in Gerdes, p. 125.

The consequences of harassment can be severe. "The far-reaching effects of sexual harassment on its victims," write Kathy Hotelling and Barbara Zuber of Northern Illinois University's Counseling and Student Development Center, can include

> physical problems (insomnia, headaches, digestive problems, neck and headaches, etc.), emotional problems including injury to self-esteem and confidence . . . , attitude changes such as loss of self-confidence and negativity toward work that can result in poor performance, loss of positions through resignations or firings, and lower wages (due to lack of raises or lack of longevity in positions).[38]

In sum, "sexual harassment discriminates against women by limiting their ability to establish equality."[39] Although feminists of all types object to such harassment, radical feminists, such as attorney Catherine MacKinnon, see it as perpetuating patriarchy. When women lose self-confidence, position, and seniority in the workplace, men can more successfully dominate them.

But some claims of hostile environment are questionable. Sommers gives examples from Pennsylvania State University and the University of Nebraska.

> Nancy Stumhofer, an instructor in the English department [at Penn State], took offense at a reproduction of the [Francisco de] Goya painting *The Naked Maja*, which . . . hung in her classroom. . . . [She complained to] Dr. Wayne Lammie, claiming that the painting was creating "a chilly climate for women." Ms. Stumhofer refused to switch classrooms and rejected a compromise plan to take down the painting while she was teaching, saying, "every female student in every class scheduled in that room would be subject to the chill. . . ." Goya's painting was removed.
>
> It does not take much to chill an environment. Chris Robison, a graduate student at the University of Nebraska, had placed on his desk a small photograph of his wife at the beach wearing a bikini. Two of his office mates, both female graduate students in psychology, demanded he remove it because "it created a hostile work environment."[40]

One problem is that *women and men often view the same situation differently.* "Men and women are most likely to agree when it comes to

---

38. Kathy Hotelling and Barbara A. Zuber, "Sex Role Stereotypes Cause Sexual Harassment," in Gerdes, pp. 94–103, at 95–96.

39. Hotelling and Zuber, p. 96.

40. Sommers, pp. 270–71.

the starkest kind of harassment," writes Glazer, "such as pressure for sexual favors from a supervisor. . . ."[41] The greatest differences in perception concern sexual joking and sexually laden compliments, although even here the gap is narrowing. For example, in 1980–81, Barbara A. Gutek, a psychologist at the University of Arizona, found that among 1,200 working men and women in Los Angeles, 67% of the men but only 17% of the women said they would be flattered by a sexual proposition. More recent studies have shown this perception gap to narrow, but not disappear.

In cases of continuing disagreement, whose perceptions should determine whether or not sexual harassment exists? Courts traditionally defer to the opinions of the so-called "reasonable man." However, if we assume that perceptions often differ by gender and that women are systematically oppressed in American society, as radical feminists claim, a "reasonable woman" standard seems more appropriate. *Under conditions of patriarchy, men are liable to view activities that oppress women as normal and therefore reasonable. Only a reasonable woman will be able to judge equitably.*

This perspective was adopted by federal district court Judge Howell Melton in response to Lois Robinson's complaint about a shipyard's environment that contained

> a Whilden Valve and Gauge calendar for 1985, which features *Playboy* playmate of the month pictures on each page. The female models in this particular calendar are fully or partially nude. In every month except February, April, and November, the model's breasts are fully exposed. The pubic areas are exposed on the women featured in August and December. Several of the pictures are suggestive of sexually submissive behavior. . . . Among the remarks Robinson recalled are "You rate about an 8 or a 9 on a scale of 10." She recalled one occasion on which a welder told her he wished her shirt would blow over her head so he could look. . . .

Many other women did not find the environment hostile, but the judge dismissed their opinions: "For reasons expressed in the expert testimony . . . the Court finds the description of [their] behavior to be consistent with the coping strategies employed by women who are victims of a sexually hostile work environment."[42] One effect of patriarchy, according

---

41. Glazer, p. 25.
42. *Robinson v. Jacksonville Shipyards*, 760 F. Supp. 1486, in Michael Weiss and Cathy Young, "Feminist Legal Definitions of Sexual Harassment Promote Injustice," in Gerdes, pp. 175–87, at 180.

to radical feminists and Judge Melton, is that victims of abuse tend to view abuse as normal and acceptable. Radical feminism requires, therefore, that the "reasonable woman" be someone enlightened by the insights of radical feminism.

The relationship between sexual harassment and radical feminism is even tighter. As Jan Crosthwaite and Graham Priest point out, hostile environment harassment is often geared not to obtaining sexual favors but "to make the victim aware of the presence of the perpetrator and her vulnerability to his sexual appraisal. . . . Leering, wolf-whistles, etc., fall into this category."[43] Also, behavior that may not be intended as harassment, such as the display of nude females, can create a hostile environment for women only because it highlights gender differences in everyone's mind. This harms women only on the assumption, basic to radical feminism, that the prevailing sex/gender system relegates women to subordinate roles. Otherwise, why would calling attention to sex apart from any real effort to gain sexual favors impair the work environment for women? *Probably many people who would not call themselves radical feminists accept claims of hostile environment sexual harassment that make sense only on radical feminist grounds.*

But if women are systematically oppressed, perhaps the criminal law should include compensating accommodations, such as the battered-woman defense.

The Battered-Woman Defense

Consider the case of *State v. Leidholm,* as described by Justice Vande Walle of the Supreme Court of North Dakota:

> The Leidholm marriage relationship . . . was . . . filled with a mixture of alcohol abuse, moments of kindness . . . , and moments of violence.
>
> Early in the evening of August 6, 1981, Chester and Janice attended a gun club party . . . where they both consumed a large amount of alcohol. On the return trip . . . , an argument developed [and continued] inside the home. . . .
>
> At one point in the fighting, Janice tried to telephone Dave Vollan, a deputy sheriff of McLean County, but Chester prevented

43. Jan Crosthwaite and Graham Priest, "The Definition of Sexual Harassment," in *Sexual Harassment: Issues and Answers,* Linda LeMoncheck and James P. Sterba, Eds. (New York: Oxford University Press, 2001), pp. 62–77, at 63.

her from using the phone by shoving her away and pushing her down. At another point, the argument moved outside . . . , and Chester once again was pushing Janice to the ground. Each time Janice attempted to get up, Chester would push her back. . . .

A short time later, Janice and Chester reentered their home and went to bed. When Chester fell asleep, Janice got out of bed, went to the kitchen . . . , got a butcher knife . . . , and stabbed Chester. In a matter of minutes Chester died from shock and loss of blood.[44]

Janice was convicted of manslaughter and sentenced to five years' imprisonment with three years of the sentence suspended. She appealed her conviction on grounds that the stabbing was a reasonable act of self-defense. This is the **battered-woman defense.**

Self-defense traditionally allows people to use force when necessary against imminent threats to life or limb. The force must be proportionate to the likely harm posed by the threat (you cannot kill someone determined to step on your toes) and only what is necessary to defeat the attack. Legal scholar Cathryn Jo Rosen writes:

> The proportionate force, necessity, and imminence prerequisites for self-defense are designed to quiet the law's uneasiness about encouraging self-help. The requirement that deadly force only be used to counter deadly force is geared to ensure that the aggressor, in fact, will commit an intentional homicide if not met with defensive force. . . . The necessity rule seeks to limit the use of self-help to circumstances in which there is absolutely no other alternative . . . ; deadly force will be used only as a last resort. Finally, the imminence requirement is meant to restrict self-defense to those situations where there is no time to turn to actors in the criminal justice system to do their designated job and save the defendant from the need to resort to self-defense.[45]

None of these conditions existed when Janice Leidholm killed her husband. He was sleeping, so he posed no imminent danger to her life. Because her life was not in immediate danger, killing was a disproportionate response. Because she had time to contact authorities to initiate proper legal intervention, self-help was unnecessary. A reasonable man

---

44. *State v. Leidholm,* 334 N.W. 2d 811 (1983), in *Philosophical Problems in the Law,* 2nd ed., David M. Adams, Ed. (Belmont, CA: Wadsworth, 1996), pp. 475–77, at 475.

45. Catheryn Jo Rosen, "The Battered Woman's Defense," *The American University Law Review,* Vol. 36 (1986), pp. 33–56. Found in Adams, pp. 384–91, at 390.

would not kill under these circumstances, and that is the standard according to traditional rules of self-defense.

> But traditional rules of self-defense may be biased against women. Rosen writes: Self-defense rules were developed to acquit a man who kills to protect himself or his family against a threatened attack from a man of similar size and strength with whom the defender usually has had only a single encounter. . . . Women, however, usually use deadly force to protect themselves under very different circumstances. Usually their male victims are larger and stronger and are not strangers. The woman's fear of the man will be influenced by her knowledge of his character and reputation for violence.[46]

Accordingly, a reasonable woman will sometimes act differently than a reasonable man. In addition, a woman who has been repeatedly battered by a man should be excused when resorting to deadly violence against the batterer if she suffers from "battered-woman's syndrome." Legal scholar Kathleen Waits writes:

> The battering of women is both widespread and dangerous. In any given year, at least one tenth to one fifth of American women are beaten by a man with whom they are intimately involved. . . .
>
> Violence between partners is often serious and even fatal. Five to 10% of women report severe beatings or use of a weapon such as a gun or knife. . . . All experts agree that the available statistics underestimate the extent of abuse [that] occurs in all social and economic groups.[47]

The battered-woman defense is used when abused women kill their abusers.

Women stay in abusive relationships in part, Waits claims, because they accept traditional gender stereotypes.

> For instance, the battered woman usually . . . takes upon herself all responsibility for the happiness of her husband and family and believes that if she just performs here wifely duties properly, all family conflict will disappear. She thinks it her duty to accommodate all her husband's demands, no matter how irrational or inconsistent. . . . Thus, when he abuses her, she blames herself. . . .[48]

---

46. Rosen, p. 384.

47. Kathleen Waits, "The Criminal Justice System's Response to Battering: Understanding the Problem, forging the Solutions," in *Feminist Jurisprudence*, Patricia Smith, Ed. (New York: Oxford University Press, 1993), pp. 188–209, at 189–90.

48. Waits, p. 191.

A woman may fail to report beatings because, believing them to be her own fault,

> she may deny their existence or severity, even to herself. . . . Further, because she is a traditionalist, she may place a premium on keeping the family intact.
>
> By the time the battered woman has been through the battering cycle a number of times, she suffers from low self-esteem [and] a state of "learned helplessness." She is oblivious to means of escape because her problem-solving abilities have been literally beaten out of her. . . . However, she is filled with rage.
>
> In many cases, the victim . . . may feel that the batterer will eventually kill her regardless of whether she leaves or stays. Her fears are well founded: a batterer usually becomes even more abusive if his partner makes any attempt to assert control over her life.[49]

The abuser is also likely to accept traditional sex roles, Waits writes. "He believes that a man should be 'the master' of the house and that it is the woman's job to satisfy all his needs and wants. Additionally, he often believes that he has the right to use violence against her in order to enforce his will."[50] Battering usually produces the effects he desires, so it actually works for him.

These are the psychological factors constituting the battered-woman syndrome, which underpins the battered-woman defense. The defense is that because of stress, learned helplessness, rage, and justified pessimism about means of escape, women suffering from the battered-woman syndrome who kill their abusers are subject to "a disability that caused a mistaken, but reasonable, belief in the existence of circumstances that would justify self-defense. It is a theory of excuse, rather than justification."[51] There is no justification because these women had the time and material means (but not the psychological ability to use those means) to end the abuse by appeal to competent authority. Taking the law into their own hands was objectively unnecessary and therefore regrettable, but it was understandable under the circumstances and to that extent reasonable for the woman in question. So it should be excused rather than punished.

Should the law accept this defense? Even traditional self-defense erodes law and order by excusing people who take the law into their own

---

49. Waits, p. 192.
50. Waits, p. 193.
51. Rosen, p. 387.

hands. The stringent requirements of proportional force, necessity, and imminence are designed to reduce the number of occasions when self-defense can be invoked. *Excusing battered women for killing their abusers opens new opportunities for killing without suffering serious legal consequences. People strongly opposed to killing will be reluctant to accept this defense.*

Radical feminists, however, may consider the defense necessary under prevailing conditions of patriarchy. They believe that our entire culture, including the legal system, tends to perpetuate the oppression of women. *Tailoring the requirements for self-defense to meet the needs and circumstances of men but not women is just another manifestation of patriarchy.* The battered-woman defense is needed to reduce women's oppression.

Many liberal feminists, by contrast, may worry that the battered-woman defense will reinforce outmoded, patronizing stereotypes about women being naturally irrational and incapable of meeting standards expected of men. Other liberal feminists, however, may consider size and strength differences between men and women, which make women more vulnerable in physical conflicts, to justify different standards of self-defense. *Equal treatment, for liberals, does not always mean the same treatment. Still, liberals generally favor treating men and women the same.*

Cultural Feminism

Cultural feminists agree with radical feminists that women are systematically oppressed. They emphasize, however, the cultural underpinnings of the present situation. Some maintain that, whether for reasons of biological propensity, societal training, or a combination of the two, women and men exhibit substantially different psychological and moral traits and that many traits associated with women are superior to some traits associated with men. So far, moral conservatives would generally agree. They celebrate gender differences and applaud women for being gentle, caring, nurturing, and civilized. But *cultural feminists, unlike moral conservatives, claim that some of the ways that women differ from men justify women having more political power in society.*

Psychologist Carol Gilligan claims that males and females in our society tend to speak differently about moral problems. Males tend to be more rule-oriented; they expect every moral problem to have a uniquely correct answer that can be discovered by correctly applying the appropriate rule. They tend to assert their rights and expect others to decide moral problems through reference to rights that social rules confer on individuals. Females tend to focus on relationships, rather than rights. They tend to see many moral problems as having no single, correct answer because the proper course will depend on the unique needs of the particular individuals involved, not on generic rules meant to govern a wide range of situations. Females tend more than males to accept responsibility for others and less than males to insist on respect for their individual rights.

Gilligan cites the work of Janet Lever, who discovered in her study of children playing games during their elementary school years that boys and girls play differently. The boys quarreled often, but quarrels never ended the game because the boys would appeal to rules and usually "repeat the play." In Gilligan's words, "it seemed that the boys enjoyed the legal debates as much as they did the game itself. In contrast, the eruption of disputes among girls tended to end the game."[52] Gilligan continues:

> Thus Lever extends and corroborates the observations of [20th-century childhood developmental psychologist] Piaget in his study of the rules of the game, where he finds boys becoming through childhood increasingly fascinated with the legal elaboration of rules and the development of fair procedures for adjudicating conflicts, a fascination that, he notes, does not hold for girls. Girls, Piaget observes, have a more "pragmatic" attitude toward rules, "regarding a rule as good as long as the game repaid it." Girls are more tolerant in their attitudes toward rules, more willing to make exceptions, and more easily reconciled to innovations.[53]

Piaget assumes the superiority of the boys' approach. Gilligan notes that the male style prevails in society, but she questions its superiority. Women's "sensitivity to the needs of others . . . lead women to attend to voices other than their own and to include in their judgment other points of view." In a complex world, cultural feminists might argue, this moral style has the advantage of comprehensiveness. More variables are considered and integrated into the analysis.

The male style has the advantage of decisiveness at the cost of incompleteness. Insisting on individual rights, the male style "is geared to arriving at an objectively fair or just resolution to moral dilemmas upon which all rational persons could agree. . . ."[54] The female style, by contrasts,

---

52. Carol Gilligan, *In a Different Voice: Psychological Theory and Women's Development* (Cambridge, MA: Harvard University Press, 1982), p. 9.
53. Gilligan, p. 10.
54. Gilligan, pp. 21–22.

focuses on responsibility. "The moral dilemma changes from how to exercise one's rights without interfering with the rights of others to how [in the words of a female law student] 'to lead a moral life which includes obligations to myself and my family and people in general.'"[55] Whereas the male style projects a unique and universally acceptable answer to all moral problems, "the responsibility conception focuses . . . on the limitations of any particular resolution and describes the conflicts that remain."[56] This book has presented many moral dilemmas and policy issues on which reasonable people may differ; it suggests that typically masculine expectations of moral reasoning are less realistic than typically female expectations.

Besides being less comprehensive and realistic than the female style, the male style threatens what gives most people the greatest meaning in life. "Favoring the separateness of the individual self over connections to others, and leaning more toward an autonomous life of work than toward the interdependence of love and care . . . ," the male style threatens relationships with friends and family.[57] It is often said that few people on their deathbed regret that they did not spend more time at the office, but many regret failure to connect better with family and friends.

In sum, cultural feminists can acknowledge that men and women are different but have good reason to think that women's ways are often superior to men's. Philosopher Rosemarie Tong writes that cultural feminist Marilyn French sees stereotypical masculine traits as power-mongering and therefore clearly inferior to feminine traits. Tong writes:

> Based as it is on the value of power-over, the masculine world can accommodate only those ways of being and doing which keep a small group of people in power. It has room for "true grit," "doing what you have to do," and "the end justifying the means" but no room for "knowing when to stop," savoring the "best things in life" (which . . . are "for free"), or reflecting on process as well as product.[58]

The world is a better place when feminine character traits prevail in society.

Although French has little respect for character traits that she identifies as masculine, many other feminists would accept the superiority of men's ways in some contexts. When decisive action is needed immediately,

---

55. Gilligan, p. 21.
56. Gilligan, p. 22.
57. Gilligan, p. 17.
58. Tong, p. 54.

considering fewer variables may facilitate faster action. Also, when a rule-governed contest needs officiating, referees should apply rules dispassionately. Basketball referees, for example, do best when they do not take responsibility for individual players' feelings.

The value of men's as well as women's styles and strengths suggests that the best person is one who exhibits the virtues of both men and women at their best. This is the ideal of **androgyny.** Philosopher James Sterba writes of androgyny:

> The ideal requires that the traits that are truly desirable in society be equally open to both women and men or, in the case of virtues, equally expected of both women and men. So characterized, the ideal of androgyny represents neither a revolt against so-called feminine virtues and traits nor their exaltation over so-called masculine virtues and traits.[59]

Equal opportunity for women and their escape from male domination require that women be able to compete with men in the marketplace, so they will need more assertiveness, decisiveness, and attention to abstract rules than is typical of the female style. By the same token, however, institutions must change to reflect the importance in life of values that women are prone to emphasize—caring, relationships, and responsibility for others.

Liberal feminists differ from radical feminists about androgyny. Liberal feminists accept the typically liberal emphasis on rights, individualism, and marketplace competition. They simply insist that women be allowed to enter the male culture if that is what they individually want. There is no call for change in men's ideals or institutions.

Radical feminists who favor androgyny, by contrast, want to change the rules of the game and the propensities of the participants. Social rules should not favor people who display only character traits historically associated with men. For example, when a company moves its operations overseas to save labor costs, it may devastate the town that has depended on it for employment. Attention merely to profit margins and property rights, preoccupations historically associated with men and embedded within the rules of the free market, suggest making the move without any compensation to the town. In an androgynous society, by contrast, attention would be paid to nonpropertied stakeholders in the decision. Maintaining relationships suggests keeping the company in town even if profit

---

59. James P. Sterba, *Justice for Here and Now* (New York: Cambridge University Press, 1998), p. 80.

is less than maximized. Or if the move is made, responsibility for others may justify compensation to town residents even when they have no legal right to it. Were these the rules of the game, moral traits historically associated with women would be as important to the company's operation as those associated with men, and both men and women would need traits of both sorts to succeed.

Instituting new rules of caring and responsibility in economic contexts is no easy task, but environmental legislation, discussed in the next chapter, does this to some extent. As for cultivating androgynous virtues, this is the task of parents, educational institutions, and (sometimes) employers. But cultural change is slow, so feminists also want help for women in the sort term regarding money and children.

Subsidized Day Care

Radical feminists, whether or not they favor androgyny, find the traditional family pivotal to women's subordination. Many therefore favor major government programs of child care so that women can have children and still earn enough money outside the home to avoid dependence on a man for material necessities. Alison Jaggar writes, if

> publicly funded and community-controlled childcare . . . were established, women would have the real option of choosing motherhood without being forced to abandon or drastically limit their participation in other kinds of work or to become economically dependent on a man. . . . The assumption of public responsibility for child care would [also] make visible the way in which child rearing is real work and would constitute an enormous step toward eliminating the public/private distinction.
>
> If women were fully active participants in worthwhile work outside the home, enjoying the economic security and self-respect that such participation would bring, it is doubtful that, from the child's point of view, a male presence would be required for successful child rearing.[60]

A male presence, suitably purged of the tendency toward domination, may yet be desired by many women, but because male participation would not be necessary, women would not be forced into subordination in nuclear families as they often are at present.

---

60. Jaggar, p. 321.

Moral conservative Phyllis Schlafly opposes publicly funded day care but agrees with Jaggar about its importance to feminism. She puts it this way, "the day-care issue . . . strikes at the heart of feminist ideology: that it is oppressive for society to expect mothers to care for their own children."[61]

Schlafly claims, first, that *day care harms children.* She writes, "a secure attachment in infancy provides the basis for self-reliance, self-regulation, and ultimately the capacity for independence combined with the ability to develop mature adult relationships." She quotes child psychologist John Bolby of London's Tavistock Clinic, who developed what he calls "attachment theory." "The primary goal of parenting should be to give a child a lifelong sense of security—a secure base from which he can explore the world, and to which he can return, knowing he will be welcomed, nourished, comforted and reassured."[62] Schlafly contends that day care interferes with attachment:

> Pennsylvania State University psychologist Jay Belsky (a former advocate of day care) concluded [in 1986] that infant day care is "a risk factor for the development of insecure infant-parent attachment, noncompliance, and aggression." Fifty percent of the day-care children he studied developed insecure attachments to their mothers and a wide range of negative behaviors.[63]

A more recent study confirmed these earlier findings, Schlafly wrote in 2001.

> The National Institute on Child Health and Human Development, a branch of the National Institutes of Health that produced a day-care-friendly report in 1996 [concluded in 2001] that children who spend most of their time in day care are three times as likely to exhibit behavior problems in kindergarten as those who are cared for primarily by their mothers.
>
> Children who spend more than 30 hours a week in day care were found to be more demanding and more aggressive. They scored higher on things [such as] fighting, cruelty, bullying, meanness, talking too much, and making demands that must be met immediately. . . . The findings held true regardless of the type or quality of day care, the sex of the child, the family's socioeconomic status, or the quality of the mother care.

---

61. Schlafly, p. 243.
62. Schlafly, p. 225.
63. Schlafly, pp. 226–27.

Schlafly believes that this study discredits Hilary Rodham Clinton's claim that it takes a village (with a day care) to raise a child.

> The "village" advocates are swarming all over the media with their feeble rebuttals. They argue, without evidence, that better quality day care might produce different results, that the real problem is that employed parents are tired and stressed, and that the study hasn't undergone rigorous peer review. Of course, there are other variables, including viewing television, the divorce of parents, and the amount of father care. But this new study is the most comprehensive to date and it finds day care wanting by a significant margin.[64]

Besides being bad for children, according to Schlafly, *federally subsidized day care is unjust because the federal subsidy must come from the taxpaying public,* which includes traditional, single-paycheck families with a stay-at-home mom.

> Employed mothers don't want to pay the high cost of employing other persons to provide the care that the children are not getting at home. The mothers want it free or at least heavily subsidized. They want the real cost of day care to be borne by the taxpayers or their fellow employees.
>
> Nothing could be more unjust. Children are the moral and financial responsibility of their parents. It is grievously unfair to impose a tax burden on those who fulfill this responsibility in order to subsidize those who have chosen a lifestyle that shifts this responsibility to someone else. This means taking from lower-income traditional families who care for their own children and giving to higher-income two-earner couples who don't care for their own children.[65]

Although beautifully stated, this misrepresents our federal tax system. Low-income traditional families do not pay any federal taxes, and may even receive money from the government in the form of the earned income tax credit discussed in Chapter 6, so a federal system to provide or subsidize day care would not take money from truly low-income traditional families. Instead, truly low-income people, whether in single-parent families or families with two working parents, would be major beneficiaries because they are least able at present to afford quality day care without a subsidy.

But Schlafly is making a second point here. She thinks *people should take full responsibility for their own decisions, including the decision to*

---

64. Schlafly, pp. 242–43.
65. Schlafly, p. 207.

have a child. Taking full responsibility disallows forcing others to provide day care for your children. According to Schlafly, child care is an individual or family matter, not a collective responsibility.

The problem with this reasoning is that it suggests equally the illegitimacy of public education. Of course, libertarians do oppose educating children at public expense. Most moral conservatives, however, favor public support for education (including school vouchers) because children's moral development affects everyone. Utilitarians and free-market conservatives favor public education because human happiness, preference satisfaction, and economic prosperity require an educated workforce. Liberal contractarians favor public education because it is necessary for fair equality of opportunity. All these arguments can be made on behalf of state-supported day care if the alternative is inadequate supervision of children while their parents work.

Moral conservatives maintain that the alternative to state-supported day care is the traditional family with a stay-at-home mom, not child neglect. This is why they compare children in day care with those in mom-care. But *even if mom-care is better for children than day care is, which remains controversial, the policy implications for government are unclear without a realistic expectation, or a government program to create a realistic expectation, that lack of affordable day care will lead to more mom-care rather than to more inadequately supervised children.* This part of the puzzle seems to be missing.

Finally, Schlafly contends that feminists favor day care and oppose the traditional family to improve their own competitive position in the workforce.

> The feminists realize all too well that they cannot achieve a level playing field in the marketplace so long as their male competitors have the advantage of full-time homemaker wives who cook their meals, tend their children, make their homes a refuge from the competitive world, and motivate them to work harder to provide for their dear ones. Feminists believe that achievement of their own career goals depends on depriving their male competitors of the advantage of having wives. *Ergo,* feminists are determined to push all wives out of the home and into the labor force.[66]

Schlafly seems to agree that having a wife at home provides a competitive advantage. This supports a key claim of radical feminism, that traditional

---

66. Schlafly, p. 236. Emphasis in original.

roles in the sex/gender system put women at a competitive disadvantage in the workplace. Schlafly's solution to the problem is for women to invest their energies at home, where she thinks they will be more fulfilled and where they can contribute most to society by raising their children well. She would probably agree that this is not true of all women, but she does not address the issue of competitive fairness for those, even if they are a minority, whose natural bent and gift is for working outside the home.

Schlafly also fails to address the problem that financial dependence poses for women's security and personal power. If there were enough charming men who would not take advantage of their wives' lack of independent income, this would not be a problem. But power tends to corrupt, and many wives have suffered from power-wielding husbands. So even if, as Schlafly claims, most women would fare best as stay-at-home moms married to fair-minded, loving, dedicated husbands, she provides no reason to think that this is a realistic option. In fact, she points out that many men have taken advantage of no-fault divorce to discard faithful wives. If this is the type of man currently available, the alternative to women's power advocated by feminists may not be security in a traditional family but insecurity, abuse, and abandonment at home and unfair disadvantage at work.

CONCLUSION

Classical liberal feminists advocate equal rights for women but seem content with social institutions and practices that disadvantage most women. Women who want marriage and family should expect to earn less than their male counterparts, including men who equally want marriage and family, because social institutions and practices make free child care and home maintenance primarily a woman's responsibility.

Under these conditions, which largely prevail in the United States, it is no surprise that moral conservatives can point to disadvantages to women of working outside the home compared to staying at home in traditional families. But *moral conservatives claim that women suffer when working outside the home primarily because human nature favors traditional families.* Such families are also naturally best for children. The fact that women in such families typically have less power than men do is no problem, according to moral conservatives, because *women do not need such power when interacting with the right kind of men. Moral conservatives count on traditional families and religious education to produce such men.*

Radical feminists claim that society is organized systematically to disadvantage women, whether in traditional families or in work outside the home. Human nature is no bar to true equality, they think, but cultural and institutional change facilitated by massive state intervention is needed to promote women's equality. In addition to state-supported day care and sexual harassment training and lawsuits, many feminists advocate such state measures as: affirmative action to place women in roles from which they have been historically excluded; comparable worth legislation that increases average pay for positions predominantly occupied by women; and legislation that helps women collect child support from absentee fathers.

The practicality of radical feminist goals remains in doubt. Perhaps women are more naturally oriented toward and suited to child care than men are, and men are naturally more oriented toward and suited to competition of the sort common in the free market. Perhaps children do best when cared for primarily by a parent at home, who will be the mother if women incline toward child care. The radical feminist case that the sex/gender system's social rules and expectations disadvantage women seems correct, but results of feminist efforts to level the playing field are mixed. Fewer women are stuck in abusive marriages and more jobs are open to women, but women work more hours outside the home, still do most of the unpaid housework, earn less than men, and tend to be poor when they are single parents. In many spheres of activity, the prospect of replacing women's values for men's, compassion and community for self-assertion and competition, is at best uncertain.

JUDGMENT CALLS

1. At one time California had a law that made it illegal (statutory rape) for a male to have sex with an underage female, but not for a female to have sex with an underage male. When challenged that the law denied males equal protection of the laws, California claimed that the distinction was needed to equalize the consequences of underage sex. The possibility of pregnancy was a deterrent to females, so the law was geared toward deterring males. Also, the state argued, detecting statutory rape typically depends on someone complaining, usually the female. If she is liable to prosecution in case the male is also underage, she is less likely to report the crime. Skeptics claimed that the real purpose of the distinction was the outmoded, sexist belief that males are better

able to decide autonomously than are females whether to engage in sex.[67] What do you think?

2. Some people think that many women who complain of hostile work-environment sexual harassment are being too sensitive to sexual comments or innuendo. James Sterba points out, however, that in the 1990s "the Senate Armed Services Committee . . . and [then] the whole U.S. Congress regard[ed] an environment in which known homosexuals are simply doing their duty in the military to be too hostile an environment to ask particularly male heterosexuals to serve in."[68] How might one try to reconcile in reflective equilibrium the view that women complaining of a hostile environment are being too sensitive but that heterosexual men objecting to military service with homosexuals are not?

3. In the late 1980s, some magazines were instructing women on how to file a sexual harassment suit while *Cosmopolitan* was telling them how to get male attention at work. *Cosmopolitan's* advice includes:

    As you pass his desk, drop a pile of papers or a purse, then stop down to gather them up. He'll help. Lean close to him, put your hand on his shoulder to steady your balance. . . ."

      If you have good legs, wear a very tight, short skirt and very high heels. Brush up against somebody in the elevator. . . ."

      Say something slightly inappropriate during a business lunch or dinner, such as "You look great in blue."[69]

    What male responses to this behavior are reasonable? How does a woman behaving in this way complicate efforts to eradicate sexual harassment?

4. Some feminists distinguish between posters in the workplace that feature nude or scantily clad women, which many women find offensive, and remarks or behavior of a sexual nature directed at individual women. In spite of the offensive nature of the posters,

---

67. See *Michael M. v. Superior Court of Sonoma County,* 450 U.S. 464 (1981), abbreviated in Adams, Ed., pp. 283–87.
68. Sterba in Gerdes, pp. 126–27.
69. "How to Make an Impact on a Man," *Cosmopolitan,* February 1989, p. 177, in Warren Farrell, "The Myth of Male Power," in LeMoncheck and Sterba, Eds., pp. 294–301, at 296.

312   Chapter 9: Feminism

Feminists for Free Expression do not think they make the work environment hostile. Only remarks or behavior directed at individual women contribute to a hostile work environment.[70] What would justify such a distinction if women are offended in both cases? What do you think?

5. Some feminists think that opposition to same-sex marriage results fundamentally from reluctance to liberate women from the sex/gender system, which assigns social roles on the basis of biological sex. Same-sex marriage gives women who want legal partners an alternative to the typically subordinate role of a woman to a man in a traditional marriage. Combined with artificial insemination, it also gives women the chance of sharing child rearing with her partner. What do you think?

---

70. See Feminists for Free Expression, "Banning Erotic Words and Pictures Will Not Reduce Sexual Harassment," in Gerdes, pp. 139–41.

10 Environmentalism

Political environmentalism stems from environmentalist belief that industrial civilization is needlessly harmful to people and other natural entities, such as animals and ecosystems. Environmentalists differ greatly among themselves, but most want state intervention to reduce damage to current and future generations both at home and abroad. They want the state to protect the public from industrial pollution, phase out government subsidies of inefficient and environmentally harmful activities, and protect endangered species. Some favor economic growth along conventional, but more eco-friendly lines. Others want the state to recognize limits to growth and support movement toward a less consumer-oriented society in which gross domestic product (GDP) is steady but human welfare improves. In either case, environmentalists enrich political debate with concern about ecosystems, species, and environmental sustainability.

Industrial Pollution

Environmentalists often point to unanticipated health problems stemming from industrial processes and products. Consider the case of Rick Feutz:

> In 1986 the Washington State teacher was building a wooden raft for his children, a job that required a lot of sawing—a lot of sawdust. Within days, he felt achy and nauseated and experienced a tingling in his hands. The problem persisted, and eventually doctors diagnosed arsenic poisoning. The price he has paid is high: he lost a third of his overall motor control, and, even today his face remains partly paralyzed.

Industrially infused arsenic in the wood is blamed for the problem, *Time* magazine's Jeffrey Kluger reported in 2001. "Ninety-eight percent of wood sold for outdoor use in the U.S. is treated with chromated copper arsenate [CCA]." The treatment "can extend the life of wood fivefold, eliminating repairs and saving millions of trees annually" but may also impair human health. Even though the chemical is injected deep into the wood, arsenic may eventually leach out and enter the human body, where it is toxic. Children could be at greatest risk because much play equipment is made of such wood. According to Richard Wiles, pesticide director for the nonprofit Environmental Working Group, "We've pretty much set up an arsenic delivery system for kids."

It took 15 years from the time of Rick Feutz's injury for significant government action. In 2001 the U.S. Environmental Protection Agency (EPA) announced that

> CCA-treated lumber sold in the U.S. will contain a warning label, and stores will be provided with stickers and signs for their displays. At the same time, the Consumer Product Safety Commission agreed to ask for public comments on petitions that could lead to an outright ban of CCA. In Florida, dozens of playgrounds [were] shut down, and Governor Jeb Bush . . . ordered a state-run wood-treatment plant to switch to another preservative.[1]

Critics attribute the slow government response to the political influence of the $4 billion-a-year wood-treatment industry, but the industry replies that its products are safe. Factory workers who treat wood and carpenters who use it show no ill effects, according to Mel Pine, speaking for the American Wood Preservers' Institute. Yet, Kluger points out, "the EPA [had] already banned arsenic for all other pesticide applications—not the kind of thing the agency does lightly."[2] What is more, effective non-arsenic-based preservatives exist, and the industry as a whole could switch to them for about $40,000 per treatment plant, not a huge sum for the industry. It seems that the industry was willing to jeopardize human health for a small gain in profitability.

Under these conditions, many environmentalists would insist that the state ban CCA completely as a wood preservative because corporations cannot be trusted to protect the public. But most of these same environmentalists would also doubt that the state would do the right thing, worrying that many in government are too sympathetic to industry concerns and perspectives. For this reason, *political environmentalists engage in deliberative democracy. They try to sway public opinion through media events and publications, influence corporations with protests and boycotts, and pressure governments with lawsuits and lobbying.*

---

1. Jeffrey Kluger, "Toxic Playgrounds," *Time* (July 16, 2001), pp. 56–57, at 56.
2. Kluger, p. 57.

Arsenic in wood typifies industry's neglect of safety, environmentalists claim. Another example concerns chemicals depleting the ozone layer that protects Earth from ultraviolet radiation. Reduced ozone protection could harm many life forms and increase skin cancer and blindness among human beings. In 1987, 37 nations signed the Montreal Protocol on Substances That Deplete the Ozone Layer, agreeing to phase out manufacture of these chemicals by 2000. This date was moved up to 1994 for some chemicals and 1996 for others owing to new evidence of danger.

Environmentalists applauded this result, but the affected industries did not. Even though they had alternatives to these chemicals, they challenged the scientific evidence of harm and resisted change. Their advocates in the U.S. Congress tried to delay action. According to Janet S. Wager, Senior Editor of *Nucleus*, the magazine of the Union of Concerned Scientists, in 1995 "Representative John T. Doolittle (R-CA) . . . introduced a bill that would postpone the chemical production ban until the year 2000. Another bill, introduced by Representative Tom DeLay (R-TX), [sought] to repeal the ban on production of these chemicals in the United States."[3] (I did not make up these names. If I had, DeLay would have suggested postponement and Doolittle repeal of the ban.)

Many environmentalists consider this typical. *Industries willingly compromise human health to maximize profit, and they have allies in government willing to do their bidding.* As a result, political environmentalism is needed to protect the public.

The Overall Benefits of Industry

Opposed to such environmentalist activism are those who believe that industry is the greatest benefactor of humanity; whatever impedes it is therefore more likely to harm than to help people. Bjorn Lomborg is a recent champion of this view. He notes that *life expectancy improves dramatically with industrialization.* For example, "in France, life expectancy in 1800 was about 30. In Denmark it was around 44 in 1845. All have ended up with a life expectancy in the 70s, with an average of 77 years for developed countries."[4] The same trend is underway in developing

3. Janet S. Wager, "Double Exposure," *Nucleus,* Vol. 17, No. 4 (Winter 1995–96), pp. 1–3, at 3.

4. Bjorn Lomborg, *The Skeptical Environmentalist: Measuring the Real State of the World* (Cambridge: Cambridge University Press, 2001), p. 50.

316 Chapter 10: Environmentalism

countries. "In 1906 life expectancy in India was about 25. In China in 1930, people lived an average of 24 years."[5] With increased access to industry's products, life expectancy in the Third World has gone up, to 41 years by 1950 and as high as 65 years by 1998, Lomborg tells us.

People are healthier as well, Lomborg claims, largely because of better public health measures, such as cleaner water, and medications effective against most infectious diseases. *Science has combined with industry also to reduce the number of people who are starving, even in the Third World*, according to Lomborg. "Although there are twice as many of us as there were in 1961, each of us has *more* to eat, in both developed and developing countries. Fewer people are starving. . . . While in 1971 almost 920 million people were starving, the total fell to below 792 million in 1997."[6] *Food is also cheaper* than ever. "The price of wheat has had a downward trend ever since 1800."[7] These improvements are due to industrial applications of scientific advances, such as better crop varieties introduced in the so-called Green Revolution. Such crops require artificial fertilizer and pesticides, to which some environmentalists object, Lomborg writes.

> But what alternative do we have, with more than 6 billion people on Earth? If we abandoned intensive cultivation and the use of pesticides, farmers would either need *more space* to grow the same quantities or end up producing *far less food*. So they would either have to take over more of the surrounding countryside or we would end up with more hungry souls among us.[8]

In short, Lomborg wants people to keep the big picture in mind—improved human life through industrial advancement. More people are living on Earth, and they are living longer and better. People are generally richer than before, with larger homes and more conveniences and "toys." What is more, "environmental development often stems from economic development—only when we get sufficiently rich can we afford the relative luxury of caring about the environment. . . . Higher income in general is correlated with *higher* environmental sustainability."[9] But government intervention in the economy can jeopardize these gains. If industry is

---

5. Lomborg, p. 51. This does not mean that most Chinese died in their 20s. Average life expectancy was only 24 because so many people died as infants. A major factor in increased life expectancy worldwide is reduced infant mortality.

6. Lomborg, pp. 60–61. Emphasis in original.

7. Lomborg, p. 62.

8. Lomborg, p. 64. Emphasis in original.

9. Lomborg, p. 33. Emphasis in original.

burdened by too many regulations in response to environmentalist complaints, industrial progress may be slowed, and people may suffer in the future. Environmentalists may not see the danger because they are so used to industrial advance that they take it for granted.

Environmentalists have many responses. First, they can agree that human life has improved because of science and industry without condoning unnecessary illness and death. Consider this medical analogy. In 1850 people did not expect surgeons to avoid infection in their patients; the causes and cures for infection were unknown. Today, surgeons use sterile technique to avoid infections and drugs to treat them. If they do not and patients die as a result, they are at fault. Similarly, if wood can be treated with non-arsenic preservatives and replacements are available for ozone-depleting chemicals, corporations are at fault if they do not alter their practices to protect the public. Such alterations do not stop industrial advance, they just direct it along more benign paths. Unfortunately, many industries seem unwilling to make such alterations without government regulation, and many governments seem unwilling to intervene without environmentalist agitation.

However, *concern with the health-impairing effects of industrial processes can go too far.* This was the view of Senator James Inhofe (R-OK), chairman of the Senate Environment and Public Works subcommittee on Clean Air, Wetlands, Private Property, and Nuclear Safety, when confronted in 1997 with proposed changes in clean air standards. The Clean Air Act requires that the administrator of the EPA review air standards every five years to ensure adequate protection for the public. Although ozone in the stratosphere protects us from ultraviolet radiation, near the surface of the earth it is a major ingredient in health-impairing smog, so few object to government attempts to limit its presence. Inhofe claimed, however, that imposing new, more stringent ozone standards would do more harm than good. He writes:

> The proposed change in the standard would triple the number of nonattainment areas [places out of compliance with EPA standards] with little to no increase in the health benefits. Such areas could lose federal highway funds and become subject to onerous mandatory federal controls. . . .
>
> State and local government officials . . . are concerned that scarce resources unwisely will be diverted away from more pressing environmental priorities such as safe drinking water and the cleanup of toxic-waste sites. The new standard will make it more difficult, if not impossible, for new industrial manufacturing and service facilities to become established and for existing ones to expand. It does not take

a rocket scientist to see that local economies will stagnate, and jobs will be lost.[10]

In sum, trade-offs are inevitable between safety and the benefits of industry. Science determines the risks of various activities, and value judgments determine which risks are acceptable. *Most people want less health-impairing pollution, but not at any cost. Environmentalists warn us, however, to be suspicious of corporate calculations.*

Limits to Growth

A second environmentalist response to a defense of industry concerns the concept of progress. Industry and government tend to equate progress with increase. The gross domestic product (GDP) should increase, the numbers of cars and other manufactured goods should increase, the number of cattle should increase, the volume of world trade should increase, and so on. Many environmentalists consider it unrealistic to equate progress with growth because, Earth being finite, growth must have limits.

Environmentalists Paul and Anne Ehrlich certainly exaggerated the limits in their 1974 book *The End of Affluence*. They wrote:

> It seems that energy shortages will be with us for the rest of the century and that before 1985 mankind will enter a genuine age of scarcity in which many things besides energy will be in short supply. . . . Such diverse commodities as food, fresh water, copper, and paper will become increasingly difficult to obtain and thus much more expensive. . . . Starvation among people will be accompanied by starvation of industries for the materials they require.[11]

Economist Julian Simon countered that there are no limits to growth because human ingenuity is, as the title of his 1981 book declares, *The Ultimate Resource*. Simon explains how people address, for example, a shortage of copper:

> Perhaps they will invent better ways of obtaining copper from a given lode, say a better digging tool, or they may develop new materials to substitute for copper, perhaps iron.

10. James M. Inhofe, "The Federal Government's Air-Quality Standards Are Too Stringent," in *Conserving the Environment*, Laura K. Egandorf, Ed. (San Diego: Greenhaven Press, 1999), pp. 110–13, at 112–13. Originally published as "Q: Are More Rigorous Clean-Air Standards Really Necessary? No: Federal Regulators Are Set to Choke Local Economies for the Sake of Marginal Health Benefits," *Insight* (April 28, 1997).

11. Paul R. and Anne H. Ehrlich, *The End of Affluence: A Blueprint for Your Future* (New York: Ballantine Books, 1974), p. 33, in Lomborg, p. 30.

The cause of these new discoveries, or the cause of applying ideas that were discovered earlier, is the "shortage" of copper—that is, the increased cost of getting copper. So a "shortage" of copper causes the creation of its own remedy.

This sequence of events explains how it can be that people have been using copper pots for thousands of years, as well as using copper for many other purposes, and yet the cost of a pot today is vastly cheaper by any measure than it was 100 or 1,000 or 10,000 years ago.[12]

There really are no limits to growth, Simon concludes:

Our supplies of natural resources are not finite in any economic sense. Nor does past experience give reason to expect natural resources to become more scarce. Rather, if the past is any guide, natural resources will progressively become less scarce, and less costly, and will constitute a smaller proportion of our expenses in future years. And population growth is likely to have a long-run *beneficial* impact on the natural-resource situation.[13]

In 1980 Simon challenged the Ehrlichs and other environmentalists to bet on the future cost of raw materials. He would bet $10,000 that any raw material chosen by environmentalists will have reduced in price a year or more after the bet was made. The environmentalists picked copper, nickel, tin, and tungsten and chose 10 years as the time frame. Lomborg writes:

In September 1990 not only had the total basket of raw materials but also each individual raw material dropped in price. . . . The doomsayers had lost.

Truth is they *could not* have won. Ehrlich and Co. would have lost no matter whether they had staked their money on petroleum, foodstuffs, sugar, coffee, cotton, wool, minerals or phosphates. They had all become cheaper.[14]

Yet, *environmentalists do have reason to claim that there are limits, not regarding raw materials for industry, but regarding food production and environmental services.* We consider food production first. Lester Brown, former President of Worldwatch Institute, agrees that agricultural productivity grew impressively during the 20th century, resulting in fewer

---

12. Julian L. Simon, *The Ultimate Resource* (Princeton: Princeton University Press, 1981), pp. 43–44.
13. Simon, p. 5. Emphasis in original.
14. Lomborg, p. 137. Emphasis in original.

320 Chapter 10: Environmentalism

starving people in the world even as population increased enormously. However, he contends, this trend cannot continue. First, productivity increases were due in part to the increased use of fertilizers and the development of new crop varieties of wheat, rice, and corn that made better use of fertilizer to grow grain for human beings and livestock. But we are reaching limits to improvements of this type, Brown claimed in 1999:

> Originally domesticated wheats converted roughly 20% of photosynthate into seed, with the remainder used to sustain leaves, stem, and roots. With the more productive modern wheat varieties now converting more than 50% of photosynthate into seed, there is not much remaining potential for increase, since scientists estimate that the absolute upper limit is 62%. Anything beyond that would begin to deprive the rest of the plant of the energy needed to function, thus reducing yields.[15]

Another major reason for crop productivity improvements has been increased use of irrigation. About 70% of grain harvested in China is grown on irrigated land. The figure for India is 50% and for the United States 15%.[16] Water is crucial to grain productivity per hectare (2.5 acres), Brown writes.

> Take wheat, for example. Three developing countries—Egypt, Mexico, and China—are in the top five . . . in wheat yield per hectare. And two industrial countries—Canada and Australia—are in the bottom five. This is because Egypt, Mexico, and China irrigate most of their wheat, while in Canada and Australia the wheat is rainfed and grown in areas of low rainfall.[17]

But *water for irrigation is running out.* Such water comes primarily from underground pools, called **aquifers,** which are being depleted. Brown tells us:

> Water tables are falling on every continent—in the southern Great Plains of the United States, the southwestern United States, much of North Africa and the Middle East, most of India, and almost everywhere in China that the land is flat. A survey covering 1991 to 1996, for instance, indicates that the water table under the north China plain is dropping an average of 1.5 meters, or roughly 5 feet, a year. . . . This area accounts for nearly 40% of China's grain harvest.

15. Lester R. Brown, "Feeding Nine Billion," *State of the World 1999* (New York: W. W. Norton, 1999), pp. 115–32, at 126–27.
16. Brown, p. 124.
17. Brown, p. 126.

A similar situation exists in India [where] underground withdrawals . . . are at least double the rate of aquifer recharge. . . . Water tables are falling 1–3 meters (3–10 feet) per year almost everywhere in India.

Another indication of a growing water shortage is the depletion of major rivers, such as the Colorado in southwestern United States, which rarely reaches its mouth at the Gulf of California. Changes in the Yellow River in China are more alarming. Tapped to irrigate corn and wheat crops, "the Yellow River . . . ran dry for the first time in China's 3,000-year history in 1972, failing to reach the sea for some 15 days. Over the next dozen years, it ran dry intermittently, but since 1985 has run dry for part of each year. In 1997, it failed to reach the sea for seven months out of the year."[18]

Problems of water scarcity are starting to depress the global grain production of wheat, rice, and corn, the grains that feed 85% of humanity. According to *Vital Signs 2003*, "in 2002, global grain production declined for the third time in four years, due mainly to drought in North America and Australia." As a result, "the harvest has slipped below demand for the last four years, pushing down the stocks of grain held in private and government stores . . . to . . . the lowest level in 40 years of recordkeeping."[19] The following year Lester Brown reported that aquifer depletion, "rising temperatures and the loss of crop land to nonfarm uses" had impaired China's grain production below levels of current consumption for four of the previous five years.[20] If aquifer depletion and these other factors severely reduce grain harvests in the future, which most environmentalists expect, world food crises could ensue.

Limited supplies of water and arable land needed to grow crops convince environmentalists that there are limits to Earth's food-producing capacity and therefore limits to human population growth. In addition, Earth's limited food-producing capacity suggests the need to conserve essential inputs, especially arable land. Economic growth through suburbanization should be limited because suburbs, new roads, and shopping malls often take rich agricultural land out of production forever.

Other limits to growth concern services that nature provides free but growing economies jeopardize. For example, some commercial developments reduce wetlands, which serve to purify river and lake water, control

---

18. Brown, p. 124.
19. Linda Starke, Ed., *Vital Signs 2003* (New York: W. W. Norton, 2003), p. 28.
20. Lester R. Brown, "Dry, with a Chance of Grain Shortage," *The Ecologist*, Vol. 34, No. 1 (February 2004), p. 12.

floods, and maintain species diversity that helps control pest species. Paying people to purify river and lake water, to control floods without wetland floodplains, and to maintain species diversity for pest control without the natural services of wetlands would be enormously expensive, if possible. Similarly, bees provide agricultural pollination services that people could hardly duplicate by hand, so industrial pollution that harms bees must be limited.

In sum, environmentalists claim, *there are limits to growth and additional limits to some types of growth, the types that reduce scarce resources such as arable land or impair natural services such as water purification and pollination. Environmentalists want government policies that keep the economy well within natural limits.*

Government Subsidies

Unfortunately, many government policies do just the opposite; they subsidize environmentally unfriendly activities. Such subsidies encourage inefficient use because they make goods artificially cheap. Consider again the use of water. Sandra Postel writes in *Pillar of Sand* that worldwide, "farmers receiving water from government-built projects rarely pay more than 20% of the water's real cost, and often pay much less."[21] An American project provides an extreme example:

> The Central Arizona Project (CAP), completed around 1993, diverts water from the Colorado River and delivers it by canal to portions of Arizona. Officials set the contract price for deliveries of CAP water to an irrigation district in the central part of the state at $2 per acre-foot . . . although the full cost of that water was $209 per acre-foot. In other words, the government charged these desert irrigators just 1% of the actual cost of the water.[22]

Water subsidies are generally environmentally irresponsible, environmentalists claim, because they encourage waste when human welfare requires conservation.

Particular water subsidies have other problems as well. Those in the American west often promote environmentally harmful meat production. Consider this: If you shower for 7 minutes each day using a normal stream of water, your showers over a 6-month period use about 2,464 gallons of

---

21. Sandra Postel, *Pillar of Sand: Can the Irrigation Miracle Last?* (New York: W. W. Norton, 1999), p. 230.
22. Postel, p. 231.

water, the same amount of water it takes to produce a single pound of beef in California. Cattle drink a lot of water, and in that dry state the crops that cattle eat need irrigation. So you can save as much water by refraining from eating a pound of California-bred beef as by refraining from showering for 6 months.[23] Tough choice. More generally, a meat-eating American requires 4,200 gallons of water per day, whereas a vegan (who eats neither meat nor such animal products as eggs, milk, and cheese) requires only 300 gallons a day.[24]

The consumption of beef has increased five-fold in the past half-century, and water subsidies, which make beef cheap, are part of the reason.[25] However, the increased consumption of meat is environmentally unfriendly for other reasons besides excessive water use. Meat-eating requires more agricultural land per person because animals use most of the food value of grain that is fed to them to move around and maintain their own metabolism. Only one fourth to one tenth of the food the animals eat becomes edible meat. People can feed themselves using less land when they eat vegetables, thereby consuming a greater percentage of the food value the land produces. Like water, good agricultural land is in short supply.[26] A study in the 1970s concluded that Earth can support only 2.6 billion people eating meat-rich diets.[27] There are already over 6 billion people on the planet. Eating meat cuts into food supplies that other people need.

The increased consumption of American meat is environmentally harmful also because the animals are commonly raised in environmentally destructive ways. In the past, animals were raised on farms where their manure was used to fertilize feed and other crops. Today, by contrast, they are typically kept in large feedlots where the concentration of animal waste exceeds the ability of the soil to absorb it. Waste lagoons where excess waste is contained are smelly and often leak. Nitrogen from the waste gets into groundwater and leaks into streams that eventually lead to the ocean where the extra nitrogen promotes the excessive growth of phytoplankton. When the phytoplankton dies, its decomposition uses almost all of the oxygen in that part of the ocean, making it a zone that is dead to

23. The Editors, "Now, It's Not Personal!" *World Watch*, Vol. 17, No. 4 (July/August 2004), pp. 12–19, at 14, in John Robbins, *The Food Revolution: How Your Diet Can Help Save Your Life and the World* (Red Wheel, 2001).

24. The Editors, p. 14.

25. The Editors, p. 12.

26. The Editors, pp. 16–17.

27. The Editors, p. 13.

other marine life. This deprives people of food and food-producing liveli-hoods from the sea.[28]

No mainstream political environmentalist suggests outlawing the consumption of meat, but they do want stricter environmental standards regarding animal waste and call for replacement of subsidies that make meat artificially inexpensive with subsidies for small-scale, sustainable agriculture.

Environmentalists would also like to curtail government subsidy of automotive travel. Such travel is generally less efficient and more environ-mentally harmful than public transportation. A train can carry as many people intercity as 16 lanes of highway designed for automobiles, thereby saving land.[29] It uses less power to transport people and causes less air pollution.[30] It is 18 times safer than driving a car.[31] It contributes less to global warming. It requires less land use for parking at each end. Similar efficiencies attend light rail within cities. Thus, public transportation is more efficient and environmentally friendly than the use of private auto-mobiles. Car travel remains as popular as it is partly because, like water and meat, it is highly subsidized.

The subsidies are many and various. For example, employers can deduct as a business expense much more for providing parking for em-ployees than for giving employees money or coupons to use public trans-portation. According to the Worldwatch Institute's David Roodman, lost tax revenues from this source alone amount to a $20 billion a year subsidy for automotive travel. In addition, general tax revenues, rather than any taxes related to automotive use, generally pay for such essential road-related services as traffic management, highway patrols, and emergency response teams. Roodman writes, "economists at the World Resources Institute (WRI) in Washington, D.C., have extrapolated from calculations for the city of Pasadena, California, to conclude that governments in the United States spend roughly $83 billion a year (1995 dollars) on these services—nearly as much as on the roads themselves."[32]

Because cars and trucks produce more health-impairing air pollution than do trains and light rail, much of our nation's health care budget goes

28. Ken Silverstein, "Meat Factories," *Sierra*, Vol. 84, No. 1 (January/February 1999), pp. 28–35 and The Editors, p. 15.

29. Marcia D. Lowe, "Back on Track: The Global Rail Revival," *Worldwatch Paper #118* (Washington, D.C., April 1994), p. 7.

30. Lowe, p. 6.

31. Lowe, p. 16.

32. David Malin Roodman, "Paying the Piper: Subsidies, Politics, and the Environment" *Worldwatch Paper #133*, (Washington, DC: Worldwatch Institute, 1996), p. 42.

to support automotive use. In addition, extensive use of automobiles requires the importation of oil, much of it from the Middle East and other politically unstable regions. Trains and light rail can be powered by electricity generated from domestically available fuel. Military expenditures to secure oil supplies needed to use cars instead of trains and light rail come from general government revenues, which is a huge subsidy for travel by car. The build-up for the Gulf War in 1991, for example, alone cost the equivalent of 40 cents per gallon of gasoline imported that year.[33] Expenses continued during the 1990s and then ballooned with the Second Iraq War in the new century.

In the early 1990s, the World Resources Institute considered national defense, pollution, noise, accidents, and other social costs that drivers do not pay, and put the total subsidy for U.S. drivers at about $300 billion a year;[34] the National Resources Defense Council put the figure at between $380 billion and $660 billion per year.[35] Most prices have increased considerably since the early 1990s. Subsidies are enormous and growing.

Political environmentalists advocate two government responses. First, governments should invest directly in public transportation to provide alternatives to car travel. Free-market conservatives and liberal contractarians should welcome such investments if public transportation improves regional economic performance, as Worldwatch's Marcia Lowe contends.

> Montgomery County, Maryland—a county of 740,000 people near Washington, D.C.—is a case in point. A long-range planning study for the county found that if urban growth continued in the usual auto- and highway-oriented pattern . . . the resulting traffic congestion would stifle further economic development. In contrast, focusing most new urban growth in pedestrian- and bicycle-friendly clusters along an expanded rail and bus system—and revising commuter subsidies to discourage the use of cars—would enable the county to double its current number of jobs and households without exacerbating traffic congestion.[36]

33. Deborah Gordon, *Steering a New Course: Transportation, Energy, and the Environment* (Washington, DC: Island Press, 1991), pp. 41–42.

34. James J. Mackenzie, Roger C. Dower, and Donald D. T. Chen, *The Going Rate: What It Really Costs to Drive* (Washington, D.C.: World Resources Institute, 1992), in Lowe, p. 47, endnote # 12.

35. Peter Miller and John Moffet, *The Price of Mobility: Uncovering the Hidden Costs of Transportation* (New York: National Resources Defense Council, October 1993), in Lowe, p. 47, endnote # 12.

36. Lowe, pp. 41–42.

326 Chapter 10: Environmentalism

Other studies show that public expenditures on public transportation improve worker productivity. David Aschauer of the American Public Transit Association, Lowe reports,

> looked at the impact of transport expenditures on worker productivity. A 10-year, $100 billion increase in public transport spending was estimated to boost worker output by $521 billion—compared with $237 billion for the same level of spending on highways. Moreover, public transport investments began returning net benefits three times as quickly as highway expenditures.[37]

Political environmentalists also advocate that the U.S. government increase its corporate average fuel economy (CAFE) standards. Because car travel is highly subsidized, current use does not reflect what people are really willing to pay. Until subsidies are withdrawn, one way to get consumer behavior to approximate what it would be without subsidies, which is the free-market ideal, is for the government to require car makers to improve the fuel efficiency of the cars they sell. Improved fuel efficiency will reduce indirect subsidies related to health and national defense.

These proposals support free-market integrity and increased productivity in keeping with mainstream economic thinking. Other environmentalist ideas, however, clash with such thinking.

Future Generations and Nuclear Waste

The environmentalist concern for future generations differs from common economic criteria. Many environmentalists want policies to be judged, as decisions in some Native American groups are said to have been judged, by their effect on the seventh generation. There is even an environmentalist-inspired product line with this title. Although some people may balk at using Seventh Generation toilet paper, *the idea of sustaining a good environment into the distant future is popular. Yet this concern sets environmentalists apart from political liberals.*

Consider, for example, nuclear waste. One reason that most environmentalists do not like nuclear power is the difficulty of protecting future generations from the harmful radioactivity of its waste. Environmentalists are joined in this concern by the Department of Energy (DOE), which intends to protect people from radioactive contamination for 10,000 years by burying high-level nuclear waste in Yucca Mountain in Nevada.

---

37. Lowe, p. 41.

Controversy continues, however, over the suitability of the Yucca Mountain site. DOE geologist Jerry Szymanski claims that although the water table is currently 1,000 feet below the proposed burial site, the future is uncertain because the area is crisscrossed with more than 30 seismic faults. A nearby earthquake could result in the water table rising, water coming into contact with hot radioactive material, the mountain top exploding, and a wide area being exposed to radioactive contamination.[38] In 1992 an earthquake measuring 5.2 on the Richter scale occurred 50 miles away.[39]

More generally, environmentalists claim that people do not know enough about geology to predict with any confidence what will happen thousands of years from now. Nicholas Lenssen writes for the Worldwatch Institute: "It is worth remembering that less than 10,000 years ago, volcanoes were erupting in what is now central France, the English Channel did not exist 7,000 years ago, and much of the Sahara was fertile just 5,000 years ago."[40] *We may not know how to protect people of the distant future from waste generated in today's nuclear power plants, yet most Americans believe that we should protect the welfare of future generations.*

Libertarians and free-market conservatives cannot accommodate the belief that present people ought to promote the welfare of future generations.

LIBERTARIANS want to protect people's rights to life, liberty, and property. It might seem that health-impairing nuclear contamination would violate future generations' right to life. But it would not, because the individual identity of future people is currently undetermined and depends in part on the energy option we adopt. For example, if we expand reliance on nuclear power to generate electricity, many new jobs in the nuclear power sector will be created. Uranium mines will reopen. New programs of study and training will be developed, and new sites of construction will exist. People will meet around nuclear-power-related education or work who would not have met had the country emphasized, for example, coal for electricity, because the places of work, such as the sites of mines, and the types of work, will be different. Some who meet doing

38. Nicholas Lenssen, "Facing Up to Nuclear Waste," *Annual Editions: Environment 94/95*, John L. Allen, Ed. (Guilford, CT: Dushkin Publishing, 1994), pp. 118–24, at 120. The article appeared originally in *World Watch* (March/April 1992), pp. 10–17.

39. "Yucca Mountain, the Ultimate Gamble," *PSR Reports* (Physicians for Social Responsibility) (Spring 2001), p. 3.

40. Lenssen, p. 120.

nuclear-power-related activities will mate and have children who would not have existed if the country had pursued the coal option.

After several generations, virtually everyone's existence will have depended on the nation's dominant energy policy. Because the infrastructure and job opportunities in a nuclear-oriented society will be different from those in a coal-oriented society, generation after generation of people will meet and have children who would not otherwise have existed. What is more, such people will mate not only with one another but with people who would have existed regardless of the nation's energy policies. The identity of the children of these couples, too, will depend on the nation's energy policies because the identity of one of the parents does. Change one parent and you change the identity of the children. Thus, within 1,000 years everyone's existence will depend on current energy policy choices.

Suppose, then, that we expand nuclear power without knowing how to contain nuclear waste effectively and as a result contaminate people who live 2,000 years from now. Have we violated anyone's rights? These particular people would not have existed if we had followed any other policy. Assuming that their lives are better than complete non-existence, we have not harmed them even if nuclear contamination impairs their lives, because the alternative for them of living with these problems was no life at all. If their lives have not been harmed, their rights have not been violated. Because libertarians reject only policies that violate people's rights, they cannot object to policies that poison people of the distant future. *Hence, libertarianism cannot accommodate moral concern for the welfare of future generations.*[41]

FREE-MARKET CONSERVATISM also fails to protect people of the distant future. Environmental economist Garrett Hardin put it this way:

> A number of years ago I decided to plant a redwood tree in my back-yard. As I did so I mused, "what would my economist friends say to this?
>
> The seedling cost me $1.00. When mature the tree would (at the then current prices) have $14,000 worth of lumber in it—but it would take 2,000 years to reach that value. Calculation showed that the investment of ... $1.00 to secure so distant a gain would be justified only if the going rate of interest was no more than 0.479%

41. This reasoning was put forward by Derek Parfit in "Energy Policy and the Further Future": The Identity Problem," in *Energy and the Future*, D. MacLean and P. G. Brown, Eds. (Totowa, NJ: Rowman and Littlefield, 1983), pp. 289–96.

per year. So low a rate of interest has never been known. . . . *But I planted the tree.*

The theory of discounting scratches only the surface of the problem. What about the quid pro quo? The quid ($1.00) is mine to pay; but who gets the quo, 2,000 years from now? Not I, certainly. And it is most unlikely that any of my direct descendants will get it either, history being what it is. . . . Why bother?

I am beginning to suspect that rationality—as we now conceive it—may be insufficient to secure the end we desire, namely, taking care of the interests of posterity.[42]

He is correct about free-market conservatism's economic rationality.

LIBERAL CONTRACTARIANISM does better; it is able to accommodate concern for the welfare of future generations, but only by altering the contractual situation precisely to get this result.

Recall that according to Rawls, if people come together behind a veil of ignorance to determine what rules to follow, they will choose rules that are fair to everyone out of the self-interested fear that when the veil is lifted, if anyone is treated unfairly, they may be the ones to suffer. But time moves in one direction only; we can harm people of the future, but they cannot harm us. So, if everyone behind the veil is of the same generation, the so-called same-time-of-entry version of the contractual situation, self-interest does not justify concern about the distant future. Of course, people may want to leave their children and grandchildren a habitable world, but such attachment does not extend hundreds, much less thousands, of years.

To address this problem, John Rawls wants the parties making a contract behind the veil of ignorance to agree to a principle of saving for future generations "subject to the further condition that they must want all *previous* generations to have followed it."[43] In this way, if the principle of savings leaves future generations with environmental contamination, the contracting parties will suffer because they are in a future generation in relation to the previous generations that followed the same principle. This makes Rawls's theory compatible with concern about future generations by tying this concern to self-interest in the original position.

42. Garrett Hardin, "Who Cares for Posterity?" in *Environmental Ethics: Readings in Theory and Application*, 2nd ed., Louis P. Pojman, Ed. (Belmont, CA: Wadsworth, 1998), pp. 279–84, at 280–81. Emphasis in original.

43. John Rawls, *Political Liberalism* (New York: Columbia University Press, 1993), p. 274. Emphasis in original.

But something is missing. Self-interest is the farthest thing from the minds of those worried that our nuclear waste will poison people 2,000 years from now. *Although Rawls accommodates concern about the distant future, which is more than libertarians and free-market conservatives can do, it is clear than the concern does not emanate from contractarianism.*[44] *We shall see that communitarianism, moral conservatism, and environmentalism do better because they supply plausible motivation for the concern.*

UTILITARIANISM might at first seem more promising because it endorses actions that produce the greatest total happiness (or preference satisfaction). Utilitarians do not discount the happiness or preference satisfaction of future people as economically oriented free-market conservatives must. Utilitarianism therefore justifies concern about people of the distant future. However, it advocates policies regarding future generations that most people reject. *The problem for utilitarianism stems from the fact that policies regarding the future can affect the size of the human population.*

If total happiness (or preference satisfaction) should be maximized, as utilitarians claim, we should have policies that promote increase of the human population because, in general, total happiness increases with increase in the number of people available to be happy. After some increase, of course, environmental conditions will deteriorate and *average* happiness will decline. But human beings are very adaptable and may remain quite happy with much less room and "stuff." Still, even when average happiness declines, further population increases are required by utilitarianism until environmental deterioration makes everyone so unhappy that total happiness, not just the average, declines. Goodness knows how many billions of people would inhabit Earth at that point. The problem for utilitarianism is that no one really thinks we should increase the human population and trash the environment merely to maximize total human happiness.

The utilitarian principle could be altered to require maximization of average, instead of total, happiness (or preference satisfaction). The problem is that people who are less happy (or satisfied) than average become social liabilities. It would be the duty of utilitarians to try to convince

---

44. For more on this see M. L. J. Wissenburg, "An Extension of the Rawlsian Savings Principle to Liberal Theories of Justice in General," in *Fairness and Futurity: Essays on Environmental Sustainability and Social Justice,* Andrew Dobson, Ed. (New York: Oxford University Press, 1999), pp. 173–98.

those whose offspring would most likely be happy, but less happy than average, to avoid or terminate pregnancy. These would be people whose prospective children are at greater risk than average of such problems as genetically influenced short stature or nervous disposition. Only people who think that discouraging such births is a good idea can be consistent utilitarians if maximizing average utility is the goal. I do not imagine that there are many such people. Utilitarianism seems a poor guide to conduct regarding future generations.[45]

Communitarians, Moral Conservatives, Environmentalists, and the Future

Mark Sagoff, research scholar in philosophy and public policy, gives plausible reasons, resembling communitarian and moral conservative views, for public policies that promote the welfare of future generations. He argues that people generally have two different frames of reference for evaluating policies. As consumers, they seek the greatest variety of the best quality products at the lowest possible prices. Free-market conservatism reflects this consumer frame of mind, because free markets are usually the best means of providing people with such products. But most people also evaluate policies as citizens concerned to do what they see as morally right or appropriate.

Sagoff discusses the Gettysburg National Military Park where the Civil War Battle of Gettysburg was fought. The Park Service could satisfy more consumer preferences at the site if they went commercial. I can imagine a mall with hip-hugger versions of Civil War uniforms and special video games "Kill the Yankee" and "Kill Johnny Reb." Kids love to play. The Park Service would never do this because their goal is "to educate the public and honor 'the valor and sacrifices of those men who fought and died on that ground for their beliefs.'"[46] Sagoff quotes long-time Gettysburg

---

45. For a utilitarian response see Jan Narveson, "Moral Problems of Population" and Peter Singer, "A Utilitarian Population Principle," in *Ethics and Population*, Michael D. Bayles, Ed. (Cambridge, MA: Schenkman Publishing, 1976), pp. 59–80 and 81–99, respectively.

46. Mark Sagoff, "At the Monument to General Meade, or on the Difference between Beliefs and Benefits," in *Environmental Ethics: Divergence and Convergence*, 3rd ed., Susan J. Armstrong and Richard G. Botzler, Eds. (New York: McGraw-Hill, 2004), pp. 524–37, at 525. Originally appeared in *Arizona Law Review* in 2001. The interior quote is from "APCWS Position on Proposed Gettysburg Development Plan" by Denis P. Galvin, Deputy Director, National Park Service, Feb. 24, 1998 (visited Mar. 26, 2000) http://users.erols.com/va-udc/nps.html.

preservationist Robert Moore: "What gives meaning to the place is the land on which the battle was fought and the men who died there. Keeping the place the same holy place, that's what's important."[47] This is a moral stand independent of consumer preference and personal benefit of any kind. It is simply what people think is right.

It is common for people in wartime to accept the citizen and reject the consumer perspective. Consider, for example, the Second Iraq War (2003). War proponents were incensed at claims made in 2003 that the war was fought over oil, because that reduced the patriotic sacrifice of our soldiers to meeting consumer demand for gasoline. If Saddam Hussein posed no threat to the United States because he lacked weapons of mass destruction, war proponents said, the war was justified by the freedom it brought to the Iraqi people. Americans with this view did not expect any personal benefit whatsoever from the success of what they saw as a noble cause expressing citizen values in a free society. Opponents of the war generally shared these values and goals, disagreeing primarily about the morality of initiating a nondefensive war and the practicality of improving Iraqi lives through foreign military intervention.

Sagoff's distinction between the consumer and citizen perspectives represents a distinction already considered in Chapters 5, 6, and 7 between the political liberalism of free-market conservatives and liberal contractarians, who incline toward a consumer perspective, and communitarians and moral conservatives, who espouse nonconsumer values and moral constraints. One important similarity between the citizen perspective and both moral conservatism and communitarianism is the concern for **holistic entities.** These are wholes that are greater than the sum of their parts, such as a choir. Individual singers may sing beautifully, but taken separately they cannot produce harmonies. Good harmony is an aspect of a holistic entity, the choir. Similarly, the effectiveness of a basketball team depends not only on the individual players' ability to shoot, rebound, dribble, and play one-on-one defense. It depends also on teamwork that can be attributed to the team as a whole, not to its members considered individually.

Communitarians are clearly interested in a holistic entity, the community. This interest justifies concern about the future because communities exist over longer time periods than do individual human beings. Communities evolve over hundreds of years. Communitarians seek long-term community improvement.

---

47. Sagoff, p. 532.

Moral conservatives also care about future generations. They want people to recognize the wisdom in practices and institutions that have withstood the test of time and been handed down to us. Respect for such practices and institutions motivates protecting them for future generations. The 18th-century English conservative Edmund Burke wrote: "People will not look forward to posterity, who never look backward to their ancestors. Besides, the people of England well know that the idea of inheritance furnishes a sure principle of conservation and a sure principle of transmission, without at all excluding a principle of improvement."[48] He objected to "changing the state as often, and as much, and in as many ways as there are floating fancies or fashions" because "the whole chain and continuity of the commonwealth would be broken. No one generation could link with the other. Men would become little better than the flies of summer." People should be mindful, therefore, "of what they have received from their ancestors [and] what is due to their posterity."[49] A 2,000-year time frame is not too long for moral conservatives, because they are religiously oriented, and religious traditions extend for such periods.

Environmentalists therefore have the company of communitarians and moral conservatives when they worry that nuclear power generates radioactive waste that may harm future generations. The community basis of objections to storing waste in Yucca Mountain is reflected in the special concern of the people and officials of Nevada. Because it is their state, their land, they take special responsibility, more than most Americans, for passing it on in good shape to future generations.[50]

Old-Growth Forests, Endangered Species, and Job Security

Environmentalists differ from communitarians and moral conservatives primarily in the legacy they value and want to preserve. Many environmental concerns are what philosophers call **nonanthropocentric**— *nonhuman entities are valued for their own sake, not merely for benefits they may provide for people now or in the future.* **Anthropocentric** concerns, by contrast, relate entirely to benefits for human beings. Up to this point, all the concerns discussed in this book, except those regarding cruelty to animals, have been anthropocentric. The exception, torturing

---

48. Edmund Burke, *Reflections on the Revolution in France* (New York: Bobbs-Merrill, 1955 [1790]), p. 38.
49. Burke, p. 108.
50. "Yucca Mountain, the Ultimate Gamble," p. 3.

animals, is considered bad even if no harm comes to any human being. The animals are important enough in their own right to outlaw cruelty to them. This is a nonanthropocentric concern.

Many environmentalists extend such nonanthropocentric concern to holistic entities, including wilderness areas, old-growth forests, species, complex ecosystems, and evolutionary processes that produce the diversity of life. These entities should be preserved not merely for benefits that may accrue to human beings, but additionally because they are valuable in themselves. Thus, extinguishing a species is not only of potential harm to human beings, on this view, but harmful in itself because species diversity and its preservation are simply good in themselves. This is equivalent in practice, Garrett Hardin notes, to treating species as sacred.[51]

Pioneer ecologist Aldo Leopold links such environmental concern to community preservation endorsed by communitarians and moral conservatives. Leopold likens ecosystems to communities and endorses an ethic that "changes the role of *Homo sapiens* from the conqueror of the land-community to plain member and citizen of it. It implies respect for his fellow-members, and also respect for the community as such."[52]

Leopold's ethic would reject continued logging in the Pacific Northwest old-growth forests. These forests contain redwoods, some of the world's oldest, and probably the world's largest and tallest, trees. Some of these trees may be 2,000 years old. They are a legacy that environmentalists want to protect because, during the last century, between 70 and 95% of them were cut down for lumber.

Threat to the remaining trees became acute only in 1986 with the takeover of Pacific Lumber by Charles Hurwitz. Before that, Pacific Lumber had

> a policy of perpetual sustained yield: mature trees were marked for selective cutting, felled, snaked out by the "cat" tractor, and milled. With more light in the forest, the younger trees matured faster; where bare spots were left, the company reseeded. . . . The sustained yield policy is economically sound, [providing] steady earnings on its outstanding shares.[53]

---

51. Hardin, p. 281.

52. Aldo Leopold, *A Sand County Almanac with Essays on Conservation from Round River* (New York: Ballantine, 1970 [1949]), p. 240.

53. Lisa H. Newton and Catherine K. Dillingham, *Watersheds 3: Ten Cases in Environmental Ethics* (Belmont, CA: Wadsworth, 2002), p. 166.

From the free-market conservative perspective, however, Pacific Lumber was underperforming. They were making money for their shareholders, but they were not making as much money as possible. Hurwitz, recognizing the potential for additional profit, paid shareholders well for the company and began increasing income by speeding up the pace of logging, abandoning expensive replanting projects, and clear-cutting large areas of forest instead of selectively cutting individual trees to leave the forest essentially intact. The results were ecologically ruinous:

> The selective cutting and replanting, besides providing for future harvests, had held the soil in place after logging, and prevented erosion of the steep slopes in the relentless rainfall of the region; under new management, the soil began to wash into the streams. . . . Erosion is bad for the slopes (which cannot then grow more trees), bad for the banks of the stream (which overflow with regular spring floods), and fatal for the salmon (which cannot breed when soil from erosion covers the gravel at the bottom of the streams).[54]

But what is ecologically ruinous and unsustainable may be economically beneficial, at least in the short run, and big business is oriented toward the short run. Publicly held companies must issue financial reports every three months so that stockholders can have timely information about their investments. Many stockholders want the largest short-term returns possible and would not mind the company devastating a forest in the process. Free-market conservative Milton Friedman held that "the social responsibility of business is to increase its profit.[55] *Individuals who favor forest stewardship over maximum profits, on this free-market reasoning, should not be allowed to impose their values on other stockholders by dictating eco-friendly policies.*

This reasoning has some appeal. Many people have pension fund investments in companies whose activities may be environmentally harmful. Should those retirees have their life savings and retirement dreams compromised because other people insist that lower profit is required in order to save some old trees? Perhaps those who believe that financial sacrifice is appropriate to save old-growth forests should sacrifice only their own money, leaving corporations free to enrich their owners by all legal means.

---

54. Newton and Dillingham, pp. 167–68.

55. Milton Friedman, "The Social Responsibility of Business Is to Increase Its Profit," *New York Times* (September 13, 1970). Cited in Newton and Dillingham (2002), p. 165.

Environmentalists needed a legal means of stopping or slowing the logging. They used the Endangered Species Act (ESA), which became law in 1973. The goal of the ESA is to avoid species loss, reflecting a fundamental value that regards species as nearly sacred, the way Hardin claimed they must be regarded if they are to be saved.

The Act charges the Fish and Wildlife Service with determining which land species are in danger of extinction. No economic considerations are to affect the listing of a species as endangered. Within a year of such listing, the Service should determine the species' critical habitat, which is the area that the species needs to continue existence in the wild, as the goal of ESA is to preserve species in their natural setting. Economic, not just scientific, considerations may affect determinations of critical habitat.[56]

Antilogging interests claimed, correctly it seems, that the old-growth forest owned by Pacific Lumber was critical habitat for the northern spotted owl, which is endangered. The owls cannot exist in newly planted forests. They require "such old-growth characteristics as broken branches that provide platforms, debris, and protective thermal cover, characteristics not found in new growth. Also, the owls' prey—squirrels, voles, rats—share the old-growth habitat and feed on the fungi that form on the decaying trees." Finally, younger tree stands provide habitat for the great horned owls, which feed upon young spotted owls. So, the endangered spotted owl needs the oldest trees in large numbers. Because so many have already been cut, "virtually all the old growth left, whether in private or public hands, must be preserved."[57] Accordingly, in 1991 a U.S. district judge ordered a moratorium on logging in the old-growth forest.

Loggers and other workers in the region complained of job loss. However, species protection was not the main cause of unemployment in the region. Most jobs were lost because lumber companies closed their mills and shipped raw lumber overseas to be processed. In addition, even if logging were allowed, at the rate of cutting before the moratorium the old-growth forest would be gone in about five years, putting an end to the jobs after the jobs put an end to the forest. Still, hundreds of millions of dollars, or more, are tied up in trees that the company cannot now cut and sell. Is this fair to the company and its shareholders?

---

56. Newton and Dillingham, pp. 162–63.
57. Newton and Dillingham, p. 160.

Property Rights and the Takings Clause

The U.S. Constitution does not allow the government to take property from private owners without providing just compensation. This is known as the "Takings Clause." It applies, for example, when a state wants to put a highway through someone's land and appropriates the land through **eminent domain.** The **Takings Clause** requires the state to buy the land at a reasonable price.

The implications of the Takings Clause are less clear, however, when the state does not want to occupy the land but seeks, instead, merely to regulate its use. Such regulation may reduce the value of the property because the owner's most lucrative use may be forbidden by the regulation. Is this a "taking" for which the state owes the property owner compensation?

A regulation is not a taking if it disallows activities that were outside the property owner's rights in the first place. These would be uses of the property that are a nuisance or harm the public. Consider this fanciful, extreme example. We have seen that burial of nuclear waste is a serious problem. I might agree to have large amounts stored in my suburban back yard if I were paid enough to afford a second home far away from any danger. Government regulations do not allow me to do this. Most people agree that the government does not owe compensation, even though this is the most financially rewarding use of my property. The regulation basically prevents me from harming other people, especially my neighbors, whose property values would be lowered and who may not have enough money to move away.

The state does not have to pay me when it forbids harmful conduct because I have no right to engage in such conduct in the first place. Any other view would cripple law enforcement. After all, the most financially rewarding use of my gun may be in armed robbery. Surely the state does not have to pay me because it forbids armed robbery.

On the other hand, consider the case of David Lucas who, writes Supreme Court Justice Antonin Scalia,

> paid $975,000 for two residential lots on the Isle of Palms in Charleston County, South Carolina, on which he intended to build single-family homes. In 1988, however, the South Carolina Legislature enacted the Beachfront Management Act . . . which had the direct effect of barring [him] from erecting any permanent habitable structures on his two parcels.[58]

---

58. See *Lucas v. Carolina Coastal Council,* 505 U.S. 1003 (1992), at 1006–07.

The legislation was justified by the state's police power, which is the state's power to prevent anyone harming the public. The legislature determined that Lucas' property was part of the beach/dune system along the South Carolina coast that

> (a) protects life and property by serving as a storm barrier . . . ; (b) provides the basis of a tourism industry that generates approximately two thirds of South Carolina's annual tourism industry revenues . . . ; (c) provides habitat for numerous species of plants and animals, several of which are threatened or endangered; [and] (d) provides a natural health environment for the citizens of South Carolina to spend leisure time which serves their physical and mental well-being.[59]

The legislature found that permanent structures and "hard erosion control devices such as seawalls [and] bulkheads" had jeopardized the beach/dune system's stability by interfering with the natural movement of sand by wind and water. So they disallowed any additional permanent structures, including the houses Lucas wanted to build.

Lucas claimed, and the court agreed, that this rendered his property absolutely worthless. Although the state did not occupy his land physically, his loss was the same as if they had. Does this constitute a taking for which Lucas was due compensation?

The matter turns on whether the state was preventing Lucas from harming the public or requiring that his property be used to benefit the public. The state owes no compensation if it is merely preventing harm, but it does if it is securing a public benefit. Unfortunately, the same regulation may be characterized either way, Scalia notes:

> The distinction between "harm-preventing" and "benefit-conferring" regulation is often in the eye of the beholder. It is quite possible, for example, to describe in *either* fashion the ecological, economic, and aesthetic concerns that inspired the South Carolina legislature in the present case. One could say that imposing servitude on Lucas's land is necessary in order to prevent his use of it from "harming" South Carolina's ecological resources; or, instead, in order to achieve the "benefits" of an ecological reserve.[60]

The Supreme Court's majority decided that the law was designed to benefit the public by preserving the beach/dune system, so, because it

---

59. *Lucas,* at 1021, footnote # 10.
60. *Lucas,* at 1024.

made the land commercially useless, the application of the law to Lucas constituted a taking. This decision supports property rights, which are extremely important. But requiring the state either to abandon a regulation or buy the affected property jeopardizes the environment. Because buying property is often expensive, the state will be able to afford relatively little environmental protection, and ecosystems may deteriorate. In fact, in Lucas's case, the state did not buy the property. Lucas promptly built his houses and moved into one of them.

Logging in the old-growth forest is similar. Such logging can be seen as harming the public because the forest is critical habitat for the spotted owl. Logging threatens an endangered species with extinction, thereby harming the nation, which is committed through the ESA to species preservation. But the opposite way of looking at the situation is also possible. Refraining from logging helps the nation, helps it secure what it values, species preservation. If this value is important to the country, the state should be willing to pay the cost. From this perspective, logging restrictions constitute a taking.

If such restrictions are ever deemed takings, lack of money may cripple state efforts to preserve species. In 1993, Pacific Lumber offered to sell one tenth of their old-growth forest holding to the government for $600 million. Would that be fair to taxpayers? On the other hand, is a lower price fair to stockholders? *It is sometimes unclear in practice how to protect other species while being fair to all human beings.*

Economic Growth

The most fundamental environmentalist critique of industrial civilization is rejection of consumerism and economic growth as fundamental values. To some extent, environmentalists again agree with moral conservatives and communitarians. As we saw in Chapter 7, moral conservatives worry that the virtues of thrift, patience, and hard work erode when society encourages borrowing to buy consumer items that promise immediate gratification. Communitarians join moral conservatives in worrying that consumerism encourages people to spend too much time at work and not enough time at home with family and friends. They also find that many consumer items, especially televisions, larger houses, and suburban sprawl, isolate people and reduce **social capital** (connections among people, social networks, and resulting norms of reciprocity and trust).

The environmentalist critique of industrial civilization is similar, but not identical. Environmentalists worry less than moral conservatives do

340 Chapter 10: Environmentalism

about maintaining traditional virtues and more about attaining a good quality of life, which they consider impossible without environmental protection. Moral conservatives seldom mention environmental limits or the value of preserving nature for nonhumans, such as spotted owls. However, the two overlap in their criticism of the gross domestic product (GDP) as a measure of social well-being. Moral conservatives recognize that much of what they consider morally unfortunate, such as divorce, adds to the GDP. Spouses hire lawyers and live apart, which costs money and adds to the GDP but detracts from social well-being, they believe. Moral conservative William Bennett's alternative measure of social well-being, the Index of Leading Cultural Indicators, therefore subtracts for divorce.

Environmentalists also use alternatives to the GDP to measure progress. If an oil spill or other pollution requires clean-up, for example, the GDP increases with expenditures on abatement. However, such pollution harms the country, so an environmentalist alternative to the GDP, the Genuine Progress Indicator (GPI), subtracts for pollution. It subtracts also for loss of natural capital, such as wetlands and nonrenewable resources, and any other environmental degradation that may add to the GDP.

These different indices, the moral conservative and the environmentalist, tend to move together with each other but against the GDP. On Bennett's index, social well-being increased in the United States along with increased GDP until the mid-1970s when, owing to such trends as increasing rates of divorce and out-of-wedlock births, the Index of Leading Cultural Indicators goes down while the GDP continues to rise.[61] Similarly, the GPI increases with the GDP until the mid-1970s and then declines owing to

> rising income inequality, declining stocks of nonrenewable energy resources (oil and gas), loss of wetlands and old-growth forest ecosystems, and the growing environmental costs associated with greenhouse gas emissions and the accumulated costs of ozone-depleting substances (e.g., CFCs).[62]

Environmentalism has a more ambiguous relationship to communitarianism. Both favor social capital because human relationships are

---

61. See Kevin Phillips, *Wealth and Democracy: A Political History of the American Rich* (New York: Broadway Books, 2002), p. 345.
62. Mark Anielski and Colin L. Soskolne, "Genuine Progress Indicator (GPI) Accounting: Relating Ecological Integrity to Human Health and Well-Being," in Armstrong and Boltzer, Eds., p. 537–46, at 540.

essential to human well-being. But communitarians favor social capital in part because it promotes economic efficiency, commercial success, and job creation. Environmentalists, by contrast, are divided on the value of economic growth and job creation. On the one hand, we saw that some environmentalists favor public transportation because it spurs economic growth. In addition, Michael Renner of the Worldwatch Institute claims that many environmentally responsible practices can create more jobs than can the environmentally damaging alternatives they replace. For example, tourism in Pacific Northwest old-growth forests can create more jobs than logging can,[63] and renewable energy, such as wind power, can create more jobs than can the fossil fuel industry.[64]

However, the main point of greater efficiency for many environmentalists is to lessen the human burden on the environment out of concern for ecosystems, nonhumans, and future generations. They see economic growth as part of the problem, and they consider job creation acceptable only when the jobs created use resources more efficiently than do the environmentally harmful and unsustainable practices they replace. *In the long run, these environmentalists think, efficiency should enable people to meet their needs and flourish in culturally rich communities with less work and less money.* For example, if public transportation is more efficient than automotive transportation, a fully developed public transportation system should eventually consume fewer resources, work-hours, and dollars. People will get where they want to go easily and cheaply while owning fewer cars, saving money, working less, and spending more time with family and friends. People will be happier and healthier while saving the environment from the degradation that accompanies building new roads and burning more fossil fuels.

Anticonsumerism and the Good Life

The anticonsumerism brand of environmentalism takes to its logical conclusion the moral conservative and communitarian critiques of consumerism. Consumerism is needed, according to mainstream economic theory, because workers use increasingly sophisticated technologies that make them ever more productive. If per-capita consumption does not

---

63. Michael Renner, "Working for the Environment: A Growing Source of Jobs," *Worldwatch Paper # 152* (Washington, DC: Worldwatch Institute, 2000), pp. 37–40.
64. Michael Renner, "Emplement in Wind Power," *World Watch,* Vol. 14, No. 1 (January/February 2001), pp. 22–30.

increase along with improvements in per-hour productivity, workers will produce more than people consume, and many workers will be fired. Lack of buying power among unemployed workers will further depress consumer demand, resulting in economic recession, which causes social hardship. So, conventional economists see the need for economic growth, which requires increasing consumer demand even if this means parents work overtime and families go into debt to buy designer shoes.

Moral conservatives and communitarians join environmentalists in decrying the negative effects of consumerism on families, neighborhoods, social capital, and mental health, but only environmentalists call for the state to support social and economic development that reduces work and consumption. For example, Gary Gardner and Erik Assadourian of the Worldwatch Institute favor co-housing, a new living arrangement with social as well as environmental advantages:

> Co-housing [is] a modern form of village living in which 10–40 individual households live in a development designed to stimulate neighborly interaction. Privacy is valued and respected, but residents share key spaces, including a common dining hall, gardens, and recreational space. . . .
>
> In a co-housing community, houses often share common walls with neighboring homes and are clustered around a courtyard or pedestrian walkway. . . . This design means that these communities often use less energy and fewer materials than [do] neighborhoods full of private homes. A study of 18 communities in the United States in the mid-1990s found that, compared with before they moved into co-housing, members owned 4% fewer cars, while their ownership of washers and dryers dropped by 25% and of lawnmowers by 75%. . . .[65]

Environmentalists favor governments encouraging such housing arrangements by providing tax breaks and preferential zoning.

In the same vein, Gardner and Assadourian applaud the Sustainable City Plan of Santa Monica, California.

> In place since 1994, the plan aims to decrease overall community consumption, especially the use of materials and resources that are not local, nonrenewable, not recycled, and not recyclable. It also seeks to develop a diversity of transportation options, to minimize the use of hazardous or toxic materials, to preserve open space, and

---

65. Gary Gardner and Erik Assadourian, "Rethinking the Good Life," *State of the World 2004*, Brian Halweil and Lisa Mastny, Eds. (New York: W. W. Norton, 2004), pp. 164–79, at 171.

> to encourage participation in community decision making. The plan uses 66 indicators to measure its progress, such as solid-waste generation, cost of living, share of major streets with bike lanes, percentage of tree canopy coverage, [and] voting rates. . . .[66]

When bike lanes make travel by bicycle safer and more people use bicycles, transportation costs and the need for money and jobs all decline. When the cost of living goes down, another positive development according to the Sustainable City Plan, people again need less money and less work. *Environmentalists opposed to a growing economy advocate living arrangements and other practices that make a good life cheaper, so people can cope with the loss of work hours.*

Environmentalists claim that after a certain level of material welfare is attained, human well-being depends on personal relationships rather than increased consumption. Some improvements in well-being are physical, Gardner and Assadourian report:

> More than a dozen long-term studies in Japan, Scandinavia, and the United States show that the chances of dying in a given year, no matter the cause, is two to five times greater for people who are isolated than for socially connected people. For example, one study found that in 1,234 heart attack patients, the rate of a recurring attack within six months was nearly double for those living alone.[67]

Other improvements concern people's emotional lives. "Again and again," Gardner and Assadourian write,

> studies suggest that happy people tend to have strong, supportive relationships, a sense of control over their lives, good health, and fulfilling work. These factors are increasingly under stress in fast-paced, industrial societies, where people often attempt to use consumption as a substitute for genuine sources of happiness. . . . In the United States, for example, the average person's income [adjusted for inflation] more than doubled between 1957 and 2002, yet the share of people reporting themselves "very happy" over that period remained static.[68]

In light of these facts, many environmentalists endorse government policies, such as those in some European countries, which encourage less work and enable people to flourish on less income. For example, "Belgium, Denmark, France, the Netherlands, and Norway now have

---

66. Gardner and Assadourian, p. 172.
67. Gardner and Assadourian, p. 169.
68. Gardner and Assadourian, p. 166.

35- to 38-hour workweeks. . . ."[69] The Netherlands and Germany have bicycle lanes that make bicycling four times safer there than in the U.S.[70] German law requires most stores to be closed after 8 P.M. weekdays and all day Sunday.[71] In these ways, European governments impair economic growth to enhance the overall quality of life. *Environmentalism seems to be the only political philosophy in the United States that clearly advocates a smaller economy to improve human well-being.* This makes environmentalism attractive to some people and repulsive to others.

CONCLUSION

Many environmentalist proposals cohere with the political liberalism of free-market conservatives and liberal contractarians. These include making corporations pay for the pollution they generate and making consumers pay the full cost of goods and services. Such theoretically uncontroversial ideas meet resistance in practice because they adversely affect entrenched interests, such as the auto, oil, and meat industries.

Other environmentalist proposals, such as protection of endangered species and rare ecosystems whether or not they contribute to human welfare, clash with property rights and anthropocentric cultural and economic worldviews. But such programs already exist by law, such as the Endangered Species Act, which we have applied for decades. Still, the values behind such programs remain controversial and implementation is understandably contested.

Finally, environmentalists agree with communitarians and moral conservatives that consumerism is bad for current people and future generations because it erodes communal ties and valuable traditions. Environmentalists add that it depletes resources and harms other species as well. Communitarians and moral conservatives in reflective equilibrium should be attracted to environmentalist proposals for government help in reducing consumerism and curtailing economic growth. Environmentalists challenge such thinkers to consider innovative, practical applications of their social critiques.

JUDGMENT CALLS

1. Independently of human intervention, over 90% of all the species that ever existed on Earth have become extinct. If extinction is

---

69. Gardner and Assadourian, p. 173.
70. Gardner and Assadourian, p. 175.
71. National Public Radio "Morning Edition," July 5, 2004.

part of the natural process, what justifies government attempts to preserve species today?

2. Some people are anthropocentric, believing that only human beings are morally important, whereas others are nonanthropocentric, believing that some nonhuman entities are important in their own right, apart from any contribution they make to human welfare. How can it be fair to use the nonanthropocentric concern of some people as the rationale for laws that constrain the behavior of everyone? Is there a fundamental right to be anthropocentric and act accordingly?

3. Many environmentalists and communitarians believe that people would be happier, more satisfied, and even healthier living in tight-knit communities within walking distance of shopping, work, and nature, and with few cars but lots of social interaction and bike paths (and maybe some granola and Birkenstocks). Why, then, don't people just live like that? Who is stopping them? Why is government intervention needed to encourage such development?

4. Many environmentalists object to genetically engineered foods, such as a tomato engineered for extra shelf life and a potato engineered to be poisonous to potato beetles (so pesticides are unnecessary). It seems that these products are perfectly safe for human consumption, yet environmentalists want the government to require labels indicating that they are genetically engineered. The companies that produce these products worry that such labels will confuse consumers. What do you think? Would it confuse consumers? Is it the government's job to require labels unrelated to product safety, such as labels of pork content that may be important to traditional Jews and Muslims who do not eat pork? What would free-market conservatives say?

5. If genetic engineering is an acceptable way to improve crops, is there any reason why it should not be used to improve people?

6. Safety is not the only concern of those who want to leave ecological riches for future generations. Many environmentalists want future people to share their enjoyment of and reverence for nature, just as many opera lovers hope that future people will enjoy opera. As Mark Sagoff puts it: "Our decisions concerning the environment will . . . determine, to a large extent, what future people are like

346 Chapter 10: Environmentalism

and what their preferences and tastes will be. If we leave them an environment that is fit for pigs, they will be like pigs; their tastes will adapt to their conditions. . . ."[72] But if this means that, once physical safety is assured, people of the future may be just as pleased with fewer species, simpler ecosystems, and more artificial environments, what justifies insisting that their preferences resemble our own (assuming that "we" have environmentalist preferences)? How might moral conservatives and communitarians differ on this matter from free-market conservatives and liberal contractarians?

---

72. Mark Sagoff, *The Economy of the Earth* (New York: Cambridge University Press, 1988), p. 63.

11 Cosmopolitanism

Cosmopolitans believe that human beings have moral obligations to one another across national borders. Consider these events in India, reported in 1993 by John Anderson and Molly Moore to the *Washington Post* Foreign Service:

> When Rani returned home from the hospital cradling her newborn daughter, the men in the family slipped out of her mud hut while she and her mother-in-law mashed poisonous oleander seeds into a dollop of oil and forced it down the infant's throat. As soon as darkness fell, Rani crept into a nearby field and buried her baby girl in a shallow, unmarked grave next to a small stream.

The authors claim that this happens often in poor countries: "For many mothers, sentencing a daughter to death is better than condemning her to life as a woman in the Third World, with cradle-to-grave discrimination, poverty, sickness, and drudgery."[1] Here is another example:

> Amravati, who lives in a village near Rani, . . . says she killed two of her own day-old daughters by pouring scalding chicken soup down their throats, one of the most widely practiced methods of infanticide in southern India. . . . "My mother-in-law and father-in-law are bedridden," says Amravati, who has two living daughters. "I have no land and no salary, and my husband met with an accident and can't work. Of course it was the right decision."[2]

Another all-too-common response to poverty is selling girls into prostitution. Freelance writer Germaine Shames gives this example: "Kham Suk, a delicate girl with fathomless eyes, hovers in the doorway of a Bangkok brothel in Thailand. Three months ago, on her 12th birthday, her

---

1. John Ward Anderson and Molly Moore, "The Burden of Womanhood," in *Global Issues 96/97*, Robert M. Jackson, Ed. (Guilford, CT: Dushkin, 1996), pp. 162–65, at 162.
2. Anderson and Moore, p. 163.

mother walked her across the border from Myanmar (Burma) and sold her to a pimp for 2,000 baht."[3]

Cosmopolitans believe that universal values require action by people everywhere to reduce the poverty and sex discrimination that leads to such horrors. Because these values are universal, writes British philosopher Nigel Dower, "national boundaries do not, with this approach, have any ultimate moral significance."[4] *According to cosmopolitans, because basic human needs and human rights are universal, states, nongovernmental organizations, and individuals should work separately and together to ensure that human needs are met and human rights are respected everywhere. Claims of national sovereignty cannot shield states from moral censure when they neglect or oppress people under their rule.*

Cosmopolitanism is controversial in part because some people believe that morality is not universal; it is based on culture. Moral obligations therefore extend only to members of one's own culture. Others accept some universal morality but believe that on many matters national borders appropriately enable political communities to promote diverse visions of the good life. Still others, political realists, maintain that universal morality does not apply to states. We discuss these views and find that we do have duties to people in other countries, but problems beset worldwide application of universal moral standards. In addition, national borders can sometimes be used to promote cosmopolitan goals.

Our Duty to Aid the Poor

Grim stories from India and Thailand touch only the surface of deprivation common for hundreds of millions of people. Philosopher Peter Unger writes:

> Each year millions of children die from easy-to-beat disease, from malnutrition, and from bad drinking water. Among these children, about 3 million die from dehydrating diarrhea. As UNICEF has made clear to millions of us well-off American adults at one time or another, with a packet of oral rehydration salts that costs about 15 cents, a child can be saved from dying soon.[5]

---

3. Germaine W. Shames, "The World's Throw-Away Children," in *Global Issues 94/95*, Robert M. Jackson, Ed. (Guilford, CT: Dushdin, 1994), pp. 229–32, at 229.
4. Nigel Dower, *World Ethics: The New Agenda* (Edinburgh: Edinburgh University Press, 1998), p. 20.
5. Peter Unger, *Living High and Letting Die: Our Illusion of Innocence* (New York: Oxford University Press, 1996), p. 3.

When the costs of administration, transportation, and repeat application are added, the cost of preventing a child dying of dehydrating diarrhea may be $3.00, not 15 cents. Still, this seems a small price to pay for a human life. Unger continues: "As is well known, many millions of children don't get enough to eat. These related truths are less well known: for each child that dies in a famine, several die from *chronic malnutrition....*"[6] This malnutrition weakens the immune system, making unvaccinated children susceptible to measles which often kills them. "Each year mere measles still kills about a million Third World kids." But measles is not the greatest killer. Pneumonia, which can be controlled with about 25 cents worth of antibiotics, "now claims about 3.5 million young lives a year, making it the leading child-killing disease."[7]

Cosmopolitans claim that neither national borders nor physical distance release people with discretionary income from the duty to save the lives of these children. The general moral principle we should follow, writes philosopher Peter Singer, is this:

> If it is in our power to prevent something bad from happening, without thereby sacrificing anything of comparable moral importance, we ought, morally, to do it. . . . An application of this principle would be as follows: if I am walking past a shallow pond and see a child drowning in it, I ought to wade in and pull the child out. This will mean getting my clothes muddy, but this is insignificant, while the death of the child would presumably be a very bad thing.[8]

Certainly, I should not let the child die in order to save time and keep my clothes clean. But what difference does it make if the child is near or far, in the United States or overseas? What difference does it make if the inconvenience is writing a check, rather than wading into a pool, and the consequence is not muddy clothes but forgoing a larger screen TV? It's a child's life. Saving it is a duty, not a matter of charity, Singer claims.

Of course, unlike saving the child in the shallow pool, transportation problems and political graft may hinder efforts to help children in the Third World. This reduces our duty to help because we have no obligation to waste money on futile efforts. But giving to such groups as UNICEF and OXFAM, with proven records of delivering help to poor people, does

---

6. Unger, p. 5. Emphasis in original.
7. Unger, p. 6.
8. Peter Singer, "Famine, Affluence, and Morality," in *World Hunger and Morality*, 2nd ed., William Aiken and Hugh LaFollette, Eds. (Upper Saddle River, NJ: Prentice Hall, 1996), pp. 26–38, at 28.

not suffer from this problem, so the duty to support the work of these organizations is like the duty to help the drowning child.

Some thinkers claim, nevertheless, that a duty to save the drowning child does not imply a duty to help starving people in the Third World, because giving food and medicine to people in the Third World promotes ecologically harmful overpopulation. Environmental economist Garrett Hardin argued in the 1970s that people dying of starvation and disease is needed to keep the human population within environmental limits. What Unger sees as a preventable tragedy, Hardin sees as an ecologically beneficial adjustment of population to resources.

Hardin opposes for the same reasons helping people in poor countries grow more food for themselves, as through the Green Revolution, which boosted rice yields in India:

> If rich countries make it possible, through foreign aid, for 600 million Indians to swell to 1.2 billion in a mere 28 years, as their current growth rate threatens, will future generations of Indians thank us for hastening the destruction of their environment? Will our good intentions be sufficient excuse for the consequences of our actions?[9]

In fact, the population of India increased, as Hardin predicted, and is now over one billion, although the pace of increase has slowed. Severe deprivation led Rani and Amravati to kill their infants long after the Green Revolution was declared a success.

But Hardin is wrong, anyway. The flaw in his reasoning is belief that population always increases with greater food availability. At the time he wrote, food was plentiful in Europe and Japan without population increase. That situation persists. Aid activists have found that empowering women (teaching them to read and giving them access to property and employment outside the home) is a reliable means of stemming population growth where food is plentiful. Danielle Nierenberg writes for the Worldwatch Institute:

> A major contributor to later pregnancies and lower fertility is at least six or seven years of schooling. When girls manage to stay in school this long, what they learn about basic health, sexuality, and their own prospects in the world tends to encourage them to marry and become pregnant later in life and to have smaller families. In Egypt, for example, only 5% of women who stayed in school past the primary level had children while still in their teens, while over half of women

---

9. Garrett Hardin, "Lifeboat Ethics: The Case against Helping the Poor," in Aiken and LaFollette, Eds., pp. 5–15, at 12.

with no schooling became teenage mothers. In high-fertility countries, women who have some secondary education typically have two, three, or four children fewer in their lifetimes than otherwise similar women who have never been to school.[10]

In sum, to stem the tide of overpopulation, women should be given more power, education, and access to health care and family planning services.[11] Helping the poor with education, food, medical services, and small business loans can save lives without contributing to overpopulation.

Another consideration that some people think differentiates saving a drowning child from contributing money to aid poor people in the Third World is the equal ability of so many others besides me to provide that aid. If I happen upon a drowning child in the situation that Singer describes, I am uniquely situated to help. If I do not help, the child will drown, and I will be at fault. But if I do not aid the Third World poor, others can help instead, so their preventable deaths are not my responsibility.

In addition, if I accept responsibility for the Third World poor, the commitment is unrealistic and unfair. It is unrealistic because it is more than I can do. It is unfair because while I do a lot others do little or nothing. Such considerations suggest that we help the world's poor primarily through state action. People in rich countries should pool their money through a fair system of taxation and then use some of that money for international aid. The aid would be international, from nation to nation or nation to private agency, rather than interpersonal, from individuals to individuals.

Peter Singer reports that most Americans support such international aid but overestimate the county's contributions. Polls conducted in 1995 and in 2000 reveal that Americans thought foreign aid constituted 15 or 20% of the national budget but that it should constitute only between 5 and 10%. In fact, however, U.S. contributions to foreign aid amount to less than 1% of the federal budget.[12]

Some theorists, however, believe that even this is too much, because states have no moral duty to help one another. Each should look out for its own interests alone.

---

10. Danielle Nierenberg, "Correcting Gender Myopia: Gender Equity, Women's Welfare, and the Environment," *Worldwatch Paper #161* (September 2002), p. 16.

11. See also Lincoln C. Cen, Winifred M. Fitzgerald, and Lisa Bates, "Women, Politics and Global Management," *Environment* (January/February 1995), p. 4 and Lisa H. Newton and Catherine K. Dillingham, *Watersheds 3: Ten Cases in Environmental Ethics* (Belmont, CA: Wadsworth, 2002), pp. 38–39.

12. Peter Singer, *One World: The Ethics of Globalization* (New Haven: Yale University Press, 2002), pp. 182–83.

Political Realism

Political realism is the view that morality does not apply to states. States should be purely self-interested, so they cannot be faulted morally for failing to help poor people in other countries. Justifying this view begins with explaining why states exist at all. Nineteenth-century philosopher John Stuart Mill points to **nationality:**

> A portion of mankind may be said to constitute a Nationality if they are united among themselves by common sympathies which do not exist between them and any others—which make them cooperate with each other more willingly than with other people, desire to be under the same government, and desire that it should be government by themselves or a portion of themselves exclusively. This feeling of nationality may have been generated by various causes. . . . But the strongest of all is identity of political antecedents; the possession of a national history, and consequent community of recollections; collective pride and humiliation, pleasure and regret, connected with the same incidents in the past.[13]

State-supported education emphasizes the common history that binds people together as a nation. In the United States we learn about Columbus, the Pilgrims, the wise Founding Fathers, the shame of slavery, the trauma of the Civil War, the perils and glories of World War II, and the triumph of good in the Civil Rights Movement. We publicly celebrate Thanksgiving and the birthdays of Christopher Columbus, George Washington, Abraham Lincoln, and Martin Luther King, Jr. to remind ourselves of people and events central to our collective memory and pivotal to our commitment to one another through common membership in a single nation-state.

The resulting sense of community membership is based on imagination, as historian Eric Hobsbawm among others points out, because the ties of nationhood that we feel do not reflect biological relationships. Instead, they come from imagining ourselves descended together from the same forbearers.[14] But, as philosopher Michael Walzer notes, when people imagine themselves heirs to the same cultural heritage they become heir to that heritage and thereby form real communities.[15]

---

13. John Stuart Mill, *Considerations on Representative Government* in *On Liberty and Considerations on Representative Government*, R.B. McCallum, ed. (Oxford: Basil Blackwell, 1948), p. 291.

14. Eric Hobsbawm, *Nations and Nationalism since 1780: Programme, Myth, Reality* (Cambridge: Cambridge University Press, 1990), p. 46.

15. Michael Walzer, *Thick and Thin: Moral Argument at Home and Abroad* (Notre Dame: University of Notre Dame Press, 1994), p. 68.

The state's legitimacy depends on this sense of nationhood. Mill writes: "Where the sentiment of nationality exists in any force, there is a . . . case for uniting all the members of the nationality under the same government, and a government to themselves apart. This is merely saying that the question of government ought to be decided by the governed."[16] The governed typically want to share their state with culturally like-minded people because the state decides what actions are permissible and what causes to support with tax funds. People are more likely to agree on these matters as they become more culturally homogeneous, resulting in state rules that most people favor. So in general, *separate states exist because separate nations exist. The state's primary task is to protect and perpetuate the nation so people can pass on their cultural heritage.*

Political realists claim that states protecting and perpetuating a nation can legitimately ignore morality. One justification for this view, put forward by Thomas Hobbes in the 17th century, is that states, like individuals, tend to be selfish. This makes them competitors, as each seeks more power for itself at the expense of others. Selfish competition knows no bounds except coercion; selfish entities behave immorally unless effective law enforcement scares them into morality through threat of punishment. Because law enforcement is absent among states, states are not subject to morality.

This view was reinforced by 20th-century American theologian Reinhold Niebuhr, who realized that Hobbes was wrong about selfishness among people; individuals do not always behave selfishly. However, he claimed, people are more selfish in groups than as individuals. For example, patriotism "transmutes individual unselfishness into national egoism."[17] Without worldwide government to coerce obedience to morality, national egoism leads to international immorality. Any other expectation is unrealistic.

What is more, if nation-states cannot expect moral behavior from one another, it would be improper for a state's agents, such as ambassadors, foreign minister, or president, to use moral criteria in crafting state policy. Like lawyers and accountants working for a client, a state's agents should advance the interests of the state within the acceptable rules of engagement. Because there are no such rules, a state's agents should ignore

---

16. Mill, p. 292.

17. Reinhold Niebuhr, *Moral Man and Immoral Society* (New York: Charles Scribner's Sons, 1932), p. 91, in Darrel Moellendorf, *Cosmopolitan Justice* (Boulder, CO: Westview, 2002), p. 144.

morality altogether. Assuming that morality imposes limits on the pursuit of self-interest, any agent using moral criteria in the selection of policies and strategies would put her state at a competitive disadvantage in a competitive world. Her state would be handicapped by morality while others were not. This would not be fair to the state she represents. So her moral obligation to the state and her fellow citizens requires that she ignore morality in international relations.

A final justification of political realism stems from skepticism about universal morality, Dower writes. Some communitarians believe that morality arises from "shared traditions, practices and institutions which . . . [do] not exist in the international area. . . . So there is no morality in international relations."[18]

A logical implication of such realism is that nations have no moral duty to supply foreign aid; they should help poor countries only so far as this serves the national interest. More alarmingly, it implies equally that nations have no moral duty to avoid despicable behavior in relation to foreigners; moral principles are expendable in the national interest.

Prisoner Abuse

Prisoner abuse is a test case for such realist reasoning. In principle, if morality does not apply to states acting to defend and perpetuate their national cultures, states responding to foreign attack should be free of moral restraint when attempting to gain valuable information from prisoners who may have aided the attackers. Such thinking may have influenced lawyers in the Bush administration to recommend ignoring law and morality regarding the treatment of prisoners taken in the war on terrorism. A Defense Department memorandum dated March 6, 2003, argues:

> As [the Department of Justice (DOJ)] has made clear in opinions involving the war on al Qaida, the nation's right to self-defense has been triggered by the events of September 11. If a government defendant were to harm an enemy combatant during an interrogation in a manner that might arguably violate criminal prohibitions, he would be doing so in order to prevent further attacks on the United States by the al Qaida terrorist network. In that case, DOJ believes that he

18. Dower, p. 29.

could argue that the executive branch's constitutional authority to protect the nation from attack justified his actions.[19]

In short, national self-defense can justify violating our own laws, international treaties (the Convention against Torture), and common moral restrictions.

This departs from past thinking and practice. Army field manuals, for example, uphold international standards for the treatment of prisoners. Anthony Lewis reports in the *New York Review of Books:*

> Secretary Rumsfeld and Vice President Dick Cheney thought the military field manuals were too restrictive. In the fall of 2002 and early 2003 they tried to change them, but JAG [judge advocate general] lawyers said the changes could not be reconciled with U.S. domestic law or treaties.
>
> With or without revisions in the field manuals, the limits on interrogation techniques were changed by Secretary Rumsfeld . . . [but] the new rules have not been disclosed.[20]

The field manuals represent American law for the military, and certain procedures are normally required to change them. In addition, the publication of new rules is legally mandatory. But *if states can pursue self-defense without limit, as realists claim, the Iraq war released the United States from domestic laws and international treaties.* It should be no surprise, then, that the International Committee of the Red Cross (ICRC) found the following violations of international law at the U.S.-run Abu Ghraib prison in Iraq:

> Handcuffing with flexi-cuffs, which were sometimes made so tight and used for such extended periods that they caused skin lesions and long-term aftereffects on the hands (nerve damage) . . . ;
>
> Beatings with hard objects (including pistols and rifles), slapping, punching, kicking with knees or feet on various parts of the body (legs, sides, lower back, groin . . .);
>
> Being paraded naked outside cells in front of other persons deprived of their liberty, and guards, sometimes hooded or with women's underwear over the head . . . ;
>
> Being attached repeatedly over several days . . . with handcuffs to the bars of their cell door in humiliating (i.e., naked or in underwear) and/or uncomfortable position causing physical pain. . . .

---

19. Quoted in Anthony Lewis, "Making Torture Legal," *The New York Review of Books,* Vol. LI, No. 12 (July 15, 2004), pp. 4–8, at 4.

20. Lewis, p. 6.

> The ICRC medical delegates [to the prison] examined persons . . . presenting signs of concentration difficulties, memory problems, verbal expression difficulties, incoherent speech, acute anxiety reactions, abnormal behavior, and suicidal tendencies. These symptoms appear to have been caused by the methods and duration of interrogation.[21]

Some prisoners died. "One," writes Lewis, "was Major General Abed Hamed Mowhoush, who had been chief of Iraqi air defenses. He was captured in October 2003 and died on November 26, 2003, in a U.S. detention facility in Iraq." At first the Pentagon said he died of natural causes, but after contradictory reports leaked out they admitted he died of "asphyxia due to smothering and chest compression. . . ."[22] Another was Lieutenant Colonel Kareem 'abd al-Jalil who died on January 9, 2004, at an interrogation facility. Again, natural causes were listed until evidence of abuse surfaced and his death was ruled a homicide from "blunt force injuries and asphyxia." Lewis adds, "those two were regular Iraqi officers, not terrorists. In American history, until now, flag and field officers of opposing armies were given great respect when captured."[23]

From a strictly realist perspective, however, Americans did nothing wrong, because morality does not apply in international relations. A treaty may resemble a promise that creates a moral relationship between the parties, but if no morality exists in international relations because morality does not apply to the conduct of states, then treaties are made for competitive advantage. The only fault in secretly breaking a treaty is getting caught, because that degrades helpful international cooperation, which pretended compliance fosters. Similarly, there is nothing wrong with torturing prisoners to advance the national interest, but getting caught is bad because then Americans held captive in war may be treated brutally as well, which harms the national interest.

Of course, a good way to avoid getting caught breaking a treaty or torturing prisoners is to abide by the treaty and treat prisoners decently in the first place. So, realists often advocate observing international norms of conduct to advance the national interest through international cooperation. However, because morality does not strictly apply to international conduct, according to political realists, the nation may, and should if the need is great, break treaties and torture prisoners. Hans Morganthau, the

---

21. Quoted in Mark Danner, "Torture and Truth," *The New York Review of Books*, Vol. LI, No. 10 (June 10, 2004), pp. 46–50, at 47.

22. Lewis, p. 6.

23. Lewis, p. 8.

chief advocate of realism in America after World War II, put it this way: "While the individual has the right to sacrifice himself in defense of a moral principle, the state has no right to let its moral disapprobation of the infringement of liberty get in the way of successful political action, itself inspired by the moral principle of national survival."[24]

International Morality

The prisoner abuse scandal illustrates that most people reject political realism. As soon as pictures of abuse at Abu Ghraib surfaced in the media, politicians denounced the mistreatment of prisoners. President Bush said that the actions of the prison guards "do not represent America."[25] Guards pictured abusing prisoners were arrested and brought to trial. No American official suggested that actions in violation of morality, law, and international treaties were acceptable if undertaken in defense of the nation. Ignoring earlier memos, which had not yet become public, officials claimed that the abuses were unauthorized actions by "a few bad apples."

But was the denunciation of prisoner abuse sincere? A political realist would advocate pretended moral indignation to make other countries think we would now exercise restraint in pursuit of self-interest when really we would not.

However, there are reasons to reject political realism on moral grounds. *Political realism contradicts the nearly universal belief that moral principles should guide conduct that has great impact on others.* For example, international relations can include war, as in Iraq, with killing and destruction. Philosopher Darrell Moellendorf asks: "How could anyone deliberating about engaging in war not be required to consider whether it is right to treat others in this way?"[26] The fact that politicians and diplomats are charged with the task of advancing their nation's interests is no excuse for ignoring normal moral constraints. After all, Dower points out:

> The duty of a company to its stockholders to maximize profits does not justify any measure to do so. A parent with special responsibilities to her child, is not justified in doing what is wrong, for instance stealing a toy she could not afford, in order to further the child's

---

24. Hans Morgenthau, *Politics Among Nations*, 5th ed. (New York: Alfred A. Knopf, 1973), p. 4. Found in Moellendorf, p. 145.
25. Quoted in Danner, p. 47.
26. Moellendorf, p. 143.

interests. . . . [In general,] the specific duty to advance the interests of others, because of the special relationship involved, does not override the ordinary moral framework of nondeception, noncoercion, respect for property, and so on. Why should governments be any different?[27]

We have seen that Hobbes's reason for thinking governments are different is that they operate in an international arena where the absence of effective law enforcement makes everyone liable to everyone else's misbehavior. Lacking assurance that others will follow moral rules justifies states ignoring those rules themselves.

But since the Peace of Westphalia that ended the Thirty Years War in 1648, states have generally accepted certain rules of international relations. These include rules acknowledging one another's sovereignty, including the right to deal with internal political matters without external interference. The rules also call for honoring treaty obligations, which are like promises. People would not make promises to one another if there were no moral principle that, absent extraordinary circumstances justifying a breach, promises must be kept. Equally, sovereign states would not make treaties without accepting the moral principle that treaty obligations must be met. Of course, promises and treaties are sometimes broken without sufficient moral justification. But imperfect compliance with a moral principle does not challenge the principle's existence.

A follower of Hobbes might still object that enforcement is necessary for real moral obligations to exist, and there is no effective enforcement of international law. But this is wrong on two counts. First, real moral obligations exist even without effective enforcement. Surely it is usually wrong for people to lie and break promises even when they can get away with it. Why would it not similarly be morally wrong for countries to lie and break treaties even when they can get away with it?

Second, states cannot always get away with it. They are liable to sanctions for violating international norms and laws. The World Trade Organization (WTO), for example, imposes penalties for the breach of international rules regarding free trade. In one case, Singer writes:

> The European Union banned the sale of beef from cattle treated with growth-promoting hormones. . . . The United States successfully challenged the ban at the WTO, with the WTO panel finding that there was no sufficient scientific basis for believing that the use of the

---

27. Dower, p. 38.

hormones posed a risk to human health. . . . When the European Union nevertheless refused to lift the ban, the WTO authorized the United States to retaliate by imposing 100% duties on $116 million of EU agricultural products.[28]

The breach of international norms can result in less formal penalties as well. The United States, the world's greatest military power, lacked international authorization from the U.N. for its invasion of Iraq in 2003, with the result that it shouldered 90% of the burden of war and occupation, whereas in Afghanistan, where it had international authorization, it shouldered a much smaller percentage of costs and incurred a much smaller percentage of casualties. Losing billions of dollars and hundreds of soldiers' lives was the informal penalty for unilateral action.

Again, one of the major concerns stemming from revelations of prisoner abuse in Iraq is that captured American soldiers may be subjected to similar treatment. This would be a significant negative consequence of the United States violating international norms. So, *states are not free to break treaties and violate international law with impunity. The breach of international rules, like the breach of domestic law, is often penalized.*

Treaties and international law can facilitate, but they cannot assure, the achievement of cosmopolitan goals. Cosmopolitans advocate moral commitment of people to one another across national and cultural boundaries without the need of international treaties or enforcement. Cosmopolitans want affluent people to care for the world's poor as we expect a passerby to save a drowning child. The treaties and international laws just considered do not amount to cosmopolitanism because they concern the obligations of states (or larger units such as the European Union) to other states (or larger units). If the EU has rules barring the importation of American beef and this violates WTO rules, the United States can impose duties on agricultural products from the EU. Individuals gain and lose, but only as members of political units. The responsible parties with treaty commitments, the right to complain about a breach, and liability for a breach, are all states or larger political units.

Even more than international trade, war is a state enterprise. A nation, the United States, not a group of individuals, attacked Iraq without international authorization. The Iraq War was paid for by government money, not voluntary individual contributions. Soldiers killing in the line of duty were shielded from prosecution because they represented their nation.

---

28. Singer, p. 61.

Thus, the issue is state monetary and military commitment, not individual commitment. Accordingly, disputes about the war, and penalties for failure to obtain international authorization, concern **international morality,** not cosmopolitanism, because it is a morality that relates nations to one another.

In sum, *political realism's claim that no morality exists at the international level is wrong. Such morality does exist. But it is morality that relates nations to one another, whereas cosmopolitans advocate a global morality with individual responsibility.*

Individual Responsibility for Crimes against Humanity

Holding individuals, not just their countries, responsible for violations of international norms is a step toward cosmopolitanism. Before World War II, it was thought that state leaders could not be tried for what they did in their official roles because states have sovereign immunity from criminal prosecution and such leaders embody the state. After World War II, however, the victors set up the International Military Tribunal to try members of the German government for **crimes against peace,** starting an unjust war, as well as for **war crimes,** and **crimes against humanity.** It is a war crime, in Singer's words, "to murder, ill-treat, or deport either civilians or prisoners of war" and a crime against humanity "to murder, exterminate, enslave, or deport any civilian population, or to persecute them on political, racial, or religious grounds."[29] Individual Germans in positions of power were tried at Nuremberg for these crimes, and some of those found guilty were put to death.

The precedent set at Nuremberg was followed in the 1990s with special tribunals established to try those accused of perpetrating war crimes or crimes against humanity in Rwanda and (the former) Yugoslavia. Slobodan Milosevic, President of Yugoslavia, for example, was accused of promoting the 1999 expulsion of ethnic Albanians from Kosovo Province, causing many deaths in the process. The Associated Press published the following interview with a boy subjected to this **ethnic cleansing.**

> Ten-year-old Dren Caka fingers the inflatable brace wrapped around his bullet-shattered right arm. . . . Dren says he was shot as Serb police slaughtered his family. . . .
>
> It begins before dawn Saturday when they claim Yugoslav police began looting and burning homes on Milos Gjic Street in Djakovica,

---

29. Singer, p. 113.

in southern Kosovo. . . . Dren and 19 women and children, including his mother and three sisters, hide in a basement. But they are quickly discovered and accused of being supporters of the Kosovo Liberation Army, the ethnic Albanian separatists. . . .

A 13-year-old girl is shot first, Dren says. Then, one by one, the police lower their guns and fire. It takes less than a minute.

"I was hit in the arm, but I fell and pretended I was dead."

The police set the home ablaze and move on, he says. Thinking everyone is dead, he starts to run. Then he hears moans from his baby sister.

"I tried to pick her up, but . . . but," Dren says before breaking into tears and pointing to his arm. His uncle takes over: "He means he couldn't lift her because of his arm. She burned to death in the house."[30]

From the cosmopolitan perspective, special tribunals prosecuting people such as Milosevic for their crimes is better than no prosecution at all. However, a major problem with special tribunals is that their establishment is a political decision, so leaders contemplating criminal activity can hope to evade eventual prosecution through political activity that thwarts establishment of the relevant tribunal. Special tribunals thus lack the deterrence of regular law enforcement. To increase deterrence, representatives of 160 states agreed in Rome in 1998 to establish the International Criminal Court (ICC) to try individuals for war crimes and crimes against humanity. Located at The Hague, the court's prosecutors can bring charges against any individuals whose government has ratified the treaty establishing the court or whose alleged crimes took place in the jurisdiction of such a country. The court came into existence in July 2002 after 60 countries ratified the treaty. Defendants cannot invoke sovereign immunity; doing one's best to advance state goals is no excuse for violating international norms.

An alternative to the ICC with potentially broader sweep is **universal jurisdiction.** It is, in Singer's words, "the right of any country to try a person who has committed crimes against humanity, irrespective of whether the country in which the crime was committed is a signatory to a convention that provides for international criminal responsibility in respect of that crime."[31] For example, even if the United States had not ratified the 1984 Convention against Torture, universal jurisdiction would allow

---

30. Brian Murphy in *The State Journal-Register* (Springfield, Illinois) (April 7, 1999), pp. 1 and 5.

31. Singer, pp. 113–14.

prosecutors in countries where torture is illegal (Spain, Jordan, and so forth) to extradite and try people alleged to have perpetrated or authorized torture at Abu Ghraib prison in Iraq.

The responsiveness of governments to such requests for extradition is currently uncertain. In the most famous case to date, the United Kingdom held Augusto Pinochet for 16 months while jurists decided whether or not to extradite him to Spain. Spain wanted to try the former dictator of Chile on charges of ordering the torture of Spanish nationals in Chile. The British court decided to extradite Pinochet but cited Chile's ratification of the Convention against Torture as a decisive factor.[32]

Some thinkers oppose both the ICC and universal jurisdiction. Henry Kissinger, former National Security Advisor and Secretary of State, notes correctly, "the notion that heads of state and senior public officials should have the same standing as outlaws before the bar of justice is quite new."[33] Cosmopolitans and advocates of universal jurisdiction, however, see no reason why "heads of state and senior public officials" should be able to evade the law. Immunity from prosecution only encourages them.

But prosecution has drawbacks as well. Recrimination and division often accompany ending a regime of terror, such as Franco's in Spain and Pinochet's in Chile. People in the affected country may know best how to heal wounds, Kissinger suggests:

> The decision of post-Franco Spain to avoid wholesale criminal trials for the human rights violations of the recent past was designed explicitly to foster a process of national reconciliation that undoubtedly contributed much to the present vigor of Spanish democracy. Why should Chile's attempt at national reconciliation not have been given the same opportunity?[34]

Perhaps Kissinger is right when he suggests that Chile may do best by ignoring past crimes, but that is not the kind of test we apply in analogous domestic contexts. We normally oppose a victim of rape achieving peace of mind by forgiving the rapist and dropping all charges. Even if that particular rapist, owing to a debilitating accident, no longer endangers the community, failure to prosecute reduces the deterrent effect of laws against rape, thereby increasing the likelihood of other women being

---

32. Pinochet was subsequently sent home to Chile because the Chilean government agreed to prosecute him there.

33. Henry Kissinger, "The Pitfalls of Universal Jurisdiction," *Foreign Affairs*, Vol. 80, No. 4 (July/August 2001), pp. 86–96, at 87.

34. Kissinger, p. 91.

victimized by other rapists. Similarly, even if Pinochet is now harmless and Chile fares best by ignoring his crimes, failure to prosecute reduces the deterrent effect of treaties against torture, thereby increasing the likelihood of other populations being victimized by other dictators.

Kissinger complains also: "The Pinochet precedent . . . would permit the two sides in the Arab-Israeli conflict, or those in any other passionate international controversy, to project their battles into the various national courts by pursuing adversaries with extradition requests."[35] Apparently, Kissinger does not want fighting extradition to distract leaders from organizing (possible) crimes against humanity.

Kissinger worries also that universal jurisdiction will be used selectively for political ends. While Pinochet has been subject to extradition, no charges have been brought against "scores of East European communist leaders—not to speak of Caribbean, Middle Eastern, or African leaders who inflicted their own full measure of torture and suffering." He is correct, but the idea of universal jurisdiction is new. Cosmopolitans hope for eventual worldwide imitation of the Pinochet precedent. If justice required prosecuting simultaneously all who break a given law, no one could be stopped for speeding, and roads would be increasingly dangerous.

Kissinger similarly distrusts the International Criminal Court. "Prosecutorial discretion without accountability is precisely one of [its] flaws. . . . Definitions of the relevant crimes are vague and highly susceptible to politicized application."[36] But by this reasoning, we should repeal laws against rape. Prosecutors have great discretion in bringing rape charges, uncertainty about the meaning of rape affects many allegations, and that meaning has changed in recent decades. Also, people sometimes allege rape for inappropriate reasons. Still, few people want to repeal laws against rape.

"Defendants will not enjoy due process as understood in the United States,"[37] Kissinger writes.[38] But the ICC allows the courts of the defendant's home state to take over the case so long as prosecution is undertaken

---

35. Kissinger, p. 92.
36. Kissinger, p. 94.
37. Kissinger, p. 94.
38. Kissinger may be particularly sensitive on these matters because, according to journalist Christopher Hitchens, he may be guilty of promoting torture and other crimes against humanity, making him liable to prosecution at the ICC or through universal jurisdiction. See Christopher Hitchens, "The Case against Henry Kissinger" Part I, *Harper's Magazine* (February 2001), pp. 33–58 and Part II *Harper's Magazine* (March 2001), pp. 49–74.

adequately. So defendants can have whatever due process their home countries provide.

Most cosmopolitans consider universal jurisdiction and especially the ICC, owing to its more uniform standards and methods, appropriate ways of holding individuals, not just states, accountable for international crimes.

Cultural Relativism and Female Circumcision

Prosecuting individuals across national borders for crimes against humanity requires general agreement on what constitutes a crime. Rape, murder, torture, and ethnic cleansing are clearly crimes, but some other practices generate controversy rather than universal condemnation. Consider, for example, the practice in Sudan of pharaonic circumcision, also called infibulation, female circumcision, and female genital mutilation (FGM). Does this practice amount to a crime against the girls subjected to it? Anthropologist Janice Boddy describes what she witnessed in 1976:

> A young girl is lying on an *angreeb* (native bed), her body supported by several adult kinswomen. Two of these hold her legs apart. Then she is administered a local anesthetic by injection. In the silence of the next few moments Miriam [the local midwife] takes a pair of what look to me like children's paper scissors and quickly cuts away the girl's clitoris and labia minora. . . . I am surprised that there is so little blood. Then she takes a surgical needle from her midwife's kit, threads it with suture, and sews together the majora, leaving a small opening at the vulva. After a liberal application of antiseptic, it is all over.[39]

Expected results of this procedure include difficulty in having sex and reduction in sexual satisfaction, Boddy writes:

> A young girl both dreads and eagerly awaits her wedding day: she welcomes the elevation in status while fearing what it implies, namely having to endure sexual relations with her husband. My informants told me that it may take as long as two years of continuous effort before penetration can occur. . . .
>
> Because they find it so painful, most women I talked to said that they avoid sex as often as possible, encouraging their husbands to

---

39. Janice Boddy, "Womb as Oasis: The Symbolic Context of Pharaonic Circumcision in Rural Northern Sudan," *American Ethologist*, Vol. 9, No. 4 (November 1982), pp. 682–98, at 683.

sleep with them only when they wish to become pregnant. Sexual relations do not necessarily become easier for the couple over time. When a woman gives birth, the midwife must be present not only to cut through the scar tissue and release the child but also to reinfibulate her once the baby is born.

Nevertheless, Boddy reports, "by far, the majority of those adults who insist that pharaonic circumcision be performed are not men but adult women. . . ."[40] Why?

Boddy's friends claim circumcision "is performed on young girls to make them clean, smooth, and pure. . . . Women say a girl who has not been purified through circumcision may not marry, and thus may not bear children and attain a position of respect in her old age." In sum,

> by removing their external genitalia, women are not so much preventing their own sexual pleasure (though obviously this is an effect) as enhancing their femininity. Circumcision as a symbolic act brings sharply into focus the fertility potential of women by dramatically deemphasizing their inherent sexuality. By insisting on circumcision for their daughters, women assert their social indispensability, an importance that is not as the sexual partners of their husband, nor, in this highly segregated, male-authoritative society, as their servants, sexual or otherwise, but as the mothers of men.[41]

Anthropologist Ellen Gruenbaum, however, finds that even if women support the practice, men benefit most. Female circumcision gives men greater assurance of female virginity at marriage and supposedly greater pleasure in intercourse because the woman's vaginal opening is narrower. The subordination of women inherent in the practice reinforces male appropriation of female labor in "biological reproduction, social reproduction (including domestic labor), and other economic work," such as farm labor.[42]

Liberal political philosopher Susan Okin is appalled by this subordination of women.[43] But Sander Gilman criticizes Okin by comparing her horror at female circumcision to 19th century horror at Jewish male

---

40. Boddy, p. 686.

41. Boddy, p. 687.

42. Ellen Gruenbaum, "The Cultural Debate over Female Circumcision: The Sudanese Are Arguing This One Out for Themselves," in *Women and Globalization*, Delia D. Aguilar and Anne E. Lacsamana, Eds. (Amhers, NY: Humanity Books, 2004), pp. 323–46, at 323–25. Originally in *Medical Anthropology Quarterly*, Vol. 10 (1996).

43. Susan Okin, *Is Multiculturalism Bad for Women?* (Princeton: Princeton University Press, 1999), p. 14.

366   Chapter 11: Cosmopolitanism

circumcision. He quotes liberal sexologist Paolo Mantegazza: "Circumcision is a shame and an infamy; and I, who am not in the least anti-Semitic . . . shout . . . at the Hebrews . . . : Cease mutilating yourselves . . . ; until you do this, you cannot pretend to be our equal."[44]

Jewish circumcision, like female circumcision, is accused of reducing sexual pleasure. However, Gilman claims, pleasure is psychological, not merely physical, so "the question of pleasure should be left to the culture that defines it." Physical complications, such as infections, are not relative to culture, but these, Gilman claims, can be addressed through adoption of modern medical techniques, as Jews have done with male circumcision.[45]

Gruenbaum joins Gilman in disparaging liberals who think women favoring infibulation are victims of "false consciousness." Gruenbaum writes that such liberals fail to appreciate "values relating to morality and honor that require pharaonic circumcision. . . ." Also, "such [liberal] responses strike many African women scholars as arrogant, especially because Western culture has its own aesthetically motivated medical disasters, such as silicone breast implants and useless cosmetic surgeries."[46]

Philosopher Martha Nussbaum, however, denies that infibulation is like cosmetic surgery. Such surgeries are performed on consenting adults, whereas pharaonic circumcision is often performed on girls between the ages of 4 and 12. Most important, circumcision interferes with capabilities that Nussbaum, in agreement with economist Amartya Sen, considers central to people leading truly human lives. Protecting and nurturing these capabilities, Nussbaum claims, is the touchstone of universal morality. Such capabilities include (but are not limited to):

> Bodily Health. Being able to have good health, including reproductive health; to be adequately nourished; to have adequate shelter.
>
> Bodily Integrity. Being able to move freely from place to place; having one's bodily boundaries treated as sovereign, i.e., . . . secure against assault . . . ; having opportunities for sexual satisfaction. . . .
>
> Senses, Imagination, and Thought. Being able to use the senses, to imagine, think, and reason—and to do these things in a "truly human" way, a way informed and cultivated by an adequate education. . . . Being able to use one's mind in ways protected by guarantees of freedom of expression with respect to both political and artistic speech. . . .

---

44. Sander L. Gilman, "'Barbaric' Rituals?" in Okin, pp. 53–58, at 53. The quote is originally from Paolo Mantegazza, *The Sexual Relations of Mankind*, trans. Samuel Putnam (New York: Eugenics Publishing Company, 1938), p. 99.

45. Gilman, p. 57.

46. Gruenbaum, p. 326.

Affiliation. A. Being able to live with and toward others, to recognize and show concern for other human beings. . . . B. Having the social bases of self-respect and nonhumiliation; being able to be treated as a dignified being whose worth is equal to that of others. . . .[47]

Infibulation clearly interferes with "bodily integrity" and "opportunities for sexual satisfaction." Nussbaum claims that sexual satisfaction is a universal value, not "a mythic construction of the male ego. Many women have reported enjoying sex a good deal, and there is no reason to think them all victims of false consciousness."[48] It is basic to human nature and human flourishing, like seeing and walking:

We all know that people who are blind or unable to walk can lead rich and meaningful lives; nonetheless, we would all deplore practices that deliberately disabled people in those respects, nor would we think that critics of those practices are giving walking or seeing undue importance in human life.[49]

Similarly, we should condemn circumcision that deliberately deprives women of the chance for sexual pleasure.

Nussbaum recognizes that eliminating female circumcision, an initiation rite central to some cultures' cohesion and self-understanding, may impair cultural continuity. But she is a liberal for whom individuals, not cultural groups are most important. She thinks a group whose cohesion requires "subordination and functional impairment" is not worth perpetuating.[50] She is also a cosmopolitan who denies the ultimate significance of national borders. She therefore supports granting political asylum to women who cross borders to escape circumcision. "The fact that a needy human being [threatened with female circumcision] happens to live in Togo rather than Idaho does not make her less my fellow, less deserving of my moral commitment."[51]

Still, Nussbaum is substituting her judgment, which reflects our cultural values, for the judgment of most women in the cultures at issue. *Cosmopolitanism risks **cultural imperialism**, the imposition of a powerful*

47. Martha C. Nussbaum, *Women and Human Development: The Capabilities Approach* (Cambridge: Cambridge University Press, 2000), p. 74.
48. Martha C. Nussbaum, *Sex and Social Justice* (New York: Oxford University Press, 1999), p. 128.
49. Nussbaum (1999), p. 127.
50. Nussbaum (1999), p. 126.
51. Nussbaum (1999), p. 122.

nation's culture on all others, unless it tolerates cultural differences. Meaningful toleration requires special respect for differences on important matters. If Nussbaum's list of essential capabilities cannot accommodate infibulation, it may be too intolerant, too ethnocentric, for universal application. On the other hand, no one suggests that we tolerate everything that a culture may favor, including slavery, murder, ethnic cleansing, torture, and rape, as these activities violate truly universal norms. Some cosmopolitans would add female circumcision to this list; others would not. Uncertainty and disagreement about universal values weakens cosmopolitanism.

Walzer's Thick and Thin

The United Nations, because it represents people from all parts of the globe, may have the moral authority to assert the universal values that cosmopolitans espouse. Such values include more than criminal prosecution of those who harm humanity. As we have seen, cosmopolitans also favor a world ethic that requires some global sharing of resources, products, and wealth. Many cosmopolitans believe that people around the world have positive as well as negative rights (see Chapter 4). **Negative rights** are individual rights to be left alone to interact with others on a voluntary basis. These include rights to life, liberty, and property, as well as the freedoms of religion, expression, and assembly. Crimes against humanity violate such rights. **Positive rights** are rights to receive help when needed to meet at least minimal levels of some basic human needs, such as food, shelter, clothing, health care, and education.

The United Nations' Universal Declaration of Human Rights includes both negative and positive rights. Articles 18, 19, and 20, for example, support the freedoms of religion, expression, and assembly, negative rights, whereas according to Article 25:

> Everyone has the right to a standard of living adequate for the health and well-being of himself and of his family, including food, clothing, housing, and medical care and necessary social services, and the right to security in the event of unemployment, sickness, disability, widowhood, old age or other lack of livelihood in circumstances beyond his control.[52]

---

52. In Andrew D. Weinberger, *Freedom and Protection* (San Francisco: Chandler Publishing Co., 1962), pp. 164–69.

If the positive rights declared in Articles 25 were honored, infants in India would not be killed as a result of parental unemployment and insufficient family income to buy food.

Michael Walzer, however, argues against the United Nation's Universal Declaration of Human Rights insofar as it includes positive as well as negative rights. Walzer, as we saw in Chapter 7, is a communitarian who believes that all claims of justice concern social meanings and these meanings differ from group to group. Walzer offers this example. It would have been unjust in medieval Europe for the Holy Sacraments to be unavailable to poor people. These sacraments were considered essential to securing eternal life, the highest good, so society paid for the Catholic Church and its important functions. But society did not pay for medical care as well, because both the efficacy of medicine and the importance of prolonged life on Earth were debatable in that society. Today, by contrast, we think it unjust for poor people to be denied medical care, because we value prolonged life on Earth. So we have state-supported medical insurance for the very poor. However, because we consider the existence and importance of eternal life debatable, we leave preparation for eternal life to religious organizations without state support. Each of these distributive arrangements is just in its social context, Walzer maintains.[53]

Claims of justice are typically contextual in this way, Walzer argues. Their dependence on social meanings makes them part of what he calls **thick morality.** They cannot be asserted worldwide because no culture or thick morality is worldwide.[54] Walzer therefore rejects the cosmopolitan view that justice requires worldwide sharing of resources and technologies to alleviate the plight of people in poor countries.

Walzer nevertheless believes that some forms of behavior are universally wrong, but he attributes worldwide condemnation to what he calls **thin morality,** which basically condemns violations of negative human rights, although he does not use this term. Walzer claims that within each thick morality there is the capacity to condemn some abuses wherever, and in whatever social context, they occur. A list of such abuses constitutes "a set of standards to which all societies can be held—negative injunctions, most likely, rules against murder, deceit, torture, oppression, and tyranny."[55] This thin moral minimum is not a free-standing morality, however. It emerges from thick moralities that, although very

---

53. Walzer, pp. 28–31.
54. Walzer, p. 8.
55. Walzer, p. 10.

different from one another, converge on several moral judgments. This convergence

> depends . . . , perhaps, on the fact that we have moral expectations about the behavior not only of our fellows but of strangers too. And they have overlapping expectations about their own behavior and ours as well. Though we have different histories, we have common experiences and, sometimes, common responses, and out of these we fashion, as needed, the moral minimum.[56]

Thus, Walzer could support the International Criminal Court's enforcement of some negative rights, even though he would not join the cosmopolitan call for rich countries to help the world's poor.

Political philosopher Amy Gutmann rejects Walzer's **cultural relativism,** the view that moral claims emanate from, reflect, and are relative to social understandings peculiar to their cultures of origin. Such relativism, she argues, disallows universal condemnation of torture, murder, slavery, and rape. Universal norms could not be justified, as Walzer claims, by finding convergence among cultures on certain moral fundamentals because such convergence is a fiction. "The dominant understanding of Nazi Germany," for example, "favored the most shocking forms of racial discrimination." Gutmann concludes, "some ethical considerations either transcend particular cultures or are immanent in every culture because of certain basic features of human nature that are . . . intercultural."[57] These basic features could be the capabilities listed by Nussbaum that justify universal recognition of both negative rights (to bodily integrity, free speech, and so on) and positive rights (to food, housing, education, and so forth). This suggests that positive rights, because they are equally basic to human flourishing, are equally universal. Global distributive justice is not thwarted by cultural relativity. The United Nations' Universal Declaration of Human Rights correctly includes positive as well as negative rights.

The Law of Peoples

John Rawls endorses universal acceptance of positive as well as negative human rights. As we saw in Chapter 6, Rawls believes that justice in a

---

56. Walzer, pp. 17–18.
57. Amy Gutmann, "The Challenge of Multiculturalism in Political Ethics,"
    Philosophy and Public Affairs, Vol. 22, No. 3 (Summer 1993), pp. 171–206, at 190.

liberal society requires that people have equal basic rights (regarding life, liberty, and political participation), that differences of income and wealth be of greatest benefit to society's poorest members, and that everyone has a fair equal opportunity to gain positions of prominence. But when he turns to world affairs, Rawls assumes that societies that are not liberal in these ways can also be decent. He calls them **decent hierarchical peoples.**

Decent hierarchical peoples are decent insofar as they avoid aggressive war, support human rights, such as freedom of religion and the rights to life, liberty, and property, and treat everyone with respect. They are not liberal, however, because they view citizens not primarily as individuals but as members of corporate bodies, each with a distinctive "common good idea of justice." A decent hierarchical society, or a corporate body within it, might be organized, for example, around religious precepts and traditions that assign different responsibilities to men and women and deny women the right to vote. Rawls contends that respect for individuals can exist in this situation if people are treated as "responsible and cooperating members of their respective groups. Hence, persons can recognize, understand, and act in accordance with their moral duties and obligations as members of these groups."[58] No one is enslaved. People cooperate because they voluntarily support the society's hierarchical conception of the public good.

In sum, Rawls accepts internationally some communitarian and moral conservative restrictions on individuals that he generally rejects domestically. He would think it wrong, for example, in a liberal society to restrict public office-holding to members of a royal family or allow a religious group within society to deny its women primary education. But he thinks it would be presumptuous and intolerant of liberal societies to impose rights to equal political and educational opportunity on societies that seem to function well without them. Peoples should be able to preserve their traditions and function communally if everyone is treated decently.

With this as background, Rawls thinks that international matters of justice should be determined by representatives of peoples, not of individuals, meeting behind a veil of ignorance. He believes that representatives of decent hierarchical peoples will agree with representatives of liberal peoples on laws governing interactions among different peoples. These include equality, nonintervention, and nonaggression among **well-ordered peoples** (liberal and decent hierarchical peoples). However,

---

58. John Rawls, *The Law of Peoples* (Cambridge, MA: Harvard University Press, 1999), p. 66.

recognizing that great poverty can impair success for a society, they will also agree that "peoples have a duty to assist other peoples living under unfavorable conditions that prevent their having a just or decent political and social regime."[59] Rawls calls these **burdened societies.** "Burdened societies . . . , lack the political and cultural traditions, the human capital and know-how, and, often, the material and technological resources needed to be well-ordered. . . . Well-ordered peoples have a *duty* to assist burdened societies."[60]

This does not mean that well-ordered peoples should provide burdened societies with wealth equal to their own. The aim is to help burdened societies become well-ordered and, Rawls writes, "great wealth is not necessary to establish just (or decent) institutions. . . . Thus the levels of wealth among well-ordered peoples will not, in general, be the same."[61] Even poverty of resources does not justify simple transfers of wealth.

> Historical examples seem to indicate that resource-poor countries may do very well (e.g., Japan), while resource-rich countries may have serious difficulties (e.g., Argentina). The crucial elements that make the difference are the political culture, the political virtues and civic society of the country, its members' probity and industriousness, their capacity for innovation, and much else.[62]

So, *the law of peoples requires help with whatever factors burden a society. It does not require transfers of wealth from haves to have-nots with the aim of material equality.*

Cosmopolitan critics of Rawls's law of peoples complain that he abandons the political liberal focus on individuals. Ultimately, they believe, justice requires respect for individuals, not for peoples or groups of any kind. Moellendorf writes in this vein, "if it is the implications of respect for persons that we are wanting to work out, the straightest route to this is a procedure that directly takes into account the interests of persons."[63]

Philosopher Charles Beitz, writing before Rawls's definitive statement of his views in *The Law of Peoples*, believes that respect for individuals can be incorporated into contractarianism to make it cosmopolitan by altering the original position from the one envisioned by Rawls. Rawls imagined people behind a veil of ignorance who did not know their age, gender,

---

59. Rawls, p. 37.
60. Rawls, p. 106. Emphasis in original.
61. Rawls, p. 107.
62. Rawls, p. 108.
63. Moellendorf, p. 16.

talents, preferences, and so forth, but they did know that when the veil is lifted they would find themselves to be members of the same society. Beitz suggests that in order to take individualism seriously at a global level, the veil of ignorance must be thickened so that people do not know that they are members of the same society. Instead, they know that some nations have better natural resources and social structures than others do, but they do not know whether, when the veil is lifted, they will be in a society that is rich or poor, well-organized or chaotic. In this state of ignorance, they will adopt principles of international sharing, even among societies living in isolation from one another, to ensure that all people can lead decent lives.

Beitz goes farther when global economic, political, and environmental interdependence is added to the equation. He reasons:

> If evidence of global economic and political interdependence shows the existence of a global scheme of social cooperation, we should not view national boundaries as having fundamental moral significance. Since boundaries are not coextensive with the scope of social cooperation, they do not mark the limits of social obligations. . . .[64]

Global social cooperation, according to Beitz, requires people to share with one another globally on the same terms that Rawls believes they should share with one another domestically. The only justification for some people being wealthier than others is that allowing them extra wealth is needed as an incentive to motivate them to use their talents to make the world in general a richer and better place for everyone. Thus, all differences of income and wealth should benefit the least advantaged people in the world. This principle emerges from people reasoning behind a veil of ignorance who know that they are engaged in worldwide economic and political interdependence but do not know if they are rich or poor. They will want the fruits of interdependence to be of greatest benefit to the worst-off people in the world because, when the veil is lifted, they may find that they are in this group. On the other hand, if they are among the world's privileged people, a worldwide system of helping the poor will not be a great burden.

Rawls, by contrast, is not a cosmopolitan; he rejects comparing people's individual well-being across different societies. The fact that most people in one society are much richer than almost anyone in a different

---

64. Charles R. Beitz, "Justice and International Relations," in *International Ethics,* Charles R. Beitz, Marshall Cohen, Thomas Scanlon, and A. John Simmons, Eds. (Princeton: Princeton University Press, 1985), pp. 282–311, at 298.

society should be of no concern to the people in the poorer society so long as the poorer society has at least the resources to provide good lives for everyone when it is well-ordered; that is, when the government is not corrupt, the society follows the rule of law, and people generally respect human rights. In short, *for Rawls, the boundary of a people, which in many cases corresponds to a national boundary, has a moral significance that cosmopolitans deny.*

Globalization

Like cosmopolitanism, **globalization** seeks to minimize the effect of national borders, but the concentration is on trade and economic integration. Globalizers advocate reducing barriers to international trade and finance, such as national tariffs, quotas, and foreign exchange controls, so that goods, services, and investments can flow freely from one country to another. When barriers to trade are lifted, globalizers reason, each country and region can specialize in what it does best.

The idea is to extend globally the system of specialization that has already made industrial nations wealthy. Within industrial nations, most workers concentrate on what they can do efficiently and use their incomes to buy whatever else they need and want. This is domestic free trade. The result has been increasing supplies of goods and services in growing economies. Global free trade extends such efficiencies worldwide, with the goal of eventual benefit to the world's poorest people. Thus, *in theory, globalization, like cosmopolitanism, discounts national borders and favors the world's poor.*

Peter Singer, who is guardedly optimistic about it, puts the argument for global free trade this way: Free trade

> should be particularly good for countries with low labor costs, because they should be able to produce goods more cheaply than [can] countries with high labor costs. Hence we can expect the demand for labor in those countries to rise, and once the supply of labor begins to tighten, wages should rise too. Thus a free market should have the effect not only of making the world as a whole more prosperous but, more specifically, of assisting the poorest nations.[65]

U.S. President George W. Bush shares this view and told the World Bank: "Those who protest free trade are no friends of the poor. Those

---

65. Peter Singer (2002), p. 56.

who protest free trade seek to deny them their best hope for escaping poverty."[66] Swedish political economist Johan Norberg describes that poverty:

> The existence from which globalization delivers people in the Third World really is intolerable. For the poor, existence means abject poverty, filth, ignorance, and powerlessness; it means always wondering where the next meal is coming from; it means walking many miles to collect water that may not be fit to drink.[67]

Globalization turns this around, he claims:

> Investments and development assistance have transmitted ideas and resources, allowing the developing world to benefit from the knowledge, wealth, and inventions of other countries. . . . Modern technology and new methods of production have stepped up output and improved the food supply. . . . We can tell from the statistics how this enhances national prosperity and reduces poverty among the population.[68]

Other thinkers challenge these claims. Consider the plight of garment workers in Bangladesh as reported by Anita Roddick for the *Ecologist:*

> The workers live in one-room dirt-floored huts, which measure about 8 feet by 12 feet and are made of scrap metal, wood, and plastic. Four or more people live in each hut. Everyone sleeps on a hard, wooden platform raised about a foot off the ground. . . . During the monsoon the workers' neighborhoods flood, and filth and sewage washes right into their homes.
>
> In these neighborhoods, up to 60 people have to share one outdoor water pump: the water is filthy. There [is] only one outside toilet—really just a hole in the ground. Early in the morning and late at night there are long lines as people wait their turn. . . .
>
> One worker said: "We feel like prisoners. There is no value in our lives. We are like slaves. Our hands are bound and our mouths are stopped."
>
> Every worker said that if their employer knew they were meeting with me, they would be fired.[69]

---

66. Frank Bruni and David Sanger, "Bush Urges Shift to Direct Grants for Poor Nations," *New York Times,* 18 July 2001, P. A1. Found in Singer (2002), p. 77.

67. Johan Norberg, *In Defense of Global Capitalism* (Washington, DC: Cato Institute, 2003), p. 13.

68. Norberg, p. 23.

69. Anita Roddick, "If Shirts Could Only Speak . . . ," *The Ecologist,* Vol. 34, No. 6 (July/August 2004), pp. 23–27, at 24.

376 Chapter 11: Cosmopolitanism

These workers do not quit because they have few alternatives after being deprived of their previously satisfying, although materially simple, way of life. Let me explain. Sixty percent of the world's people, writes development economist David Korten, do not live in poverty, even though they lack material abundance. They are, or were when Korten wrote in 1995,

> members of the world's sustainer class, they travel by bicycle and public surface transport; eat healthy diets of grains, vegetables, and some meat; buy few prepackaged goods; and recycle most of their wastes. Although their lifestyles do not correspond to our vision of consumer affluence, neither is it a vision of hardship.... [They can have] a high and satisfying quality of living.[70]

Such people live in traditional communities and have traditional rights to farm or herd and to gather many free products of nature from nearby forests and streams. They pay little or nothing for the right to use these means of sustenance, so the land generates little cash income. Instead, resources and work simply meet local people's needs.

Globalization encourages world trade that deprives people of such materially simple, but satisfying styles of life. World trade encourages rich people who own such resources to kick peasants off the land and divert its productive potential from meeting local needs to meeting the needs or wants of affluent people in rich countries. Thus, for example, a diverse forest is logged bare and planted in coffee or eucalyptus groves to grow products that meet few local needs but generate cash income and foreign exchange though international sales. The people who traditionally farmed small plots in the forest and used its diverse output of different tree and animal species for food (fruits, nuts, meat), housing, shade, recreation, and so forth, are simply pushed off the land. Their satisfactory lifestyle has ended, and destitution begins. In these desperate circumstances they often have no choice but to become squatters in urban slums, kill infant daughters, sell girls into prostitution, and work in factories under slave conditions. Consider this:

> Two thousand new garment factories opened in Bangladesh between 1994 and 2003. In that period apparel exports from the country grew by more than 300%—exploding from $1.5 billion in 1994 to $4.9 billion in 2003....
>
> Shouldn't this be an example of the magic of trade? If so, why are 2 million mostly young female garment workers being stripped of

---

70. David C. Korten, *When Corporations Rule the World* (West Hartford, CN: Kumarian Press, 1995), p. 180.

their rights—in their own words, trapped like slaves, paid just a few pennies an hour, working exhausting hours and seven-day weeks, living in utter misery, and sacked, penniless and worn out, when they reach 35 years of age?[71]

In sum, *world trade may often lower consumer prices in rich countries by condemning newly destitute people in the Third World to work under sub-human conditions.*

This affects relatively poor workers in the First World. The consumer products they buy are cheap, but they tend to lose their already poorly paying jobs to overseas competitors who work for next to nothing. This is why many cosmopolitans believe that globalization, as currently organized, is unjust. It harms more than it helps poor people in both rich and poor countries.

National Borders and Fair Trade

Some people want what they call **fair trade** to replace free trade. Third World governments, they think, should impose a decent minimum wage, guarantee workers the right to organize unions, and require many safety and environmental standards common in the First World. This will help Third World workers make decent wages under humane conditions and help First World workers keep their jobs.

But such government mandates and restrictions may impede the international flow of goods and services, so proponents of globalization generally oppose them. The World Trade Organization (WTO), which promotes and regulates world trade, opposes such restrictions on world trade by distinguishing products from processes. In general, they think, a country can exclude a product that is dangerous or harmful in some way, but it cannot exclude a product out of concern for the way it was produced. For example, the European Union (EU) disallowed the importation of American beef that had been given artificial growth hormones. The EU claimed, without convincing evidence, that eating beef treated with these hormones may harm human health. The WTO protected free trade, deciding the case in favor of the United States and requiring the EU either to allow the importation of this beef or suffer retaliatory duties. They chose the latter course.[72]

---

71. Roddick, p. 26.
72. Singer, p. 61.

In another case, the United States wanted to exclude tuna caught in nets that kill many dolphins but decided that WTO rules disallowed this exclusion as an unacceptable restraint of trade. In two other cases, fear of successful challenge before the WTO deterred Europe from prohibiting importation of furs from countries that allow animals to be caught in steel-jaw leg-hold traps and cosmetics that had been tested on animals.[73]

The WTO distinguishes products from processes that may be harmful to the environment or destructive of human dignity in order to protect free trade from unfair exclusions. If processes could justify excluding products, they say, many countries would violate free trade agreements by excluding foreign competitors of local industries, claiming that foreign competitors use unacceptable processes. This could ruin free trade.

However, excluding consideration of production processes may encourage cheap production methods that harm workers and the environment. WTO opponents want individual nations to disallow importation of improperly produced items. This amounts to using national borders to protect people from predatory global business practices. *National borders may be morally insignificant as cosmopolitans claim, but they remain practically important to protect poor people and the environment.*

Many cosmopolitans recognize also that industrialization in today's wealthy countries occurred under state protection. The state provided or largely financed a physical infrastructure (roads, ports, railroads, public health measures regarding sewage), legal infrastructure (courts, police, patent laws), financial infrastructure (banks, a common currency), and human infrastructure (compulsory education and near universal literacy). The state also protected infant industries from foreign competition so they could grow by meeting domestic demand. Global competition was introduced gradually as industries became efficient enough to compete with reasonable prospects of success.

The International Monetary Fund (IMF), complains Nobel Prize-winning economist Joseph Stiglitz, lends money to poor countries on condition that they do just the opposite of what worked in the past. The IMF wants countries to open their borders immediately to international competition and reduce government expenditures even if this requires cutting back on public health measures, physical infrastructure development, and universal education. This is a formula, Stiglitz argues, for keeping poor countries poor. Their infant industries are nipped in the bud, and they never develop the physical infrastructure and human capital needed for

---

73. Singer, pp. 60–62.

industrial success. The most successful Third World countries, such as China and South Korea, developed in the late 20th century by ignoring the IMF's advice.[74] But this means that globalization should often be stopped at the border if free trade is to be fair. *Again, national borders foster fair trade that helps poor people.*

CONCLUSION

Cosmopolitans favor equal respect for all people on Earth irrespective of national borders. In Charles Beitz's words, "state boundaries have a merely derivative significance. There are no reasons of basic principle for exempting the internal affairs of states from external moral scrutiny, and it is possible that members of some states might have obligations of justice with respect to persons elsewhere."[75] Such cosmopolitan views support universal jurisdiction and the ICC so that government officials incur criminal responsibility for crimes against humanity wherever those crimes occur.

Cosmopolitans argue that people in wealthy countries have a duty to help the world's poor. This can be done as individuals, as contributors to international nongovernmental organizations (NGOs) such as UNICEF and OXFAM, and through government aid. But the world's poor often need government protection from predatory practices of global business. National borders remain important in this respect.

JUDGMENT CALLS

1. Poor people in the United States often take dangerous and un-pleasant jobs, such as picking fruit and working in coal mines, which affluent people avoid. Perhaps it is only natural, then, for poor people in the Third World to take jobs considered too dangerous or unpleasant for workers in rich societies, such as work in chemical factories without all the safety precautions required in the United States. Advocates of fair trade may be eliminating needed jobs in the Third World. What do you think?

2. How important are national culture and sovereignty? What considerations favor allowing a country that likes dolphins to exclude

---

74. Joseph E. Stiglitz, *Globalization and Its Discontents* (New York: W. W. Norton, 2002), especially pp. 182–86.
75. Charles R. Beitz, *Political Theory and International Relations* (Princeton: Princeton University Press, 1979), p. 182.

importation of tuna caught in nets that kill many dolphins along with the tuna?

3. What differences are there between excluding a product because its production involves killing dolphins and excluding one because it is made with child slave labor? Should American age and wage limits be applied worldwide? If not, what should the limits be, and who should decide?

4. If national borders have no ultimate moral significance, should people (who are not criminals or terrorists) be able to cross borders to live wherever they choose, or can cosmopolitans justify restricting immigration?

5. Using the CIA, in 1973 Henry Kissinger apparently helped Augusto Pinochet violently overthrow Salvador Allende, the democratically elected president of Chile. Pinochet seems to have tortured political opponents after taking power. Should Kissinger be arrested and tried before the ICC? What would be the charge?

6. In 2003 the United States attacked Iraq, claiming self-defense against Iraq's weapons of mass destruction (WMD). It seems that Iraq had no WMD. Should President Bush and his advisors be held internationally liable for crimes against peace? Was the war justified by the Iraqi's need to escape the rule of Saddam Hussein? Does cosmopolitanism support wars to liberate oppressed people?

 # Conclusion

We have now investigated the merits and limitations of two forms of democracy, aggregative and deliberative, and eleven different political philosophies: theocracy, utilitarianism, libertarianism, free-market conservatism, liberal contractarianism, communitarianism, moral conservatism, multiculturalism, feminism, environmentalism, and cosmopolitanism. Each of these expresses fundamental political thoughts popular among Americans. Although none suffices to explain completely the foundations and functions of the state, together they constitute the philosophical bases of almost all current American political thought on controversial political matters.

Familiarity with these views has several benefits: It sheds light on the thought processes behind most Americans' political judgments; it helps people choose political positions with more self-conscious awareness of the trade-offs involved—which ideals are being sacrificed or compromised for which others; it helps people choose more defensible positions; and it helps people articulate their positions in ways that other Americans understand and appreciate, because they share the underlying ideals. By thus improving political judgment and communication, the study of political philosophy can facilitate deliberative democracy.

The goal of this concluding chapter is to illustrate these benefits in relation to three controversial matters: abortion, the genetic engineering of human beings, and immigration. In each case I use several political philosophies to understand different sides of the debate and to choose a position in reflective equilibrium. Others may not share my conclusions, but my reasoning will provide insight into the bases of my judgments and illustrate the utility of political philosophy.

My reasoning also illustrates **political principlism.** As we saw earlier, **principlism** is the view in moral philosophy that no single principle of ethics gives reasonable guidance in all situations. People should therefore appeal to different principles in different contexts.[1] Political principlism makes the same claim about the underlying principles of political philosophy. This book is filled with illustrations supporting the view that *different political principles are needed to address different political questions.* What is more, *there is no fixed hierarchy among such principles.* The most important principle in one situation may be relevant, but of lesser importance, in others. *Reflective equilibrium requires good reasons supporting such selective use of political principles.*

Abortion

Freedom is the watchword of American patriotism, yet many Americans object to the freedom of American women to have abortions. I consider first politically liberal and utilitarian arguments for and against abortion rights, because both sides of the debate invoke liberal and utilitarian considerations. I find that political liberalism ultimately favors abortion rights when combined with considerations of deliberative democracy and state neutrality regarding religion. The strongest arguments against abortion rights come from moral conservatives, whose approach echoes some environmentalist concerns.

Throughout this discussion, *I focus on the political question of whether state power should be used to prevent abortions, not the moral question about whether or when abortions are morally justified.* Although these questions are related, they are not the same, because *the law often permits people to do what is morally wrong. Individual freedom would suffer if people were free only to do what is right.* For example, even if careful moral analysis showed the sacrifice of animals in religious rituals to be morally wrong, the principle of religious freedom would preclude state prohibition.

Liberal and Utilitarian Arguments for and against Abortion Rights

Political liberals (libertarians, free-market conservatives, and liberal contractarians) emphasize the importance of individual rights. For this group of thinkers, disagreements about abortion center on whose rights are

---

1. This view receives its classic expression in Tom L. Beauchamp and James F. Childress, *Principles of Biomedical Ethics*, 4th ed., (New York: Oxford University Press, 1994), especially Chapters 3–6. The first edition, which introduced the term *principlism,* appeared in 1979.

most important, those of pregnant women or those of the unborn. Proponents of abortion rights side with pregnant women and opponents with the unborn.

Libertarians generally favor abortion rights. They champion individual liberty and consider abortion rights integral to that liberty. *State restrictions on abortion interfere with body self-ownership. Because pregnancy occurs within individual women and competent adults should have the right to decide what happens to their own bodies, no one should interfere with a woman's decision to terminate her pregnancy.* State abortion restrictions, on this view, violate the respect for individual choice in the personal sphere that governments owe to all competent adults.

Proponents of abortion rights (often called pro-choice) also appeal to liberal contractarianism and classical liberal feminism, claiming that abortion rights are needed to secure social and economic justice for women. We saw briefly in Chapter 9 that *many feminists consider abortion rights necessary for women to have fair equality of opportunity in society.* Without abortion rights, for example, an unplanned pregnancy and resulting unwanted child can jeopardize a woman's education or career advancement and even doom her and her family to poverty. No birth control is completely effective, and some women are precluded by medical conditions from taking the most effective kinds. Demanding sexual abstinence of career-minded women but not men would be unrealistic and unfair, pro-choice advocates claim. So, without abortion rights all young women are disadvantaged in competitive educational and career contexts because admission committees and employers would reason correctly that a woman's professional contribution is subject to greater uncertainty than a man's, regardless of her intentions. Playing the odds, they will favor men over women. To have fair equal employment opportunity, a goal shared by liberal contractarians and classical liberal feminists, women must have safe abortions available not as a substitute for birth control but as a response to birth control failures.

A third politically liberal argument for abortion rights appeals to free-market conservatism. The economy grows fastest and provides the greatest array of goods and services when people are encouraged to use their talents in the most productive ways. The marketplace is generally the best arbiter of productive contributions. *Only when women have abortion rights can the marketplace operate free of considerations,* such as interruptions due to unwanted pregnancies, *which interfere with marketplace efficiency.*

Utilitarians may join political liberals, observing that people generally prefer self-determination and a growing economy, so abortion rights promote the satisfaction of most people's preferences. In addition, without abortion rights, more unwanted children would be born, and many would be treated poorly by their parents. This would make them unhappy and jeopardize societal happiness as unloved children are more likely than others are to display criminal tendencies in later years. Finally, some women seek abortions because they already have more children than they can handle. Requiring them to continue additional pregnancies would put an enormous strain on them and their families.

Liberal arguments, which stress individual rights, can also be used against abortion rights. Opponents of abortion rights (variously called pro-life and antiabortion) argue that freedom must not include killing innocent human beings, which is how they characterize abortion. The linchpin of their case is the claim that *the unborn killed by abortion is a human being with the same right to life as other human beings.* Here are some of their arguments.

First, the *unborn in a human pregnancy is not only alive but clearly human.* From the moment of fertilization, it has its own unique (unless it is an identical twin) human DNA, and early in its development it exhibits signs of human life, such as fingerprints, brain activity, and sensitivity to pain.

Second, *denying that the unborn has a right to life justifies infanticide as well as abortion,* pro-life advocates claim. This can be argued in two ways. *Gestational development from fertilization through infancy and childhood is a gradual, continuous process.* There is no moment of radical change, not even birth, to justify attributing a right to life to the newborn but not the unborn. Thus, if a newly fertilized egg lacks a right to life, so will the newborn it becomes, and the newborn's right to life cannot be used to argue against infanticide.

In addition, *the reasons that pro-choice advocates give for denying unborns a right to life suggest that newborns also lack this right.* Pro-choice advocates say that because unborns, like nonhuman animals, lack such common human traits as reasoning, language, and artistic ability, they have no right to life. But the same is true of newborns, pro-life advocates point out. We respect the right to life of newborns because of their *potential* for distinctively human traits, so fertilized eggs with the same potential deserve the same respect. Reflective equilibrium requires, pro-life advocates conclude, that anyone opposed to legalizing infanticide should oppose legalized abortion as well.

Utilitarians may also support the pro-life position. Women unable to obtain abortions but not wanting to raise a child resulting from an unwanted pregnancy can have that child adopted. The pregnant woman still suffers some interruption in her life, but a child gets to live and a family wanting to raise a child has its wishes fulfilled. *Adoption rather than abortion may maximize preference satisfaction.*

On balance, liberalism supports the pro-choice better than the pro-life position because opponents of abortion rights lack persuasive arguments that the unborn has a right to life. For example, *the argument that rests on the gradual and continuous nature of gestational development from fertilized egg to newborn is unsound.* The argument assumes that if development is gradual, then no new rights emerge at various points. But this is not true in other contexts. A newborn develops gradually into someone who is eventually 30 years old. There are no dramatic biological breaks along the way. Yet, the newborn lacks the right to vote that citizens acquire at age 18, the right to drink alcohol that comes with turning 21, and the right to be a member of congress that awaits citizens at age 25. *Gradual development can result in the acquisition of rights,* so abortion opponents cannot infer from the gradual development of the unborn from fertilized egg to newborn that the newborn has no more rights than the fertilized egg. Newborns might have a right to life that fertilized eggs lack.

In addition, *abortion rights can coexist with bans on infanticide because the bans reflect a natural human impulse to nurture newborns.* This impulse is probably common among humans because groups that did not nurture their newborns failed to survive. Human evolution has not given people a similar natural impulse to protect fertilized eggs, so no one naturally reacts the same way to fertilized eggs as to newborns. For example, people have funerals and mourning periods for the death of newborns. The same would be required for miscarriages at the earliest stages of pregnancy if fertilized eggs were the moral equivalent of newborns. Nobody does this when a newly fertilized egg miscarries.

What is more, *treating all fertilized eggs the same as newborns is medically and socially dysfunctional.* Owing to genetic and other anomalies, at least 40%, and probably more than 70% of fertilized eggs fail to develop into newborns, making anomalies afflicting fertilized eggs humanity's greatest health problem, if such eggs are considered fully human. In that case, we should try to protect these eggs as we try to protect newborns by developing treatments to save as many as possible. The likely result would be additional millions of genetically impaired infants with lifelong, debilitating medical problems, including severe mental retardation, whose care would require more money than we currently spend on health care for everyone else. No one advocates this. *When it comes to saving lives, even abortion opponents distinguish fertilized eggs from infants.*

386 Conclusion

Theocracy, Religious Freedom, and Deliberative Democracy

Many abortion rights advocates claim that attributing rights to the unborn, and forbidding abortion on that basis, is theocratic; it violates people's religious freedom by imposing an essentially religious view on everyone. We saw in Chapter 1 the importance of respecting religious differences and avoiding theocracy.

Sometimes pro-choice people substantiate the charge of theocracy by noting the predominance of certain religious groups, such as the Catholic Church, in the pro-life camp. But the prominence of a religious group in a cause does not make that cause religious. Religious groups support many secular causes, such as feeding, housing, and educating the poor. State efforts to improve society would be hampered if it could not join forces with religious groups on such matters.[2]

However, many religious people claim that the unborn has a right to life because God has endowed it with an immortal soul. If this were the basis of state legislation, it would impose a religious view on society at large because beliefs about immortal souls are clearly religious. But many pro-life advocates point to scientific findings, not theological propositions, to justify attributing a right to life to the unborn.

Nevertheless, pro-choice advocates claim, attributing rights to the unborn, especially to newly fertilized eggs, is religious even when supported by scientific facts. As explained in Chapter 1, *for political and constitutional purposes, religious beliefs are those, like belief in the existence of God, that can be argued for and against, but every bit of reasoning on one side can be countered by the other side with evidence and reasoning of equal significance to uncommitted minds.* This does not make all uncertain and disputed conclusions, such as the guilt or innocence of O. J. Simpson for double homicide, matters of religious belief. Although we may never have definitive proof, we know the kind of evidence that could result from methods of inquiry integral to our common way of life that, were it available, would convince uncommitted minds. Regarding God's existence, by contrast, nothing that anyone could find using methods of inquiry integral to our common way of life could convince such minds one way or the other. So it remains an article of faith.

The prohibition of using such articles of faith as bases for legislation stems not only from the principle of religious freedom but also from the fundamental premises of deliberative democracy. Deliberative democracy

---

2. See Peter S. Wenz, *Abortion Rights as Religious Freedom* (Philadelphia: Temple University Press, 1992), pp. 62–63.

presupposes that people can engage in meaningful exchanges of ideas and information that hold the prospect of their coming to agreement on public policies. Because articles of faith are not amenable to alteration through exchanges of ideas and information backed by methods of inquiry integral to our common way of life, their use in political discourse conflicts with the practice of deliberative democracy.

Belief that newly fertilized eggs have the same human rights as newborns, like belief in God's existence, is an article of faith. Such eggs are alive and have human genetic codes; most healthy ones will become human infants in time. This suggests that they are human beings with human rights. Yet such eggs are single cell beings, so they lack cell, tissue, and organ differentiation characteristic of infants and other human beings. They lack brains and all functions associated with typical human beings. Like most single-cell beings, and unlike typical human beings, they can divide and become two out of one. After some cell divisions they can be frozen and then thawed years later without apparent damage. These characteristics suggest that newly fertilized eggs are so different from typical human beings as to lack the human right to life. *No arguments using methods of inquiry and reasoning integral to our common way of life can convince uncommitted minds either way about the rights of newly fertilized eggs.*[3] This implies that religious people should be free to follow their religious beliefs regarding abortion but not to impose them on others through restrictive legislation, as this would violate religious freedom and conflict with deliberative democracy.

But abortions typically take place several weeks after fertilization. When does the unborn become enough like a newborn to merit the same protections? **Viability,** the ability of the unborn to live and continue development outside of the woman carrying it, is often considered the time when the unborn merits full protection. At that point, the reasoning goes, the unborn is just like a newborn except for location. However, this reasoning is flawed. If medical science ever comes up with an artificial placenta where fertilized eggs can develop into babies without human pregnancy, newly fertilized eggs will be viable. Yet they will remain as different from typical newborns as they are at present. *We need a stable, secular standard that relies on similarities between unborns and newborns to justify attributing rights to the unborn.*

Many such standards have been proposed, for example, that a heartbeat justifies attributing rights to the unborn because a heartbeat is

---

3. For a more extended version of this argument that relates it to the Constitution's Establishment Clause see Wenz, especially Chapter 6.

proof of life. But this is no good. Many differences remain between a newborn and an unborn with a heart beat. It is still a religious judgment, in the sense used above, whether or not these differences justify denying the unborn a right to life. The same problem besets the acquisition of reflexes or brain waves as the standard. However, *when the unborn differ from newborns only in ways that we generally consider irrelevant to the attribution of rights, its rights have a secular basis. This occurs at about 24 or 26 weeks of gestation.* At this time the unborn has all the basic anatomical attributes of a newborn. It is like a newborn that is small, weak, and requires temporary life support, which is given by the pregnant woman. In our society we do not deny rights to those who are otherwise people except that they are small, weak, and require temporary life support. At this point, then, secular standards justify attributing human rights to the unborn.

Abortion after this point may still be justified, I believe. American parents are not legally required to risk their lives or health to save their children, such as through life-saving kidney donations. So, women whose pregnancies jeopardize their lives or health should be permitted abortion even after the unborn has a child's right to life. Otherwise, to be fair, all parents, fathers as well as mothers should be required by law to jeopardize their lives and health when needed to save their children. Feminists might wonder if we have no such general requirement precisely because it would apply to fathers as well as mothers.

In any case, absent threats to life or health, abortion should, on the reasoning above, generally be disallowed after about 24 or 26 weeks of gestation. Such limitations will seldom impair equal opportunity for women. But this reasoning does not yet reflect moral conservative and environmentalist views.

Moral Conservative and Environmentalist Views

The preceding reasoning relates abortion primarily to individual rights, of women and the unborn, which is a political liberal approach. But this orientation misses issues that many pro-life advocates consider central. Here is a symptom that something is missing. On a purely individualist plane pro-lifers want to reduce abortion as much as possible, because each abortion is really murder. One way to do this without committing any crime of equal magnitude is to promote the use of contraceptive methods that prevent fertilization. Yet pro-lifers often oppose the use of such contraceptives and oppose vigorously school instruction in their use. Why? They are not being inconsistent political liberals; they are being consistent moral conservatives.

Sociologist Kristin Luker explains the moral conservative worldview of pro-life activists in California whom she interviewed in the early 1980s. One activist told Luker:

> [What] I find so disturbing [about] the whole abortion mentality is the idea that family duties—rearing children, managing a home, loving and caring for a husband—are somehow degrading to women. And that's an idea which is very current in our society—that women are not going to find fulfillment until they get out there and start competing for a livelihood with men and talking like men, cursing and whatever. . . .[4]

Luker found that most pro-life activists consider men and women fundamentally different and complementary by nature. Both men and women find maximum fulfillment in nuclear families where men take primary responsibility for earning money and women for taking care of the house and children. Whatever weakens such families is bad for society, and this includes women working outside the home. One pro-life activist thought that pro-choice people have "helped destroy the family because they want to make it so free for the woman to go to work, like with the child-care centers and all the rest of it."[5]

Abortion also helps to destroy the family:

> I think having abortion as an alternative—as a way out, I guess— makes it easier for men to exploit women than ever before. I think they are less inclined probably to take responsibility for their actions or to anticipate the consequences of their actions as long as abortion is available. And I think it makes it harder for women who do not choose to engage in premarital sex to say no. . . .[6]

Without the availability of abortion, according to this pro-life activist, *women would be more likely to refuse premarital and extramarital sex, and this would strengthen commitment to marriage and family.* The availability of contraception has the same effect, which helps to explain why pro-life people often oppose contraception.

Opposition to contraception also comes from related natural-law reasoning. An activist told Luker: "You're not just given arms and legs for no purpose. . . . There must be some cause [for sex], and you begin to think, well, it must be for procreation ultimately, and certainly procreation in

---

4. Kristin Luker, *Abortion and the Politics of Motherhood* (Berkeley: University of California Press, 1984), p. 160.

5. Luker, p. 162.

6. Luker, p. 162.

addition to fostering a loving relationship with your spouse."[7] Couples using natural family planning (NFP) instead of contraceptives bolster this reasoning. NFP is an updated version of what used to be called "the rhythm method." Married couples wanting to avoid pregnancy have sex only during those days of the month when the wife is not fertile. One woman said:

> It's really a whole new way of life for a married couple because it demands very close communication, to have to communicate with one another every day about their fertility. I think that's so beautiful. They both learn about one another's bodies, and it creates a tremendous closeness, and I think it demands a very mature love. Because, you know, a husband sees that he can't just demand love from his wife . . . if she's fertile and they just can't afford to have another child right then.[8]

For married women pursuing careers just like their husbands, and for families focused on the material advantages of two incomes, an unplanned pregnancy is an obstacle to achievement, so reliable contraception is essential for couples with an active sex life. But for women dedicated to homemaking and for families that value children more than wealth an unplanned pregnancy is an adventure and opportunity, not an obstacle, so reliable contraception is not essential for couples with an active sex life. The imperfections of NFP are preferable to contraception methods that tend to degrade women and family life. Luker summarizes the pro-life position this way:

> Pro-life people object to every step of the pro-choice logic. If one values material things too highly, one will be tempted to try to make detailed plans for acquiring them. If one tries to plan too thoroughly, one will be tempted to use highly effective contraception, which removes the potential of childbearing from a marriage. Once the potential for children is eliminated, the sexual act is distorted (and for religious people, morally wrong), and husbands and wives lose an important bond between them. Finally, when marriage partners who have accepted the logic of these previous steps find that contraception has failed, they are ready and willing to resort to abortion in order to achieve their goals.[9]

These sentiments cohere not only with moral conservatism but also to some extent with environmentalism. *Environmentalists, like moral*

---

7. Luker, p. 164.
8. Luker, p. 166.
9. Luker, p. 171.

conservatives, worry that preoccupation with material advantage leads people to attempt excessive control over nature. Such attempts often result in grave environmental and social problems because human abilities to plan and control are more limited than people think. Environmentalists therefore recommend reducing consumption and living within natural limits. Moral conservatives see themselves as advocating essentially the same things regarding family life and sexual activity when they oppose contraception, abortion, extramarital sex, women's careers, and child day-care centers designed to foster women's careers.

Many environmentalists nevertheless favor abortion rights. First, they worry about increases in the human population that threaten ecosystems and ultimately humanity. Abortion curtails increases in the human population to some extent. Second, *empowering women seems essential to population control.* Moral conservatives advocate domestic roles for women, which they see as dignified and empowering. But in a society in which almost all necessities must be bought with money, power follows money. Women homemakers who rely on men for money lack the power of women working outside the home for incomes of their own.

In small communities where social pressure from neighbors ensures that men meet their family obligations, such as among the Amish or ultra-orthodox Jews, homemakers may have the power and dignity that moral conservatives desire for them. In these contexts, as Chapter 8 on multi-culturalism suggests, the community may be justified in expelling people who violate moral conservative norms about extramarital sex, abortion, and other matters. Many men outside of such communities may also meet their family obligations, providing their wives with security and treating them with respect. Unfortunately, however, it seems that such men are not plentiful enough for every woman who wants marriage and a family to find one. Denying such women abortion rights jeopardizes their equal opportunity in the marketplace and equal power at home.

Summary on Abortion

I believe that moral conservative and some environmentalist thinking supports restrictions on abortion rights that may be wise in some contexts, but not in the United States at this time. Other environmentalist insights, concerning overpopulation, for example, support abortion rights. Liberal political perspectives that emphasize individual rights of both women and the unborn favor abortion rights because the pro-choice position rests on the uncontroversial rights of women, whereas the pro-life position rests on the uncertain rights of the unborn. Adding considerations of religious freedom and deliberative democracy leads me to conclude that only at 24 to 26 weeks of gestation is the unborn enough like a newborn to have legally recognized rights. In sum, the reflective equilibrium I reach by combining relevant facts about abortion with the insights of political theories gives more weight to libertarian, free-market conservative, liberal contractarian, liberal feminist, and deliberative democratic thinking than to moral conservativism, so I favor abortion rights, at least before 24 weeks of gestation.

Many issues regarding abortion remain. For example, if abortion is legal, does that make it always moral? Is it moral for abortion to be used for sex selection? Should waiting periods be required before abortions are performed (to give women an opportunity to reconsider)? Should minors be able to have abortions without parental consent or even notification? Should the state pay for abortions desired by poor women receiving state medical aid? Recourse to relevant facts and to the political philosophies in this book can help answer these difficult questions.

Genetic Engineering of Human Beings

Genetic engineering uses knowledge in genetics to alter life forms through the manipulation of genes. The resulting organisms can differ from those possible through natural evolution or traditional breeding techniques because genetic engineering allows genes from very different species to be combined; for example, genes from peanuts may be inserted into corn and genes from fish into tomatoes. Although some agricultural uses of genetic engineering are controversial, the greatest controversies concern the application of genetic engineering to human beings. This is our topic.

Most of the applications discussed here are not yet available, and insurmountable technological difficulties may prevent some from ever being developed. But we should consider now which applications are desirable and worth pursuing, and which should be prevented *by law*, because once a potentially harmful technology exists it may be too late to decide it should not be used.

Types and Uses of Genetic Engineering

Genetic engineering has the potential to be therapeutic, to cure some serious, genetically linked diseases, such as Huntington's disease and cystic fibrosis, which cause great suffering and result in early death. **Genetic therapy** can be either **somatic-cell therapy** or **germ-line therapy. Germ**

cells are the sperm and ova that carry genetic information to the next generation by combining to create newly fertilized eggs and, ultimately, new human beings. Germ-line therapy alters genes in germ cells to avoid disease in future generations. **Somatic cells** are all the cells in your body except the germ cells. Somatic-cell genetic therapy is the manipulation of somatic cells to cure disease.

Cystic fibrosis may be susceptible to cure through somatic-cell therapy. Patients with cystic fibrosis have lung tissue that performs poorly owing to the cells containing a defective gene. If a virus containing the proper gene can infect these somatic cells and replace the defective gene with the normal gene, the disease could be cured. The cells with corrected genes do not live forever, but they divide before they die, thereby passing on their entire genetic code to new cells in the lungs. In this way, the normal gene can remain in the lung tissue for the life of the patient. The patient is cured. But the genes in the patient's germ cells are still defective, so the patient can still pass on the defective gene to a child.

Germ-line therapy replaces defective genes in people's germ cells, so defects are not passed on to future generations. This has the advantage of preventing disease in future generations instead of curing it after it appears. In addition, some genetically linked diseases, such as Huntington's disease, cannot be cured with somatic-cell therapy because the somatic cells with defective genes are not accessible to viral manipulation. Genetic therapy for Huntington's disease requires the alteration of germ cells.

Genetic engineering can also be used to enhance human beings rather than cure disease. **Genetic enhancements** are of two kinds. First, people can be enhanced to make them less susceptible to diseases that are not of genetic origin, such as the common cold. Enhanced people will have genetic codes that enable them to withstand environmental contamination better than people with normal genetic codes do, so they will be sick less often. These are **disease-related enhancements.** Second, genetic enhancements may enable people to have more traits that they desire, such as greater height, leaner figure, longer attention span, better memory, more mathematical aptitude, better eye-hand coordination, and so forth. These are **desire-related enhancements.** In both cases, genetic engineering is most efficient and useful when it takes place through the germ-line, so that beneficiaries can pass enhancements on to their progeny.

Political Liberalism, Utilitarianism, and Genetic Engineering

Many political liberals favor the development and use of genetic engineering of all these types. Libertarians believe that the state should not prevent individuals from doing what they want with whatever they own, so long as they do not harm others directly. Genetic engineering poses no direct hazard to others, and the benefits of allowing people to be cured from debilitating diseases are obvious.

Free-market conservatives agree and add that genetic engineering of all these types has potential economic benefits. Fewer people with debilitating diseases translate into more available workers and lower healthcare costs for business. Enhancements that improve resistance to diseases caused by environmental assault may reduce pressure for costly pollution abatement. If fewer people get sick from certain chemicals used in manufacturing, for example, industry may be allowed to use those chemicals instead of more costly alternatives. Desire-related enhancements that improve people's memory, attention span, stamina, imagination, and so forth may benefit the economy by improving worker performance and fostering the invention of new products and industrial processes. And genetic engineering itself may become a big business that stimulates the economy.

Many liberal contractarians also support genetic engineering. Disease harms people not only directly but also indirectly by impairing equality of opportunity. People afflicted with cystic fibrosis, for example, lack the opportunity to climb the corporate ladder. People who are unusually susceptible to other diseases, such as colds and flu, are also at a competitive disadvantage compared to people with more robust immune systems. Genetic engineering can thus help some of society's least advantaged members, which, according to Rawls's difference principle, is essential for justice.

Political liberal Ronald Dworkin defends genetic engineering against charges that in constitutes improperly "playing God:"

> There is nothing in itself wrong with the detached ambition to make the lives of future generations of human beings longer and more full of talent and hence of achievement. On the contrary, if playing God means struggling to improve our species, bringing into our conscious designs a resolution to improve what God deliberately or nature blindly has evolved over eons, then the first principle of ethical individualism commands that struggle, and its second principle forbids, in the absence of positive evidence of danger, hobbling the scientists and doctors who volunteer to lead it.[10]

Bioethicists Allen Buchanan, Dan Brock, Norman Daniels, and Daniel Wikler generally endorse Dworkin's view in a book, *From Chance to Choice*, exploring the implications for justice of advances in genetic engineering.

10. Ronald Dworkin, *Sovereign Virtue: The Theory and Practice of Equality* (Cambridge, MA: Harvard University Press, 2000), p. 452.

Increasing human control of our genetic code enables people to replace nature with technology and therefore chance with choice. They write: "What we have taken to be moral progress has often consisted in pushing back the frontiers of the natural, in bringing within the sphere of social control, and thereby within the domain of justice, what was previously regarded as the natural, and as merely a matter of good or ill fortune."[11]

Finally, many utilitarians may also favor genetic engineering. It promises to give people what they want, thereby improving the satisfaction of preferences. People want to be free of genetically linked diseases as well as colds and flu resulting from weak immune systems. People also desire certain enhancements, such as greater height, better looks, more intelligence, and improved athletic ability. So what's not to like?

These theorists agree that the state should not forbid the genetic engineering of human beings, whether for purposes of therapy or enhancement.

Liberal Contractarian and Environmentalist Objections

Although many thinkers who want to promote justice favor development and use of genetic engineering, others are in opposition, especially to enhancements, and favor state prohibitions. Francis Fukuyama, for example, worries that many enhancements will either increase inequality and injustice or be futile (but costly and dangerous), because they only provide **positional goods.** People seek positional goods primarily to improve their social standing. But because social standing is comparative, one person's gain is another person's loss.

Many desire-related genetic enhancements are positional goods in this sense. Consider height, for example. Fukuyama writes, "height confers many advantages on individuals who are above average, in terms of sexual attractiveness, social status, athletic opportunities, and the like. But these advantages are only relative: if many parents seek to have children tall enough to play in the NBA, it will lead to an arms race and no net advantage to those who participate in it."

> Fukuyama applies this reasoning to intelligence as well: A society with higher average intelligence may be wealthier, insofar as productivity correlates with intelligence. But the gains many parents seek for their children may prove illusory in other respects. . . . People want smarter kids so that they will get into Harvard, for example, but competition for places at Harvard is zero-sum: if my kid

---

11. Allen Buchanan, Dan W. Brock, Norman Daniels, and Daniel Wikler, *From Chance to Choice: Genetics and Justice* (Cambridge: Cambridge University Press, 2000), p. 83.

becomes smarter because of gene therapy and gets in, he or she simply displaces your kid.

Futility is one problem; justice is another. Fukuyama writes: "This kind of genetic arms race will impose special burdens on people who for religious or other reasons do not want their children genetically altered; if everyone around them is doing it, it will be much harder to abstain, for fear of holding their own children back."[12] In addition, the enhancements may have negative health effects that cannot be anticipated and will not be recognized for decades, yet parents will often enhance their children to promote competitive success. This is similar to the use of performance-enhancing drugs in sports. Such drugs are usually banned because they have, or may have health-impairing effects and also because their voluntary use by some competitors makes their use by other serious competitors compulsory.

The greatest problems of justice, however, concern society's least advantaged members. Germ-line enhancements are likely to be very expensive because they will require in vitro fertilization (IVF), which is fertilization of the egg in a test tube, manipulation of the resulting embryos to effect the enhancement, and then implantation. In 1991, before subsequent cost increases, IVF and implantation alone cost $10,000 per procedure, according to Burke Zimmerman, writing in *The Journal of Medicine and Philosophy*. This explain why, Zimmerman writes, "in general, the poor or lower-income families in the Western world utilize IVF [to have children] far less often than [do] the middle and upper economic classes." The differential use of enhancements would be greater because "the . . . genetic modification strategy would be much costlier . . ." than IVF plus implantation.[13]

We saw in Chapter 6 that gaps between rich and poor in the United States have been increasing since the mid-1970s and show no signs of abating. Medical insurance will not likely cover desire-related enhancement because they will at first be experimental and will later be considered optional, like much cosmetic surgery. Without insurance coverage, the poor and even much of the debt-ridden middle class will be unable to enhance their children. Rich kids already benefit from better schools, extra tutoring as needed, and helpful social contacts. If desire-related enhancements become available, they will have the additional advantage of what could literally be called better breeding.

---

12. Fukuyama, p. 97.
13. Burke K. Zimmerman, "Human Germ-Line Therapy: The Case for Its Development and Use," *The Journal of Medicine and Philosophy* 16: 593–612, at 607.

What is more, these people would not only pass their genetic advantages on to their children but could also have their children additionally enhanced. Those children could do the same with the following generation, and so forth. The result after several generations could be a genetic aristocracy.

Let us now consider health-related enhancements. These, too, can cause problems of justice in societies in which access to genetic enhancements is *less than universal.* The authors of *From Chance to Choice,* although in favor of developing and employing genetic technologies, articulate the problem well. They recognize that *people who are genetically enhanced to improve their health will have a competitive advantage in the job market because they will be less likely to miss work for health-related reasons.* In addition, Buchanan and company write, "if affordable health insurance continues to be largely employment-based, as it currently is in the United States, and if employers continue to offer health insurance, then they would have an added incentive to hire those who had benefited from genetic enhancement and to shun those who had not."[14] This will increase the job-market advantage of those who enjoy other employment-related advantages of wealth—superior education and personal contacts.

Additional problems could beset the less privileged and therefore unenhanced part of the population if many others received health-related enhancements.

> Standard employment contracts . . . might come to be geared to the health needs of those who have benefited from these enhancements. The number of sick days allowed to employees without loss of wages might decrease significantly. . . . In these circumstances, those who lack access to the interventions in question would face severe limitations on employability because they would be unable to meet prevalent expectations for work performance. They would be disabled relative to their social environment in the way that people with chronic illnesses are in our present social environment.[15]

Although the authors of *From Chance to Choice* raise these difficulties, they do not oppose enhancements, because they are writing about policies appropriate in "*a just and humane society.*"[16] My concern is with development and use of enhancements in contemporary America, where more than 40 million people lack health insurance and gaps between rich and poor are increasing. In this context, it seems that liberal contractarians

---

14. Buchanan et. al., p. 97.
15. Buchanan et. al., p. 297.
16. Buchanan et. al., p. 4. Emphasis in original.

should oppose legalizing desire-related and health-related enhancements owing to their tendency to promote injustice.

Environmentalists also have reason to oppose legalization of health-related enhancements. In a just and humane society where everyone is enhanced (to promote fair equality of opportunity), enhancements may enable people to live with environmental contaminants—such as PCBs, radiation, and other carcinogens—without getting sick. But such *contaminants travel the globe and will harm people in societies too poor to afford such enhancements.* And if we stray so far from reality that we imagine all humanity so enhanced (a stretch of the imagination in our present food-rich world where currently 40,000 children die every day from the effects of malnutrition), we still have other species to consider. *We cannot realistically enhance all other life forms.* Thus, even in a society (or world) where all people are treated justly, health-related enhancements for people jeopardize other forms of life because they encourage increased use of toxic chemicals. Environmentalists oppose such enhancements for this reason.

Communitarian and Moral Conservative Objections to Enhancements

The availability of desire-related enhancement in a society that has not yet achieved complete justice is likely to erode our sense of community. We have seen that such enhancements could lead to a genetic aristocracy if enhancements are left to the free market. Such a differentiation among people may weaken community bonds. Even the politically liberal authors of *From Chance to Choice* write:

> For all we know, it might turn out that if differences among groups . . . became pronounced enough, they would not treat each other as moral equals. History is replete with instances in which human beings have failed to empathize with their fellows simply because of quite superficial differences in physical appearance or even in customs and manners.[17]

Biological differentiation through germ-line enhancements can erode the sense of community needed for people to live together harmoniously.

Moral conservatives may envision a worse scenario. They emphasize human tendencies toward immorality and therefore the constant need for religious and other training to combat such tendencies. Germ-line desire-related enhancements may be more power over nature than people can handle morally. Oxford scholar C. S. Lewis observed two generations ago,

---

17. Buchanan et. al., p. 95.

"what we call man's power over nature turns out to be a power exercised by some men over other men with nature as its instrument."[18] A moral conservative would therefore predict that people with genetically engineered advantages will use them to gain and retain power over other people, such as by obtaining positional goods that confer competitive advantage in a competitive world. Because this advantage disappears when other people have access to the enhancements, *the enhanced elite will probably try to prevent widespread access to enhancements.*

The privileged may do this by noting that enhancements are very expensive. The state cannot pay for them without raising taxes on the wealthy, which depresses the economy by discouraging wealthy people from being productive. So enhancements must remain in the free market where only the rich can afford them. Would most Americans accept this? As noted in Chapter 8 on deliberative democracy, the concentration of wealth in the United States helps the rich manipulate the majority. So the wealthy may be able to convince the majority to keep enhancements in private hands.

Suppose, however, that people share the technology widely. Francis Fukuyama considers this plausible because "it seems highly unlikely that people in modern democratic societies will sit around complacently if they see elites embedding their advantages genetically in their children."[19]

But the prospect of most or all people's genetic lines being enhanced is equally worrisome, Fukuyama thinks. His reasons, which I find convincing, are essentially moral conservative considerations. Fukuyama believes that our morals and political philosophies are guided by our beliefs about human nature. He defines human nature as "the sum of the behavior and characteristics that are typical of the human species, arising from genetic rather than environmental factors."[20] He believes that much of morality is underpinned by natural emotional reactions embedded in human nature.

> We ... parse language for evidence of deceit, ... engage in reciprocity, pursue revenge, feel embarrassment, care for our children and parents, feel repulsion for incest and cannibalism, attribute causality to events, and many other things as well, because evolution has programmed the human mind to behave in these species-typical ways.[21]

---

18. C. S. Lewis, "The Abolition of Man," in *Philosophy and Technology: Readings in the Philosophical Problems of Technology,* Carl Mitcham and Robert Mackey, Eds. (New York: The Free Press, 1972, 1983), pp. 143–150, at 143.

19. Fukuyama, p. 158.

20. Fukuyama, p. 130.

21. Fukuyama, p. 143.

400 Conclusion

Such facts about people explain the universal appeal of some moral propositions, such as the Golden Rule (reciprocity), and widespread revulsion at practices that people engage in only when severely deprived, such as infanticide.

Political philosophy counts on such natural emotional responses. Nationalism, for example, would be impossible without a natural susceptibility to group loyalty. International intervention to relieve people from oppression would not be possible in a democracy without appeal to citizens' natural sympathy for the oppressed. Social welfare programs to help destitute families similarly depend on sympathy. State attempts to provide equality of opportunity appeal to a natural sense of justice and fairness.

If people design human beings as they see fit, these natural emotions and the morality and political philosophies they underpin, may be lost. Without an unchanged human nature, there is no telling what people may do with their new powers. Moral conservatives believe that we should, therefore, defer to the natural order in these matters.

One reason people should defer to nature is that human control over nature often has unexpected, negative consequence. Environmentalists join moral conservatives on this matter. Fukuyama writes: "Ecosystems are interconnected wholes whose complexity we don't understand; building a dam or introducing a plant monoculture into an area disrupts unseen relationships and destroys the system's balance in totally unanticipated ways."[22] The genome is similarly complex. "Once we move beyond relatively simple single-gene disorders to behavior affected by multiple genes, gene interaction becomes very complex and difficult to predict. Recall the mouse whose intelligence was genetically boosted by neurobiologist Joe Tsien but which seems also to have felt greater pain as a result."[23] Achieving changes that we desire may build into the human genome other changes that prove destructive or evil.

Even changes we desire may not be good. *We may lack the wisdom to know what is good for us.* If we could design people today, for example, we would likely make people less aggressive. But aggressiveness is part of our nature because it was adaptive during evolution, and more passive people may, Fukuyama writes, "stagnate and fail to innovate; individuals who are too trusting and cooperative make themselves vulnerable to others who are more bloody-minded."[24]

---

22. Fukuyama, p. 97.
23. Fukuyama, p. 92.
24. Fukuyama, p. 98.

Genetic engineers may also want to make life more rational and fair by trying to give everyone maximum equality of opportunity. One reason people have unequal opportunities is that their nuclear families of origin are different. If we could design people to be happy when raised collectively, this problem could be solved. Collective rearing of children would also solve the problem of people preferring family over state when conflicts arise. Political philosophers since Plato have found nuclear families impediments to the rational regulation of citizens. Fukuyama points out in this connection that "all real-world communist regimes targeted the family as a potential enemy of the state. . . . Maoist China engaged in a prolonged struggle against Confucianism, with its emphasis on filial piety, and turned children against parents during the Cultural Revolution in the 1960s."[25] People seeking genetic control over humanity may, therefore, target our natural sentiments of family loyalty and affection, which moral conservatives would oppose.

In reflective equilibrium, if find these moral conservative concerns compelling. Genetic enhancements are simply too dangerous. These fears are reinforced by liberal contractarian concerns about justice and environmentalist concerns about the protection of nonhuman nature. However, therapeutic genetic engineering to cure specific diseases may still be allowed, if they are policed vigorously to ensure that they do not advance, either by intent or mistake, genetic engineering for enhancement.

Abortion and Genetic Engineering for Enhancement

Moral conservatives have similar concerns about abortion and genetic engineering. In both cases, they reject what they see as too much control over nature. Unlike many environmentalists, their greatest fear is not that attempts at control will be futile or backfire. Instead, they believe that successful control over nature replaces God's system with human choice. God's system exposes people to what scientists consider mere chance, such as the chance that natural family planning (NFP) will result in an unplanned pregnancy or the chance that someone's genes will make him unusually short or mathematically challenged. Moral conservatives do not reject all human attempts at control; they endorse NFP to control fertility and education to teach math. But they also endorse limits on replacing natural (God-given) chance by human choice. These limits, although based on what they see as God's plan, are not theocratic, because the rationale for respecting such limits emphasizes secular goods. Overstepping

---

25. Fukuyama, p. 99.

the limits, moral conservatives claim, reduces human well-being by weakening the family and other natural (God-given) structures that people need to control antisocial tendencies.

I side with liberals against moral conservatives on the abortion issue and with moral conservatives against liberals regarding genetic enhancements. I am not being inconsistent. I use the same moral principles when considering these two issues, but I reverse their priority. This would be inconsistent only if I lacked good reasons for doing so, and I think I have such reasons.

Society today is organized without genetic enhancements; a decision to forego developing such enhancements will not, therefore, disappoint anyone's legitimate expectations or take something away that people already have. In fact, such enhancements may prove impossible to engineer; not every bad idea succeeds. If successful, of course, disease-related enhancements have the potential to prolong life and avert suffering. But deviating from the natural order in unprecedented fashion courts disaster. *I therefore consider it essential for general human safety that we retain natural human limitations and emotions. It is particularly important to preserve the emotional bases of sympathy and loyalty that underpin our basic moral and political imperatives.*

Abortion is different because the cat is already out of the bag. The ideal that pro-life people uphold is already lost, yet tolerable human life persists. Few Americans today forego material goods in order to spend more time and energy developing family relationships. Instead, most Americans are consumers who replace family time with work time in order to afford more material goods. Most Americans also live outside of traditional communities and do not know their neighbors, so they can easily escape strong social pressure to conform to the traditional norms of married life. In particular, men can abandon women with ease, and when they do women are often poorly equipped to maintain a decent standard of living for themselves and their children. Women might do better under traditional conditions marrying faithful men for their lifetimes, just as moral conservatives contend, rather than working outside the home. But in our context that choice is too risky for the state to require it of all women. Abortion is needed by women who choose not to take that risk and should therefore be legally available.

Immigration Policy

Should the United States continue the trend of increasing immigration? From its founding until the 1920s the United States had few barriers to immigration. Then the door was substantially closed by federal legislation limiting immigration and favoring newcomers from such northern European countries as Britain, Scandinavia, the Netherlands, and Germany. In 1965 a less restrictive immigration law eliminated the preference for northern Europeans in favor of immigration from any part of the globe that united families and supplied America with the workforce it needed. Additional preference was given in 1980 to refugees who credibly feared persecution if returned to their homelands. The result of these changed laws was, write Peter Duignan and Lewis Gann of the Hoover Institution, that "immigration levels rose to over one million a year, not counting undocumenteds; immigrants overwhelmingly came from three areas, Asia, the Caribbean, and Latin America (85%), and the ethnic pattern changed dramatically away from Europe to Asia and Latin America"[26]

Immigration may cause dramatic increases in our population. According to Christopher Jencks, writing in the *New York Review of Books* in 2001, net immigration to the United States has increased by about 3% per year since the major immigration reform of 1965. If this continues, "America's total population in 2050 will be over half a billion—about twice the current figure," and almost all of that increase will be due to immigration.[27] People of European ancestry will no longer be a majority. This reminds me of the old Chinese proverb: if we do not change direction, we are likely to arrive where we are headed. Do we want to go there?

Cosmopolitanism

Cosmopolitans believe that national borders have no ultimate moral significance. People are people wherever they live. It is a fundamental American belief, announced in the Declaration of Independence "to be self-evident, that all Men are created equal, that they are endowed by their Creator with certain unalienable Rights, [and] that among these are Life, Liberty, and the Pursuit of Happiness." Human equality depends, therefore, on the intrinsic nature of human beings, not on their talents, origins, locations, or abilities. One basic human right is freedom of movement. The United States properly castigated communist countries during the Cold War for failure to allow their citizens to emigrate. But the right to emigrate means little if there is no corresponding right to immigrate.

---

26. Peter Duignan and Lewis H. Gann, "Introduction," in *The Debate in the United States over Immigration*, Peter Duignan and Lewis H. Gann, Eds. (Stanford: The Hoover Institution Press, 1997), p. 14.

27. Christopher Jencks, "Who Should Get In? Part II," *The New York Review of Books* (December 10, 2001), pp. 94–102, at 97.

404 Conclusion

According to the logic of this cosmopolitan argument, *there should be no border controls at all aimed at controlling immigration.* The only justified controls would be to protect the country against the entry of people who threaten national security.

Economist John Isbister puts the cosmopolitan argument this way:

> As a mental exercise, one could ask how a law passed by the residents of New York City that restricted the permanent entry of Americans who were not city residents would be judged. Leaving aside the fact that it would be unconstitutional, would it be morally justified? The people of New York could offer some good reasons for the law. New York is already crowded and cannot tolerate further population growth, they might argue. The sanitation system is close to breaking down, the schools are crowded, the welfare system is bankrupt, the homeless shelters are inadequate, and the unemployment rate is rising.
>
> These sorts of arguments would not prove convincing to most Americans, who would find the restrictions on personal freedom too onerous. . . . The interests that New Yorkers have in restricting entry, although perhaps meritorious, are not of sufficient weight to permit such massive violations of the rights and interests of outsiders. New York cannot justify its own immigration policy, morally.
>
> Reasoning by analogy, it is hard to find an ethical justification for the United States' restricting entry across its borders. In fact, it is harder, since the people of the United States are privileged, vis-à-vis the rest of the world, in a way that the residents of New York are not, in comparison to other Americans. New Yorkers could argue plausibly that [Americans] denied entry could find comparable amenities in other cities. [However,] the great majority of immigrants and potential immigrants hope to enjoy a significantly higher standard of living in the United States than they experienced in their home countries. Immigration controls on the U.S. border therefore restrict access to privilege.[28]

Multiculturalism

Multiculturalists may join cosmopolitans in support of increased immigration. Increased immigration promotes cultural mixing. For people who believe that a good society encourages many cultures to commingle, the trend since 1965 for immigrants to come from Asia and Latin America rather than Europe is a positive development.

---

28. John Isbister, *The Immigration Debate: Remaking America* (West Hartford, CN: Kumarian Press, 1996), pp. 126–27.

Free-Market Conservatism

Free-market conservatives also welcome immigration if this promotes economic prosperity, their bottom-line goal. But opinion is divided on the matter. Some free-market conservatives give four reasons for believing that increased immigration leads to economic prosperity. First, immigrants typically work for lower wages than natives, leading to higher profits, which stimulates investment and ultimately improves productivity. Second, some immigrants have special skills, such as in the technology sector, lacking in sufficient numbers in the American workforce. Immigration is needed to supply high tech firms with needed employees. Third, immigrants increase the population, which increases the demand for goods and services. Finally, increased immigration from around the world improves the ability of American companies to understand and respond to consumer demand in other countries. This is important in a global economy.

On the other hand, argue some economists, lower wages can impede investment in technology needed for long-term economic growth. Companies look to technological change to reduce the need for labor when labor costs are high. Lower labor costs could reduce rather than increase investment in technological innovation. The United States could increasingly resemble Third World countries where labor costs are so low that technological innovation seems unnecessary.[29]

Second, an increasing population requires increasing public services of all kinds. Some people claim that immigrants are over-represented among those receiving public assistance, and expenditures on public assistance require taxes that can interfere with economic growth. There may be some truth to this. To the extent that immigrants receive lower wages than most other Americans do, they will qualify (typically after five years' legal residence) for social services designed to help poor workers make ends meet. At the same time, however, these poor people may stimulate the economy by supplying needed services at minimal cost to employers. In addition, most economists conclude, immigrants generally pay more taxes than they receive in public benefits, and they receive fewer public benefits than do most Americans.[30]

The big exception concerns education. Immigrants entering the United States to work are typically young adults. The United States gains their skills without having had to spend money educating them but must spend

---

29. See Isbister, Chapter 6, pp. 138–63 and 176–77.
30. See George J. Borjas, "Immigration and Welfare: A Review of the Evidence," in Duignan and Gann, pp. 121–44.

a great deal educating their children, and immigrants tend to have more children than most other families in the United States. Many immigrant children do not speak English. Educational quality suffers in some communities unable to keep up with the increasing demand for schools and teachers.

Finally, immigrants increase the size of the population, contributing to crowding, which drives up prices for real estate. When real estate prices increase without any corresponding increase in productivity, the country is poorer, other things being equal, because people have less money to invest or to spend on other consumer items.

In sum, *the economic value of immigration is uncertain. I would therefore not want to decide the issue one way or the other on this basis.*

Libertarianism

Libertarians may dispute the cosmopolitan claim that people have a natural right to settle wherever they want, by likening a state to real estate. Just as people who own real estate can usually deny entrance to others, people inhabiting a country should be allowed to keep foreigners out, libertarians might reason.

The analogy is flawed, however. Property rights in real estate are needed for economic reasons; they give people the incentive to improve the land. As we have just seen, the economic argument for restricting immigration is uncertain at best. In addition, property owners enjoy the right to exclude others because they are presumed to have gained ownership by legal means. Americans did not gain control of North America by legal means. We stole it from Native Americans. In general, libertarianism seems an unhelpful guide to immigration policy.

Communitarianism

Communitarians may also want to restrict immigration. They may see restricting immigration as a way to protect the common culture that unites Americans and underpins communal bonds. Although the United States is a nation of immigrants and 100 years ago the number of immigrants per year compared to the total population was greater than at present, past immigrants quickly learned English and assimilated to a relatively common American life. Coming mostly from Europe, they were less culturally diverse than the current group of immigrants. Peter Brimelow, a senior editor at *Forbes* and *National Review* magazines, writes:

> For the first time, virtually all immigrants are racially distinct "visible minorities." They come not from Europe, previously the common

> homeland even for the 1890–1925 Great Wave about which Americans were so nervous. Instead, these new immigrants are from completely different, and arguably incompatible, cultural traditions. . . .
>
> There is no precedent for a sovereign country undergoing such a rapid and radical transformation of its ethnic character in the entire history of the world.[31]

Previous waves of immigration posed less danger to American cultural integrity because the American birthrate was high,[32] and immigrants dispersed themselves around the country. Today, immigrants often cluster more effectively in one locality, such as Cuban immigrants in Miami, and change the locality to suit themselves rather than assimilate into American culture.[33] This results in part from current law favoring immigration that reunites families.

Although I think these concerns have some weight, they do not convince me that immigration should be greatly curtailed absent evidence that attempts at assimilation are failing. *I am content so long as children are still learning English and American history in school and assimilation is taking place.* I do not want the country to place multiculturalism ahead of communitarianism and start allowing Hmong marriage-by-capture, for example, or Sudanese female circumcision. This is a feminist as well as a communitarian concern. But I do not see any tendency at present toward such changes in American law.

Environmentalism

Environmental concerns, on the other hand, do give me pause. As noted earlier, additional people require additional space. Besides increasing the price of real estate, population increase reduces land available for wild nature. Jencks writes:

> Most Americans want to live *near* a densely populated area, because that is where the best jobs are mostly located. But few Americans want to live *in* a densely populated area. They keep moving out of central cities and high-density suburbs to more remote suburbs where they can get bigger houses and bigger yards for less money.

This increases commuting distances and thereby transportation-related pollution.

---

31. Peter Brimelow, "The Case for Limiting Immigration," in Duignan and Gann, Eds., pp. 102–20, at 107–08.
32. Brimelow, p. 107.
33. Brimelow, pp. 105–06.

The greatest problem with immigration is not that it results in more people living on Earth, but that it results in more people adopting the environmentally destructive American way of life. Jencks points out:

> The United States currently accounts for almost 25% of the world's carbon dioxide (CO_2) emissions, making it the leading contributor to global warming. Americans produce twice as much CO_2 per capita as the British, Germans, or Japanese. All else being equal, doubling America's population will double our emissions.[34]

Americans seem unwilling to curtail environmentally destructive consumption, so population increase here threatens the environment if immigrants assimilate and share in America's abundance.

Liberal Contractarianism and Deliberative Democracy

An alternate worry stems from the possibility that most immigrants and their descendants will not attain the American dream. In economic theory, introducing many unskilled people working for low wages should lower the wages of all Americans with few skills. It is a matter of supply and demand. Increase the supply of unskilled workers, and the price for their services goes down. At the same time, cheaper labor means cheaper services for the rich (gardeners and nannies) and more profits for corporations and stockholders. The result is *increasing gaps between haves and have-nots in society.*

This can be seen historically, writes immigration opponent Roy Beck. "Despite having democratic institutions, abundant resources, and a reputation as a workingman's country, America during . . . periods of 19th-century immigration surges was a land of jarring inequality."[35] Christopher Jencks adds: "Claudia Goldin, an economic historian at Harvard, has shown that between 1890 and 1915 wages grew more slowly in those American cities where the proportion of immigrants grew fastest."[36] Inequality declined quickly when World War I interrupted the flow of immigration; returned after the war; and then declined again after immigration was curtailed in the 1920s. Without immigrants, employers had to raise wages. This justified investments in capital equipment that made workers more productive and allowed further increases in wages. New technology also required a more educated workforce, Beck writes.

---

34. Jencks, (December 10, 2001), p. 97. Emphasis in original.
35. Roy Beck, "The High Cost of Cheap Foreign Labor," in Duignan and Gann, Eds., pp. 145–67, at 153.
36. Christopher Jencks, "Who Should Get In?" *The New York Review of Books* (November 29, 2001) pp. 57–64, at 57.

American parents realized that they would need to spend more money to help their children gain a better education. This contributed to lower birthrates and thus to slower labor force growth and thus to tighter labor markets and thus to higher wages, which pushed manufacturers to push the skill levels of their workers even further. In this cycle of productivity and wage gains—each feeding on the other—the United States became a middle-class nation.

But since 1965, Congress has denied the country the opportunity for this "virtuous circle" by flooding the labor markets with foreign workers.[37]

From the liberal contractarian perspective, the problem is not primarily negative effects on economic growth, but increasing unjustified inequality. As we saw in Chapter 6, economic inequality has been increasing in the United States since the mid-1970s. However, Beck concedes, with so many variables, such as the "massive restructurings of the economy and domestic social mores, as well as changes in trade laws and global competition . . . , it is not easy to determine how much of the depression of U.S. wages and increase in economic disparity is the result of increased immigration."[38] History and economic theory nevertheless suggest that the impact of immigration is significant.

Poor American workers are not poor by global standards, so cosmopolitans may not object to the American poor becoming a bit poorer if this is what it takes to help truly desperate people in the Third World. However, *both deliberative and aggregative democracy, we saw in Chapter 8, suffer from inequality within our country. The constant and growing underclass that unlimited immigration could create and sustain threatens our most cherished political institutions.*

Jencks's summary of the case for limiting immigration reflects concerns that I label communitarian, liberal contractarian, and democratic.

In a world where billions of people live close to starvation, no nation is rich enough to guarantee all its workers decent wages or working conditions unless it also limits the number of unskilled workers entering its labor market. Political support for both public education and the welfare state requires some sense of solidarity between haves and have-nots. Support for public education has already collapsed in California, at least in part because so many white California voters see the children in the schools as "them" and not "us." . . . Fifty years from now our children could find that admitting millions of

---

37. Beck, pp. 153–54.
38. Beck, p. 152.

poor Latinos had not only created a sizable Latino underclass but—far worse—that it had made rich Americans more like rich Latin Americans.[39]

I conclude that immigration must be limited to promote justice and democracy in the United States. But, out of respect for the cosmopolitan ideals that I share, I think immigration should be at the highest level compatible with the assimilation of immigrants, the reduction of gaps between rich and poor, and the maintenance of decent wages for all Americans. I do not know if current levels of immigration are appropriate by this standard and can suggest only remaining open to policy changes as new information emerges. As for environmental quality, it should be preserved through government incentives for people to live in more compact spaces, using less land and fossil fuels. In short, as the population density in the United States approaches that in Western Europe, we should adopt and further develop their strategies for environmental protection.

Political Philosophies Right and Left

The title of this section is a play on words. Americans often think of political philosophies as right or left, conservative or liberal. I hope this book reveals that our political thinking is much more complex than this dichotomy suggests. Just as successful gardeners may say they have tomatoes right and left, because they have so many, we have political philosophies right and left. Each philosophy highlights the importance of one or more political principles. Few Americans are content with only one or two philosophies or principles. Instead, we appreciate and use at least several of these philosophies and principles, preferring one on some matters and another on other matters. Thus, we cannot think clearly and understand ourselves or one another if we try to force our thinking into conservative or liberal stereotypes.

In examining the issues of abortion, the genetic engineering of human beings, and immigration, for example, I found several philosophies and associated principles helpful. My conclusion regarding abortion resembles views commonly called liberal, but I found moral conservative considerations most persuasive regarding genetic engineering. I found so many views about immigration to be persuasive that my conclusion is somewhat ambivalent and cannot be classified as either liberal or conservative.

---

39. Jencks (December 10, 2001), p. 102.

However, although I altered the priority I assign different philosophies as applied to different issues, I did not contradict myself. I did not violate the need to strive for reflective equilibrium.

In sum, the vocabulary of multiple political philosophies helped me sort through the various considerations that seemed important, appreciate arguments from more than one perspective, and reach a conclusion backed by consistent reasoning that I could communicate to others. I hope this book will help you address and participate effectively in public discussion of controversial political issues and moral conflicts that you consider important.

Glossary

act utilitarianism   Utilitarian view according to which actions are judged by their individual effects.

ad hoc assumption   A belief that people adopt without good reason except to win an argument.

aggregative democracy   The form of democracy in which adult citizens influence state laws and policies primarily through voting in periodic elections.

altruism   The belief and the actions inspired by belief that every human being's welfare is equally important.

anarchism   The political philosophy according to which states should not exist.

androgyny   The state of being equally male and female, or having in equal measure virtues associated with men and women.

anthropocentric   Describes value systems centered entirely on human welfare.

aquifer   Underground water, often used for drinking water and irrigation.

authenticity   Acting in accordance with one's true identity.

autonomy   The ability of individuals to act in a self-determined manner.

battered woman defense   Defense against prosecution used by women who kill or injure men who have repeatedly battered them.

burdened societies   Societies that lack the political and cultural traditions, the human capital and know-how, and, often, the material and technological resources needed to be well-ordered.

civil liberties   Freedoms associated with the Bill of Rights (the first ten amendments to the United States Constitution), including the freedoms of religion, assembly, and speech.

civil rights movement   Organized protests against Jim Crow laws and practices.

civil society   All social interaction not subsumed by the state or the economy.

communitarianism   A political philosophy according to which personal identity involves group membership and the state should foster maintenance of practices that advance social solidarity and perfectionist ideals over individual autonomy.

community   A group of persons united principally by their identification of themselves as the present bearers of, and participants in, a tradition.

consequentialism   The belief that what makes actions, laws, and policies right or wrong is not their nature but their consequences.

cost-benefit analysis   Decision-making procedure that favors adoption of actions and policies that maximize social wealth as measured in monetary terms.

crimes against humanity   Murdering, exterminating, enslaving, or deporting any civilian population, or persecuting civilians on political, racial, or religious grounds.

crimes against peace   Actions that start an unjust war.

cultural defense   Defense against criminal charges based on defendant's cultural background.

cultural imperialism   The imposition of a powerful nation's culture on others.

cultural relativism   The belief that moral requirements stem from culture and therefore vary according to culture. There is no universal morality.

decent hierarchical peoples   Peoples who avoid aggressive war and treat all human beings with respect but deny to individuals much social mobility and individual autonomy.

deliberative democracy   The exercise of popular influence on state laws and policies through communication among citizens using a variety of means in a variety of venues.

democracy   The form of government in which most adults have significant voice in determining state laws and policies.

desire-related enhancements   Genetic engineering to alter an organism to desired specifications where disease is not at issue.

difference principle   The principle in John Rawls's political philosophy according to which inequality in society is justified only so long as it maximizes benefits to society's least advantaged members.

dilemma of selfishness   *See* prisoner's dilemma.

diminishing marginal utility   The principle whereby the more people have of something the less additional welfare they derive from more of the same.

discount rate   The annual percentage rate by which the current monetary value of something that will exist in the future is reduced to reflect the time lag.

disease-related enhancements   Genetic enhancements that improve an organism's ability to avoid disease.

division of labor   The practice of dividing complex tasks into simpler ones and assigning different simple tasks to different people in order to improve efficiency.

earned income tax credit   Government payments to families or individuals who worked to earn their living but whose income is still very low.

economic theory of law   The theory that laws have generally evolved, and ought further to evolve, to assign rights and duties in such a way as promotes behavior that maximizes economic efficiency.

eminent domain   The right of the state to acquire property from individual property owners as needed for public purposes.

encumbered self   An individual whose identity is constituted in part by her association with particular other individuals and/or with groups.

entitlement theory   Robert Nozick's theory of justice, according to which people have just ownership of property if they acquired it through just means from someone who had just ownership of it. Resulting inequalities among people are irrelevant to justice.

environmentalism   The view that industrial civilization is needlessly harmful to people and other natural beings, such as animals and ecosystems.

equal consideration of interests   The view whereby the welfare of each individual human being counts equally in the calculation of a law or a policy's effects and in the evaluation of its acceptability.

equality of opportunity   The equal legal right (formal equality) of everyone to compete for favored positions in society.

equivocation   Changing the meaning of a key term in the middle of an argument.

Establishment Clause   The first clause in the First Amendment to the Constitution of the United States. It says, "Congress shall make no law respecting an establishment of religion."

ethnic cleansing   Expelling civilians from a geographic area on the basis of their ethnic identity.

ethnocentrism   Belief that one's own ethnic group and/or its culture are superior to others.

external goods   Goods resulting from an activity that are not specific to that activity, such as monetary rewards.

externality   An effect of an action that is not considered in the agent's calculations of benefits and costs.

external protection   The protection of minority cultures against the corrosive influence of the country's dominant culture.

fair equality of opportunity   The equality of material means (of the sort that the state can distribute) to compete for favored positions in society.

fair trade   International trade conducted under provisions that require protection for workers and the environment.

feminism   The belief that no person should be disadvantaged because she is female.

formal liberty   The freedom to do whatever the law does not forbid.

freedom of expressive association   The constitutional right of people to organize for a cause without having to include in their organizations people who do not support that cause.

free market   A system of voluntary exchange of goods and services in which consumer demand is the primary determinant of the nature, quantity, and prices of goods and services.

free-market conservatism   Political philosophy according to which the state should promote economic growth by supporting free trade.

free rider   A person who benefits from a public good without contributing to its creation or maintenance.

genetic engineering The use of knowledge in genetics to alter life forms through the manipulation of genes.

genetic enhancements Genetic engineering to improve an organism.

genetic therapy The use of genetic engineering to cure or avert disease.

germ cells Cells that carry genetic inheritance to the next generation; sperm and ova in human beings.

germ-line therapy Genetic therapy through alteration of genes in germ cells.

globalization Economic integration across national borders.

government People in positions of official power who are authorized to act on behalf of the state.

harm principle The principle whereby the only justification for the state to restrict individual liberty is to prevent individuals from harming one another.

hedonic calculus The calculation of proper actions or rules by estimating the net amount of pleasure that the actions or rules would produce.

hedonism The belief that pleasure is the only good and pain the only bad.

holistic entities Entities composed of many individual beings, such as a basketball team composed of individual players or an ecosystem composed of individual plants and animals.

humanistic ethics Ethics based entirely on human reason and emotion.

incapacitation The removal, at least temporarily, of a criminal's ability to commit a certain kind of crime.

individualism The ethical belief that emphasizes the importance of individual rights, liberties, and opportunities.

informed consent A patient's agreement to a medical treatment after information about the treatment has been communicated and understood by the patient.

inspiration Whatever triggers discovery of an idea.

internal goods Goods specific to a type of activity, such as the visual imagination specific to chess or a portrait painter's ability to communicate her subject's character.

internal restrictions Restrictions placed on members of a minority culture by that cultural group to discourage defection from the group.

international morality Morality that applies to states in relation to one another.

intimate association The personal relationships in private life characterized by informally gathering for dinner, sharing a vacation, and the like.

Jim Crow Laws and customs in the American South after the Civil War designed to subordinate, segregate, and humiliate black people.

justice Giving each person her due and treating like cases alike.

justification Evidence or reasoning that supports the acceptance of an idea.

laissez faire The economic theory that favors free-market transactions unencumbered by government regulations.

liberal contractarianism Political philosophy according to which the state should promote economic growth without creating inequalities that harm society's least-advantaged members or denying people civil liberties or fair equality of opportunity.

libertarianism   Political philosophy according to which the main foundation of the government is the human desire for and right to individual liberty, and the government's primary function is to guarantee such liberty.

Locke's proviso   According to the philosopher John Locke, the belief that people have a right to appropriate unowned natural resources for their own individual welfare only so long as sufficient resources of similar type and quality are left for others to do the same.

material liberty   The ability to do as one likes, unhampered by insufficient material means.

maximin   The principle of choice according to which people choose in risky situations to make the worst possible outcome for themselves as good as possible.

moral conservatism   Political philosophy according to which people have natural tendencies toward antisocial behavior, so the state should promote religious training and traditional practices, including traditional family structures, to maintain social well-being.

multiculturalism   The belief that society should respect many cultures because no single culture, including our own, has a monopoly on insights or practices that promote human flourishing.

nationality   The commonality of customs and ideas among people that inspire mutual sympathy and a desire to live together that these people do not share with others.

natural law   Law based on what appear to be naturally occurring phenomena; such phenomena are often considered to indicate God's will.

natural rights   The rights that some thinkers believe individuals have by nature; these include rights to life, liberty, and property.

negative rights   The rights to be left alone to interact with others on strictly voluntary bases—for example, the rights to life and liberty, including the freedoms of speech and religion.

nonanthropocentric   Describes value systems that are not centered entirely on human welfare.

original position   The situation of people making a hypothetical social contract in John Rawls's political philosophy.

ought implies can   The view that it makes no sense to require the impossible, so a requirement implies that its performance is possible.

paternalism   The overriding or restricting of rights or freedoms of individuals for their own good.

patriarchy   The rule and systematic subordination of women by men.

perfectionism   The belief that the state should sponsor a particular vision of virtue and the good life.

personal revelation   A special communication from God, such as in a dream or apparition, indicating what God wants the individual to feel, believe, and/or do.

pluralistic political philosophy   The belief that several political philosophies provide important insights and that no one such philosophy suffices to provide adequate guidance in all situations.

political environmentalism   Political philosophy according to which the state should intervene in the economy and society to reduce or reverse the negative impact that industrial civilization has on people and other natural beings, such as animals and ecosystems.

political liberalism   The political philosophies that emphasize individualism; these include libertarianism, free market conservatism, and liberal contractarianism.

political philosophies   Organized views about the need for states, their foundations, and their functions.

political principlism   The position that no one political philosophy suffices to give reasonable guidance in all political contexts. People should therefore appeal to different political philosophies, with their different associated principles, in different contexts.

political realism   The view that morality does not apply to states.

positional goods   Goods that benefit individuals only insofar as they confer social advantage in comparisons with other people (as height does).

positive rights   The rights—for example, food, shelter, clothing, health care, and education—to receive what one needs, from others if necessary, to meet at least minimal levels of some basic human needs.

practice   A socially defined, complex activity with internal goods whose achievement requires development of skills or virtues that are specific to that kind of activity.

preference utilitarianism   Utilitarian view according to which the goal of actions, laws, and policies is to maximize the satisfaction of individual preferences.

principlism   Ethical view according to which no one principle of ethics provides adequate guidance in all situations. Several independent principles are needed, and no definitive hierarchy among them can be established.

prisoners' dilemma   A situation in which people acting to get the best outcomes for themselves as individuals create an outcome that is worse for everyone than cooperation could have produced.

progressive taxation   Tax policies and laws that tax people at a higher percentage rate as their total wealth or income increases.

psychological egoism   The belief that everyone always acts selfishly all the time.

public accommodation   An establishment that serves the general public, such as a restaurant or a car rental company.

public goods   Good things that no one can benefit from unless many other people benefit as well.

reasonable pluralism   The existence in society of many different styles of life, values, and goals among people who are reasonable enough to want to get along peacefully with everyone else in society.

redlining   Banking practice of refusing to write home mortgage loans to blacks or other minority members for housing outside of certain parts of town.

reflective equilibrium   The state of logical consistency among a person's views achieved, as needed, by altering judgments regarding individual cases and beliefs in general propositions covering those cases.

rehabilitation   Assisting criminals to gain skills to be economically and socially successful without recourse to crime, which they no longer find attractive.

rule utilitarianism   Utilitarian view according to which actions are to be judged by the tendency of the rule they accord with to produce the best consequences in the long run.

school vouchers   Government vouchers that parents can use at private schools to pay for their children's education outside the public school system.

selfish   Characteristic of people who take action taken without sufficient regard for the welfare of others or the disposition toward such action.

selflessness   Characteristic of people who take actions in accordance with the belief that agents should not count their own welfare among the considerations relevant to practical decision-making.

sex/gender system   A system of thought, action, and policy within patriarchy that subordinates women by associating biological sex with gender-specific social roles.

sexual harassment   Unwelcome sexual advances or allusions that inhibit equal employment opportunity for women by diminishing the chances of success for women who reject the advances or by creating a hostile work environment for women who find the allusions offensive.

shadow prices   Hypothetical market prices of goods not in the marketplace; these are used in cost-benefit analysis and are based on questionnaires and on inferences drawn from the prices of goods in the marketplace.

social capital   The connections among individuals and social networks, and the norms of reciprocity and trustworthiness that arise from them.

social contract tradition   Political philosophies according to which governments are founded on the consent of the governed through an actual or hypothetical contract.

somatic cells   All cells in the body that are not germ cells.

somatic-cell therapy   Genetic therapy through manipulation of genes in somatic cells.

state   The organization in society that can wield more power than any other organization can and that claims the right to determine how force may be used in that society.

takings clause   Clause in the U.S. Constitution that disallows the state taking property from individual owners without just compensation.

theocratic view   Political philosophy according to which state law should reflect the dictates of a particular religion.

theories of justice   General accounts of which rewards and burdens people are due and which differences among people or situations justify different treatment.

theory of deterrence   The belief that people obey laws because they are scared off by the prospect of punishment if they disobey.

thick morality   Moral requirements applicable to people in a particular culture that reflect the particularities of that culture.

thin morality   Moral requirements that apply universally, regardless of culture.

Title I   Government program that provides extra educational help in basic academic skills to children, most of whom are from poor families.

tradition   A history or narrative in which the central motif is an aspiration to a particular form of life, to certain projects, goals, and ideals.

traditional welfare programs   Government programs to help the poor that did not stress personal responsibility to escape poverty through work.

tragedy of the commons   Tendency of people to overexploit and thereby degrade a resource held by them in common.

two moral powers   According to John Rawls, the sense of justice and the personal conception of the good that he believes people generally have.

unencumbered self   An individual whose personal identity is independent of her association with any groups or other individuals.

universal jurisdiction   The ability of prosecutors in any country to extradite and try people regardless of their residence for war crimes and crimes against humanity.

utilitarianism   Ethical and political philosophy according to which proper actions, laws, and policies maximize net good, either happiness or preference satisfaction.

veil of ignorance   The ignorance of personal identity that characterizes people making a social contract in John Rawls's political philosophy.

viability   The ability of the unborn to live and continue development outside the woman carrying it.

war crimes   Illegal actions taken while at war, such as murdering, ill treating, or deporting either civilians or prisoners of war.

well-ordered peoples   Liberal and decent hierarchical peoples.

Index